BETH CHATTO'S
DAMP GARDEN

BETH CHATTO'S
DAMP GARDEN

MOISTURE-LOVING PLANTS FOR YEAR-ROUND INTEREST

PHOTOGRAPHS BY STEVEN WOOSTER

EDITED BY ERICA HUNNINGHER

CASSELL
ILLUSTRATED

TO THE MEMORY OF ANDREW CHATTO

Original edition first published in the United Kingdom by
J.M. Dent Ltd in 1982
Revised paperback edition first published by Orion Books
Ltd in 1998

This fully revised and illustrated edition first published in
Great Britain in 2005 by Cassell Illustrated
a division of the Octopus Publishing Group Ltd
2–4 Heron Quays, London E14 4JP

British Library Cataloguing in Publication Data
A CIP catalogue record for this book is available from
the British Library

ISBN 1 84403 045 8
EAN 9781844030453
10 9 8 7 6 5 4 3 2 1

Designed by Nigel Soper
Horticultural consultant Tony Lord
Index by Hilary Bird

Typeset in Bembo
Printed and bound in China by Toppan

Above: *Butomus umbellatus*
Page 1: *Trillium erectum*
Page 2: *The water gardens in late June*
Page 3: *Iris x robusta* 'Gerald Darby'
Page 6: *Zantedeschia aethiopica* 'Crowborough'

Contents

Preface

THIS REVISED AND ILLUSTRATED edition of *The Damp Garden* brings up to date the story of making a garden on a site that contains every type of damp soil from moist silt to sticky clay, in both sunny and shady situations. (I started making what has become The Beth Chatto Gardens more than forty years ago, in 1960.) Sections of the original text have been reduced either because the information no longer applies or to make room for Stephen Wooster's beautiful photographs. The A to Z of plants has been adjusted to take in changes in nomenclature and to reflect some of the lessons I have learned over the years — plants I can no longer recommend are omitted, for example, and I have added others I've come to know more recently.

Rather than giving a comprehensive account of moisture-loving plants, I focus on those I grow around the ponds and in other areas of retentive or spring-fed soil in my garden. Among them are many well-loved hardy perennials which will not thrive in dry conditions, but which do well in most gardens with adequate rainfall. A few of the shade-tolerant plants described in my book the *Woodland Garden* also appear here, since they were found in woodlands which have plenty of rain, such as in Japan and parts of North America. In Great Britain and other northern temperate regions often overcast skies and comparatively low summer temperatures mean we can sometimes grow plants, such as hellebores, in an open situation which need more shade or moisture in their native home where summer temperatures are higher.

It is almost sixty years since I first wandered in the mountains of Europe with my late husband, Andrew Chatto, and more than twenty years since he wrote about the homes of garden plants for *The Damp Garden*. Re-reading the summary of his life-long research (Chapter 8) reminds me of how much I have learnt by seeing plant communities *in situ*. I hope you will be as fascinated as I am still to discover how many of our familiar garden plants originated in the wild throughout the temperate world. Of course it is neither practical nor desirable to try to copy nature, but knowing something of a plant's origin and association helps us not to stray too far from the conditions it prefers and needs.

Zantedeschia aethiopica, the Arum Lily, is handsome in leaf and flower and grows well in deeply prepared soil kept moist in summer.

ELMSTEAD MARKET 2004

Introduction

I N MY FIRST BOOK, *The Dry Garden*, and more recently in the *Gravel Garden* and the *Woodland Garden*, I have written about gardening on poor sand and gravel soil. I also have some very damp land on the same site, and in this book I tell the story of its development as a garden. I describe not only the many beautiful plants which previously I had no chance of possessing, but also the trials and errors which occurred as I laboriously learnt something of the art of managing a boggy meadow.

I live in a highly developed part of the country and sometimes feel sad that many young people growing up today will not have the evocative memories that those of us have who were children before the Second World War – of playing and wandering in copsey places, dusty lanes or wet-legged meadows, where each season we looked out for the flowering plants that we took for granted would always be there, part of our world, part of the fabric of our lives. When I was a child a hedge, together with the ditch that had provided the soil bank on which the hedge had been planted generations before, provided the shelter and spring-moist atmosphere needed by sweet violets and pale clumps of primroses. On dusty roadsides we found tall purple knapweed, scabious, yellow toadflax and great stands of Cow Parsley, their star-topped seed heads always used to make 'fairy wands' in autumn. In spring the shining golden King Cups edged the little brook meandering through the low-lying damp meadows, dotted about with lilac Lady's Smock and contented

Mixed planting in the Canal Bed, on either side of the remains of the original spring-fed ditch, includes *Onoclea sensibilis,* the Sensitive Fern, *Primula bulleyana*, and *Iris* 'Sibirica Alba'.

cropping cows. As the summer days lengthened we would look out for the tiny baby frogs which, disturbed by our plunging through the long grass, would leap ahead of us like grasshoppers, tiny clammy-wet creatures, appealing because they were so vulnerable. As we chased them we stumbled across a colony of slender spotted orchids, a rare sight even in those golden days of childhood.

As I grew up the Big Machines moved in. The utilization of the land was under constant revision. Greater efficiency in farming decimated the hedges and drained and ploughed the water-meadows; networks of new roads had to be made, conurbations of new homes built – all of this has created very different associations.

Many people will be growing up, making homes and starting gardens who have not had these carefree nature lessons when we unconsciously absorbed something of the needs of plants. I had never heard the word ecology in those days, nor did I connect wild plants with gardening as I understood it then. But before long I was involved in making a survey of our local salt marshes as part of my college studies. With the highly informed help of Andrew Chatto, my future husband, I started an interest, which has lasted all my life, and directly influenced my gardening. By studying the marshes in detail I learnt how marvellously plants adapt themselves to their environment, and also how that environment can change in a matter of a few metres or yards, and that each section has a slightly modified plant community.

Salt marshes may seem a long way from cultivated gardening, but I learnt important lessons there. Plants have adapted themselves to almost every kind of condition, no matter how unpromising. They will tolerate a great deal. But they are also sensitive and will not establish themselves in a situation that differs markedly from their natural environment. As conditions change in my own garden from dry gravel to silt, from damp to bog, so I must consider what I will plant that will tolerate the change.

In this book I discuss most of the plants that I grow which are omitted from *The Dry Garden* and the *Gravel Garden*. Some which I include in the *Woodland Garden* also appear here because they thrive more easily on retentive soil. While many, or most of them, do not need, and would not thrive in, really wet conditions, neither will any of them tolerate drought during the growing period. They require soil that does not dry out and, in some cases, a sheltered environment, providing some shade from direct hot sunlight and shelter from wind, which can cause immediate wilting of large soft foliage, even though there be ample moisture underfoot.

While I discuss the making of my ponds, and the plants I have put in and around them, I do not describe how pools in general, either natural or artificial, may be constructed. Nor do I include more than a fraction of the plants that actually grow

Snowdrops (*Galanthus*) provide late-winter delight beneath *Cornus alba* 'Sibirica', the Westonbirt Dogwood, which has the most brilliant red stems in winter. These make handsome contrast with the Ghost Bramble, *Rubus cockburnianus*, growing in heavy clay soil on the opposite bank.

INTRODUCTION

in water. I have too little experience of either, and shall stick in the main to the things I have learnt through trial and error.

I may tend to overstress the need for dampness for certain plants in the garden, but I should remind you that my part of East Anglia has a very low average rainfall (50–55cm/20–22in per year). Half of that falls in summer, but it is then often whisked away by a couple of days of destructive drying winds. Also the foliage of trees, bushes and plants themselves prevents some of this precious moisture reaching the roots. Those who live in areas of heavy rainfall will probably grow many of these plants with no trouble.

There is, however, another point I should like to make. I am advocating the idea of gardening without regular resort to watering. Although I have ample supplies of water in the form of large spring-fed pools which we have made, we rarely irrigate the garden. I try to plant each different section with plants chosen for their ability to survive there, whether it be in hot, sunny, totally drained gravel, dry shade (as I describe in *The Woodland Garden*) or heavy clay, saturated at the pond edges, or in meadow silt watered by springs which run just beneath the surface; or yet again, areas where enough moisture is conserved because of shade, shelter from wind and the ample addition of humus, both in the soil and protectively as a mulch. Of course I do not disapprove of watering plants well in at planting time. But it is always when we most badly need to use the garden hose that we may be unable to because of serious water shortages. My theory of gardening without irrigation would make it impossible for many people to contemplate growing such plants as astilbes and Globeflowers (*Trollius*), and even some of the Knotweeds, for example. I confess that in my previous garden there were many plants I craved. I planted them, and suffered as I watched them wither away in utterly the wrong conditions no matter what I tried to do to please them. So I abandoned the idea of growing damp-loving plants and stuck to those I could grow reasonably well. Since 1960 I have been creating a garden on a site that has almost every kind of problem from free-draining gravel to deep silt fed by underground springs; leading me to search for the right plant for the right place, and eventually turning the problems into advantages.

The underground springs keep the water level constant in my five garden pools, even in severe drought. The water splashes quietly from one pool to the next, in gentle gradient, to flow through the Canal Bed and under a Weeping Willow, where it merges with the reservoir. The springs are derived from rainwater which seeps down through porous soil until it reaches the practically impervious clay beneath. Here it must travel over the surface of the clay towards the lowest point, small trickles of water meeting up with others, so that if you could skim off the porous soil you would see a system of small tributaries leading to the main ditches (see the

Hosta fortunei
'Albomarginata'
finds the right
degree of shade
beneath the Golden
Weeping Willow,
Salix × sepulcralis
var. *chrysocoma*, to
produce large sage-
green leaves variously
variegated: some
are broadly edged
with white; others
more shaded may
be half-white.
Smilacina racemosa
and *Polygonatum
× hybridum*, Solomon's
Seal, make good
companions.

diagram showing a section across the garden on pages 18–19). This precious water travels through the lower garden and is led to the reservoir to be stored for use in time of drought. There is a large outlet pipe at the far end to take the surplus away downstream through an alder wood.

Occasional visitors who come to me for advice on what they should plant in a water garden add as an afterthought that the level of water drops 1m/3ft in summer! Sometimes it is a farm pond, sometimes a moat, and sometimes a river in full spate whirling past the bottom of the garden. Another time it may be a low-lying piece of puddled clay that is wet and soggy all winter, but bone-dry and fractured in summer. None of this, of course, will do – at least, not as it stands. Soil for damp-loving plants must not be allowed to dry out during the growing season, when the plants will be seeking moisture. At the same time, for the vast majority, neither must it be waterlogged. I describe how we have dealt with badly drained soils in Chapter 7.

Damp gardening when it is successful is possibly one of the most beautiful forms of gardening. If it sounds like hard work I can assure you that, unless nature provides for you, initially, it is. Both the careful preparation of the site and the subsequent management of the soil (ideally suited for the germination of weeds) require considerable effort, followed by skilful planting.

THE BETH CHATTO GARDENS

THE PLAN SHOWS THE WHOLE GARDEN. The main damp areas about which I write as they developed are the four ponds and the canal bed that make up my Water Gardens, the moist shade beds on retentive meadow silt and the north-facing clay bank. Stock beds to the north and the ditch running along the east side of my Wood Garden also come into the story.

Above: Water Gardens (1)

Above: Stock Beds (5)   *Below: North-facing clay bank* (9)

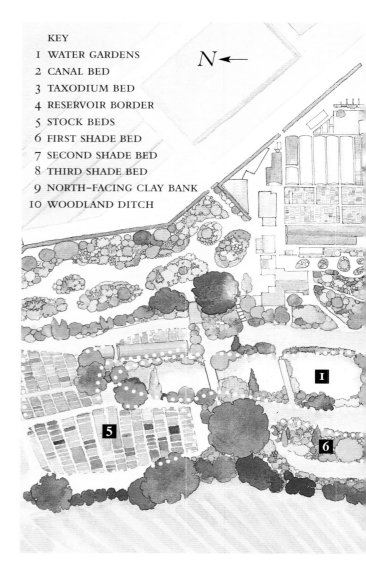

KEY
1 WATER GARDENS
2 CANAL BED
3 TAXODIUM BED
4 RESERVOIR BORDER
5 STOCK BEDS
6 FIRST SHADE BED
7 SECOND SHADE BED
8 THIRD SHADE BED
9 NORTH-FACING CLAY BANK
10 WOODLAND DITCH

N ←

Above: Third Shade Bed (8)

Above: Canal Bed (2)　　　　*Below: Woodland Ditch* (10)

I | Starting from Scratch

ＦIRST I MUST SHOW YOU THE SITE as it was when we stumbled through it one late November afternoon, making the final decision that this isolated and derelict piece of land was going to become our home. Several fine oaks threw rugged silhouettes against the skyline, supported by a couple of towering dark hollies alive with quarrelsome sparrows fighting over accommodation. Mountainous piles of blackberries ran into wickedly prickly thickets of sloes, with nettles and marsh thistles filling the remaining spaces.

Down the centre of a long and narrow hollow, a spring-fed ditch ran from north to south. The Water Board sent a couple of men along it once in a while to clear it because the free flow of water was vital to the drainage of the fields which surrounded us. Gradually the ditch had deepened and low banks of mixed clay and gravel had built up alongside to be colonized by Rosebay Willowherb, nettles and coarse grasses until the next spring-clean. A stately alder rose out of a muddle of stunted oaks while a group of Arthur Rackham-like willows visually closed the northern end.

Most of Essex is dead flat; in any case, few builders would consider putting a house into a swamp. But here, for us – if we could persuade a builder to build us a house – was the possibility of making a garden on different levels, with running water and, perhaps one day, a pond.

For those who have real valleys, I hasten to repeat that ours is a very shallow

Bog Arum, *Lysichiton camtschatcensis*, flourishes at the water's edge in the area known as the Canal Bed, which is the remains of the spring-fed ditch leading to the farm reservoir. The Bog Arum was was one of the first plants I used in my new Damp Garden and has been here for more than forty years. It must have very deep, damp soil.

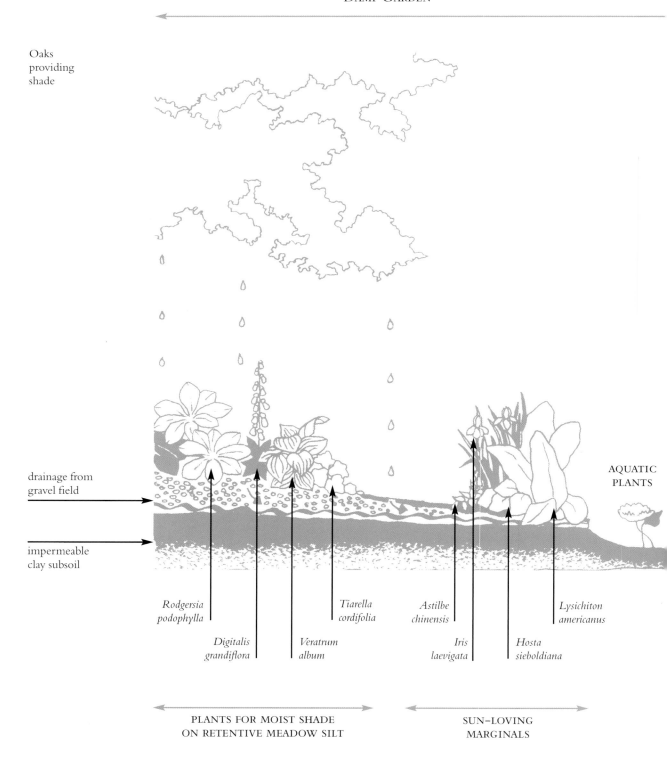

Oaks
providing
shade

drainage from
gravel field

impermeable
clay subsoil

AQUATIC
PLANTS

Rodgersia
podophylla

Digitalis
grandiflora

Veratrum
album

Tiarella
cordifolia

Astilbe
chinensis

Iris
laevigata

Hosta
sieboldiana

Lysichiton
americanus

PLANTS FOR MOIST SHADE
ON RETENTIVE MEADOW SILT

SUN–LOVING
MARGINALS

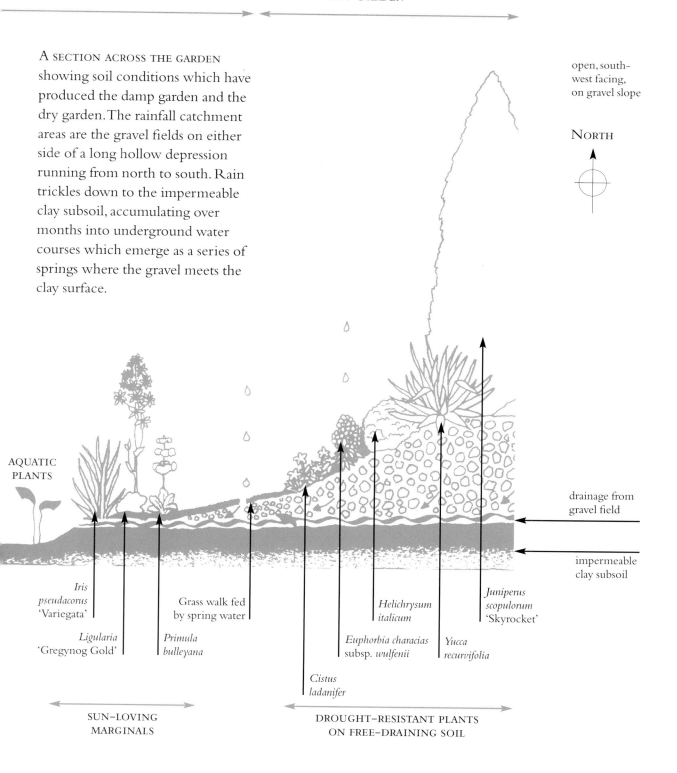

DRY GARDEN

A SECTION ACROSS THE GARDEN showing soil conditions which have produced the damp garden and the dry garden. The rainfall catchment areas are the gravel fields on either side of a long hollow depression running from north to south. Rain trickles down to the impermeable clay subsoil, accumulating over months into underground water courses which emerge as a series of springs where the gravel meets the clay surface.

open, south-west facing, on gravel slope

NORTH

AQUATIC PLANTS

drainage from gravel field

impermeable clay subsoil

Iris pseudacorus 'Variegata'

Grass walk fed by spring water

Helichrysum italicum

Juniperus scopulorum 'Skyrocket'

Ligularia 'Gregynog Gold'

Primula bulleyana

Euphorbia characias subsp. *wulfenii*

Yucca recurvifolia

Cistus ladanifer

SUN–LOVING MARGINALS

DROUGHT–RESISTANT PLANTS ON FREE–DRAINING SOIL

depression. This whole area was formed about 500,000 years ago by the melting of the Devonian Ice Cap which covered most of the country approximately 370 million years ago. The glacier ground its way over land to deposit, as it melted, a layer of clay many feet thick, incorporating nodules and grains of various rocks and chalk, from the hills it had passed over. This layer is what we call chalky boulder clay. The glacier did not come beyond Colchester but the melting ice water did, gushing over the east coastal strip and laying down banks of gravel where the current was strongest, sand and silt where it was quieter and still. All these gradations of soil lay on 4.8 hectares/12 acres of land, part of which we proposed to turn into a garden. Our small stream cut itself a shallow course through the gravels and silt to the ancient London clay, which lies beneath us.

The wasteland was overgrown by different groupings of plants, because of the different soil types, reminding me of the salt marshes which varied from salt to fresh water. We had willows and marsh thistles in the wet hollow, tall stands of bracken on the drier sandy slopes, wild roses, sorrel and bare stones on the uppermost gravels. Overall the soil was acid. An analysis showed the pH to be as low as 4.0 in places.

On either side of the ditch, unseen beneath the tangles of undergrowth, were springs, which enter our land from east and west. The cultivated farmland, which lies on either side of us is higher, as much as 6m/20ft higher than the lowest level of the garden, and is, predominantly, a gravel soil overlying the clay base. The rainfall, especially winter rain, trickles very slowly down through this open-textured soil to the clay beneath, which it cannot easily penetrate. So water runs along the surface of the clay, joining up into underground tributaries, which eventually find their way on to our land, emerging finally at the ditch level as a row of springs. The ditch was thus continuously fed by water that had fallen months previously. With our few centimetres or inches of summer rainfall either blown away by devilish winds, or dried up the next day by the sun, the thought of all this underground water was intoxicating.

We could see very little of it then, but as we squelched our way up through the hollow that long-ago November evening, the white mist curling among the russet stands of head-high bracken and mouldering the last of the blackberries, I felt that this place was right for us. I had no idea of the way the garden would evolve, but I could hardly wait to make a start.

The first thing to decide was where our house should stand. Among our friends was a young architect who, on being taken to the site, immediately saw the possibilities. The result was a plan for a simple, low-lying, split-level house to be built into the warm, west-facing gravel bank, at that time overlooking the ditch. Months of planning and preparations went by. At the same time I was busy in my Colchester garden, boxing up seedlings and cuttings, trying to preserve as much as I could of the first seventeen years of our gardening life together.

CLEARING THE SITE

Eventually the day came when we followed the bulldozer down the quarter mile headland (unmade farm roadway), which led from the main road through the farm to our wilderness. The last hundred yards or so ran along an old boundary hedge. We stopped at an ancient pollarded oak with a magnificent umbrella head. Between this bastion and an equally ancient holly, yards on at the top of a slope, was the place where our house would stand. Old rabbit netting and barbed wire – which years before had kept grazing cows in the damp hollow from invading Andrew's apple orchards – had to be cut. We cut, and tugged, and tore ourselves, but by the end of the day a roadway had been levelled out of the headland, and three shallow platforms had been made on the south-facing slope on which the house would stand.

Next day, Percy, on the bulldozer, started to clear the site for the garden. In some ways it was a pity. I know that my husband, a more devoted naturalist than I am, thought so; and a speck deep inside me can see his point of view. For so many years this piece of land had been a haven for all kinds of creatures. One early morning a vixen had been seen playing with her cubs. A badger had a set up on the warm sandy bank, well hidden by bramble tangles and bracken beds. Grass snakes sunned themselves on the remains of straw bales. But not all was idyllic. Lazing one day on the edge of the ditch, fascinated by caddis worms, teasing them perhaps by giving them bits of stick to embellish their pebbly coats, my reverie was shattered by the screams of a rabbit being chased relentlessly through the brushwood by a stoat. Now humans were invading, for better or worse!

It always alarms me how quickly large machines change the landscape. Within a few hours the impenetrable tangle of blackthorn was crushed into a vast heap to be burnt. We had marked the straight limbed oaks we wished to keep, and the hollies, of course, were not touched. The alder stood alone now on the edge of the ditch. Opposite it, some distance away, was the vast oak complemented by the equally massive holly. Between these trees and the site where the house would stand there was nothing, not a blade of grass. The ditch, several feet deep, lay parallel to the house site but separated from it by a level stretch of moist silt.

At the very end of this long tongue-shaped piece of land we had a small reservoir, made several years previously to irrigate the farm. It had been constructed by scooping out the 'valley' bottom, and piling the clay across the end, so collecting the spring water that ran down through our land. A large outflow pipe took the excess water further downstream through an alder wood. Some repair work was being done to this at the same time as we were bulldozing. The owner of the dragline at work there walked over to see what was going on. Immediately he saw from *his* viewpoint. 'I know what you want, Mrs Chatto!' he said. 'A nice Lily Pond.' 'Yes,' I said, uncertainly, 'that would be nice.' Looking at the large empty area we had created – the straight line of the ditch, the unfamiliar scale of the few huge trees we had left – I could not be helpful. However, he was not a man to let the grass grow under his feet. In no time his vast machine was trundling over my 'garden' as easily as a wheelbarrow. He dipped the large scoop into the ditch a number of times, brought out several tons of bright yellow clay and laid it around the edge of a large muddy hole. It seemed a huge hole at the time, and the pile of clay looked totally unmanageable. Percy's fire of brushwood was sending up sparks like fireflies into the dusk. Both machines moved off home.

I was pleased with the cleared ground. The soil – soft black silt, full of humus from decades of falling leaves – looked good. We thought we knew what we would do next with that. But 'Mrs Chatto's Lily Pond' was not right. I could not tell myself why, but I knew it was wrong.

SOIL PREPARATION

The next tool we used was our own tractor, with the subsoiler attached. Land that has lain for a long time can become very compacted; roots cannot easily penetrate; there may be bad drainage and certainly lack of air. When breaking up a new piece of ground we always use the subsoiler, a great curved piece of strong steel, facing forward, which, drawn behind the tractor, sinks in about 2ft/60cm deep, bursting up the compacted soil. I love to walk behind the tractor and watch the soil lift and crack on either side of the deep spike. The soil has to be right. If it were very wet the tool would just slide through like butter – which might be useful to start off some drainage – but when it is the right degree of dampness the land fractures, which is better.

In many gardening books double digging is recommended to open up the soil. It is not easy to find someone, able and willing, to do this heavy work. But I do think in entirely new gardens, where the soil may have been compacted by very heavy machinery, perhaps to level the site before building, some deep digging should be done initially – if not overall, then for individual trees and shrubs. Simply by doing that I have, on occasion, in gardens where I have been asked to help, had an unwelcome shock finding all kinds of unexpected features beneath soil level (like large pieces of buried hardboard, or the swillings out of the concrete mixer which had set like a laid path, a foot beneath the surface). Once the hard pan, whatever it may consist of, has been broken I would prefer to maintain the texture of the soil by adding as much humus as possible to the top layer, and allowing the worms and soil bacteria to build up the soil structure.

With our subsoiling done this is how things stood. Three shallow platforms represented the house. All the land on the house side of the ditch had been cleared (apart from the marked trees). From its west side the house overlooked the ditch, beyond which were still the dark masses of blackthorn, and overtopping them was the ancient farm boundary hedge containing oaks, a crab apple, holly and hazelnut. Crowning them all was the finest oak in the district. I felt puny beneath it.

I had never before started a garden from scratch and felt rather nonplussed by the size of the area cleared and its absence of features. It was a bit like facing these large empty sheets of foolscap and wondering where to go next. So I was thankful to follow Andrew's ideas, which were based on ecological groupings rather than park-like landscaping.

We had in mind to create several different gardens, influenced by our memories of plants in the wild and subsequent reading of plant associations. So, the area between the alder and the large oak was to become a Shade Garden. The Lower Ditch area, which ran alongside would become a Water Garden. The open silty soil on the south side of the house would, for the time being, act as a nursery bed until we had sorted ourselves out. The fairly level areas of starved gravel on the approach to the house and which lay all round it on its upper levels could only become our Mediterranean Garden, the making of which I described in *The Dry Garden,* and subsequently in *The Gravel Garden*. 'The Lily Pond', although lying across that part of the ditch which flowed past the west window of the house, I managed to ignore. Quite soon, as a gesture, I planted a large Pampas Grass on the edge of it, but I could not imagine what else to do and anyway there were more important things to be done – like making paths.

MAKING PATHS AND PREPARING TO PLANT

By now I have learnt one or two useful tips about paths. When starting from scratch paths need to have a definite objective, and to return if possible by a different route. By their very nature they make openings among the screen of trees and shrubs to be planted, so make sure the path will lead your eye as well as yourself to a pleasant vista. Again it is wise to follow the contours of the land and let your path take the gentler slopes, remembering that before long you will be pushing a heavy barrow up or down the slope. Andrew had these things in mind as we shuffled our paths in the soft soil. We left a much wider curving strip throughout the whole length of the garden alongside the ditch. Later we sowed it all down by hand with a fine grass seed mixture. Much later the narrow grass paths and the beds they contained were simplified as the garden developed, and I began to get a feeling of the scale of the garden to come. But initially it was right that we designed to a scale we could manage ourselves.

Although the land had been broken up by the subsoiler it still had to be levelled and dug. It was full of roots, especially blackthorn and bracken. We had several men working on our fruit farm (of which this patch of land was the wasteland, too wet, or too dry, to plant commercially). But there was rarely time in the year when they could easily be spared. So we did our own digging. There was plenty of time. The house took nearly a year to build. I thought at the time that the garden would take the rest of my life. Now I know that one lifetime is not half enough. After seventeen years of chalky boulder clay in my Colchester garden, only seven miles away, I found it very enjoyable to dig in this soft, almost stoneless soil, full of the leaf-mould of ages. I took pleasure in following down as deep as I could the black rope-like roots of bracken, which in places interwove the soil like a fishing net. Subsequently I learnt that it could be killed by spraying with a systemic weedkiller, but that is not a quick process either; it takes months to be effective. It is still the thing to do if you happen to be a hill farmer and are trying to clear extra grazing land. However, in small areas, where digging is possible, it is I think the best way, for breaking as much of the root as you can causes the milky-white sap inside to bleed and so helps the destruction of whatever you leave behind. For years afterwards odd pieces of bracken appeared in my garden; some still do. I try to remember to weed them out when the frond is mature, pulling the stem away from the deep root, so wounding it again. Gradually it dies out. For those who may wonder why I am so intent on the destruction of something which looks so attractive, especially in spring uncurling among bluebells, I will say more explicitly that left to itself it forms dense tangles, more than head high, much too rampant for a garden. Proper ferns are a different matter, and will come later.

As the digging progressed we ferried over our boxes of plants, small shrubs and young trees, and planted them in rows, in a nursery area, till we had time to sort them out. Almost the first night the local rabbits found the new menu to their taste, so we hastily erected some old netting as an enclosure. But before we could contemplate any permanent planting we had to face up to the trouble and expense of putting a proper rabbit-proof fence around the perimeter of the area we thought then was to be our new garden.

THE FIRST SHADE BED

Thus far you may have felt excluded by so much attention to preparations, especially with earthmoving machinery – although I can assure you that the cost, in relation to the type of work done and the time saved, was not exorbitant. But now I propose to tell you something of the making of our first Shade Bed, which in itself could be a complete small garden for someone who has a shady site and soil that does not dry out excessively. Of course sometimes, by the very nature of being shady, gardens are often dry as well. This is especially the case where there is too much root competition from trees and shrubs, and too low rainfall in the growing season. Where every inch is precious I have been told of an idea to keep questing roots out of a bed particularly desired for choice plants. It is to dig down a deep slit trench, as close to the trees or shrubs as you dare, and insert a sheet of corrugated plastic, or even high-gauge black polythene.

The soil of my first Shade Bed was deep and black, with a damp area along the lower side where a spring ran just below grass level. At one point, when digging an extra-deep hole for a shrub, we hit the old land drain which had been laid long, long ago to carry this spring off the land above. Not pipes as we use today but tile drains, that is, a pipe made in two halves, one lying on the other like a lid. We also came across the curious greyish-white substance called 'gley', caused by the humus acids from the top layer of soil bleaching the silty soil beneath. We wondered immediately if anything would grow on such barren-looking soil, but elsewhere it had been thrown on the surface by the bulldozing, and within weeks the finest crop of Fat Hen, *Chenopodium album,* a common farm weed, was thriving on it.

The first tree we planted to create shade was *Paulownia tomentosa,* native to the warm temperate parts of China. It is generally seen now planted as a specimen, since the Chinese have destroyed most of their natural forests to make way for crops. It is a member of the foxglove family and its flowers, carried on long upcurved shoots, look like large, frill-lipped, pale blue foxgloves. In early June they open from soft chamois velvet buds, with no leaves unfurled to detract from their exotic beauty. Visitors seeing the flowers dropped on the green grass wonder where they have come from, looking in vain from left to right, not thinking to look at the great tree above their heads. Some years the branches sweep down to eye level and then we are all bewitched. Our tree loved the rich, deep soil and shot up like a rocket, all of 2m/6ft a year. But it paid the price for such exuberance, for several large, brittle limbs were torn off by autumn gales; rough pruning! The large, soft, heart-shaped leaves, which do not expand fully till mid June, make pretty dappled shade for the large bed beneath.

More trees planted for shade were *Liriodendron tulipifera, Catalpa bignonioides, Liquidambar styraciflua,* a pink-flowered *Robinia* (torn to pieces by wind), *Picea omorika* and *Ginkgo biloba.* What a list, far too many for the space available, and there were shrubs as well. The blue-berried *Symplocos paniculata* was ruined by the sticky spit from aphids in the oak above. A *Neillia* made a thicket of stems (useful for pheasant cover, in suitable places), was pretty in leaf and flower, but menacing here.

I have found that though, in places, I have underground moisture, I do have to restrict the number of trees and shrubs that suck it up greedily in dry summers, leaving my plants between famished.

At the beginning some shade was already provided by the high canopy of alder and oak, so I planted great clumps of hostas backed by tall stands of Solomon's Seal, *Polygonatum* × *hybridum,* and the common fern, the Male Fern, *Dryopteris filix-mas.*

We have directed a strong spring on one side of the Wood Garden into a shallow ditch. It provides damp soil for the gigantic *Gunnera tinctoria,* the Sensitive Fern (*Onoclea sensibilis*) and a host of candelabra primulas, set off by large-leaved hostas, including *H.* 'Frances Williams' (*sieboldiana*).

Among them, for ground-cover, I planted *Tiarella cordifolia* and *Geranium endressii,* both of which spread quickly, making a carpet of pretty foliage as well as providing a foam of white or pink flowers in spring. Lily-of-the-Valley seemed the right thing to plant, bluebells were already there (why not keep them?) and the Welsh Poppy, *Meconopsis cambrica,* in orange and lemon, added to a spring picture of simple charm. *But* the bluebells and Lily-of-the-Valley spread far too well, pushing their way through clumps of *Tellima* and jostling poor Bowles' Golden Grass, *Milium effusum* 'Aureum', almost out of existence. The poppies too were into everything. After a few years my ruthless character could stand it no longer and all those invasive creatures had to come out and be banished to places where I felt they could do less damage.

The upper side of this bed was drier, partly because of tree roots, so I planted it with things that enjoyed spring and early summer moisture. Pretty *Corydalis solida* is very welcome there early in the spring, while erythroniums have increased well.

Erythronium dens-canis, and *E. californicum* 'White Beauty' do especially well. They come up through carpets of *Viola riviniana* Purpurea Group (previously, but wrongly known as *V. labradorica*), which I find invaluable for awkward conditions. Dwarf vincas and *Leptinella squalida* are the only things that have made a satisfactory carpet over the roots of *Acer davidii*. This is a most beautiful small tree, especially in winter when its green and white striped bark is tinted red and the young twigs are coral against a blue sky. I think it should be in grass. It makes such a loofah-like mat of roots.

On the lower damper side of this bed are hybrids of *Primula vulgaris*; *P.* 'Guinevere' and *P.* 'Lady Greer' look well mixed up in backgrounds of pink- and purple-leaved ajugas. Very striking too are a few clumps of *P.* Cowichan Garnet Group. I love best the darkest garnet colours, velvet soft, with the merest glint of a golden eye. Various forms of *Anemone nemorosa*, including the fragile-looking lilac-blue bowls of *A. n.* 'Robinsoniana' run now with *Tiarella*, while *Potentilla rupestris* looks right with sprays of pure white flowers on rosy-pink stems. × *Heucherella alba* 'Bridget Bloom' has settled happily and flowers over a long season in this bed, but the ordinary heucheras would not put roots down into the sour black silt.

In a drier section, where a big oak root may be coming near the surface, epimediums have made most satisfying thickets of growth. Especially easy is *E.* × *versicolor* 'Sulphureum' and nothing is more beautiful in the spring when, if you have remembered to cut off the old leaves in February, it will be covered with nodding sprays of tiny primrose-yellow flowers; heart-shaped leaves most tenderly suffused with tan over pale green will quickly follow. As the leaf strengthens the colour drains away, to become russet again with autumn frosts, remaining so all winter. I have other delicate epimediums to tell you of in more favoured spots elsewhere, but I value none more than this.

Thalictrum aquilegiifolium was an easy settler, holding its large mauve-pink or white powder puffs high above most things. Its green seed heads also add something to the scene among stands of *Lilium lancifolium* and dark blue *Aconitum*. *Thalictrum* seedlings appear where I would not think of putting them, and grow to an astonishing height, peering through the lacy foliage of the golden cut-leaved elder, *Sambucus racemosa* 'Plumosa Aurea'.

Camassia leichtlinii has also seeded generously in among hostas with tall graceful stems of pale cream-coloured stars. Not quite so delicate, but much admired, is the double form *C. l.* 'Semiplena'. This needs a deep, rich soil to make the large bulbs which send up stout stems, over 1.5m/5ft tall, heavily set with double cream rosettes. Snowdrops – among which appeared a particularly fine looking one now known as *Galanthus plicatus* 'Beth Chatto', tall stemmed with globular flowers and grey leaves – I plant and divide every few years to build up stock. Ivory-white *Narcissus* 'Thalia', and *N.* 'Tresamble' please me more than too much bright yellow, looking especially lovely among the forget-me-not blue of *Brunnera macrophylla*, whose large leaves handsomely cover the gaps when both flowers have long gone.

For autumn glory colchicums, including the peerless *Colchicum speciosum* 'Album', slowly multiplied.

Alongside this Shade Bed, separated by a wide curving grass walk, ran the ditch, about 1m/3ft wide with fairly shallow sloping banks. We had no experience of growing water-side plants, and we made the usual mistakes. Probably the worst was being in too much of a hurry and not making proper preparations. But to begin with it did not show up too badly.

The worst weeds along the bank-side were rushes, grasses of course, and nettles. Although we had dug the roots out initially the soil was full of weed seed, and in those early days we had no ideas about mulching – at least we had seen hop waste used at Kew Gardens, but considerable effort among local breweries produced not even a whiff. It seemed it all went to fertilizer firms, in which case we could not afford it, not in the amounts we would be needing. We could only cope with the

The damp stock beds are situated in low-lying, partially spring-fed, heavy soil where we can grow late-flowering perennials and grasses which would not stand a chance in our free-draining gravel soils. Here various forms of *Miscanthus* in flower create a prairie-like effect, billowing above the taper-like crimson flowers of *Persicaria amplexicaulis* 'Atrosanguinea'.

weed problem on this especially difficult type of soil, where native weeds germinate freely and rapaciously smother newcomers, by planting large and vigorous co-operators who would do some of the work for us.

We planted quick growing shrubs like *Cornus alba* 'Sibirica' whose china-blue berries set among crimson autumn leaves are followed by brilliant red stems all winter. The lovely green and gold variegated *C. a.* 'Spaethii' made a great shrub more than 2.5m/8ft high, and far more across. Several bushes of *Viburnum opulus* 'Xanthocarpum' looked charming in early summer covered with lacy 'maid's caps', while in autumn we seemed to have weeks of pleasure from the large clusters of marble-sized berries, butter-yellow, gradually turning transparent amber. The crimson-fruited *V. opulus* was there as well. So too was *V. betulifolium,* which made an enormous screen, but was most reluctant to berry. Why, I wonder? Thinking the first plant needed company, perhaps from a different clone, we bought two more, which shot up with equal vigour, but only an occasional bough was hung with the characteristic tiny glittering berries.

OVERLEAF
A view across the low-lying Canal Bed, either side of the spring-fed ditch, towards Shade Bed 2, which, with its east-facing side, provides an open, sunny site for perennials that need retentive soil.

We planted *Aralia elata*, the Japanese Angelica Tree, which makes in one season tall, linenprop-like prickly stems topped with handsome pinnate leaves, the second year producing a froth of white blossom followed by wide heads of tiny purple-black berries on crimson stems. But this too had to go further afield. Its suckering habit was insufferable among border *Phlox*, Black-eyed Susan, *Rudbeckia fulgida* var. *speciosa*, and other robust perennials.

Persicaria campanulata was a great success. A rapid colonizer with surface roots so not a menace, it makes ideal ground-cover in damp soil where something large is needed. In spring it appears as a close cover, but during the summer the crowded stems elongate to about 1m/3ft. All late summer and autumn they are topped with loose heads of tiny rose-pink flowers.

Fallopia sachalinensis we planted also, and magnificent it looked in its wild setting. Great jointed bamboo-like stems, 3–4m/10–12ft high, carry large oval green leaves while strings of typical white flowers emerge from every leaf axil. But it is a formidable underground worker so beware of putting it anywhere you would regret. *F. japonica*, and *F. j.* var. *compacta*, were both there, invincible among native weeds but practically ineradicable themselves – a pity, because they are both very handsome. They had to be removed, but fortunately I could find for them a distant wilderness where I hope I shall not live to regret my decision. Tall grasses like *Miscanthus sacchariflorus*, *M. sinensis* 'Gracillimus' and *M. s.* 'Zebrinus' made splendid contrast in form to these gigantic herbs.

Having read that *Rheum palmatum* looked splendid among water-side plantings I tried to establish some pieces, but they looked more and more miserable. When I dug them up I found their great crowns were rotting. The soil was too wet for them. However, in later years I have planted more, not far from the water, but on raised ground so there is no danger of water-logging. They do look almost tropical in luxuriance, and are needful near the lush water-side plants, in place of *Gunnera* if that is too massive for the situation.

We had prepared a rich, deep bed for *Gunnera tinctoria,* which was making good headway until we had a particularly cold winter. Our plant was being so slow to produce those rusty-backed funnels of new leaves that we went to investigate and found that a family of water voles had lived all winter in its huge starchy heart and eaten it out, leaving, like a cheese, the outer rind. Offshoots did survive, but it was a wasted year or so. I have also had *Phormium tenax* chewed off at their heavy bases by these little creatures. When we first began the garden they were so unused to humans they were quite fearless. Not at all repulsive, unlike the scabby land rats against which we wage incessant war, they are neat little creatures, with sleek brown coats and shining beady eyes. Endearing, in fact, as Ratty himself. But their eating habits are as deadly to water gardeners as are rabbits elsewhere. We had to deal with the problem in due course by making low support walls (see pages 43–7).

Naturally I tried to grow candelabra primulas and blue *Meconopsis* (of all things in windy Essex!), but the situation was not sufficiently under control. Anything small was eventually lost, either because I could not give it enough attention, or because the coarseness of the soil did not favour it.

I should not like to forget to mention a plant that I associate very much with the early days of the Damp Garden. We had planted Himalayan *Impatiens glandulifera*. When well grown this imposing annual makes transparent stems, as thick as your wrist at the base, standing easily 2–3m/6–8ft tall. In late autumn its curious sweet scent floats on the moist air of still evenings. I stand and look into its extraordinary shaped flowers, made in two parts, which open like a medieval knight's hinged helmet. Andrew takes a ripe pointed seed pod and puts it in my hand, telling me to hold it close – knowing that in a few seconds I will jump in alarm as it bursts like a broken spring to toss its seeds for yards. That is the trouble. We had, at times, forests of seedlings. In our primitive beginnings it did not matter. It looked in keeping. But as I wished to grow more and more unusual plants I knew it would have to be checked.

Now we tend to weed out every seedling we find so that sometimes I am concerned that there seems not to be a single plant left. But I need not worry. Tucked into the wilder places, perhaps around the great clumps of bamboo, enough seedlings escape to flower and toss their seeds where no harm can be done.

By midsummer 1960 the house was finished, and as much of our seventeen years of plant collecting as we could decently manage was heeled in, lined out, or comfortably planted somewhere. Then we concentrated on paving and planting round the house. With so much empty space, more trees were needed to frame the house and to shelter the plants I hoped I could grow. I sometimes say it is not difficult to cover the bare earth when making a new garden; much more patience is needed to paint the sky. Time dragged as I waited for the trees to reach the roof level of our low-pitched mushroom-like house.

Another interesting problem was to adapt to the unfamiliar scale created by a three-hundred-year-old oak, dominant under a wide Essex sky, set in undefined space. I felt this most keenly one day when I carried a handful of snowdrops in green leaf and planted them beneath the oak. I stood back to admire the effect and felt chilled by the loneliness of that little bunch. There needed to be many frames within frames to ease the transition in time and space. An oak wood, with trees of mixed years, with ivy curled round their trunks and carpeting the ground below, becomes with time the setting for a ballet of snowdrops, bunched and drifting to catch your breath.

2 | Beginning the Water Gardens

WITH THE REST OF THE GARDEN UNDER WAY I looked again at the Lily Pond and thought I knew what was wrong – it was too small for the setting and too round. It was a heady spring day, long white clouds in a blue sky. Suddenly I saw that, instead of a small round pond, I needed a long stretch of open water to repeat the shape of my white-boarded house, to reflect the clouds and the majestic oak, which stood almost opposite the house. I broke the good news to Andrew who, while not exactly discouraging, thought it was out of the question. The expense would forbid it.

Then came one of those curious coincidences which make you feel as though life is already mapped out for you, and you are merely following the white line. Within a few days, who should I meet in the village but my friend with the dragline. He began the conversation. How was the Lily Pond? What could I say? I said, 'Why don't you come and have a look at it?' The outcome at the end of an entertaining and reassuring morning, during which Mr Crees walked up and down our hollow (hanging on to a vibrant hazel twig), was that he could easily do what I wanted for £20! Twenty pounds then was worth a great deal more than it is today, but that morning to me it seemed very reasonable to drown a lot of weedy rubbish, to get rid of the dry steep sides of the ditch, to create shallow boggy edges. I could already see primulas – in sheets!

Once again the dragline, that huge and seemingly cumbersome machine, edged

The Weeping Willow (*Salix alba* 'Tristis') was a garden-warming present when we moved into our newly built, split-level house in 1960. I hoped it would grow to be a partner to the ancient oak nearby, so that both would be in scale with the ponds I planned to make. It has done that, and gives pleasure all year round.

ABOVE LEFT: Part of the original wilderness, before we had begun to clear dead trees, brambles and blackthorn.
ABOVE RIGHT: The first pond, in about 1965, showing ancient oaks which form the west-facing boundary and cleared land before any planting had begun.

its way delicately down the slope at the garden entrance, followed by a bulldozer, for we had decided to go further and open up the overgrown boggy meadow beyond the pond as far as the ancient boundary hedge. There was already a crossing over the ditch made above a small brick culvert. It was decided to open up this little dam and raise the level of the water by ramming wet clay into the culvert, lay new pipes at a higher level and replace the topsoil. This would cause the running water to flood the land behind. It was also decided, because of the gentle slope of the land, that instead of making one long sheet of water we would divide it by two dams placed across the middle, so forming a second and third pond, each at slightly higher levels. This involved moving the minimum of soil. The effect when done was, and still is, just as I wished. I realized at the time that it would have been better if more clay had been removed from the bottom of the ponds, as they were rather shallow, and I was afraid they would silt up. However, to cart away the abominable clay would have entailed expense we could not afford – and where to? (After about twenty years, we partially drained the ponds, deepened them in places, and subsequently use our own tanker to suck out some of the silt.)

I am always in a state of dither when the dragline is at work. So much happens so fast. Can I visualize how it will look when the piles of oozing scooped-up clay, heaped to make dams across the middle of three seemingly vast scraped holes, have settled and the water has found its new level? It must not come too high and flood the grass walk below the house. At the same time will it be high enough to cover a particularly awkward wet patch?

While the topography of the garden was being remade the bulldozer was making short work of the wilderness beyond. Great thickets of blackthorn to which we had become accustomed, even admired for a brief space when 'frosted' with blossom in April's 'Blackthorn winter' – all were being swept away, and a new wide expanse of brown meadow silt was being exposed. For the first time we could see all of the boundary trees: six oaks, a couple of immense hawthorns, a fine crab apple and several decrepit hazelnut bushes.

It was no use being impatient at this stage. The land had to settle. During the summer we let the meadow silt run down to its native grasses, and while there were undesirables like great prickly rosettes of marsh thistle, and soft grass (*Holcus mollis*), which makes enormous floppy tussocks so big that one will fill a barrow, we managed to control it well enough for the time being with our old farm Hayter pulled behind the tractor.

My first bog borders lay between the mown grass and the edge of the water where we could see them from the house. We dug and carted away in barrows as much of the clay as we had the strength and willpower to do. Then we carted as much decent topsoil and rotted compost as we could find and piled that on top to hide the beastly yellow stuff.

PAINTING THE SKY WITH TREES

Next we thought about suitable trees. We planted three Swamp Cypresses, *Taxodium distichum*, tiny things, knee high, and a *Metasequoia glyptostroboides*, or Dawn Redwood as many people, understandably, would prefer to call it. Both of these are leaf-losing conifers; both take, like ducks, to water. The Swamp Cypress, from the Everglades of Florida, has smaller frond-like leaves, soft and mossy-green. Before they drop in autumn they slowly turn a rich foxy-brown. Knowing they would take many years before they made their mark in the landscape we planted quick growing willows to give some height. The great oak still remained aloof in the background, so to bring it into the garden I planted a Weeping Willow between it and the water. By the water's edge I planted *Gunnera tinctoria*. Today the willow makes a tumbling mass as tall as the oak. It unites visually with the oak from across the water, and together with the vast parasols of the *Gunnera* leaves they create a harmonious group in scale with their surroundings.

When the dams were sufficiently settled they were prepared for grass. This was Harry's job. Harry, over the years, made it possible for me to follow behind his careful preparations and plant my garden. Halfway across one of the dams, which lies opposite my bedroom window, we planted a *Salix babylonica* var. *pekinensis* 'Tortuosa', better known as the Twisted Willow. On the whole I do not like 'tortured' plants. I think the contorted hazelnut is shockingly hideous in summer, its poor leaves so twisted and malformed that one immediately thinks it must be riddled with aphids. In winter, of course, it is a different matter; there is something attractive about those corkscrew curling twigs and branches. But where to plant it, so that you will not come across it in summer?

The Twisted Willow is not nearly so deformed, but I think *it* is best in winter, when every gracefully curling branch and twig sparkles as the sun is reflected from its polished surfaces. The young leaves, slightly twisted, look particularly pleasing if you cut a few boughs in early January, bring them into the house, and let a jugful become an indoor mini tree, decked in the tenderest green leaves long before the buds have burst outside. (Eventually the willow grew too large for the dam, its roots gave way, and I was not sad to have it removed.)

Near the first little dam we planted *Prunus* 'Taihaku', the Great White Cherry, well above the water on a little bank. Among earlier tree plantings we had had a *Liquidambar styraciflua*, the Sweet Gum, but in autumn it never managed more than the dirtiest of nettle-green colouring where I had expected a warm conflagration of crimson and scarlet. From somewhere I had obtained seed, and now with several little saplings to choose from I picked out the one which looked most promising and planted it in a group with the white-flowered cherry and another *Metasequoia*. They have all grown into a most companionable group: the *Metasequoia* rapidly made a tall slender accent, as lovely in winter with its cinnamon-brown bark as it is in summer clothed in larch-green. The leaves of the *Liquidambar* glow like garnets in the short days of autumn, a total contrast to the ice-white clusters of cherry blossom in spring. They grow to the constant sound of water as it falls from the hidden pipe laid beneath the little grassed dam, and drops several feet into the widened ditch, over which they cast a cool shade. For long enough the steep sides of the bank and the sight of the pipe emerging from it bothered me. But I planted *Hedera helix* 'Parsley Crested' thickly and soon both bank and pipe were disguised by a green shawl of crinkled leaves, which solved my weeding problem in that awkward area.

PLANTING AT THE WATER'S EDGE

We came at last to the exciting moment of putting herbaceous plants into the damp soil. Water does not travel far sideways in heavy soil, so it remains really wet a comparatively short distance from the water's edge. Here we planted various forms of marsh marigold, *Caltha palustris* and *C. p.* var. *radicans* 'Flore Pleno', the double-flowered form which makes such a long-lasting display but does not, to my mind, have quite the charm of our common King Cup with its brownish stems forming a graceful mound, each single cup filled with a boss of rich golden stamens. With heaps of wet ground to cover perhaps my favourite is *Caltha p.* var. *palustris*. Planted on the edge of a low wet place it will root itself into the soil, or fling out yard-long stems which root into the water, eventually making great rafts many feet across if you will let it. The large round leaves stand up well above the water, no less handsome than the leaves of water-lilies, perfect to unite large areas of land and water.

The Water Forget-me-not, *Myosotis scorpioides*, quickly settled in, seeded and made drifts of blue among the spring golds. Water iris, especially *Iris laevigata*, *I. versicolor* and the handsome *I. v.* 'Kermesina', also multiplied.

We had decided that large herbs would, on the whole, stand a better chance of survival than anything more refined. The largest we were aware of then was *Eupatorium purpureum*, whose dark plum-coloured stems easily soar over 2.5m/8ft, topped with wide flat heads of fuzzy cinnamon-pink flowers.

Members of the meadowsweet family were another obvious choice, especially *Filipendula rubra* 'Venusta' which sent its strong roots down into the clay, spreading around its tall stems set with dark vine-like leaves. As time has passed one of the prettiest sights now, in summer, is that of the fluffy pink heads, like candyfloss, poised high against the fresh green columns of the Swamp Cypresses. Not so tall, and keeping itself in a well-controlled clump, is the pale pink form of *Filipendula purpurea*. Close again to the water I planted my two favourites of the European

The autumn gold of the Great White Cherry, *Prunus* 'Taihaku', is reflected in the ponds nearest the house, while *Pontederia cordata* and *Caltha palustris* var. *palustris* soften the edges of the mown-grass dam which divides them.

mountain meadows, *Trollius europaeus* with *Persicaria bistorta* 'Superba', the soft yellow globes and thick pink pokers reflected in the dark water. The *Persicaria*, with its mounds of great dock-like leaves (always causing the same kind of tediously obvious comment – as does *Gunnera*), is invaluable ground-cover in wet clay soil.

Along the mown grass edge, furthest away from the water, I planted hostas. Especially handsome is *H. sieboldiana* var. *elegans* – its quilted, bluish leaves make an incomparable focal point – while the exquisite grass, *Molinia caerulea* subsp. *caerulea* 'Variegata', almost steals that honour, especially in the autumn when it becomes almost totally white.

It is not easy to find plants which remain evergreen by the water-side. Most disappear completely, so that the contrast between summer lushness and the desolate drabness of winter can be painful. I value the Pampas Grass, *Cortaderia selloana*, and *Phormium tenax* for their big bold outlines, in winter especially when they help to take the eye off the empty wastes.

I try to leave the tall stately clumps of *Miscanthus* for as long as I can in winter. In autumn they withdraw their colour, becoming columns of palest straw. *M. sinensis* 'Gracillimus' survives the wintry gales with scarcely a curling wisp out of place, elegant to the end, but the 3m/10ft (and more) stems of *M. sacchariflorus* fluttering with tattered ribbons have usually to be cut down before they have made a fine mess.

All of these plants, in their season, add something to the varied pattern of leaves and flowers at the water's edge. But there are two plants, which for me are high points in the design. From spring to autumn they dominate.

The first is *Lysichiton americanus*, the Bog Arum. In early April, when the cold wet soil is bare but for twigs and dead leaves, cobra-like heads emerge, tipped and shaded with green. As this fades away the huge spathes reflect rich yellow in the clear water. Inside are sheltered slim spadices, which slowly form green club-like heads of seed, caviar for the water voles. There is more to come. At this time only the very tips of the leaves are showing at the base of the thickly clustered flower stems, but surging up from 1m/3ft or more below the sodden clay they come, pushing aside the spent spathes, and making a leaf cluster, shining green, as spectacular as any flower for months to come. Thinking how to describe these impressive leaves, I am reminded of one, among a group of young students, who irreverently rocked with mirth at the enormous 'spinach', which had suddenly caught his eye and imagination. Recovering my balance I appreciated that he had noticed the plant, and am grateful now for the simile because they are not unlike a well-grown Spinach Beet, though four times as big, and stronger and smoother in texture. I once cut a mature leaf to take to a lecture; it was as tall as I was.

The second and most dramatic plant by the water-side is *Gunnera*, whose enormous leaves, 1.2–2m/4–6ft across, can stand more than head high, offering shelter from a sudden shower of rain. Not everyone admires it. Its sheer size, rasping texture and outlandish fruiting body undoubtedly contributed to the emotion of a lady who observed, matter of factly, that it really was quite hideous. Although I could not agree with her I was amused by this unexpected opinion in place of the usual comment of 'Oh, look at this gigantic rhubarb,' which of course it is not.

Our plants of *Gunnera* came from a garden in the last sad stage of decay. The shallow moat had vanished completely beneath a meadow of rush and water grasses, the flowering plants long gone. Once or twice a year the banks were scythed. Tidied up with the rest (maybe in full leaf, but no matter), were the remnants of *Gunnera tinctoria*, their huge parasols reduced to pygmy proportions. I could not believe they were the real thing. But time and care (with annual dressings of old muck) healed and they recovered their majestic grandeur. Without them, and the towering feathery pennants of Pampas Grass, *Cortaderia selloana* 'Sunningdale Silver', the scale of the garden could overwhelm smaller plants. (I may have said it before but in a smaller setting I have used an ornamental rhubarb, *Rheum palmatum* in place of *Gunnera*.)

Our first plants were of *Gunnera tinctoria*. It grows wild in Chile, with *Cortaderia selloana*, backed by a forest of the Antarctic Beech, *Nothofagus*, while feathered stems of climbing bamboo disappear above them. This spectacular scene is illustrated in *Die Vegetation der Erde*, by Dr Karl Reiche, who stands four-square beside his photographic paraphernalia, dwarfed by these giants among plants. This wonderful picture stretches the mind, and is the answer to a sensitive gardener who, when advised by me to plant Pampas Grass as a feature near her water garden, ventured hesitantly that it might look suburban. In the wrong setting it might look out of place, but suburban never!

In the wild *Gunnera tinctoria* stays near the shelter of the forest, but the Pampas Grass can also be found alongside water courses, all over the wide pampas, or prairies, where there is little but grass and sky for miles and miles. *G. manicata*, which grows even larger and taller than *G. tinctoria*, comes from southern Brazil, which is considerably warmer. It is necessary to cover both forms well, to shelter the coconut-sized resting buds, which have no outer protection, only the first leaf wrapped round like a parcel. When the plants are young, additional comfort like straw or bracken will be needed, but we saw down the stout prickly stems of our established plants and press them upside down over the knobbly seed heads, which hold them down like gigantic hatpins. By early April the upturned funnels of folded leaves are pushing through the battered remains; so it is time to remove them. But some years late May frosts have killed the new leaves; they stand crisply mummified while I wait anxiously to see what will happen next. Within a few weeks new leaves

BETH CHATTO'S DAMP GARDEN

have emerged from hidden reserves and the show is on, a little later.

My second, narrower bed beside the water I filled at last with primulas. *Primula japonica, P. pulverulenta, P. florindae* and *P. bulleyana*, mixed up with *Iris ensata*, the little double *Cardamine* and a few astilbes. It was colourful – too colourful for my liking, too many star-performers grouped together. However, we pressed on, and before long we had made borders round two of the ponds, so tempting was it not to waste any damp ground.

Beguiled by a picture in Frances Perry's book, *Water Gardening*, that has haunted me for years, showing a great curve of lake-side with at least a thousand blooms of Arum Lily (*Zantedeschia aethiopica*), I planted two or three clumps. We made shallow baskets of old wire netting, filled them with upturned turves, well-rotted muck and topsoil, set the roots among it and lowered the lot into the water, hoping the water rats would not get them. They have established and increased, but I shall never see the luxuriance of that mysterious garden in the picture – could it be a warmer district than here?

WEEDS, WATER VOLES AND OTHER WILDLIFE

By now we had learnt a little about gardening in boggy land. The most frightening thing was the way the weeds grew. No thought of hoeing – everything had to be pulled, dug or slurped out of the squelchy ground or it immediately took root again. Along the water's edge knitting needle clumps of Common Rush, pretty as could be when young, became a major issue, back-breaking to lift with the slime running down the front of your anorak and into your wellington boots. Not only that, but the edge of the bed on which you have piled your precious topsoil would crumble down into the water as you prised out some particularly tenacious weed. Something had to be done.

There was another problem. It was the water rats, or more correctly, water voles, who were becoming too troublesome to be tolerated. Imagine, on one of our few soft, still summer evenings, that you are dreaming round the garden counting your blessings (and failures). Or, you are tearing yourself away from a bit of blissfully uninterrupted planting to go indoors to make supper. Suddenly either mood is shattered by the loud crunching of teeth on something not easily spared. It may be the fine stand of bamboo by the little wooden bridge now at the far end of the garden. It is almost bound to be water iris. Remains of enormous clumps of *Iris pseudacorus* have been seen to float on the surface like shredded wheat. In spring I have found heavy tillers of *Phormium tenax* that could be lifted out of the soil, baseless. I could go on, monotonously for you, maddening for me.

Riddling their way through the pond-side borders the water voles undermined the banks with their exits and entrances, below water level. The edges fell in; plants

A variety of different leaf shapes and textures clothes the pond edge, but would not make a satisfactory picture without the huge, handsome leaves of *Gunnera tinctoria*, which will expand to as much as 1.5m/5ft across. The curious, club-like fruiting stem can be seen at the base of the plant.

OVERLEAF
In early spring the naked stems of *Darmera peltata* rise from creeping rhizomes, bearing wide heads of starry pink flowers. Large, parasol-shaped leaves follow, making mounds of eye-catching splendour. *D. p.* 'Nana', which is more suitable for smaller areas, develops, in my garden, the richest autumn colour of the two. Both thrive in boggy soil.

Rheum 'Ace of Hearts' is a handsome foliage plant for retentive soil, its tall, branching flower spikes of palest pink a bonus in early summer. To the left of the *Hosta* is the lovely *Filipendula purpurea* 'Elegans', with flat heads of deep rose flowers that change to bronze-red seed heads and create a feature for weeks into late summer.

fell out. Even the lawns became undermined by these busy little bodies. What to do? Neither of us was born with guns in our hands, so although we possessed a four-ten we were not very efficient with it. The water voles plopped out of our plants as soon as they heard us coming and we did not have the cat's patience to wait. What is more, there were plenty of families both up- and downstream to come and take their places.

Then Andrew had a bright idea. We remembered the edging around the lakes at Kew Gardens, preventing the banks from disintegrating. They had driven in strong poles, of elm perhaps, vertically, and packed close together so that the finished effect, a few inches above water level, is a necklace of round wooden blocks (about 15cm/6in across as I remember), set all round the water's edge. This is called piling, and must be extremely laborious and expensive. We could not see our way to piling with wood, but we could make a substitute. We could lay our hands on old angle irons (new ones are costly), and we could buy, not too expensively, hollow concrete blocks. We would sink the blocks around the edge of the pond and stabilize them with an angle iron driven through both ends of the blocks into the hard soil beneath.

Once more Harry took over this heavy job. The flow of water had to be stopped by blocking the entrance culvert with clay, and our handy little pump chugged away for a day or so lowering the water level so that he could see what he was doing. In most places two blocks deep were sufficient, making a 46cm/18in wall, with irons about 1.2m/4ft long driven through them. Sometimes three or four blocks were required where the hard bottom was deeper, and I saw irons 2m/6ft long disappear through the blocks to rest just at the top level of concrete. When finished the top of the blocks was about 5cm/2in above the water line, and I think Harry was as delighted with it as we were, having taken great care to make the curves natural and pleasing.

It may *sound* horrible. I confess that throughout the operation I had felt Gertrude Jekyll's sensitive eye looking down on me in reproach. But, said to myself, I must try to be practical as well as aesthetic. A garden is by its very nature chaos controlled (more or less), but we do not want that control too apparent.

As I had hoped, the hard edging soon weathered, plants flopped over it; *Iris* and *Pontederia* grew happily against it. I hardly think that, in most places, you would notice it. We decided to edge the dams as well; the final effect of neat mown grass walks crossing the broad stretches of water is very satisfying. They are pleasant places to sit, surrounded by lush plants, and to feed the ducks and watch a red-finned rudd surge beneath an astonished drake to tip him off course as both of them aim for the same crumb of bread.

On early summer mornings I often see a heron from my window, immobile in shallow water or marching stiffly up and down the dam, alert for the slightest sign of movement in the house. Sometimes I see him lunge like a spear, then throw up his head and struggle mightily to ease a big fish down his long neck. There are plenty of the native fish for him and to spare; he helps keep a natural balance. Sometimes the shallows look like marmalade with thousands of tiny suspended fish warming themselves in the sun. I like to think the kingfisher has a taste of those. One memorable day I walked back to my digging to find him, unbelievably, sitting on the handle of my spade.

After making the low support walls gardening around the ponds became much less hazardous. The sound of chewing ceased, and I could crouch on the narrow edge of the blocks to weed my beds in comfort; yet I am aware that I have contributed to driving the bright-eyed water voles almost to the point of extinction, which is a sobering thought.

3 | The Shade Beds

L OOKING FROM THE HOUSE, across the ponds, the view disturbed me. It needed a more comfortable background. There was, of course, the great oak, which dominates the garden wherever you stand. It stood at the end of the boundary row of miscellaneous oaks and oddments. Too many oddments. Elders, naturally, were seeded everywhere, with blackthorn suckers and Goat-willow between the glaring gaps. Beyond the gaps we have glimpses of the neighbouring farm, under plough, or golden with corn, while a distant mixed hedge of mature trees and brushwood adds considerably to the view. But I dread this being axed during some particularly cold spell when nothing more useful can be done. I felt we needed to plant more trees and shrubs, in groups, in the grass, and far enough away from the boundary not to be affected by overhead shade.

One warm day, walking over the rough grass discussing the proposed tree planting, someone dropped a hot match – in a flash the grass crackled and fire ran quickly ahead of us, in spite of damp soil underneath. Beating with branches and stamping our feet we had a hot and anxious time before it was controlled.

I shall not list the names of all the trees and shrubs we planted to make a windshield and background screen for our ponds. Suffice to say that plant we did, and as usual more than enough so that changes had to be made as crowding became apparent. The trees and shrubs were planted in rough grass that was cut two or three times a year. I used to enjoy sweeping up the long grass with a big wooden rake,

Angelica archangelica is a huge, stately biennial umbellifer for the back of a bank or large border that does not dry out. In its second year, stout branching stems rise among the broadly divided leaves; these are topped with handsome heads of cream, Cow Parsley-like flowers. The young, tender hollow stems are very aromatic and, preserved in sugar, are used in confectionery.

imagining I was on holiday in Switzerland as I 'toiled' up and down my slight slopes. The hay I piled around the trees to act as a mulch, leaving a few inches of bare ground round the base of the trunks so that mice would not be tempted to sit under cover and chew round the bark in winter.

As the trees grew, the little round beds they stood in were enlarged to prevent too much root competition from the grass. One or two trees stood still for several years after planting. Feeling there was not much to lose I slit the bark vertically from top to bottom with a sharp knife. I was pleased to see the split widen and the trees begin to make new growth. Such a drastic method can be worth knowing if trees become bark-bound; an old countryman had shown me how to do it years before.

By the late 1960s Andrew's health had deteriorated too badly for him to continue running the farm. It had to be sold. The thought of leaving the wasteland and the garden, well-started, I found unbearable. It was agreed that I could start a little nursery to help pay someone to help me. I had learnt to propagate many things for the garden. There were always plants to spare. So I began, with one girl, a few frames made from railway sleepers, and Harry, who asked to stay with me when the farm was gone.

An old way of life was over. A different life began. The garden had to be maintained, but alongside it I had to learn to balance the books. Making and selling plants had to have priority. However, I made time still to plant, and one day I planted both the green-and red-leaved forms of *Rheum palmatum* in two groups in front of my young trees. The effect was inspiring. There were already bulbs in the grass, the colchicums especially looked effective, but they had not suggested to me, as these handsome big leaves did, that too much of this moist meadow soil was wasted under grass. I had big groups of *Hosta*, with perhaps *Astilbe* or *Ligularia* in mind, with room to spare for plants unknown. I dragged hosepipes in a wide arc around one of my tree groupings, and asked Harry to clear the turf.

When I wish to extend the garden, I equip myself with all the hosepipes I can find in order to take away from one bed, or add to another. In case I have not made myself clear I should explain that a hosepipe laid on the ground is the easiest way of suggesting a new curving outline. I also have by me a bundle of small canes to push into the grass on either side of the hose to hold it in position here and there. Then I take a half-moon edging blade, make a shallow cut on either side of the hose, remove it and pick out the narrow strip of turf with a border fork. There is the new outline of bare soil lying on the ground until such time as the rest of the turf can be removed, and the soil properly prepared for planting. By aligning the new curves with those already laid down you make sure that they flow naturally and easily, not fussily, like contrived scallops.

Then I was ill. For four months I did not see the garden or the nursery. When I returned it was with a few new ideas, including the following:

1. I am not indispensable.
2. It is a waste of energy worrying about what cannot be done tomorrow.
3. Much better to reserve my energy for what I can do today.
4. Simplify wherever possible, without sacrificing interest.
5. Use all available aids.

This may sound childishly obvious to you, but I was glad to have been shaken into seeing it for myself.

Before long the grass was cleared around all my young shrubberies. The uncovered soil appeared damp. In one place it was wet where a spring from the farmland behind came near the surface. The west wind was also a problem from this quarter, so I fastened a fine mesh Netlon windbreak to the rabbit-netting fence, which we had put behind the boundary oaks. I did not care for the look of it, but more recent plantings on the bank of holly, laurel, yew and *Cotoneaster* have hidden it, and have themselves done better because of this protection from wind which blows uninterrupted across open fields.

Slowly the trees and shrubs became effective, and the water gardens too started to look attractive, so we began to take more interest in the grass. There is always too little time to care for it when all available help is required for more important jobs, but the time comes where poorly kept grass spoils the effect. Our trouble was that the land remained wet far too long in the spring. Often it was late May, and still the small Hayter would become stuck in wet places – I remember sinking in those same wet boggy places long years before we ever thought of making a home there when we went blackberrying along the mountainous bushes laden with fruit:

> And never was queen
> With jewellery rich
> As those same hedges
> From twig to ditch. (*Walter de la Mare*)

All of that delicious poem would stream through my mind as we filled our baskets to make dark jelly. Were strands from those drowsy afternoons binding us to this soil then? We were not aware of it.

Drainage is not a simple matter in fine close-textured soil. It packs down tightly, almost as bad as clay. To begin with we made T-shaped trenches across the wettest patches to pick up the water and carry it down to the ponds. We put in short land drainage pipes and covered them with gravel before filling in with topsoil. Then a particularly wet February showed that this was not enough, so Harry dug a deep ditch where the original ditch must have been made generations before to catch the line of springs from the adjoining land. It is always a pleasure to see a craftsman dig a good ditch, the sides so straight and clean, sloping slightly so that they do not immediately cave in. I would like to say that we found some relic of times long past, a coin perhaps, dropped from the pocket of the first digger of my ditch. But we did not. Only a rather curiously shaped green glass ginger-beer bottle with its rattling marble, and the name of its maker, and town, Colchester, moulded in the glass.

The banks of spoil were removed, to be used elsewhere. We never have waste soil. It is a precious commodity, whatever it may be like, and will inevitably come in handy one day. Often our problem is finding enough of the kind we want. If it is heavy it will go eventually to some place needing body. If it is the poorest gravel it will be ideal for draining wet land, or making up pathways. If it is a solid wet clay it is the only thing for repairing dams. The new ditch was a success, carrying away the surplus surface water, but not drying my tree and shrub plantings too much, or the grass walks which improved in texture.

The cleared ground between the shrubs was deeply dug to aerate it. Once more I had a new home for plants. But before I describe them I would like to tell you something of their neighbours.

The spine of trees and shrubs in the centre of the large, somewhat elliptical-shaped bed, is dominated by *Malus tschonoskii*. I love the shape of this wild apple from Japan. It is so upright you might think it a poplar when not in leaf, while the autumn colour is the most brilliant we have, the richest scarlet. The flowers are inconspicuous, unlike most flowering crab-apples, but flower it must, because in November I can search the ground beneath for little yellow and red fruits. We split a few and sow the pips. I did have several other wild crab-apple trees in this area, thinking it would be pretty to have a little grove of them flowering in the grass. But the blossom of most ornamental trees is so fleeting that unless you have parkland to fill I think the room they take is not justified. So, the broad-headed ones were removed.

Although it does take up a lot of room I kept *Parrotia persica*. This has made a great, wide, hazel-like shrub, but it provides a fine background for other things, and its autumn colour, especially now it has a little shelter and the new growth does not get so whipped about, is really magnificent. I like the funny little flowers too. Absurd for such an elephantine shrub, they are just little tufts of raspberry-red stamens.

Cryptomeria japonica, the Japanese Cedar, likes moist soil so I planted it at the dampest end. It has made a graceful pyramidal shape to which my eye is gratefully led in winter. Other evergreens with interesting form are two or three *Picea omorika*, which I probably use too much, but they are so beautiful, take up little room and associate well with soft-leaved trees and shrubs. So anxious have I been to make a screen that I have also planted different forms of *Chamaecyparis lawsoniana*, including *C. l.* 'Pendula', and *C. l.* 'Stewartii', though I am not really certain if they look right. But I must give them time. Too artificial looking trees, if I can use that phrase, can look out of place, especially in a very rural setting.

The same remark could apply to variegated hollies, but I planted a couple in the back. They are very slow growing. (I cannot understand how rabbits can have such a passion for holly. Although the garden is surrounded by rabbit netting, inevitably the occasional youngster squeezes through, or a gate is left open, so every holly has to be individually netted.)

Mahonia japonica slowly made bulk beneath the tall *Malus*; I love the odd leaves enamelled red in winter. Another evergreen I planted is *Osmanthus delavayi*. 'One of China's Gems' says *Hillier's Manual*, but not in my garden. It sits looking very thwarted, which is not the same thing at all as being slow growing. In April, when properly grown, its twiggy, neat-leaved branches are wreathed with clusters of small, white, tubular flowers, most sweetly scented. Perhaps my soil is too sour for it.

I planted *Stephanandra incisa*, and *S. tanakae*, both because I have seen them in other gardens looking a dream in autumn, their prettily shaped leaves a mass of honey-gold. But not with me.

These failures give me the space to try something else but meanwhile precious years have gone, and I still have gaps. However, only by trying, sometimes again and again, can you find what suits your soil and climate.

I should think that more young trees of the cut-leaved Japanese Maple are planted and lost every year than almost anything else. They are under-storey large shrubs or small trees from forests in Japan. They need a sheltered environment, especially from cold east winds, with moist, not waterlogged soil. I was given seed from the famous Westonbirt maples. I picked out the three strongest seedlings and, rather to my surprise, they hung on through several severe droughts and now make substantial growth. The character of my bed will change considerably when all these trees and shrubs look more mature.

Finally, on the old hazelnut bushes in the far background, I threaded *Rosa filipes*, which fills the air with scent from a tangle high above our heads, and the golden-leaved hop, *Humulus lupulus* 'Aureus', mingles both with it, and also trails its beautifully shaped golden leaves across the bed beneath and between dark green clumps of *Helleborus × hybridus*.

Since my new bed looked very big, and the trees were still not big enough, I chose large herbs for the centre, hoping to provide height, bulk and colour – although not too much at a time! I planted *Eupatorium purpureum* again because it

For the large garden, the Wild Garden or lakeside, *Eupatorium purpureum* subsp. *maculatum* 'Atropurpureum' makes a sensational plant in late summer, a fit companion for *Gunnera tinctoria* and the larger forms of *Miscanthus,* stately Japanese grasses.

is so good. Nearby I liked the creamy plumed heads of *Aruncus dioicus* although they do not flower together. *Rheum palmatum* 'Atrosanguineum' looked sumptuous in the spring. First the scaly stumps produce large polished cherry-red buds, almost the size of a cricket ball. The enormous leaves then emerge, pleated and puckered, tinted dull purplish-red all over as the newly born human can be, but as they expand the reddish tinge fades away from the upper surface, lining the underside with soft magenta, a sight to warm your heart on a cold April evening. Good, rich, vegetable-garden type soil is all these great plants need to do well.

Ligularias soon fill up a large empty space. One of my favourites is *Ligularia przewalskii*. Its tall tapering spires of clear yellow flowers look very good rising 1.5m/5ft above neighbouring plants. When I was planting this bed I had not yet come across the fine hybrid called 'The Rocket'. I find this genus, some members of it anyway, rather clannish, so I sometimes look for other members of the same genus to keep each other company. (Red and puce astilbes look quite dreadful nearby I think!)

Persicaria amplexicaulis 'Atrosanguinea' needs plenty of room because by autumn it can be 1.5m/5ft tall, a softly bulky plant crowded with thin tapers of tiny red flowers while occasional leaves become brilliantly coloured, with crimson, yellow, bronze and green markings, vivid as any tropical plant. On thinking over that statement I am wondering if the colour occurs more frequently on poorer soil. This plant takes over in midsummer from *Euphorbia griffithii* 'Fireglow'. Certain euphorbias succeed in hot, sunny, well-drained situations, but this one, although happy in sunshine, revels in deep, rich soil. The spreading roots send up branched stems 1m/3ft high, with handsome red-veined leaves, and every tip shoot developing in succession a flat cluster of soft tomato-red flowers. I think it is because these flowers are small, held lightly, with green light reflected among them, that from a distance the colour appears to be soft rust.

Euphorbia sikkimensis also likes cool, damp conditions. You cannot overlook its new young shoots which appear so early in spring with the first gentian-blue flowers of *Pulmonaria angustifolia* 'Munstead Blue'. The smooth white underground shoots of the *Euphorbia* thrust up pale stems immediately topped with glass-red shoots, flower-like against the bare earth. They spend the rest of the summer

The pale pink tapers of *Persicaria amplexicaulis* 'Rosea' make interesting verticals among the sweet-scented Border Phlox or with the large pink Coneflower, *Echinacea purpurea*. Here it grows beside a tumbled branch of *Persicaria polymorpha*, which makes a tall columnar accent above lower plants, including hostas, rudbeckias and low grasses.

growing green and tall, retaining red veins and stems. Then, suddenly, in late summer, you are surprised to see wide flat heads of gentle yellow-green flowers pushing above something else.

I planted astilbes but they did not look right, so they went elsewhere. *Actaea simplex*, which we used to call *Cimicifuga* (Bugbane), looked magnificent, although I cannot say I have it growing in abundance. How I wish I had. There are several different kinds, all most desirable. I am trying to build up stock, but it takes a long time. Perhaps I have not yet learnt the art. I have learnt that they dislike hot sun on their leaves, no matter how moist it may be underneath.

Hostas I chose as a buffer between these groups and because their bold foliage is a relief, both in shape and colour. In full sunlight I think that *Hosta sieboldiana*, or *H. s.* var. *elegans* is the most successful. They need plenty of humus, occasional dressings of old muck, and then time: many years of undisturbed growth to produce really huge leaves. I have one vast group that takes over quite easily from *Rheum palmatum* 'Atrosanguineum' which, when it has sent up its 2m/6ft spire of tiny carmine-red flowers, takes a rest and retreats rather shabbily into the background. I planted a big group of *Hosta fortunei* 'Albomarginata'. It produced plenty of large leaves and increased in girth, but it was in no way remarkable, the leaves remaining green with only a narrow white margin. Plants taken from the same group and planted elsewhere, in fairly dense shade, are unrecognizably different, being boldly variegated with some leaves hidden within the clump are almost entirely white.

I managed to germinate *Veratrum nigrum*, and gave it a place of honour. I almost think it is a plant you need to inherit, it takes so long to become stupendous. My single plant, with its curving pleated leaves, could have been sufficient alone, but when it sent up a tall dark stem topped with a proud branching head of maroon star-shaped flowers, I thought I had a treasure. Since then I have seen an established clump, inherited from a plant-minded mother-in-law, which stood taller than I, and was an experience to walk round. Then, idling one day with Farrer's *The English Rock Garden*, I began to read his opinion of these statuesque mountain plants. His introduction led me to expect the ultimate in beauty, but he ended with explosive contempt for these flowers of 'unmitigated dinginess'. Such an unexpected viewpoint, expressed so forcibly, found me helpless with laughter. The cult of flower arranging has been responsible for helping us to look and see plant forms with fresh eyes. Certainly green, both in leaf and flower, has probably never before been so fashionable. Imagine the rush there would be now, if we could suddenly supply hundreds of *Veratrum viride*. Whatever would Farrer think?!

Two tall plants that found themselves foot-room before more permanent neighbours had covered the gaps were foxgloves and an Ornamental Tobacco. I particularly love white foxgloves, *Digitalis purpurea* f. *albiflora*, and allow some seedlings to settle where they will, thinning out too crowded colonies or removing any that threaten to spoil something more lasting. I have learnt to weed out any that have purple leaf stalks as these plants will have purple flowers. Pretty though they are in the wild, I care less for them in the garden. I have two other colour forms of the native foxglove, which add something special to early summer flowers. One is primrose-yellow, the other soft apricot-pink. Among the young *Hosta* leaves, with yellow *Paeonia mlokosewitschii*, or white *P. emodi*, they look serene. But I have had them seeded together with *Thalictrum aquilegiifolium*, all poking their heads through the arching branches of *Rubus* 'Benenden' in bridal splendour, and the effect was devastating.

Nicotiana sylvestris I have lost sight of for several years, but I think I prefer it for its effect (where there is room) to *N. alata* which is, I admit, a very pretty thing for flower arranging, with its loose stems of blotting-paper green flowers. But in the emptier days of my big borders I loved to see *N. sylvestris* with its handsome columns of large matt green leaves topped with elegant heads of long tubular white flowers, gleaming faintly in the falling dusk, scenting the damp air.

By the end of the first season the progress of this bed was so encouraging I felt that more could be done with an extra metre or yard of grass round the edge than waste time mowing it. So the bed was extended. It has become a habit of mine to create the garden this way. In doing so I have found that I need to keep a comfortable balance between the width of the grass walks and the beds. Going back to my first damp border: I was now looking for low or medium-sized plants that would taper the profile of my big bed into the broad grass walk which separates it from the water garden.

Perhaps the plant which stood out most exotically as a feature was *Rheum alexandrae*, that is, when it flowered – it is, unfortunately, rather reluctant to do so. Perhaps it needs a softer climate than we have in East Anglia. This relative of common rhubarb and docks grows wild on the Chinese–Tibetan border, in damp mountain grassland. I first saw it at the Inverewe Garden, Ross-shire, where it was staged, dramatically, as foreground to a water garden. It was meant to take your breath away, and did. The leaves, not at all like the other big ornamentals, remind me in shape of the ribbed plantain, but shining, brighter green with wide pale veins. Stiff above them stand 1m/3ft stems, pagoda-like, with large parchment bracts sheltering the clusters of little dock-like flowers hidden beneath them. It was unlike any other flowering plant I had seen. I planted it in two different places. Where it was drier it flowered reasonably but looked discontented. Where the soil was much wetter the plants increased, but rarely flowered! There must be some place where it will do both well. (I no longer have it, and realize I do not have the conditions it requires.)

The long-lasting, fluffy spires of astilbes are tantalizingly desirable in sun or part-shade, but succeed only where there is sufficient moisture throughout the growing season. Do not be too efficient in tidying up the dried stems and rich brown seed heads since these provide good shapes and warm touches of colour to the winter landscape.

More cream, or rather soft yellow, accents are made with perennial foxgloves. *Digitalis lutea* perhaps has rather too small flowers for some people, but I find its close-set, narrow tubular flowers rather interesting. Sometimes a hybrid appears in the garden crossed with *Digitalis lutea* and *D. purpurea*, the purple-flowered native, which has escaped my eye. The offspring is a pretty thing with slightly larger creamy flowers flushed with pink. It lasts quite well as a perennial. When I think of it I split it up, and it seems to appreciate this, as it cannot set seed itself. *D. ferruginea* is as unlike our flamboyant native as could be. It has narrow smooth leaves, and sends up a wand-like stem set halfway down its length with little round buds. They open short roundish trumpets of copper-yellow, netted with brown veins. *D. grandiflora* and *D. ciliata* I think have interbred in my garden. Both produce good-sized yellow flowers, with *D. ciliata* making taller stems. Neither is less desirable than the other. They and their offspring, if such they be, all last in flower for weeks in midsummer. The semi-shady patches would be dull without them, and it is a relief to know they will stay where you put them and return next year.

Around the sunny edges I planted quick-growing carpeters like the ajugas. *A. reptans* 'Burgundy Glow' has clustered leaves in warm shades of pink and cream, and I like to set it off with the darkest glossiest form I call *Ajuga r.* 'Atropurpurea'. These bump into *Viola cornuta* in shades of blue and white, and all go as near as they dare to the big clumps of *Hosta*. Further along I planted a generous patch of my favourite *Astilbe* 'Sprite'. From spring to winter it is a joy. First comes its neat ferny bronze foliage followed by wide delicate sprays of shell-pink flowers not more than 30cm/1ft high. These slowly become russet-brown seed heads which remain to warm the chill of winter. Another virtue of *A.* 'Sprite' is that it provides a buffer, as the hostas do, to keep the stranglers apart. Nearby is *Pratia angulata* 'Treadwellii'. Little prostrate stems run about over the damp soil starred with stemless white flowers. By autumn they have become currant-sized pink berries nestling on a moss-green bed, remaining some time after the tiny leaves have gone.

This bed still receives full sunlight for much of the day, but both the background of oaks, and some of the new trees and shrubs do now afford welcome shade where it is needed. Such places provide a setting for the kind of planting I love best. There is a corner, shaded overhead, with *Cryptomeria japonica* and *Weigela florida* 'Foliis Purpureis' with chocolate leaves and dark pink flowers providing the background. Several crowns of a lace-like fern, *Polystichum setiferum* Acutilobum Group, make a frame for the dangling yellow flowers of *Uvularia grandiflora. Anemone nemorosa* 'Allenii' opens its lilac-blue saucers filled with golden stamens when touched by the sun, but when the sky clouds over their wine-stained buds nod modestly above the dark leaves of *Viola riviniana* Purpurea Group.

The variegated *Hosta undulata* lightens this quiet scene and tones with another group created by *Hydrangea paniculata*, which I find less formidable than *H. p.* 'Grandiflora'. If you have never seen *H. paniculata* then try to imagine a cream-coloured lace-cap *Hydrangea*. Take a handful of these round lacy mats, each diminishing in size, and place them one above the other until you have a cone-shaped inflorescence separated by short lengths of stem, each mat consisting of an outer ring of large sterile flowers, the inside filled with small fertile flowers. With *H. p.* 'Grandiflora' the arrangement is similar, but all the flowers are sterile. It makes larger, more showy heads, but sometimes I think it looks overdone. Much depends, of course, on the setting to decide which one you prefer.

The driest and shadiest side of this bed looks best in spring when *Erythronium* 'Pagoda' and *E. californicum* 'White Beauty' delight me with their beautiful olive-mottled leaves and crowds of little lily-like flowers in yellow and cream. The deep rose-pink of *Dicentra formosa* takes over in May. It provokes admiration all season with its pewter-blue ferny foliage.

Another traveller is the variegated strawberry, *Fragaria vesca* 'Variegata', but it never really becomes a pest because it is so easily pulled up. It continues to look very pretty when some of the more showy plants have had their day.

Hostas and Daylilies are excellent for smothering weed seedlings, and make good contrast for carpeting plants like ajugas and the scrambling *Viola cornuta*. Here is the sweet scented *Hemerocallis lilioasphodelus* with *Hosta* 'Spinners'.

COPING WITH WEEDS

By the time most of this was planted I was beginning to worry about the amount of weeding I had set myself, and my helpers. Not that I dislike weeding. I would go so far as to say that gardening without weeding would lose much of its charm. I think there is no better way of getting to know plants than working among them. Ensuring that they are not being attacked or invaded, you find yourself at close quarters, able to study exactly the petal formation, feel the texture of a leaf. You smell strange perfumes, aromatic or pungent from bruised leaves, emerging bulbs or disturbed roots. Sometimes you step on plants, smash your heel into a tender shoot, which is sickening of course. But crouched low among tall herbs you have a child's view of the garden. Like Alice in Wonderland, you feel yourself in another world — seeing a new garden from unfamiliar viewpoints. Down to earth, you can curb invasions before the weak have fallen to the strong. You move things around, break something up — jobs which rarely get done by saying 'I shall go out and divide those …'! You learn to know your plant seedlings as well as the native weeds and rejoice when something unexpected appears; curse yourself also for having allowed pepper-pot seeders like poppies or foxgloves to make unnecessary work by scattering armies of their offspring in the wrong place. You find gaps and sense the kind of planting needed there.

Weeding can be both a delight and a lesson. It can also be a great bore. Or worse, a nagging worry, either because you feel you cannot cope and the sense of frustration saps your energy or, if you are fortunate enough to have some help whether it be paid or blackmailed, it is maddening still to find yourself going three steps forward and two back because the same boring jobs have to be done too often. Weeding can be tiresome, very tiresome, or impossible. I infinitely prefer a large patch of nettles to the same area of annual meadow grass. With a border fork a nettle comes up easily enough, its tough yellow roots pull clean, leaving the soil behind. Annual meadow grass, chickweed, groundsel and the rest, which soon form a tight turf, have to be hoed or forked and removed, taking away barrowloads of good topsoil. You leave the bed – there are other things to be done – for a month or six weeks and return to find the same misery. Even valued ground-cover plants like *Vinca*, *Hedera*, *Tiarella* and *Ajuga* can, if the conditions are poor for them, be overrun by the native inhabitants.

Where there is complete chaos I find the situation has only one solution. No more fiddling about. Remove carefully everything you still wish to keep and heel it in, in a reserve border, which can be quite small. Dig out everything else thoroughly – plants infested with weed roots, all deep-rooted and running weeds. Next dig in anything nutritious that you can lay your hands on – garden refuse composted, well-rotted muck, and a sprinkling of bonemeal. While I used peat initially in making this garden, we have replaced it with other materials such as crushed bark and mushroom compost. Organic fertilizers, like dried blood and bonemeal, are concentrated and costly. Used sparingly they add vital elements to the plants' diet, but without humus as well to improve the soil texture it would be like taking vitamin pills and little else.

MULCHING

I was concerned about the time spent doing unnecessary and unpleasant weeding, concerned too about the amount of topsoil being peeled off my garden like pieces of old carpet. So I made the momentous decision that I must spend money to reduce weeding to a pleasurable level in order to save ourselves time to do something more advantageous. I decided that once my beds were planted I must cover them with a sterile mulch which would depress germinating seedlings and prevent the removal of good soil. In addition, it would gradually improve the structure of the soil and conserve moisture.

Initially I bought coarse shamrock peat, which was delivered in large wrapped bales. We broke them open on a big sheet of polythene laid on the grass. Then, the bed having been freshly weeded, we used our weeding buckets to spread the peat, about an inch or more thick, all over the bare soil and among the herbaceous plants. Today I use other organic materials. I also use baled straw, spread thickly, among trees and shrubs, or very large plants, which could not be smothered, and in the centres or backs of borders where it would not be unsightly.

By the time I was ready to start another large bed I had discovered crushed bark.

When pine logs are stripped in the Forestry Commission forests the bark is put into a pulverizer, where it is crushed and then sorted into various grades. It is unwise to use freshly pulverized bark, however. I like to buy one year, let it stand in great heaps to decompose a little, and then use it the next year.

Now, after several years of using bark, I really have an aversion to naked soil. The reddish-brown bark looks attractive, footmarks do not show, and on warm days the bark smells delicious, bringing back memories of holidays in the Alps. Another advantage is that heavy rainfall cannot cap the surface of the soil. It follows that the structure beneath remains open, so water can trickle gently through the mulch into the soil beneath. Not least, the soil remains damp far longer than soil which is exposed to driving winds and sun.

It is not usually necessary to add fresh mulch every year, as it breaks down slowly. At the end of even the first year of planting I find that the plants have done so well that they will be covering more than half the surface. And that is what I aim to have, the plants themselves providing natural soil-cover for most of the year.

How often do we apply it? Once we have thoroughly mulched a bed it could, in theory, last two or three years because the bark disintegrates very slowly. By the end of the growing season at least half of the original bare soil will have been covered by the plants themselves, which grow so much better having had protection for their roots instead of constant interference from forking and hoeing. The important thing is not to disturb that total cover; any little nodule of soil left on the surface will, when moist, sprout some kind of weed. However, I always have second and third thoughts about my planting, so inevitably there will be breaks made in the mulch where I have been putting in new finds, as they have become available. A bucketful, or barrowload, of fresh bark soon covers the disturbed patches. Sometimes, we put two layers on a new bed, the first shallow while the plants are still small, then, when they have grown a little higher we add more. I make a point of walking by young plants to see that they have not been buried. Both the wind and scrapping birds can toss the bark about which can smother small plants as well as weeds. At the beginning of the new growing season it is a good idea to follow the spring clean-up with just enough bark to cover any bare patches of soil. There is no need to add it where the layer has not been disturbed. Try to watch plants that are heavy seeders. Fresh seed scattered onto the mulch will happily germinate down into the warm, damp medium. A mulch will only stifle seedlings that are struggling up from beneath it.

It would be wrong to give the impression that the garden becomes totally weed free after mulching. There are always a few persistent scramblers for the light, which manage to emerge triumphant, like chickweed, but most seedling weeds and especially annual meadow grass, which I consider the worst pest, are defeated.

We walk over the beds to remove the survivors, carefully so as not to disturb the mulch, adding more if any soil is left showing. Finally, the depth of mulch must be generous. It is false economy to apply a thin dressing – robust weed seedlings will thrust their way through it.

Another point to remember is to apply your mulch when the ground is thoroughly wetted deep down. Sometimes, in autumn, I feel that we need a good snowfall to wet the soil, because once my fine silt has dried out it can receive all the winter rain that falls and still, in some places, be dry. But snow melts slowly and seems to sink well down. When it does snow we are soon frustrated, for little work can be done, but there are advantages we cannot see at the time. Some springs, on my very dry soil, I am unable to mulch because the soil is still too dry. Once the bark is put down it takes a tremendous amount of rain to wet it and the soil beneath. Like peat it absorbs a lot of water before it can begin to soak down into the soil.

MORE PLANTING IN SUN AND SHADE

I have been trying to decide how I shall describe more of my damp-loving plants, fearing that it may be as boring for me to write as it will be for you to read if I do not introduce it from a different angle. The beds which contain these plants are, in effect, one long continuous curving border, broken in two places by grass walks which enable you to see both shady and sunny aspects without having to take in all of one side at a time. Perhaps I should explain what I am hoping to achieve as I steer the garden through its various phases of development. A garden is never finished, never just as you think it should be. Rarely comes that magical moment, captured when everything is there together, the matured planting, the light and your state of mind. The next year you may stand at the same spot, but it will not be the same – the picture, and your mood, will have changed.

Whether your garden is very small or covers acres, there are perhaps a few basic principles of design, which apply to both. I think a garden needs to have a sense of wholeness, a harmonious feeling overall. But that does not mean that the same pattern should be repeated throughout, still less that the same plants will be dotted about indiscriminately regardless of conditions. The tiniest garden can provide different conditions – a hot sunny patch, a cool shaded corner – which will provide areas for different themes. In simplest terms, the hot spot may be filled with silver- and grey-leaved plants, a scented *Cistus* or stately *Verbascum*. The dark corner could be restful all the year round using ferns, hellebores and trailing ivies. To place the plants in these two groups together would not necessarily be wrong, but some would do less well than others and, to my mind, they would not look so well. Grey-leaved plants are protected from the drying effect of hot sunlight by the felty covering over their leaves. The second group of plants is adapted to cool, dim conditions. Reduced to very simple examples it becomes basically commonsense. The interest begins when you start to search for all the subtle variations on the theme you have in mind, which will fit your situation.

Again, consider shapes. A haphazard collection of trees and shrubs could become a monotonous hedge-like obstruction. I prefer to plant in groups, with spaces between so that you may see the view beyond through the gaps. This gives depth to your design. I try to keep to this principle in a small garden, a small bed, even a sink garden. I make a dominant group, which is the main centre of interest, while every plant, large or small, contributes something to the shape as well as the colour of the design.

How has all this worked out in the second half of my long broken border, which is separated from the ponds by wide grass walks? The side which faces the ponds lies in the sun for much of the day, but the back of the border is cool and shady, overhung by the ancient oaks and sheltered by the groups of trees and shrubs along its centre. The soil remains fairly damp on the sunny side in all but exceptionally dry summers. The shady side is drier, more affected by roots. It is an indication of the type of soil, and the effect of springs coming nearer the surface, that the low-lying wide grass walks have remained emerald green ever since they seeded down, while grass elsewhere in the garden, on the upper level, on gravel soil, burns biscuit brown without a fortnightly shower in summer. And that we rarely have!

Now, to return, once again, to the second half of the Long Border. By the time I was ready to take up the turf and use the good soil beneath for more unusual plants, most of our original planting of trees and shrubs had passed the spindly stage and some were already making interesting features. A few, regretfully, had to be removed as we had made our usual error of putting too many in too little space. It might have worked if we had stayed with trees and shrubs. The major trees would have eventually shaded out the others, but trees can be lopsided, grown close against one another for a very long time without much harm to either. But mine is the constant search for root space, for the kind of tree that will allow plants to grow beneath or around them, hopefully during my lifetime. So a beech, maple and horse chestnut had to go. One would need a park to accommodate the many fine trees one would like to grow. On the other hand, in the average garden, with only ornamentals like flowering cherry or laburnum, attractive though they are, there is no touch of stateliness in the design. A tree, which does, in time, add grandeur to the garden is *Quercus coccinea*, the Scarlet Oak (sadly lost in the storm of 1987). This tree is like *Liquidambar*, I suspect, in that seedlings from it vary in the intensity of autumn colour. Ours is not spectacular, but it has already made a young tree of noble aspect throughout the year. For a week or so in spring I think it is as beautiful as any blossoming tree, when the tiny emerging leaves are like little pleated fans, silvery pale, held against a blue April sky.

As a companion to the oak we planted *Liriodendron tulipifera*, the Tulip Tree, with its curious shaped leaves looking as though all the tips had been carefully cut off with scissors. Although the flowers are very beautiful, they can easily be missed. One day I was lucky enough to be at Kew at the right time to see a splendid isolated specimen in full flower, hundreds of upturned pale green cups painted inside with orange. My tree does not flower so spectacularly, but in autumn the rich honey colour of its leaves carries your eye above everything else.

In the shelter of the oak, hoping to protect it a little from cold spring frosts, I planted *Pieris* 'Forest Flame', a presumed hybrid between *P. formosa* var. *forrestii* 'Wakehurst' and *P. japonica*. So often, no sooner have the young shoots unfolded in late April or May than they are reduced to pulp by a murderous frost. But sometimes we are lucky, and can marvel as the young terminal leaves go through a long phase of change, from polished red through tender pinks and cream to green. It is not surprising that everyone who sees it wants to possess it.

Much easier, and making fine bulk, is a purple-leaved hazelnut, *Corylus maxima* 'Purpurea'. The young pleated leaves open rich chocolate-purple, this colouring draining slightly in high summer, but lightening and brightening to reddish tones in autumn. As contrast to this heavy purple colouring I planted *Rubus idaeus* 'Aureus' beneath it. Now I have a carpet of cool yellow around the massed stems as this golden-leaved raspberry has sent its runners through the fine soil, producing fresh yellow foliage all summer on short stems, none more than 45cm/18in long.

For blossom and perfume there is *Syringa sweginzowii*, Chinese Lilac, of great elegance and charm. Its small oval leaves are not overpowering for the long loose panicles of palest pink tubular flowers, which are carried on every shoot. *Rubus* 'Benenden' forms part of this group. It makes a stout frame from which cascade arching branches garlanded with large white blackberry-like flowers. But although it is spectacular at its best, the flowering season is short. I think it may move on one day to a place where its exuberant growth can be allowed more space, in grass perhaps, with masses of the late-flowering, sweet-scented *Narcissus poeticus* var. *recurvus* beneath it. It has now found a home in my Little Grassy Wood (see *Beth Chatto's Woodland Garden*).

I left the space beneath and immediately around this group of trees and shrubs free, except for *Rubus tricolor*, hoping it would cover the soil, which becomes dry on the surface, partly because of roots, partly because the leaf canopy does not allow much of the light summer rain to penetrate. Now this rampageous ground-coverer is coping very well, and will need to be curbed when it reaches the boundary of its allotted space. I like the way it sends out long prostrate runners, then quickly fills the space between with side shoots so that before long you have a carpet of shining, dark green leaves, grey backed, with soft red bristles set all round the young stems. I also planted it at the top of a very steep clay bank, where I think little else would flourish, and already it is beginning to hang down a curtain of trailing stems to hide the raw clay. Like all brambles it roots down at the tip, useful when you need more plants. Although rampant it is not difficult to control, being lax and soft to handle. Where space is limited watch it each spring, and cut back then if necessary. I have been told that this bramble is not very hardy. That may well be so in very cold and exposed districts. Here in East Anglia there is little between us and the bitter north-east winds from Russia, but my plants are sheltered among shrubs, partially protected by the straw mulches which are put down until the ground-covering plants have carpeted the empty spaces. Some years the overwintering leaves of *Rubus tricolor* have been singed by cold, but the plants have never suffered.

With these strong-growing trees and shrubs as the background and apex of one end of my bed I began to plant tall strong-growing plants just in front of their shade perimeter. *Macleaya cordata* I found had not liked my poor starved gravel elsewhere, so I thought I would try it here, in the sun. Its graceful heads of coral buds and pale creamy flowers look well among the rustling stems of *Miscanthus sinensis* 'Silberfeder'. This superb grass, 1.5m/5ft high, makes an elegant fountain (not so overpowering as *M. sacchariflorus* might have been) and it flowers regularly, pale fawn and brown feather dusters, folded and furled when wet, silken and silvery when dried in the wind.

Several inulas complete this group of herbaceous giants. *Inula magnifica* must be one of them. All of them have enormously long, coarse, but handsome dock-shaped leaves. All send up stout towering stems over 2.5m/8ft high; they can only be contemplated where they will have ample room. Among mine I have three distinctly different types of flower, but no one has yet been able to help me identify them with certainty. One has a tapering head of closely set, hard, knobbly buds, which open smallish yellow daisies in a spire, eventually forming an interesting seed head for decorating a large space like the church. I planted some of these by the water-side where they look very suitable, in scale and form. Provided they are not situated where they catch the wind they remain stiffly upright without staking. My two other giant inulas each have similar foliage and majestic height, but one is topped with wide branching heads of large yellow daisies with the narrowest, almost thread-like petals; the other has orange petals, with brown centres. Nearer the front of the border I placed another, *Inula hookeri*, more suited to smaller gardens, although it is invasive. It makes good cover because of this, with spreading clumps which send up many stems, about 75cm/2½ft topped with unusual furry green buds which open greenish-yellow daisies.

Yet another similar plant is *Telekia speciosa*. Not so tall as the other giants, it has similar heads of large yellow fine-rayed daisies over great mounds of huge heart-shaped leaves. To retain their look of distinction watch for damage by slugs or snails for it is the perfection of the great leaves that contributes to the scene. Some of

Telekia speciosa, it must be admitted, is for the wild garden. Well-watered it grows over 2m/6ft tall, with stout branching stems clothed in large, heart-shaped leaves and bearing heads of large yellow daisies whose many petals are finely shredded.

these great daisies are invasive, and could be a menace in unsuitable places, but they are ideal in rough grass where they can add drama to a scene that might be monotonous, but which would also be impractical to garden in detail.

Another great plant, which could be used for the same purpose is *Rheum palmatum*. When I was thinking of what to use to bring the eye forward from the tall herbs in the background I chose an especially fine form, which may be *R. p.* var. *tanguticum*. This wonderful plant, which has much richer coloured foliage than *R. p.* 'Atrosanguineum', starts the season in a void before the tall herbs have begun to make their mark. Very early in spring the *Rheum* buds are unfolding, continuing to do so for weeks to come, so that gradually there is a huge overlapping pile of curved and slashed leaves, purplish-red and ruched above, raspberry-pink beneath, slowly maturing to green above but retaining the strong carmine tint on the undersides. From among this pile, one or two great reddish buds emerge, each with a single enveloping scale from which unfolds a 2–2.5m/6–8ft flowering stem dangling with tiny sprays of white flowers (not pink, as has *R. p.* 'Atrosanguineum'). This is a plant I waited long to possess. For weeks, for months, its leaves remain an important feature, framing the view as you look beyond, diametrically, across the sloping grass and clear water, to another planted on the far side of the pond. Placed among plants with smaller fussier leaves, these noble plants have a stabilizing, architectural effect.

Towards the edge of this large group is a planting of *Geranium maculatum*, a choice member of a genus in which it is hard to choose a favourite. The cool lilac flowers in early summer are followed by mounds of parasol-shaped leaves, with frilly-edges. They sometimes have rich orange and red tones in autumn. To complement this group I planted *Dicentra spectabilis* nearby. To mark the *Dicentra*, which fades away by late summer, are clumps of *Pulmonaria saccharata* 'Alba'. I was given this plant by Elizabeth Strangman. It is so much better than *P. officinalis* 'Alba', which is a wishy-washy plant by comparison. (Poor thing! Why haven't I found a grouping that would enhance it?) But *P. saccharata* 'Alba' has large trusses of pure white flowers followed by great rosettes of undulating dark green leaves handsomely spotted with white, decorating their share of the scene until winter withers them away. By early March the clustered flower buds will unfold, long before the basal rosettes appear, to charm no less than do the snowdrops.

I hope it is not becoming monotonous, my obsession with leaves, but if a plant has beautiful leaves, it is, I think, the best reason for growing it. If it has good flowers as well that makes two good reasons. Although not exactly short yet of room to grow plants I still have to be selective. Those that go off quickly in both leaf and flower must be placed where their absence is not noticeable, so plants which continue to furnish, even if it be with quite plain good green foliage, are welcomed. After all, nothing but spotted and splashed leaves herded together would be quite upsetting.

Most people know *Aruncus dioicus*, which is not unlike a huge *Astilbe*. It makes such a handsome stand of light green foliage, never troubled by pests. I like best its early stage of development before the great creamy plumes have exploded into foaming flowers, when the sprays are delicately lined with tiny round buds, only a few breaking. Not everyone has had the chance to meet *Aruncus dioicus* 'Kneiffii'. It makes a smaller plant, with leaves so finely shredded you would not be blamed

The lovely Goat's Beard, *Aruncus dioicus*, thrives in part shade in my Wood Garden. Many years ago, when I first began to learn about the homes of wild plants that now are familiar to us as garden plants, I saw it with *Thalictrum aquilegiifolium* overhanging a mountain stream in the Swiss Alps. I realized why I could not hope to succeed with these plants in sun-baked gravel.

for failing to recognize it. Above this fretted frame are the same ivory plumes, reduced in scale. To add body to this dainty group without overshadowing it I planted *Heuchera cylindrica* 'Greenfinch'. For most of the year I enjoy its tidy clumps of heart-shaped leaves, beautifully mottled green and silver. By midsummer they break the low line of edging plants with a forest of straight stems a yard high, topped with closely set spikes of green flowers.

While thinking of related shapes it also helps to group together plants whose flowers look well together. On the cooler side of this corner group, close to the grass edge, is a combination of plants slowly forming a picture. These are three fritillaries that seem to prefer heavier soil than their Mediterranean cousins flourishing elsewhere on my sun-baked gravels. *Fritillaria meleagris* can still be found growing wild in a few damp, low-lying meadows in England. None has more sinister charm than this, our own Snake's Head Fritillary. Like the Lenten hellebores it can be found in all shades. Those with white tapering bells, squared at the shoulders, are faintly shaded and chequered with green. Others are dark greyish-plum, with occasional in-betweens of palest pink, delicately veined and patterned in minute mosaics. Standing taller is *F. verticillata*, which produces very narrow strap-like leaves along the flowering stem, to become tendrils, with curling tips at the top of the stem. This adaptation may be a means of ensuring that they can haul themselves up into the sunlight when growing in the wild in grassy meadows. The flowers are shallow open bells, almost whitish-green, chequered inside with brown. The large angular seed heads surrounded by dried curling wisps of leaves are equally attractive.

All fritillaries seem to have very individual characters. I have special feeling for *Fritillaria pallidiflora*. Shorter than the other two, it is sturdier looking, with thick stems set with broad wax-grey leaves which taper up the stem, bending with the weight of several large citron-yellow angular bells, overlaid with green and faint tan veining. If you tip them up you will see the tan repeated inside, around the base of the stamens.

For these treasures *Epimedium grandiflorum* provides a background of newly made leaves, small and heart-shaped, echoing with softest tan. Soon there will be sprays of little mauve-pink flowers, on thread-like stems, and the leaves will mature green.

Astrantia major 'Sunningdale Variegated' produces clumps of almost strawberry-shaped leaves brilliantly variegated with cream, yellow and green. Much later in the year, in late summer and autumn, these will have faded to green, and the scene will have changed as the plant sends up tall, branching stems which carry hundreds of green and white posies, stained pink in the centre, for weeks and weeks.

Meanwhile, in spring, carpets of dark purple-leaved *Viola riviniana* Purpurea Group cool the group and separate it from the starfish-shaped clumps of *Pulmonaria longifolia*, whose variegation is somewhat muted as it carries its clustered heads of small gentian-blue flowers.

A curious form of *Helleborus purpurascens* (I think that is what it is) sits on the edge of the group, massed with short, stout flower stems each carrying several smallish cupped flowers of a dingy, dusky purple. The insides are lined with greyish-green and filled with fresh green anthers set around dark purple ovaries. The subtle tones of *Primula* 'Guinevere' seem just right with this strange plant. Purplish-brown stems carry heads of many light lilac-pink flowers, with leaves neat and narrow, shaded and veined maroon.

Another spring group is based on *Valeriana phu* 'Aurea', whose bright yellow, divided leaves set off *Euphorbia sikkimensis* with leaves, stems and veins in strong vermilion-red running through leafy soil. Cream and yellow erythroniums, including *Erythronium californicum* 'White Beauty' and *E.* 'Pagoda', reflex their petals, each fluttering stem rising out of a boat-shaped base made by the broad succulent leaves, faintly marbled brown. *E. revolutum* has not yet established itself so abundantly. As yet it has only one flower to a stem, a rich rosy-red, paling slightly at the tips of the pointed petals. *Dicentra formosa alba* marks this ephemeral little treasure with drooping clusters of greenish-white heart-shaped flowers held over spreading clumps of pale ferny foliage. In the background among the shrubs are creamy-white *Narcissus* 'Tresamble' and *N.* 'Thalia' making an entrance among pale gold ribbons of *Milium effusum* 'Aureum', Bowles' Golden Grass.

We have been led around the border to the Long Walk, shaded by the boundary oaks. Spring is the loveliest time here while there is still enough sunlight for flowers. Later in the year hostas and ferns, with shade-loving plants like *Actaea*, provide quieter patterns.

Euphorbia amygdaloides var. *robbiae* usefully invades the drier soil over the roots of shrubs while its running shoots appear through tight carpets of *Vinca minor* 'La Grave' both in flower together, although the *Euphorbia* lasts much longer.

Dominating another picture is the golden cut-leaved elder *Sambucus racemosa* 'Plumosa Aurea', forming a tender background for *Smilacina racemosa* whose softly pleated leaves clasp green stems which end in a fluffy spike of cream, citrus scented flowers. It is supposed to set red berries, and sometimes shows every sign of doing so, but although I watch, full of expectation, they never materialize – I don't know why. Some years it happens that the *Sambucus* and *Smilacina* have just expanded to perfection when *Paeonia obovata* var. *alba* rises among them, her perfect round globes of white petals protecting precious crimson ovaries inside. All too ephemeral, these few perfect events, but remembered forever.

Paeonia 'Late Windflower', although single, and white, is quite different. It makes a slowly increasing clump, the leaves as they appear being more dissected, richly shaded in browns and tan. Maturing green they form a large loose mound over which nod open shallow saucers filled with golden stamens.

4 | Developing the Water and Bog Gardens

BY THE SUMMER OF 1972 I had become very discontented with the mixed planting of trees and shrubs that continued downstream below the top three pools and decided that a mirror of water was needed to lie between the old and the new Shade Gardens. It would widen the area visually, and reflect the beautiful white trunk and branches of *Betula utilis* var. *jacquemontii,* which stood alone in a broad grass walk. Originally the idea had been to cover the steep dry banks of the ditch with shrubs to smother the native weeds. This had been achieved. In summer it looked lush and copsy, but it was far too twiggy in winter, with not enough evergreens. As the Shade Gardens gradually developed on the opposite side of the water from the house garden these shrubs formed a visual barrier and, when one day I was asked if the garden opposite belonged to me, I knew what had to be done. But it is always a sad business taking the mattock and axe and destroying years of one's life, together with the trees and shrubs. Fortunately I was able to spare the best bit of planting, the fine *Metasequoia, Prunus* 'Taihaku', the Great White Cherry, and the *Liquidambar* which became the apex of a revised planting to frame the new pond.

MAKING ANOTHER POND

On 9 January 1973 I had a thyroid operation. On the morning of the 22nd, from the house, I saw the large crane of the dragline go lumbering towards the cleared and waiting site. In my diary I wrote that 'I felt shattered and excited – both!' I remember that I felt scared suddenly to make important decisions, which I would

It is good to see what a range of handsome plants thrives in heavy soil provided it remains damp and does not dry out like concrete. Here hostas, rodgersias, *Iris* and *Gunnera* provide supporting foliage while the Globe Flower (*Trollius*), geums and the pink pokers of *Persicaria bistorta* 'Superba' add early summer colour.

TOP LEFT: Harry clearing for the third pond. ABOVE LEFT: Clay from excavating the third pond settling to form the dam. TOP RIGHT: The new dam levelled for grass and the concrete pools that lower the water into the remaining ditch. ABOVE RIGHT: Hollow-block edging supports the sloping banks.

have to live with, like them or not. However, I pulled myself together and went out to meet my friend, Mr Crees, to discuss a plan of campaign. Mr C. is one of those eminently capable men who always inspire confidence. But while I was invigorated by his enthusiasm for our project I was worried lest I was not in a fit state to evaluate what he and his vast machine were about to do. For two days the sound of the machine carving up my garden disturbed my peace of mind. From time to time I went to watch. Gradually the steep narrow ditch was opened out. As the shape of the pond gradually emerged the clay was laid across the lower end to form a dam. The digging and building had to be estimated carefully so that the final water level would lie comfortably in the hollow. By four o'clock of the second day the man and machine had done their work. I stood at a distance and surveyed the empty hole, and the great heap of piled clay across the far end.

The overflow from the pools above was splashing into the small stretch of ditch, screened by the original planting, which now led into this new pond. It would take two or three days to fill. There was remarkably little spoil to be cleared: most of it was built into the dam which, of course, lay high and rough and would need several months to settle. The mown grass that led towards the pond showed very little damage, so carefully had the great machine been manoeuvred round the site.

At that stage, as with the foundations of a new house, the pool seemed too small. But if it were larger, I told myself, that would have created bigger problems removing the spoil. I spent the evening ironing, comforted by the sweet smell of domesticity, and went to bed very tired and slightly confused!

Before the water reached the top of the dam we had to dig a narrow trench in the clay to let it cross over and slither down the slope in a muddy trickle to fall into the last section of ditch which remained at the lowest end of the garden. There was no more we could do then but wait for the dam to settle.

Late summer is the time I prefer for earth-moving jobs. By then the flush of plant and weed growth has slowed up and we feel we can (sometimes) spare time for improvements. One might think that winter would be more suitable, and occasionally it is. But especially where heavy soil is involved, it is best to handle it when it is neither sodden wet nor baked concrete dry. Another consideration is that I cannot think properly when I am shuddering with cold.

So, near the end of July 1973, we turned our attention once more to the pile of clay which had now settled, and grown quite a crop of weeds, intermingled with surviving plants which had been swept up by the crane bucket. These included the gigantic *Fallopia sachalinensis,* which had looked positively tropical towering out of the ditch, but must now be banished elsewhere.

There were two major decisions to make. I wanted to change the point where the water would leave the pond so that it did not remain a pond with a ditch entering and leaving in a straight line. What worried me was how it would descend from the dam into the lower ditch. I did not like the muddy trickle, which was already showing signs of wearing away the clay. Andrew decided that what we needed were two more small pools, made of concrete, to hold up the water and let it spill gradually down to the lower level. This seemed a marvellous idea, and we sited them to one side of the dam so that it almost appeared that the flow of water was taking a natural curve. Before they could be made, or the pipe laid across the dam, the continual flow of water had to be diverted. Harry made a new channel for it to run outside the area where all the work would be taking place. Then a trench was dug across the dam, sufficiently deep to bury the concrete pipes, plus enough soil above on which grass could grow. Only rarely now do we see the telltale signs across the mown grass.

Next the little artificial pools were marked out, and their levels staked. It was not easy to make a good base in the soft buttery clay, but between them Andrew and Harry laid down all the broken rubble and stone they could find, held in position by angle irons well driven home. Pig-netting was laid on top of this and finally concrete, smoothed and shaped into two shallow basins with a slipway between. When it was sufficiently set the water was redirected through the pipe, and by the next morning the two little pools were spilling over and joining the ditch.

Before long Harry had levelled the dam, and finally brought topsoil to spread over the clay before he sowed it with grass. Within a few days a film of green was to be seen. By the autumn it had merged with the wide grass walks on both sides and the new pond looked as though it had always been there.

Before I could think of planting I knew we had to do a lot more to the soil. We had originally made a small water garden along one side of the ditch. Here I had learnt that the ornamental rhubarb, *Rheum palmatum*, and several other plants will rot if the soil is waterlogged. Too soon native weeds had overtaken my exotic plant introductions, which had never been happy in the solid, sticky clay. So, for more than a year we had emptied our wheelbarrows of weeds onto the land on both sides of the lower ditch. We had also carted out spare compost from the great heaps stacked to rot, and all the waste pot soil from the nursery. All this helped to make a new topsoil, so that when I came to plant I had a good texture in which to work, and in which my plants could establish themselves before their roots reached the wet clay beneath.

The final stage before planting was to make the hollow block edging which was so successful round the first ponds. When Harry came to edge the lower ditch he widened it and set his blocks so that the water curved round from the little pools into a final stretch, which sweeps under a little wooden bridge. We can now stand here and listen to the gentle splashing of water among a lush planting of water-loving plants.

This final straight stretch of water was the reason for the name the Canal Bed, the wide area of damp, low-lying land on either side. To maintain the correct water level, about 5cm/2in below the top of the blocks, Harry built another little dam at the very end of our ditch where it disappears under a great clump of bamboo into our neighbour's reservoir.

Now our water levels are constant throughout the year. However many weeks of drought we may have had, the underground water keeps all the pools topped up. Occasionally, after very heavy rain, the levels may rise an inch or two, but never enough to flood the surrounding land. We do have to watch carefully, especially in winter, that the exit pipes are not blocked by sticks and fallen leaves.

THE CANAL BED

Although it does not have a very attractive name I sometimes think that this is the most popular bed in the garden, possibly because it is such an unaccustomed oasis of lush planting to be found in our dry Essex farmland. The sound and movement of water and perhaps the sight of a mother duck with her brood of ducklings sailing along the 'Canal' help to suggest that 'God's in his Heaven and all's right with the world', in spite of the mess that we seem to be making of it.

The area planted is about 28m/90ft long, 14m/46ft across, with the raised water level of the ditch widened to about 1.5m/5ft across running through its length. There are two trees giving light dappled shade, more or less in the centre: one of the original oaks, *Quercus robur*, and the other we planted, *Q. palustris*, which has now made a fine young tree. Beneath this I planted an *Acer palmatum*, and two or three *Viburnum plicatum* 'Mariesii' to make a bosky centre and background.

I have already remarked that there seem to be few evergreens, either woody or herbaceous, for the water-side. *Phormium* seemed the obvious choice for a dramatic evergreen, and plants are sited near the dam as exposed features. Certainly they have become irreplaceable in this important bed. *P. tenax* Purpureum Group with wide purplish-brown leaves makes a most handsome clump, almost 1.5m/5ft high in my garden, but can be more in softer climates. The variegated forms of *P. tenax* vary, the hardiest I think is not the brightest coloured, but the new young leaves are very attractive, and for the rest of the year they retain creamy-white margins. *P. cookianum* makes a smaller plant, still a useful feature in the small garden, and useful to me in this bed, in another grouping. There are many beautiful variegated and purple forms of *Phormium* available, which have been introduced from New Zealand, but they are unreliably hardy.

Most winters the phormiums survive, but the occasional bad winter, when alternate wetting and freezing, accompanied by wind frosts out of the North, finds them shriven to the base in the spring. With luck they recover, but it takes two or three years before they regain their former splendour. So, we wrap ours up with bundles of straw surrounded by sheets of polythene to protect the greater part of the leaves and leaf-bases from the searing winds. It takes two of us to run round them with long lengths of twine – usually our last job before Christmas. I cannot say that I like the look of our efforts, rather like untidy old crinolined ladies all winter, but it is worth the trouble, and the unsightliness, to preserve these magnificent garden ornaments. Just occasionally I am defeated to find that a family of water voles has spent the winter in such cosy comfort and has eaten away a large part of a fine clump! (We have discontinued this practice now we have warmer winters and our plants are well established.)

I was anxious to conceal the edges of the little concrete pools, but not at all sure

OVERLEAF
This harmonious group is part of a promontory situated at the end of one of the ponds. The retentive, heavy soil supports the arching bamboo and the spectacular *Phormium tenax*, in flower, soaring above rodgersias, astrantias, damp-loving irises and astilbes. *Hosta* 'Spinners' makes a full-stop plant on the border-edge between low carpeting plants, *Persicaria affinis* 'Superba' and *P. vacciniifolia*.

how dry, or moist, the soil would be. It is, of course, useless to put bog-loving plants in bone-dry soil alongside any kind of artificial pool if you have not made proper provision for some kind of underground watering. I think, however, that we were lucky, or perhaps I should say inefficient, as our cement layers for the little pools are not watertight. (With a little more experience I think I can say we would have been lucky if they had held water – we have had the experience of waking and seeing the large pools opposite our house windows almost emptied, once by burrowing water voles, and again by an insufficiently rammed dam.)

The small pools ooze water gently into their surrounding banks, which is, of course, ideal. The water level is easily maintained by the constant flow throughout the entire water course. I tried several plants as cover, but those, which have lasted and saved me endless weeding are *Persicaria affinis* and *Leptinella potentillina*. I would not have dreamt that this little plant would have liked such a position. It is recommended for crevices in paving, but fortunately my bank is to its liking, and it has crept all along the concrete edges of the pools, hiding them completely.

As an alternative feature to the phormiums I planted a sprawling bush of *Salix repens* var. *argentea*. Sprawling sounds awkward and untidy; I don't think this plant is either. It is a low, gracefully spreading bush on the rim of the small upper pool, breaking the curved grass edge of the dam. For weeks in early spring it delights me. There is a wealth of long thin branches studded with silken pearl-sized buds, which slowly swell until the bush becomes alight with silvery white. Suddenly the buds burst into yellow fluffy catkins, beautiful as mimosa. When they have faded I prune the bush quite hard, taking most of the strong stems back to the base, leaving just enough to keep a reduced shape. The strong rootstock soon replaces them with fresh long branches covered with glistening silver leaves. They add grace to the corner for the rest of the season, and do not impede the cover of *Persicaria* and *Vinca minor* 'La Grave', which clothe the bank beneath it. The white-flowered form of *Colchicum autumnale* pushes up near the drier grass edge with narrow polished leaves in spring, and crowded clumps of small goblets on tall stems in autumn.

March finds *Lysichiton* just emerging along the water's edge. I planted several, both the yellow *L. americanus* and the white *L. camtschatcensis* whose leaf clusters are slightly smaller, and whose first surprising flower makes me think that a white duck has just flown in – but the resemblance is only fleeting as the flower opens into a perfect spathe of purest ivory. One clump was not enough. Beneath *Prunus* 'Taihaku' I planted several of my seedlings, hoping to see their reflections and those of the great showy clusters of cherry together as I looked down into the water from the edge of the Middle Dam. Some seasons it comes just right, on a day of blue skies, with little puffs of white cloud. For me such a performance is as stirring as a great stage production, takes far longer to produce and is never repeated quite the same again.

I value the shapes of plants, especially those which make good verticals, thus lifting the eye into the distance. Here are the stately spires of *Veratrum album*, still in bud, found wild in Swiss alpine meadows, avoided by grazing cows. In deep moist soil it takes time to make an imposing clump.

The drumhead primulas, *Primula denticulata*, like the heavy soil of the Canal Bed, but do not need to take up precious space at the water's edge. Showing colour there with the lysichitons are several forms of *Caltha*. Our own native *Caltha palustris* is as beautiful as any, luxuriating in the black, soggy soil, surrounded by little lilac drifts of the double Lady's Smock, *Cardamine pratensis* 'Flore Pleno', both original inhabitants of this marshy piece of land long before we came. (The single form of *Cardamine* is native.) Lasting longer but making almost too solid clumps of colour for my liking is the double Marsh Marigold, *Caltha palustris* var. *palustris* 'Plena'. They are prettiest, I think, partly opened when they show green centres. Both flop usefully over the hard block edge, which prevents all the carefully accumulated topsoil from sliding down into the water. More block-smotherers are the Water Forget-me-not, *Myosotis scorpioides*, which floats yards of flowering stem out in the water, and several kinds of musk. The most robust of these with me are *Mimulus guttatus*, the Monkey Musk, and *M*. hose-in-hose. This latter has soft copper-coloured flowers, one sitting inside the other.

To conceal my edgings still more I encourage *Caltha palustris* var. *palustris* to float out into the water, and add *Iris laevigata* and several clumps of *Zantedeschia*, the Arum Lily, to break up the straight stretch of the 'Canal'.

Beneath the oaks on either side of the water where it is less moist, I let white foxgloves seed among huge-leaved forms of *Hosta sieboldiana*. I am never sure if it is my soil, or if I have perhaps an extra-good form, but certainly some of the *Hosta* clumps are elephantine. They mingle with *Rodgersia*, which likes moist but not waterlogged soil. I also think it likes a little shade in the hottest hours of the day. Certainly the beautiful *Astilboides tabularis* needs a sheltered site to retain the perfect symmetry of its huge dimpled, round leaves. *Rodgersia aesculifolia* is also planted there. Sadly, once these great plants begin to spread, a large bed quickly becomes a small one, and you wish you had half an acre of these special, precious conditions. It always amazes me how small and few are the areas I have for really specialized conditions, whether cool, shady, moist and well-drained – or, elsewhere, warm and sunny with deep fed soil! As time goes by we gradually create new situations by growing shelter and improving soil conditions, but by then the first ones often need remaking too. That is the pattern of growth. Nothing remains the same, there is always change, and part is improvement, part deterioration.

Big clumps of *Lysimachia* rise above the bulky foliage plants. *Lysimachia punctata*, common though it may be, is a joyful sight with its stiff spires of bright yellow, and here it usefully colonizes a poor piece of soil beneath the original oak, drifting into *Luzula sylvatica* 'Marginata' which can also make bad soil look positively lush. It looks so pretty too in May with its sprays of little brown and yellow tassels and finally, and not least, it is still fresh and green all winter.

Here the *Veratrum album* is in full flower with *Iris* 'Sibirica Alba', *Primula bulleyana* and the Sensitive Fern, *Onoclea sensibilis*, which spreads in moist soil.

BETH CHATTO'S DAMP GARDEN

I learnt from reading Gertrude Jekyll to put *Thalictrum flavum* subsp.*glaucum* and *Veratrum* near the water-side. The fluffy heads of pale greenish-yellow thalictrum flowers are held high on grey stems which carry stiff fan-like sprays of bluish leaves, wonderful contrast for the stiffly pleated leaves of *Veratrum*. Around the garden I have three flowering forms of *Veratrum* – white, acid-green and maroon-purple.

Ligularia 'The Rocket' makes another lofty plant – 2m/6ft spikes of smallish yellow flowers set along purplish-black stems. These giant herbs grow up to take the place of the many candelabra primulas and water irises, which have decorated the water's edge in the early summer and do not mind too much being overshadowed later in the season.

Large, round leaves are provided by *Ligularia dentata*. Although its roots may be in water, wilting can occur temporarily with sudden heat in early June. But this is one of the few plants, I think, that has superb foliage and superb flowers, especially in the form *L. d.* 'Desdemona'. As they emerge in spring the newborn leaves are small and purplish-red with a shiny wet look, but they quickly expand, smooth and large as saucers, bronzed-green above, shining mahogany-red beneath, poised on red stalks. Add to this colour scheme large heads of thick petalled daisies the colour of orange peel standing 1.2m/4ft above the foliage, and you will agree that this either deserves the most special place in the garden, or cannot be accommodated at all! (Unfortunately they can be shredded by slugs.)

Senecio smithii is a large daisy-plant that was given to me by Eric Smith, but he tells me it was named before his time. It was introduced as early as 1895 from southern Chile and the Falkland Islands. It must have really wet soil, anything less and it will be a poor thing. Well-grown it makes nice-looking clumps of large puckered green leaves with pale backs. The thick flower stem, about 1.2m/4ft high, supports a close-set, roundish head of medium-sized white daisies with greenish-yellow centres. It is not an obviously showy plant, but the shape of the flower head intrigues me. The fluffy seed head, which follows is attractive too. It flourishes in the well-watered Shetland Islands.

There is planting that I remember all year, and anticipate all spring. After the prostrate Silver Willow has lost its catkins, and the *Lysichiton* spathes are dragging in the mud, the yellow-leaved form of *Iris pseudacorus* is at its best. Last year's leaves lie curled like pale wood shavings round the base of the new leaves which are a most delicate harmony of butter and cream. (By midsummer they will be scarcely distinguishable from the green-leaved form.) Nestling among them is *Cardamine raphanifolia*, which seems to be a perfect complementary harmony with its large trusses of cool lilac flowers.

Just opposite, across the little pools which now look quite natural with their softened edges of *Leptinella* and a few moss-covered stones, is a little 'field' of cotton grass in full flower, and dancing among it is a corps de ballet of *Primula pulverulenta* Bartley hybrids, the palest pink version, with slender stems powdered white. Further downstream is the lovely old wine-coloured form, which I should not like to be without, *P. pulverulenta* itself.

The running fern *Onoclea sensibilis* joins in this reckless party, and I know that before long it will be out of hand, if it is not so already. But for a brief while I can stand on my little bridge looking up the 'Canal' towards the small brimming pools which spill and splash among these exquisite plants. The great phormiums, both dark and light, make a strong accent in the middle ground between the Canal Bed and the Bog Gardens above and are framed in the background by the great oak, weeping willows and Swamp Cypress and finally calmed and united by the New Pool and wide mown grass walks. For a brief moment there is complete harmony.

In our first garden, where we struggled with chalky boulder clay and destructive droughts, our enthusiasm for gardening was declining by the middle of July, and sank lower and lower until we were rescued by the autumn (sometimes delayed till winter) rains. As the summer days went pitilessly by, often drearily overcast, the grass withered to nothingness, few flowers were worth looking at, and only my drought-resisting foliage plants provided relief from the weary scene.

I have since learnt how to cope more efficiently with drought and dry soil, as I still have plenty of both, but although my Damp Garden has problems just as severe – probably more so – the great advantage is that plants can be found and grown without hindrance to prolong the flowering season from earliest spring to the back end of autumn, without a break. But please do not think that the garden is a perpetual blaze of colour. That would be dreadful, surrounded as we are by agricultural crops. There is a time, in midsummer, when everything does seem to be in flower at the same time but, mercifully, that does not last. The quieter seasons always seem to me to be the best, when it is possible to be pleasantly surprised by colour rather than satiated by it.

Astilbes are coveted, understandably, by almost everyone who sees them. Everything about them is good. Beautiful foliage, often warmly tinted, often delicately divided into fernlike fronds, is topped with tapering spires of tiny fluffy flowers in many shades from creamy-white through pastel pinks to rich dark reds or purplish puce. It is not likely you will care for all of them – certainly you will not plant them all together. To make a choice among the many fine hybrids is bewildering, but I find I prefer the slender open spires rather than the short dense heads, which look rather like upturned dish mops. Almost always I go back to the species, or near species. They really prefer part shade combined with moist conditions and I have not yet a sufficiently suitable area to show off many of these beautiful plants. Of the large forms I planted only two white ones. *Astilbe rivularis*

BETH CHATTO'S DAMP GARDEN

attracts me because of its noble form, with impressive foliage and 2m/6ft stems of arching plumes made up of small greenish-white flowers developing into an interesting seed head; but it does demand a lot of space. *A.* 'Professor van der Wielen' is smaller, and more generous with its flowers, but they still make large, gracefully arching sprays.

Two small astilbes are favourites for the edges of my cool damp borders. The first is a hybrid of *Astilbe simplicifolia*, of which there are several delightful garden forms, some with bronze-green leaves and short but light open heads of rosy-pink flowers. *A.* 'Sprite' is possibly the best known and loved of these dwarf astilbes; given moist soil and not too much scorching sun it flowers for weeks in the late summer with pale, almost flesh-pink flowers set in an airy spire, about 30cm/1ft high. With soft clumps of finely cut bronze leaves the season carries on into autumn, when the flowers are replaced gradually by the warm chestnut-brown seed heads.

Astilbe chinensis var. *pumila* is, I think, an underrated plant. Its foliage is flatter and broader and the little shoots spread around to make very competent ground-cover. They send up barely branched flower spikes, about 23cm/9in high, which continue to elongate and provide light mauve-pink tapers for weeks – I could say months – into the late autumn. I find the regimented ranks of seed heads equally attractive, remaining so all winter, until they are cut down.

Another unusual *Astilbe* is *A. chinensis* var. *taquetii* 'Superba'. It flowers late in the warm Indian summer we often have as autumn in East Anglia. Slender spires of vivid cyclamen-purple on 1.2m/4ft stems are very welcome when there is little risk of other colours clashing. There are usually a few flowers nearby on *Lysimachia ciliata*, another uncommon plant but one that gives excellent value from the moment it pushes its milk chocolate-coloured leaves through the ground in spring. It makes running clumps of fine stems moderately set with leaves which are topped for months with loose heads, not spikes, of little dangling pale-yellow flowers.

I must not leave out two foliage plants which dominate the bridge end of the Canal Bed. Each year *Physocarpus opulifolius* 'Luteus' sends up tall, elegant, 2.5m/8ft branching stems, clothed with prettily shaped leaves of a really clear yellow, which remain throughout the growing season. As soon as its rather inconspicuous flowers have shown themselves I prune the strong stems back to within 1m/3ft or so of the ground, keeping a reduced shape for effect. If you neglect this pruning the bush becomes a shapeless tangle, and the foliage is not nearly so clear and brilliant. It stands on one side of the Canal like a great arching bower while opposite, repeating the colour, is a fountain of golden grass-like leaves made by Bowles' Golden Sedge, *Carex elata* 'Aurea'. How fortunate for us that Mr Bowles went to the Norfolk Broads and kept his perceptive eyes to the ground. When all the colour

I like the free-flowing habit of this shrub, *Physocarpus opulifolius* 'Luteus', whose lemon-yellow leaves in spring and early summer act like a burst of sunlight on a dull day. To promote plenty of new strong growth, this shrub needs to be pruned to a framework after flowering.

OVERLEAF
In the lowest part of the garden, where underground springs help maintain damp soil conditions, I planted *Rhododendron* 'Sappho', the yellow-leaved *Physocarpus opulifolius* 'Luteus', which draws the eye all summer long, and *Viburnum plicatum* f. *tomentosum*. In early summer the viburnum's layered branches are so crowded with white lacecaps that it looks like a vast crinoline; in autumn the leaves turn to rich colours. The pink pokers of *Persicaria bistorta* 'Superba' weave beneath these shrubs, partnered by the tomato-red flowers of *Euphorbia griffithii* 'Dixter', intermingled with *Matteuccia struthiopteris*.

has gone from the flowers, and only the seed pods of *Primula*, *Iris* and *Veratrum* remain, these two plants dominate the scene.

Late autumn is the time of the grasses. The great ones, all the different *Miscanthus*, add grandeur to the centre of the bog beds, while *Molinia caerulea* subsp. *caerulea* 'Variegata' has also outstayed any flowering plant as a feature. Throughout autumn it declines gracefully into a small ivory shower as its flower stems and leaves gradually whiten.

On the opposite side, also placed against the mown grass edge, are low tuffets of *Carex oshimensis* 'Evergold', which have been brilliant all summer but will be more appreciated throughout the winter. With every narrow leaf of this green and yellow grass-like plant, curved and outlined against the bare earth, it is one of the very few plants that will remain, of all this rich summer glory.

Two more small willows at the bridge end of the bed are *Salix lanata* and *S. hastata* 'Wehrhahnii'. *S. lanata* takes a long time to be even as big as a gooseberry bush; I have to be careful that it is not smothered by its neighbours. It is a willow from the far north. During the great drought of 1975 I was fortunate to be able to go to Norway, and was very excited to see this willow just opening its catkins beside melting pools of snow, in mid July. With us, of course, it produces them in spring, exceptionally large and woolly pale yellow catkins. The leaves are unusual too, being broadly round covered with silky hairs. *S. hastata* 'Wehrhahnii' is about the size and shape of a good blackcurrant bush. It has attractive polished purple-brown young shoots, which carry round white catkins, woolly and snow-white as those cotton wool 'buds' you can buy at the chemist. At the base of it is *Verbena corymbosa*, an eccentric member of a family most of which will only survive in my hot, dry, gravelly garden. This one runs about in moist soil, producing small heads of violet-mauve flowers endlessly throughout the summer, and is no deterrent to the clumps of *Trollius chinensis*, which grow up through it. But I think the time is not far off when it will have to be removed, as it is rather too exuberant for this limited space.

In shallow water, against the mown-grass edge, I planted *Iris laevigata* 'Variegata'. The young white-striped leaves in spring draw the eye, as do the violet-purple flowers in midsummer. My white-flowering form is one I have grown from seed. To an expert it may have its faults, but as I am not yet acquainted with any that may have romantic-sounding Japanese names, and long pedigrees, I look upon mine with fond ignorance and admiration. I think it is beautiful. Large, pure white, floating petals – for a brief while it lights the scene.

At the end of the summer I can often find flowers of *Caltha palustris* var. *alba*. It is the first Marsh Marigold to appear in spring. In early March my clumps are tightly packed with buds, like small white eggs, or perhaps marbles, at ground level. They push up quite quickly, regardless of icy conditions, until each plant is a tidy mound of round green leaves, studded with shallow china-white saucers. These first flowers drop their petals to form round green seed heads filled with shining jet black seeds, but new flowers still continue to come for weeks and weeks. There seems to be hardly a day in the summer when I cannot find a flower tucked away somewhere on one of my plants. By midsummer there is little room for weeds in the Canal Bed. The problem is usually to find the time to see that the strong do not subdue the weak in this overloaded bed.

THE TAXODIUM BED

A few treasures have slipped across the bridge into a little continuation bed made around a Swamp Cypress, *Taxodium distichum*, which now stands about 7.5m/25ft high. Here one of the many springs that travel beneath the surface of my Shade Beds and grass walks has been dug out and runs across the surface as a shallow ditch, at right angles to the 'Canal'. On either side of this little ditch I planted *Matteuccia struthiopteris*, where its beautiful shuttlecocks of fern fronds catch the light in early summer making a tender green background for the first Blue Poppies, *Meconopsis betonicifolia*. In the background are two more great ferns, outlined against a huge bamboo, *Pseudosasa japonica*, which shields the whole bed from the south. *Osmunda regalis*, the Royal Fern, is well known, loves to be planted at the water's edge, and cannot have too many helpings of well-rotted leaf-mould or compost. They take many years to show their best.

Blechnum tabulare is one of those rare treasures, a really magnificent evergreen for the bog garden, as well as being a very distinctive and unusual fern. It does need a sheltered situation to preserve its great leaves through a bad winter, and probably makes far more imposing plants in the warm, wet West Country than we can manage in East Anglia. But I enjoy my plants, which are slowly increasing, producing each year a few more of those broad, dark green leaves that look as though they had been stamped out of leather.

Thinking back to the Blue Poppies, I have been obliged to give them up. They grow wild in the Himalayas, high in the cloud belts which drench them daily with fine dew. It is the dry air as much as dry roots, which kills them in many gardens.

I treasure a fine but uncommon *Persicaria* in this bed of specialities. I have not yet found enough of just the right conditions for it to flourish really well. It is one more of my plants, which lays claim to the water's edge but where, if I do not watch continuously, plants can be overlaid and smothered by their more successful neighbours, such as the vigorous musks. This plant is *Persicaria milletii,* which thrives best with its roots thrust deep into continuously wet soil where it makes slowly increasing clusters of narrow dark green leaves. Tall slender stems carry thick short heads of flowers the colour of ripe loganberries, and about the same shape. These

The hybrid *Lysichiton camtschatcensis × americanus* is larger in leaf and flower than either of its parents. Here it makes splendid contrast to its colourful companions, candelabra primulas and the pink pokers of *Persicaria bistorta* 'Superba'.

flowers are produced from late summer until the frosts, not in great quantities, but each flower remaining fresh for weeks. When I am searching for seed I can only tell, as one does with a ripe loganberry, by the slight darkening of the crimson bloom, that the seeds may be formed and ready for collection. Often I am surprised to rub an almost perfect-looking flower head in the palm of my hand and see, with delight, the shining chestnut-coloured seeds.

I have two more persicarias, which are similar in habit but less demanding of situation. Both will grow in full sun, provided the soil does not dry out. A fairly stiff soil with enough humus suits them well. The first is *Persicaria bistorta* subsp. *carnea*,

BETH CHATTO'S DAMP GARDEN

which is a really worthwhile border plant, being tidy of habit and flowering for weeks throughout the summer. Produced in abundance, the flower heads are bright, but a much lighter colour than *P. milletii*, on the salmon side of pink. *P. macrophylla* also makes similar clumps of neat narrow leaves, but has flowers that veer towards the purple side of pink. Like the old fashioned roses, and some of the border Phlox, it is a colour impossible to describe, of such a beautiful luminous tone, you remark on it immediately.

Beside *Persicaria milletii* I planted *Carex grayi*. This is a plant that might be enjoyed by many flower arrangers. Above its grass-like leaves it holds tall sprays of curious seed heads, round clusters of inflated capsules, interesting and unusual, both green and when dried brown.

Diphylleia cymosa, the Umbrella Leaf, sends up a few of its large double-lobed round leaves. I wonder how long that splendid clump has grown with its back to a great bluff of stone in the rock garden at Kew. Must I be patient, or shall I need to move my plant to a more suitable position where its constitution will be more suited? Then perhaps it will also produce heads of insignificant flowers to be followed by bold blue berries on crimson stalks. Graham Stuart Thomas calls it 'most unusual and dignified' – I think so too, but where shall I find a position to match?

Absurdly different, but very lovable, are the wee species of *Trollius*. They are a charming excuse to sit down on the grass and peer into their glistening faces. *T. pumilus* makes little clumps of bright green finely cut leaves above which stand enamelled yellow cups on thin branching stems. *T. yunnanensis* is similar, but taller. *Primula secundiflora* droops its plum-purple flowers, slightly dusted with greenish-white meal, while a group of *Dodecatheon* seedlings produce variation in their dart-like flowers, which are sometimes called 'Shooting Stars'.

Around the base of the Swamp Cypress, *Taxodium distichum*, which forms the centre of this small bed, I planted five or six clumps of *Kirengeshoma palmata*. Every year I look forward to this unusual and beautiful plant. Its fresh leafy stems are arched over by the heavy sprays of creamy-yellow shuttlecock-shaped flowers, which are produced from late August to the end of September. Nearby I planted *Astilboides tabularis* for its unique effect. The light green leaves are almost perfectly round, slightly frilled at the edges, while the tall leaf stalks are attached to the centre of the leaves causing an indented 'dimple' on each upper surface, which can be as much as 1m/3ft across. A pile of these beautifully shaped leaves (even 45cm/18in across) looks very spectacular and scarcely needs the drooping heads of creamy-white flowers which tower above them, handsome as they may be. Where there is not enough room for *Gunnera*, this plant might be considered, provided there is adequate protection from sun and wind, and the soil is perpetually moist. It creates both drama and tranquillity among more fussy-leaved plants.

5 | The North-facing Clay Bank

IN THE LATE 1970s I decided that the north-facing bank that lies on the southern boundary of the garden would become a home to plants that would not thrive elsewhere in my garden. The bank, backed by three or four fine elms, was formed many years ago from spoil from the reservoir. At the lower end, on the edge of the reservoir, a golden Weeping Willow, *Salix sepulcralis* var. *chrysocoma*, and the stately Silver Willow, *S. alba*, we had put in as substantial cuttings were now mature trees. An alder was placed, visually about the middle of the bank. It produces quantities of catkins in spring and is a fine feature. But with the loss of the elms through disease, much character had gone, and slowly, I wanted to recreate a leafy, shady atmosphere.

The bank is 115m/375ft long, and about 11m/36ft deep, that is from the edge of the walk to the top of the bank, and as much again from the top of the bank, dropping to the ditch on the south side. For many years we had piled our weeds and garden rubbish all over this bank, using it as a compost heap – not very beautiful, but it was out of the way and available. One of the problems with above-average-sized gardens can be the long trek with trolleys and barrows to either the bonfire site or compost heap; I am finding it necessary to screen suitable sites with quick-growing shrubs. These valuable sources of combined topsoil and composted plant waste are then at hand to be put back into the beds from which they were originally taken.

Replanted since I first made use of it, this north-facing bank is home to a long-lasting display of foliage and flowers. *Astrantia* 'Hadspen Blood' jostles with the ladder-shaped fronds of the Mountain Fern, *Blechnum spicant*, while the terrestrial orchid, *Dactylorhiza × braunii*, flaunts tapering heads of crimson-purple above the dark leaves of *Heuchera micrantha* var. *diversifolia* 'Palace Purple'. The variegated *Persicaria virginiana*, blue-leaved *Hosta* 'Halcyon' and the ribbon-like leaves of *Hakonechloa macra* 'Aureola' carry the scene well into autumn.

My bank was nothing but sticky plasticine-like clay with a small accumulation of decomposed weed waste spread over it. When our neighbour bought and enlarged the reservoir, and large machines were again working on my boundary, I arranged for the dragline to scoop out a few bucketsful of field soil. This was easily done, several hundredweight at a time, I should think, dumped as easily as teaspoonfuls of sugar, while the machine stood on the farm headland.

Harry, had by now been joined by Keith, and together they tackled the job of making a new garden from this unprepossessing site. I do not care for steeply sloping banks, they are awkward to work and walk on, and rain tends to run off, rather than soak in. A slippery, slithery bank does not offer comfortable resting-places for plants or people, or suggest individual groupings.

We had plenty of good logs so we decided to terrace the bank to make three gently sloping levels. As the work progressed the new levels were top-dressed with plenty of rotted compost and grit, for the soil that had been added was of a close, heavy texture, usefully water-retentive but cold and sticky in winter, liable to cake if it was allowed to dry out in summer. Before planting began these top-dressings were forked into the soil below, and I hope the worms have helped to integrate the whole.

CREATING MORE SHADE

The mature willows gave part shade at one end of the bank, but it was not nearly as leafy as I would have liked it to be throughout its length. To create some shade I planted on the edge of my neighbour's headland fast-growing trees to compensate for the loss of the elms. I always grieve to see really big trees disappear from the landscape, knowing that it takes more than one lifetime to grow such fine specimens.

Populus balsamifera, the Balsam Poplar, shot up, 2m/6ft a year, to a great height, filling the air with its resinous scent on memorably warm days in early spring. *P. × canadensis* 'Aurea', the golden-leaved poplar, takes a few years to make its mark, but it is a beautiful companion for the tall Silver Willow which also shoots up 2m/6ft a year once it is established. I added *Salix babylonica* var. *pekinensis* 'Tortuosa' to the group. All these trees stand on the farm side of my bank, separated from it by the little stream. Eventually I hoped they would create a large screen to filter the sun but from where their roots would not greedily invade my bank.

This group of leaf-losing trees needed some evergreens to create interest and solidarity in winter, so to the top of the bank I added *Picea omorika*, my favourite slender spruce, and several interesting hollies. *Ilex × altaclerensis* 'Camelliifolia' has beautiful leaves with scarcely a prickle, large and shining, of a dark purplish-green in winter. When mature it would make a fine pyramidal shape to lead the eye up into the alder and poplar beyond it. To one side of the dark green holly I placed

I. aquifolium 'Flavescens' to make strong contrast. The young leaves are totally butter-yellow and, as the old leaves mature, the pale tint remains only at the tips of the leaves. But the effect of the bush is softly yellow, all the year round.

Eucryphia × *nymansensis* 'Nymansay' is growing very well, already making a stately column of foliage and producing its clusters of cupped white flowers for weeks in late summer. Two shrubs of *Pieris* have also taken well, flowering abundantly even while young plants. *P. japonica* Taiwanensis Group carries large clusters of waxen white Lily-of-the-Valley-like flowers. They are closely 'threaded' on to drooping stems set in pale olive-coloured bracts, the whole delicate colour scheme contrasting with the rich green of the narrow leathery leaves. There is a second display in late spring when the new young shoots unfold rich bronze-red. These shoots can be seen from the farm, and caused great interest when they first appeared above the bank. Some years we are lucky and these tender flower-like shoots are not damaged, but our treacherous spring frosts can, and often do, harm them. I am always astonished how quickly they produce new shoots, less vividly coloured but still attractive. The other *Pieris* is, I think, *P. japonica* in its pink form. The shrub has smaller leaves and deep rose-pink buds, which open palest pink. They are held by dark copper-coloured bracts, attached to dark stems. Both these beautiful early flowers need to be brought into the house to admire their unique quality, their very sumptuousness, so early in the year. It is not easy to appreciate them while being hurried along by the cold east wind, nor in the garden will you detect the strange faint scent which is released by the warmth of a room.

Lower down the bank, nearer the path, is a planting of another early flowering shrub, *Ribes laurifolium*. This relation of the Flowering Currant has long racemes of hellebore-green flowers. Each little pale flower has a darker green centre. The old leaves have a very matt, almost silk-like finish, while the younger ones have red stems, with red veins and shading on their backs. It is a quiet little shrub, but valued because of the pallid tones of its flowers and their early appearance.

Finally, to create more immediate but light shade on my bank's cool terraces, I planted *Acer negundo* 'Variegatum', the Box Elder. This makes a small light tree with smooth green twigs and leaves delicately variegated, giving almost the impression of sunlight. *A. n.* 'Variegatum' has irregular white edges to its leaves, *A. n.* 'Elegans' has yellow.

As well as creating shade, the other necessity was to mask the top of the bank. Standing on the grass walk and looking up, the top level of the bank is well above head height, disappearing as it were into the sky. It looked to me too much like an ancient burial mound. Some trees and shrubs screened this effect, especially in summer, but the spaces in between still bothered me. I planted clumps of *Iris foetidissima* var. *citrina*, *Mahonia repens* and *Vinca minor*, all to cover the bare clay.

Eventually I hope the skirts of my shrubs will completely screen the top edge in summer, if not in winter. On the rear side of the bank I planted bush willows, *Salix gracilistyla* and *S. daphnoides*, with smooth purple stems overlaid with white bloom, to emerge over the top in fine fan-like shapes as another background feature, interesting in winter, lush and leafy in summer.

On the top terrace of the north-facing garden side I planted a few more shrubs, among them *Aronia × prunifolia* 'Brilliant', which caught my eye on Messrs Hillier's stand at the RHS Great Autumn Show, and very pleased I am to have it, especially in autumn when every little leaf changes gradually to brilliant red. It has small clusters of white flowers in spring, rather like hawthorn, followed by shining black fruits.

Not all the plants that I added to this bed were necessarily the ones that would stay there. With most new beds I find myself adding far too many things, which I hope will do well there, but which are also experiments. Or they may merely be temporary residents, put there to grow and increase a little while I am finding, or making, a better situation for them.

PLANTS WHICH TOLERATE HEAVY SOIL

The soil on the terraces is heavy, intermixed with vegetable waste, fine grit and a little field soil, but almost solid clay at the top of the bank between the shrubs. I had a pressing need to find somewhere for my collection of double primroses – so they were the first plants to arrive here. They flourished exceedingly well, quite unlike anywhere else in the garden; even the more delicate double white made most healthy-looking clumps of rich green leaves.

The best time to divide primroses is during flowering, if you can bring yourself to tear them to pieces when you have waited all year to see them. But that is what I do to get young pieces established before we have any real heat to wilt them. We reduce the leaf surface by half at least, pot the special ones, that is those we have least of, and shelter them in a shaded tunnel.

If I find too many blossoms being picked off by mischievous birds I push a few short twigs into the soil and weave a web of black cotton over the plants, which is effective without being unsightly.

We do not, as yet, have many genuine old-fashioned varieties of double forms. I have mentioned the double white, *Primula vulgaris* 'Alba Plena'. We also have *P.v.* 'Lilacina Plena' whose massed stems of rosette-shaped blossoms bury the light green leaves. The colour is a delicious cool lilac. *P.* 'Marie Crousse' makes an excellent contrast, with light claret-coloured flowers edged with silver. In between these colours I have another pinky-mauve double, which I think came originally from Margery Fish. All these have rather lax flower stems with perfectly formed rosettes which open well.

For several years now we have assiduously sown seed of Barnhaven origin, and have acquired a few fairly good doubles. I cannot say they are really good because I have seen the amazing ones that the late Jared Sinclair had at his fascinating nursery in Cumbria, and I judge mine by his. But each spring we hover optimistically over the last year's batch of seedlings, looking for the buds, knowing that only the fat ones will produce a double flower, and that rarely a good full double. So you can see why it is they are rare, and if ever you are offered one you might wonder whether money can buy the years of care that have produced it, not only the nursery's care but the breeders whose patience is legendary.

As with laced polyanthus primulas, it is essential to divide the double primulas at least every two or three years. If they have been neglected the leaves become smaller and smaller, sprouting from a crowded ugly-looking knobby base. These knobs must be cut away as completely as possible. Each new shoot is usually attempting to produce clean white roots at its base, but those that do not can be boxed, or potted up and kept moist and sheltered until they have done so.

Although I am, I confess, ensnared by the double primroses (and double forms of *Primula auricula* too) I do on the whole prefer single flowers. I have two single-flowered primulas that look well at the base of my bank, near some especially large-flowered seedlings of a purple *Helleborus × hybridus*. One is *Primula* Cowichan Garnet Group with garnet-red velvety petals, the other *P.* 'Guinevere' which in spring has crinkly purplish leaves which set off large heads of pale mauve-pink flowers held in purple calyces. These are separated by a large patch of sombre-coloured spidery plants of *Ophiopogon planiscapus* 'Nigrescens'. This impossible name is well suited to an impossible-cannot-be-real looking plant. 'Whatever is that?' is how it is inevitably addressed by anyone meeting it for the first time. Related to *Liriope*, this strangely attractive plant from Japan spreads flat clusters of smooth, strap-shaped leaves of the darkest purple shade – indeed they are almost black. They send up short clusters of little violet-coloured flowers, which set sprays of shiny black berries in autumn.

To make sharp contrast with these strange plants I chose *Bergenia* 'Abendglut'. (Both are evergreen.) I love the *Bergenia* genus. Although they do look tatty for a brief while in late winter–early spring when the old leaves are deteriorating, the new ones come so quickly, are so fresh, so well shaped and always provide interesting balance and change of shape and texture, so often needed in a new planting. Not only do they remain evergreen, many of them assume rich tints of bronze, russet-red and carmine throughout the winter. Here, on this bank, with the dusky hellebores, primulas and strap-leaved *Ophiopogon* they add large rosettes of crinkle-edged round leaves, and double flowers of vivid rose-pink.

As spring grows more confident, green cut-leaved carpets of *Viola gracilis* will be smothered with rich violet-purple flowers. From reading I am not certain if this is the true form. It has delicately twisting petals, which give the flower a butterfly appearance.

Around and through the mats of *Viola* appear the erythroniums. So quickly they come and go I look each day to make the most of them. First comes *Erythronium dens-canis*. Folded oval leaves push a firm tip through the soil and expand to soft sage-green, heavily mottled and spotted with chocolate-brown. The large flowers hang folded on cold dull days, but immediately the sun warms them they flare back like cyclamen petals to show off the blue powdered anthers. They are generally cyclamen-pink in colour but seedlings do vary; some are almost white. I like to plant *Corydalis solida* nearby with low trusses of little amethyst-blue flowers out at the same time, which disappear as quickly. Fleeting as these little treasures are, they are some of my most valued plants, coming at the end of winter when spring still seems very reluctant, except for the mating birds which sing all day long, oblivious of the cold winds and snow showers that are part of March.

Erythronium revolutum comes a little later. It has narrower leaves and slightly taller stems of rose-pink flowers, while *E. tuolumnense* has large shining green leaves and branching flower stems which carry several small turkscap flowers of rich yellow.

Two or three big patches of *Primula denticulata*, in shades of lilac, reddish-purple and white start opening their balls of flowers at ground level, gradually lengthening their stems and expanding their leaves over several weeks. I like their great rosettes of pale green leaves, which remain handsome for the rest of the summer.

The variegated form of Solomon's Seal, *Polygonatum falcatum* 'Variegatum' is slowly increasing in a pocket all to itself. It has smaller leaves than the familiar *P. × hybridum*. The fat buds emerging through the soil are pink, and so too are the leaf stems, while the leaves are narrowly outlined with white. I have elsewhere a very small amount of *P. × h.* 'Striatum', which is very heavily variegated, each leaf slightly twisted and strongly striped with cream and green. It makes a much smaller plant, both in height and leaf size, because it is so variegated. It is keenly sought but increases very slowly, having so little chlorophyll. I think it is more interesting than beautiful, but I thought it worthwhile to mention the difference between the two.

Among the plants that were new to me was *Cardamine pentaphylla*. Apparently it is more than three hundred years since this plant was first described, occurring in mountain woods of west and central Europe. I have been slow to catch up with it. Flower buds and folded leaves emerge together, both tinted purple and almost invisible against the leaf-mould, but as each unrolls the finely cut leaves become green while the flowers open soft rosy-lilac. Lovely as these are I was perhaps even more impressed by the curious clusters of scaly white roots, which produce this delicate structure.

Looking at the purplish-pink buds of the variegated Solomon's Seal, thrusting up taller every day, smooth and streamlined as icicles, my eye was caught by two or three large plants of *Euphorbia amygdaloides* 'Purpurea' growing beside them. This coloured form of our native Wood Spurge varies considerably from seed; we have selected an extra-dark form. In the March sunlight the colour was enhanced by the yellow-green curtain of the Golden Weeping Willow, *Salix × sepulcralis* var. *chrysocoma*, which makes a backcloth to this end of the bank. All winter the shoot tips of the *Euphorbia* are a rich purplish-red but in late March, as the tip arches over, the young leaves stand up like a turkey's crest and as the light shines through them the colour brightens almost to brick-red. Over the weeks the heads will gradually expand into large clusters of emerald-green 'eyes' and the colour will drain from the mature leaves, which become dark blue-green. But after the seed has set, new shoots with red leaves will appear to make interest for the autumn and winter.

Among the low carpeting plants along the edge of the grass walk are different coloured forms of *Prunella*. This plant enjoys full sun and relatively dry soil, but it prefers a heavy meadow-type soil and will easily shrivel and die in poor light soils without adequate rainfall. *Prunella* has strong purplish-blue flowers in the wild, but the form called *P. grandiflora* 'Loveliness', which has light lavender-blue flowers, is more often grown in gardens. There is a good white form, and also very attractive is the one which makes a glowing carpet of raspberry-pink flowers.

Another low-growing plant I enjoy in spring I obtained as *Geranium dahuricum* (of gardens). As the leaves emerge through the soil in neat, round clumps each one is a combination of pink, apricot and cream, with no green at all, making a pastel patch of colour against the dark soil. As they mature the finely cut leaves turn light green. The flowers are soft lilac. Dahuria is a region of south-east Siberia and north-east Mongolia, so this little plant can stand intense cold. Like most geraniums it requires a well-drained soil but is not a drought-loving plant.

Some of the mossy saxifrages make tidy cushions studded with rose or white flowers in early summer. Two I grow more for their leaves than their flowers, which are white. *Saxifraga* 'Bob Hawkins' makes quite large rosettes of leaves edged with white in summer, flecked with touches of crimson in winter. *S.* 'Cloth of Gold' makes much smaller rosettes in a lovely cool shade of yellow.

The *Phlox* genus provides something for almost every type of garden. The drought-tolerant forms, such as *P. douglasii* and *P. subulata*, flourish in the well-drained upper garden, but the cool soil of the bank suits *P. adsurgens* much better. Low tangled mats of small leaves are lost beneath quantities of round salmon-pink flowers. *P. a.* 'Wagon Wheel' is a selected clone of this popular plant, with flowers less rounded and petals slightly separated, producing a more star-like effect. It is different, but I would not say it was better.

I planted *Phlox divaricata* subsp. *laphamii* 'Chattahoochee' in several parts of the

garden to see which suited it best. The sunny gravel is too exposed and starved in times of drought. My plants look best where the bank soil has been lightened with plenty of grit and garden compost. The first winter I was shocked to see them wither and die with the frosts – or so I thought. But in early spring I was relieved and delighted to see many new purple-tinted shoots pushing through the old stems.

A small plant that has found a congenial home on the lowest level of my bank bed is *Gentiana farreri*. In the autumn, from among close-packed mats of narrow, bright green leaves, emerge large upturned trumpets of a most startling blue, unlike any other gentian blue, with the colour intensified by the sharp white throat.

A handsome Japanese grass provides brilliant contrast and is equally demanding of attention for far longer, from the time its fresh leaves unfold in spring until the late autumn frost. *Hakonechloa macra* 'Aureola' is a tiresomely awkward name for this gem among grasses, whose leaves arranged in soft arching clumps remind me of coloured ribbons, vividly variegated gold and buff with warm touches of bronze.

I spent a long while finding a suitable place for *Chiastophyllum oppositifolium*. You would think with its rather succulent rosettes of leaves that a dry place would suit it, but it comes from steep rocky foothills in the Caucasus, which suggests that it is probably happiest with its roots tucked into some humus-filled crevice, preferably facing north. That is where its charming catkin-like sprays of bright yellow flowers would best be displayed. Lacking rocky crevices, at least I now have healthy-looking clumps on the edge of my cool border.

Iris setosa is making good contrast. I have two forms. Among the larger plants I put *I. setosa* itself. It makes clumps of soft green leaves and in May–June produces quantities of light purple flowers on not too leggy stems, about 60cm/2ft long. These are followed by round, pale, greyish-brown seed pods, good for picking. The dwarf form, with flower stems of less than 30cm/1ft, looks charming among the mat-forming plants.

Two unusual hydrangeas are already making bulky features without any sign of fainting in warm weather. One is the curious *Hydrangea macrophylla* 'Ayesha' which I originally grew as a cutting given to me many years ago by the late Norman Hadden. The wide, rather flat heads are packed with thick-petalled, seemingly half-closed buds, which look not unlike lilac blossom. Each thick petal is deeply cupped and slightly crinkled which helps to create this effect. On the bank my shrub has greenish-white buds which open pink, probably because of the fresh soil lifted over from the farm, which must be neutral. Elsewhere in the garden, where the soil is acid, the flowers are slightly grey-blue. Here too, on this north-facing bank, I also planted *H. aspera* subsp. *sargentiana* with its large leaves of almost shining velvety texture. I find that all my lace-cap hydrangeas look and do best in deep, rich soil in partial shade. Some I have sheltered beneath the ancient oaks where they have

I value highly the weed-smothering properties of the hardy geraniums, the Cranesbills, but have learnt where to take care with those which colonize too freely, in particular the enchanting *Geranium endressii* which takes over if left to itself. Bold contrast of form among hardy geraniums is made with the yellow-leaved *Hakonechloa* and *Hosta* 'Halcyon'.

OVERLEAF
The terrestrial orchid, *Dactylorhiza* × *braunii*, a frothing cloud of *Peltaria alliacea* and *Lilium martagon* form an attractive group in midsummer, while the yellow-ribbon grass, *Hakonechloa macra* 'Aureola', and the two hostas, *H.* 'Halcyon' and *H.* 'Frances Williams' (*sieboldiana*), furnish this spot on the north-facing bank throughout summer and into autumn.

grown well, though a prolonged autumn drought sometimes shortens the length of flowering, withering the beautiful gentian-blue florets of *H. macrophylla* 'Mariesii Perfecta' before its time. But other possible sites, where the soil remains moist, in the hollow of the garden, can become frost pockets in winter as the cold air sinks into the lowest-lying land, killing the tender flower buds.

The lowest end of the north-facing bank is the dampest, and is almost completely shaded from the south by the tall White Willow, *Salix alba*, and the familiar Golden Weeping Willow, *S.* × *sepulcralis* var. *chrysocoma*, planted behind the bank. Just before we reach the shade, we are stopped by a plant that disturbs more people than it pleases. It is *Carex buchananii*, without even a touch of green. It makes a small fountain of stiff buff and pinkish-copper stems which erupt into arching sprays of flowers and filaments. Standing isolated, every wisp and line reflecting the light, I find it beautiful, but some people think it looks dead. I had been racking my brains to know what to put under it – something very flat like a carpet – when suddenly I thought of *Acaena microphylla* and planted a few pieces round the base. They settled in immediately, in time to show me that their rosy burrs might be just what was needed to harmonize with the *Carex* and to weld several other unusual plants nearby into an interesting group. *Ophiopogon planiscapus* 'Nigrescens' is just below the *Carex*. The tiny bronze-green leaves of *Acaena*, shaped like minute rose leaves, can thread harmlessly among those black strap leaves.

Like a waterfall dripping into the deep reservoir behind them, the willows create a background for a collection of ferns. (I seem to have little collections of ferns wherever I can find both shelter from sun and wind, and where the soil does not become too dry in midsummer.) None of the ferns I planted here will stand waterlogged soil in winter, nor will the rest of the plants I put with them.

I was given a plant of *Dryopteris erythrosora* by Reginald Perry when my husband and I visited him at his nursery and had the unforgettable experience of being shown every rarity he possessed. Do jewellers have the same joy running fine stones through their fingers as plantsmen do sharing their love of good plants? They cannot have more, of that I am sure. We associate ferns with particularly tender shades of green. *D. erythrosora* catches your breath in spring when the young leaves are warm bronzy-red, especially beautiful caught in the low rays of the evening sun. As they mature they become a rich glossy green.. When I first had *D. goldieana* I could see nothing gold about it, but after it had settled down I found that the young fronds are pleasantly tinted yellow and carry on growing to make a fine feature over 1m/3ft in height.

I put *Hypolepis millefolium* on the very edge of the little path that leads to the back of the bank. I am confused between this and *Dennstaedtia punctilobula*. There is a difference, I believe, but perhaps not enough to worry about in the garden.

The unrolling fronds of *Dryopteris erythrosora* are flushed red, fading to bronze and finally bright green. As they mature new fronds are produced throughout summer, so this fern attracts attention well into autumn.

Both are very pretty with finely divided leaves like low and dainty bracken, but both are vigorous underground travellers and will ruthlessly march through anything. *Dennstaedtia*, for all its fragile appearance, obliterated a bed of variegated Lily-of-the-Valley. I think they are ideal where there is plenty of room, in shade or part shade, and where they will not menace choice plants. If you do plant them unwisely they are not difficult to eradicate – sorting out your treasures from among them is more bothersome.

I also planted *Polystichum aculeatum*, the Hard Shield Fern, one of the best we can grow, making tall distinguished-looking clumps of firm fine-cut and shining leaves which remain throughout winter. *P. munitum*, sometimes called the Christmas Fern, is similar in texture to *P. aculeatum*: they both have hard, smooth and leathery leaves. But the sickle-shaped leaflets attached to the central stem of *P. munitum* are not divided, they are entire, like the flattened teeth of a comb with slightly serrated edges. Each frond, standing waist high, makes an impressively strong feature winter and summer.

Rather like a scaled-down version of *Polystichum munitum* is *P. lonchitis*, the Holly Fern. Although at a casual glance this fern looks similar it is but half the size, and looking more closely you notice that each leaflet is edged with tiny curving prickles, hence its name. Another curious feature with both these ferns is that at the base of each leaflet, on the upper edge, close to the main stem, is a small upstanding point, like a little thumb. Each fern makes a beautiful simple design as you hold a frond against the light, so very different from the intricate, lacy structure of *Polystichum setiferum*, which is fuzzily complicated.

The simplest fern shape must be *Asplenium scolopendrium*, best known and loved as the Hart's Tongue Fern. There are many selections, some quite horrible, I think,

Beth making some
adjustments to the
Reservoir Border
in 1985.

with curly crested tips. I have one or two such plants, but I cannot admire them. The great charm of this fern, for most people I am sure, lies in the wide, slightly undulating, ribbon-like fronds. I have one which seems to make particularly long and elegant 'tongues'. I also have the more unusual *A. s.* Crispum Group in which the side margins look as though they had been scalloped with a small goffering iron (used in Victorian times to iron starched frills on babies' pillow-cases and maids' caps. My Victorian mother possessed one.) The hedge bottoms of the West Country are often crowded with the common Hart's Tongue Fern – they are not difficult to grow, when conditions are right – but they rarely survive hedge bottoms in dry and windy East Anglia. As with many other plants it has something to do with a humid atmosphere, as well as sufficient moisture at the roots.

Snowdrops look just right among the winter-green ferns. I split up my clumps to spread them around, immediately after flowering, sometimes in full flower. They do not resent this, but flower the next year most rewardingly. I am always glad to move plants when I can see that it would be nice to have this or that transferred to another place. To wait until a plant has died down (bulbs especially), often means that I forget it until it is too late, and then I cannot find it, when all the leaves have gone. Fortunately it is ideal to move snowdrops in green leaf.

Among my fernery I planted two elegant shade-loving plants. The first to flower is the white Lady's Locket, *Dicentra spectabilis* 'Alba'. This lovely plant has delicate-looking pale green leaves, which are just right for the pendulous lockets of ivory. As they open, the big round leaves of *Brunnera macrophylla* 'Hadspen Cream' will be slowly developing and will continue to produce new leaves until the arrival of autumn frosts. This is yet another plant which we owe to Eric Smith who first selected it and then made it possible for us to treasure it in our gardens. It differs from *B. m.* 'Dawson's White' in having a much gentler degree of variegation. The leaves are not startlingly green and white, but have a much lighter green background, irregularly bordered with primrose-yellow.

Actaea 'Elstead' pushes through the soil very finely divided purplish-tinted leaves, which mature to dark green with purplish branching stems. Not until autumn do we see the spires of purple-tinted buds, which open into tiny fluffy cream flowers.

To eventually hide the back of the clay bank, I planted a young scion from my beautiful Golden Yew. I knew it would take time, but was worth the wait. For more immediate effect, and directly beneath the willow branches, I planted various ivies, not variegated, all green leaved, but some are curled, others heavily veined or cut, all busily sending out long runners to hold and drape the clay with a living shawl. Among them I planted a very unusual arborescent type called *Hedera helix* f. *poetarum* 'Poetica Arborea'. It slowly makes a dome-shaped bush covered throughout the winter with clusters of developing fruit which, by spring, will have become not black, but orange. I was surprised and pleased how well the ivies have grown in this sticky, solid clay at the back of the bank. Admittedly I gave them a hand by chipping out holes of a reasonable size and filling them up with compost.

A pretty little single white primrose, *Primula* 'White Wanda', has something of the crinkled dark leaves of *Primula* 'Wanda' and is scattered among the ferns to follow the snowdrops, while several large clumps of *Carex oshimensis* 'Evergold' are a joy all the year round. The *Carex* is in the sunshine, next to *C. buchananii*, which I should have said is not reliably hardy. I always keep a few plants in a plastic tunnel protected with a few handfuls of dry straw.

The more unusual hostas are gathering strength in this favoured place. Already many years have gone into their making, many years from the life of Eric Smith and others who are specializing in this kind of foliage plant. Once hostas were considered coarse plants, to be tucked into the back of the shrubbery. They are fine among shrubs and will, in my experience, do much better there than exposed to full sun on poor soil. The yellow-leaved forms particularly must be protected from scorching, and I am finding that the glaucous blue-leaved ones both look and do much better with a little shade. A small group, which took my fancy for several weeks during the summer was made with *Meconopsis betonicifolia*, *Primula bulleyana* and a small blue-leaved *Hosta*, one of Eric Smith's *Hosta* Tardiana Group crosses. Unbelievably, the blue of the poppy petals did not kill the extraordinary wax-blue of the *Hosta* which grew beneath it, while the brilliant orange of the individual *Primula* flowers, set in whorls around slim stalks, was threaded among the poppies, making a perfect complementary harmony.

Hosta sieboldiana can flourish in more open situations provided it is well fed and mulched, but the most enormous leaves are produced in partial shade with ample

moisture. It is part of my spring routine to go round with environmentally friendly slug bait and sprinkle it among the newly unfolding *Hosta* leaves, and those of *Veratrum* too, both of which are ruined when riddled with holes. For the rest of the season we rely on the deterrent effects of crushed bark and a large bird population.

The golden bamboo, *Pleioblastus viridistriatus* (syn. *P. auricomus*), adds to the fresh, almost spring-like tones of yellow and light green that remain as features all summer on my cool bank. If I remember to cut down the old foliage in early spring the new canes come springing up, tall and unhampered, looking much brighter and fresher without last year's tattered remnants.

Into deep, deep pockets of pure leaf-mould and garden compost I planted *Cardiocrinum giganteum*. Each year the shiny heart-shaped leaves grow more numerous and larger, so the bulbs must be building up strength. What a thrill it will be when a flower spike emerges, after so many seasons of looking and checking to see that they still survive. After flowering, after that immense effort when the stout stem may have been 3m/10ft tall from which dangled long greenish-white trumpet flowers followed by huge, equally handsome seed pods – after all that, the bulb will die and we shall start again to watch the offsets build their way up.

I am reminded of a story about Gertrude Jekyll, whose patience was being sorely tried one day by a less practised visitor who repeatedly told the great gardener how lucky she was to have such marvellous soil. They were passing a pit a little way in from the edge of the woodland path along which they were walking. Just then a donkey appeared, its side panniers loaded with garden refuse – cut down plants, weeds and fallen leaves. All were tipped into the hole and a layer of the fine sandy soil was forked into the pit before another load arrived. 'That,' observed the lady tartly, 'is my marvellous soil.' And I've no doubt she explained that it would be a year or two yet before the mixture became sweetly decomposed and fit for a new planting of *Cardiocrinum*.

Another lily, which likes rich, damp soil is *Lilium pardalinum*, the Leopard Lily, from California. I have a fine variety called *L. p.* var. *giganteum*. It hangs its scarlet spotted flowers from stems over 2m/6ft high, above all the plants on the bank bed. The bulbs are curious, not individual bulbs like all other lilies I know, but clustered masses of scaly clumps, which can be broken up. I see that the Royal Horticultural Society Dictionary says '*Bulb rhizomatous*' – that's just right, in two words, but it would not prepare me for the surprise I had when I first dug up one of those curious clusters.

It is more than twenty years since I wrote about the north-facing bank. Since then inevitably the planting has changed as trees and shrubs have matured. But many of the groups I planted originally have been retained elsewhere because they worked well at the time.

Hosta sieboldiana is still one of the most reliable hostas to make a great effect, acting as it does here like the full stop at the end of a long sentence. It takes several years for one plant to achieve maximum size. *H. s.* var. *elegans* is even more spectacular, its superb grey leaves more deeply veined and quilted than those of *H. sieboldiana*.

6 | Large-scale Water Gardening

N OT MANY PEOPLE HAVE THE PRIVILEGE of planting around the edges of a large stretch of water and those who have may perhaps find it to be more of a burden than a privilege, which is a pity. By the careful choice of comparatively few plants, a really magnificent piece of landscaping can be achieved with the minimum of upkeep. I think it is largely because owners do not know what to plant that many opportunities for improvement are overlooked.

Water gardening on the landscaping scale is a quite different affair from the marginal plantings I have considered in a garden setting. I am not sure if I have stressed sufficiently the amount of work involved in maintaining marginal planting, unless it be on a very small scale. When conditions are warm and moist, weeds and plants all romp away merrily if not kept strictly under supervision. But with care, and knowledge, in planting and management, choice subjects can be preserved together in some of the most beautiful plant combinations in gardening.

The owner of a lake-side or farm reservoir starts from quite a different angle. On a large scale there is neither room nor time for delicate plants that need protection from giants and invaders. These in fact can become desirable in the right circumstances, that is, where there is ample room.

In large-scale planning it is, I think, well understood that the end result must fit harmoniously into the natural environment. Groups of native trees will, on the whole, look best and be more likely to survive long after our time than too many

These are the first two ponds that we made by constructing grass-covered dams across the spring-fed ditch. The sides are supported by hollow concrete blocks, securely fixed by angle irons driven through them into the hard clay beneath. In blossom is the Great White Cherry, *Prunus* 'Taihaku', and in the foreground the Water Hawthorn, *Aponogeton distachyos*, which produces flowers throughout the summer. The boat corresponds to the wheelbarrow on dry land – essential equipment for grooming and clearing pond plants and weeds.

exotics, which can create an unnatural look. That does not mean that we should shut our eyes to the host of suitable trees and shrubs that occur in similar situations elsewhere in the world. Although rhododendrons have been planted successfully around artificial (and natural) lakes, where the soil is not waterlogged, they are not what I have in mind in East Anglia and would certainly be a disaster around an exposed reservoir. But if you are surrounded by sheltering stands of birch and pine in the west or the northern counties of the British Isles, they would fit as harmoniously as do hollies and laurels with us. Evergreens are particularly needed in winter to contrast with the bare stems of deciduous trees.

Simple, but devastatingly invasive plants like the Common Reed, *Phragmites australis*, and the Reed Mace, *Typha latifolia*, commonly but erroneously called Bulrush, can be used with great effect in natural surroundings where there is ample room and depth. Avoid at all costs planting such things where the water is shallow overall for they will completely colonize it, and the water will vanish.

The same applies to floating plants. When considering water-lilies – which surely could be seen more often on stretches of still water – you have to remember that there are varieties suited to varying depths of water. If the water is shallow and you plant a lily which prefers greater depth it will pile itself up into a great huddle of leaves with no room for flowers to float to the surface.

Planting around the farm reservoir which ends my garden began in the autumn of 1976, my ambition being to cover the raw clay and fringe the naked perimeter around the empty stretch of water with trees, shrubs and robust plants.

The various colour-stemmed dogwoods draw me out into the winter-garden, especially to the banks of our small nursery-reservoir where they bring life and colour to an otherwise bleak scene. I like to stand close to the bright, lipstick-red stems of *Cornus alba* 'Sibirica', the Westonbirt Dogwood, spot-lit by low winter sun, and then turn to see the acid, yellowy-green stems of *C. sericea* 'Flaviramea' on the opposite bank, reflected in the clear, still water. Colonizing the water's edge is the Common Reed, *Phragmites australis*, while the Ghost Bramble, *Rubus cockburnianus*, forms a silvered 'birdcage' in the distance.

SOME TREES AND SHRUBS

Willows are the obvious choice for sticky, wet soil. It was not until I had room to experiment that I began to appreciate them. Apart from the well-known Weeping Willow I had tended to dismiss them as having long, narrow, green leaves – nothing really very striking. But with closer acquaintance I have learnt to value them, not only because they thrive in soil that few other trees stand, but also because of their variety and grace.

In Hillier's *Manual of Trees and Shrubs* there are several pages of willows to choose from, with the sizes ranging from creeping dwarfs (charming in the rock garden) to noble trees and bulky shrubs, which were what I needed. We already had the fine *Salix alba* and several mature specimens of the Golden Weeping Willow, *S. × sepulcralis* var. *chrysocoma*. We allowed to remain an ancient *S. fragilis*, or Crack Willow, well named because it has weak joints. After strong winds we have to pick up the litter of branches scattered over the grass walk. This willow grows on a steep bank overhanging the water. Years ago an ivy berry must have been dropped by a roosting bird for now there is a dark, heavy mass around the base and halfway up the great trunk. The ivy roots must not become waterlogged, but the willow can delve deep into damp soil beneath the reservoir. Together they make a mature feature, which I am reluctant to remove, despite the advice of the man on the bulldozer to get it out of the way before it fell down! It shows no sign of doing that and, in spite of the mess it occasionally makes, I shall continue to admire its great head against an empty Essex sky while I wait for my own plantings to balance it. (The Hurricane of 1987 brought down the Crack Willow.)

With this large empty landscape there was room for repetition. In the spring I cut several straight branches from my original *Salix alba*, trimmed them and stuck them in the ground like pea-sticks. (Not in a row, but singly where I needed a tall feature!) They soon sprouted new leaves, and are now fine trees.

Another variety of *Salix alba*, *S. a.* var. *sericea*, the Silver Willow, has quite the most striking foliage of all my willows; it is less vigorous than *S. alba*, which is one of the loveliest sights for the water-side being of such noble proportions with graceful branches which sweep down over the surface of the water. Their long, narrow leaves are the whitest, shining silver, so they stand out brilliantly all summer long from among the other shrubs, making lovely reflections in the dark water.

One of the first willows we planted for its catkins was *Salix aegyptiaca*. It quickly shot up strong wands, 3–4.5m/10–15ft, and was always the first to be wreathed with large, bright yellow egg-shaped catkins, often in February. It was originally planted in the garden to provide height while we were waiting for the Swamp Cypresses, *Taxodium distichum*, to make their way more slowly into the important features they are today. Eventually the *Salix* had to be removed as it detracted from the cypresses and was beginning to damage one of them, competing for air space. It is hard to destroy a tree you have planted, but it was less painful than it might have been because in recent years the catkins were never so fine as when it was a smaller and more vigorous sapling. Cuttings rooted easily and made over 2m/6ft in the first year, so fresh young saplings have been planted out and I shall hope to keep them pruned as shrubs where we can easily see the handsome catkins, rather than let them develop into rather lanky trees.

Quite a different-shaped bush, the very opposite in fact, is *Salix udensis* 'Sekka'. This willow causes great interest among flower arrangers, quite understandably, because occasional stems become fasciated, that is, they look as though several stems have been stuck together halfway along their length and then squashed flat under a heavy weight. This induces the free ends, studded with catkin buds, to splay out into an irregular curved outline, which can be a complete arrangement in itself. Dropped into a jug of hot water and glycerine it will, on removal, remain perfect, complete with half-opened 'pussy flowers' for ever, until you grow tired of it. But unless you have plenty of room to spare there are many more useful shrubs for flower arrangers – and the fasciated branches are few and far between, even on my shrubs which must be 4m/12ft across but not more than about 2m/6ft high. The great majority are straight and are strongly grown shoots, which give me more pleasure for several weeks in the early spring. The dark purplish stems hold round, polished buds which open first to white then pinky-grey before they suddenly expand into long and narrow yellow catkins, a lovely sight when the whole bush is covered. Because of its spreading shape I value this willow in summer for the amount of bare ground it covers and have planted it at the water's edge, where the banks of the reservoir shelve down steeply and the intensive root system binds the soil and prevents subsidence.

Another splendid selection of *Salix alba* is subsp. *vitellina* 'Britzensis'. I think it produces the most vividly coloured stems of all. Orange-tinted at the beginning of winter they gradually deepen to startling shades of orange and scarlet-red, illuminating the water's edge as they are caught in welcome winter sunshine, perhaps on a frosty day or, better still, when a layer of snow covers the ground. Such a day is good for the more subtle-coloured stems, which are needed for contrast, for the various 'Violet' willows. I have *S. daphnoides* and *S. acutifolia* 'Blue Streak', both of whose young blackish-purple stems are coated with a fine waxy bloom.

More willows, for height as well as bulk, include the Twisty Willow, *Salix babylonica* var. *pekinensis* 'Tortuosa'. I think this tree is enchanting in spring, when its new leaves are emerging, but in high summer I cannot really admire the twisted leaves close to. I really enjoy these trees in winter, when they catch the light along their polished, buff-coloured corkscrew branches. The Twisty Willow makes a large tree in my wet soil, but I have noticed them growing much smaller in London, near to Marble Arch I think, where they rise above island beds of other shrubs. Obviously this is a less advantageous site, but the result so far is very attractive as they have grown tighter, smaller in scale, like elegant narrow fans of pale spiralling twigs.

Salix 'Erythroflexuosa' is a cross between *S. × sepulcralis* var. *chrysocoma* and *S. babylonica* var. *pekinensis* 'Tortuosa'. In its second year from a cutting it had already made a stout little trunk of a warm ochre-yellow colour, while the spiralling branches are a rich chestnut.

Two more willows please me because they quickly make large shrubs, invaluable for masking the bare reservoir banks. The first is *Salix elaeagnos*; I think that might be its name, but apparently *S. elaeagnos* subsp. *angustifolia* is surrounded by confusion. The definition in Hillier's *Manual* sounds like my shrub, which is large but graceful, its wand-like branches tinted purple and densely set with long, very narrow leaves of a dull leathery green above, and white beneath, which look very pretty as a gust of wind ruffles them.

Even more delicate in leaf is *Salix gracilistyla*. Pale translucent leaves crowd polished olive-green stems. Yet despite its tender appearance this willow stands out conspicuously on the edge of the water, being one of the most vigorous, and quickly forming a tidy, rounded shrub. In winter pairs of pointed buds show up as soon as the leaves have dropped, while in spring they are among the first to swell into small, neat, furry grey catkins flushed with pink.

From among the smaller willows I included several bushes of *Salix hastata* 'Wehrhahnii' and *S. repens* var. *argentea,* which I have described in Chapter 4. I planted groups of them on the curve of the grass walk that edges the wide slope leading down to the water's edge. It may be, in years to come, that we shall catch only glimpses of the water between the trees and shrubs, when they are full of leaf in summer time, but I am thinking that the level must drop when the water is pumped for irrigation and then we will be glad of the screen. Fortunately there seems to be ample water, and thus far it has not dropped much more than 60cm–1m/2–3ft. This kind of fluctuation does no harm to strong-growing trees and shrubs, as their roots will have penetrated deep into the wet clay beneath.

Another possibility, which can make an interesting feature where space is limited, is *Salix purpurea* 'Nana'. It makes a small bush, roughly 1 × 1m/3 × 3 ft, consisting of very thin, dark purplish-black shoots. They are smooth and inviting to touch, with masses of fine shoots growing straight upwards to make a neat, tidy shape. The leaves are in scale, small and narrow, dark grey-green above, light beneath. One bush alone can be used as a feature. I massed several on the edge of the reservoir where their dense but tidy shapes please me in winter. They are sometimes recommended for making a low hedge in damp soil. This sounds a good idea, for they do not need cutting as frequently as other coloured-stem willows. However, it is a pity to neglect them entirely; they do slowly grow larger. Mine are now head high, time they were pruned to a basic shape to encourage bright new shoots. Most willows take kindly to pruning where space is limited for where they grow too tall, large or ungainly. They benefit by being reduced to a basic framework.

I knew it would be difficult to tear myself away from the willows, which once I passed by. I cannot describe all those I grow now, but will mention finally one, which always fascinates visitors with its very unusual catkins. It is *Salix gracilistyla* 'Melanostachys'; you will remember the name if you think of the dark mood, melancholy. Before the leaves appear, matt, sooty-black catkins slowly swell to show a glimpse of red before they burst into yellow fluff.

Although we are already beginning to enjoy a bosky, leafy look around the reservoir in summer, winter and spring are inviting too, with many different coloured stems, curious twisted shapes, and the seared remains of sedges and grasses. The wide expanse of water is alive too, with mallard duck in winter plumage.

On the higher, drier slopes I planted Silver Birches, alders and hollies. The Balsam Poplar, *Populus trichocarpa*, is growing at a tremendous rate to take the place of the stately elms, and fills the air with its special sweet fragrance when there are still few signs of spring. I hope its searching roots can do no harm here, with only the farm headland to invade. My original tree became a menace in the garden, throwing up suckers along the edge of a border far removed from its trunk, where its roots had been cut by the edging tool.

Populus × jackii 'Aurora' also had to be ejected from the garden because it has the same greedy habits. There is room for it around the reservoir, and its large, oval, creamy-white leaves, tinged with pink, make good contrast with the narrow green leaves of many of the willows. It needs to be hard pruned every few years to encourage the variegation; this can be attended to at the same time as the willows are pruned. Those we value for their vigorous, whip-like growths should be cut every other year in early spring, before the buds begin to break. If they are left indefinitely they become a crisscross of old and new stems, which are not only short, but poorly coloured.

I must not forget *Populus × canadensis* 'Aurea', the beautiful Golden Poplar. This is not quite so vigorous initially but does in time make a very large tree, a perfect companion for *Salix alba*, the White Willow. I know of a mature planting of these two beside a railway viaduct which spans the road, with low-lying land on either side. Together they create a scene that is very satisfying. The fine trees tower high above the elevated railway, their straight trunks complementing the pillars of the arches while their graceful branches, fluttering with silver and golden leaves, soften the good brickwork.

One of the most beautiful trees you can plant in damp soil is *Alnus glutinosa*

'Imperialis', the Cut-leaved Alder. If you have room plant a little grove of them. You will be enchanted when they are only a few feet tall and for someone's grandchildren you will have endowed a magic circle, their columnar trunks supporting a canopy of delicate, lace-like leaves.

Dogwoods are planted for their coloured stems. The most vivid enamelled red stems are made by *Cornus alba* 'Sibirica', better known perhaps as *C. a.* 'Westonbirt'. I like its clusters of grey-blue berries, which show up against the plum-red autumn leaves. *C. sericea* 'Flaviramea' makes similar terminal clusters, but they are pearl-white. I picked a few branches and put them into a jar with the cupped white blossoms of *Anemone × hybrida* 'Honorine Jobert' and the double white form of *Saponaria officinalis,* which grows round its feet. All three looked good together, so unexpectedly fresh in late autumn. *Cornus sericea* 'Flaviramea' needs regular hard pruning to produce the straightest and brightest yellow-green shoots, but if you like to have the berries you must let it go for a year or two. By planting several, and pruning them alternately, you can have both.

Two 'ghost' brambles look good in the 'wild garden', but like all wild gardening must not be neglected if you wish for the best effects. *Rubus cockburnianus* makes the largest bush in my garden. I cut the old stems to ground level each year just as the new canes are emerging. *R. thibetanus* is similar but daintier. Its leaves are even more fern-like, so heavily coated with silky hairs that they appear soft grey above, almost white beneath.

I have a third bramble, not often seen but always admired when sprays of its flowers are put in a vase, where they will last for days. *Rubus ulmifolius* 'Bellidiflorus' looks very like our common blackberry, except that its long flowering shoots are covered with double flowers. Pale grey buds open to tightly packed, lilac-coloured rosettes. My bushes are planted in heavy soil. Each spring I trim them to leave a tidy, compact shape, which will produce the coming season's flowering shoots. I cut off the long trailers, which were made the previous summer because they are tip-rooting and would soon spread far and wide.

I should, at this stage, explain that while some of my plantings may make the Reservoir Garden look as though it were all too easy, that was not quite the case in the beginning. In fact I suspect I almost lost Harry, in more ways than one, in those early days of planting. It had slipped my mind that he cannot swim, so it was not the state of the soil alone which caused dark silences and stiff lips. There we were, especially on the farm side opposite our garden, slithering up and down the wet clay with nothing to stop us going into 5m/16ft of icy water below. The old tractor with its buck loaded with gritty compost stood above us on the farm headland. We dug holes as best we could in the wet clay, so solid and sticky we had to stop and cut it off our spades and boots with a knife. Drainage slits had to be dug

OVERLEAF
Nothing enhances the mirrored surface of a pond like rafts of water-lily pads with upturned faces of flowers peeping among them.
Among several unknown varieties are *Nymphaea* 'Rose Arey' and *N.* 'James Brydon'. Since they increase rapidly, once established, the boat is required to reduce them, usually in early autumn while we can still see what needs to be done.

beneath the holes, else they filled up like wells with water whenever it rained. The gritty soil was carted to the holes by the bucketful – we could not use a barrow. It was very slow, very dirty work, with little to show at the end of a long day but small twigs lost in the dusk and a lot of dirty tools to clean, not to mention clothes and boots. The first year there was a poor response for all our efforts, but I reminded myself that it was asking a lot for anything to grow in heavily compacted clay. I could be thankful most things were still alive. The next year was better, and I was encouraged to go on, to plant a few more things each year, until now I marvel that so few years have passed since we began the Reservoir Garden. Once a year, usually about July, the coarse grasses, rushes and buttercups which have also colonized the banks are scythed and we sprinkle a handful of base fertilizer around the trees and shrubs. It would be better if it were done earlier no doubt but, like the farmer, we have no time to spare earlier. Before long I think they will not need that small assistance, but will themselves smother the native weeds. Now, twenty years on, enough trees have grown on the farm side of the reservoir to screen out the open fields, form a shelter belt from the west winds and 'paint the sky'.

On my side of the reservoir I allowed a much wider area for planting, and used a few more exotics to blend with the garden. I could not resist planting two more Swamp Cypresses, *Taxodium distichum*. Although they lose their leaves in winter their tall, narrowly pyramidal shapes have now pierced the skyline, as they do in the garden. I also repeated *Thuja plicata*. The tree we planted in the early nineteen-sixties dominates a mixed group summer and winter, but is especially valuable in winter. I tend to stress the importance of evergreens in the garden. They are not planted as solid and continuous barricades, but where the planting is most successful they form the basic core of the main groups. Some deciduous trees and shrubs make very attractive outlines when planted as specimens, but many others, especially if herded together, can produce a dull shapeless tangle in winter. I have not found it easy to find evergreens that both look well and do well around the exposed reservoir. On the drier banks hollies have been the most successful and long lasting, always good with Silver Birches. There are many to choose from; a careful study of the Holly Walk at Kew is very helpful. The variegated ones look better, I think, in more formal settings, but in natural landscaping those with rich glossy foliage and good berries are preferable. Among these *Ilex aquifolium* 'J.C. van Tol' is one of the best.

In a more sheltered corner I planted bamboos. *Pseudosasa japonica* forms lush masses of dark glossy green leaves and makes imposing thickets several metres or many feet high and across. Much more elegant is *Fargesia nitida*. It does not sucker so freely, but extends slowly as a compact circular clump. Bamboos can be restrained by digging out the suckers which transgress beyond their allotted territory, but it is tough digging. I tend to associate them with large gardens, but I once visited a garden on the outskirts of London on a long, very narrow sloping site about 8m/26ft across where the enclosing high, and rather unsightly, walls had vanished behind magnificent stands of fine-leaved bamboos, alternating with wall shrubs and climbers. Every inch beneath was full of plants, hostas and ferns predominating, surrounding little pools. The step-ways (no space was wasted by making a definite path), consisting of laid blocks or rocks, veered from one side to the other, instead of making two narrow boring borders down each side. On consideration I wonder if the construction of the little pools was designed to keep the roots of the bamboos in their place. Nothing seemed to be suffering while the natural effect of dappled shade created by the lacy bamboos overhead was quite astonishing. Such a situation would prevent the scorching of their foliage by extra-severe frosts, which we sometimes have in the open.

Fargesia murielae is very similar to *F. nitida*. The most obvious difference is the colour of the mature canes, which are stained dark purple on *F. nitida*, and whose leaves are slightly narrower, altogether creating a very dainty yet distinctive appearance. The stems of *F. murielae* remain green, and the leaves too have a rather softer effect, being light pea-green in colour. Both these bamboos can be grown successfully in large tubs, provided you do not neglect to water them adequately and feed them occasionally.

Another bamboo which had to be banished to the outer garden is *Sasa veitchii*. This invasive plant successfully colonized the steep clay banks where it forms thickets about 75cm–1m/2½–3ft high. The dull purplish canes carry wide, stiffly held leaves, forming plain green ground-cover all summer. But in autumn the colour is withdrawn from their edges, leaving a pale straw-coloured border, which gives a bold variegated effect lasting all winter. In the right place, where there is ample room and it cannot force strong shoots through herbaceous plants, it is both admirable and useful.

I have written elsewhere of the bad habits and bean-pole like structure of *Aralia elata*. It found its home in the heavy clay soil around the reservoir where it is far less trouble, obviously finding it more of an effort to thrust up too many suckering shoots. Instead the main rods have shot up above the surrounding bamboos where they now display their huge elegant leaves, creating an almost tropical effect, backed by the falling curtains of weeping willows. In early autumn they are topped with large fluffy heads of tiny creamy flowers, adding to an already exotic picture. The flowers can be seen more easily on a smaller specimen of *Aralia elata* 'Variegata' which I placed on the opposite side of the grass walk that runs along the reservoir border. Close to you can see the pretty pink stems which support the elderflower-like mass of creamy flowers, but I doubt if I shall see many of the small purple-black berries which are sometimes set on the plain-leaved form. But they are not the main reason for growing this shrub. It is the magnificent foliage, quite the most dramatic and beautiful (provided you like variegated plants) of any variegated shrub. I imagine that, because it is partially stunted by variegation, the habit is less gawky, the thick prickly stems branch much nearer the ground, and eventually create quite a low broadheaded tree. The leaves are enormous, almost 1m/3ft long and half as much across, handsomely divided and irregularly bordered and splashed with creamy-white. The suckers which come up from the base are from the plain stock and must be removed. I no longer have either of these aralias, but in suitable conditions they are worth growing.

I am nearing the boundaries of my land (tucked close up against them in most places!) but there are still vast quantities of trees, shrubs and plants that I do not know and cannot hope to grow because I have not the space. Time too becomes more precious and each year is noticeably shorter. So I have learnt to be more selective. It is tempting, and sometimes sensible, to repeat plants which have been successful elsewhere, but one needs new ideas from other people, other gardens, other countries sometimes, to bring a fresh look to the garden.

Berries provide highlights in autumn, and some of the best are produced by the Guelder Rose, also called Water Elder. *Viburnum opulus* can be found wild in Britain on the edge of woody places or in hedgerows, usually not far from a running ditch or marshy place and more commonly, I think, on chalky soils where the rich green leaves turn to brilliant pink and crimson autumn tints. I see but a ghost of that colour on my wet clay, but the berries are lovely. I grow two selected forms. One is *V. o.* 'Notcutt's Variety' which is more vigorous in every way than the wild form, with stronger growth and larger clusters of luscious-looking transparent red berries. The other, *V. o.* 'Fructu Luteo', has large pea-sized berries which start green and slowly change to a pale and opaque creamy butter-yellow. These marble-textured berries are quite exquisite, hanging over the rim of a container, when arranged with something else that may be stiff and upright. But that is not all. As they ripen the colour deepens to translucent amber and, as the leaves fall, may still be seen hanging in heavy clusters. Some years the birds have ravaged them but my little half-Siamese cat, Emma (short for Emacia, she was brought to me, skin and bone) has such a restless, busybody nature that she may have been something of a deterrent. I tried spraying some of my berried trees and shrubs, and others, like cherries and *Forsythia,* which have their buds systematically stripped by bullfinches, but the birds usually win in the end. I cannot blame them. When the ground is iron-hard and icy blasts sweep the garden I like to think there is some food and shelter available. (Since the commercial apple orchards have been removed we seldom now see bullfinches.)

I have described elsewhere the Japanese *Viburnum plicatum* 'Mariesii'. There are several forms, all extremely beautiful, their horizontal branches loaded with creamy lace caps. The one called *V. p.* 'Pink Beauty', with flowers which turn pink as they age, continues to produce new flowers, for months it seems, until the autumn.

I would not put any of these forms of *Viburnum plicatum* into such wet soil as *V. opulus*, but they all need deep rich soil. A *Viburnum* which so far has defeated me is *V. betulifolium*. When properly suited it is one of the most amazing sights in autumn, with infinitely more grace and elegance when in fruit than our rather heavy *V. opulus*. Imagine a large open shrub, more than 3m/10ft high and across, much branched and so loaded with dainty sprays of small glassy red berries that you can see it from afar, glowing red in the distance. I remember seeing it like that in the Valley Gardens at Windsor, but although I have grown bushes easily that size and introduced others planted alongside to encourage fertilization, only the meanest little clusters of berries have appeared, sometimes one branch only. Why, I wonder? My original planting was scrapped when we made the last pond, and new ones have been planted beside the reservoir, but I still wait to be dazzled by their splendour. Meanwhile I quite enjoy their shape and their leaves, which are small and oval, like birch leaves.

GIANT HERBACEOUS PLANTS

Just as some trees and shrubs proved too large, or invasive, for the garden, some of my more vigorous herbaceous plants have also gravitated to this outer garden. They *must* be vigorous to thrive in the heavy soil, with the minimum of attention. Those that certainly would prove a menace elsewhere will probably, eventually, be overcome here, squeezed out by invading trees and shrubs. However, nuisance value has not been the criterion for selecting plants for this outer garden. Large-scale planting needs large and imposing plants, so naturally several groups of *Gunnera tinctoria* were among the first to be planted. We placed them well above the water's edge, making extra-large holes and filling them up with barrowloads of garden compost. Every other year we heap farmyard manure among them to encourage the production of spectacular leaves. They take several years to establish a starchy base and strong root system to support their magnificent superstructure.

Further away from the water, where the soil cannot become waterlogged, are groups of ornamental rhubarb. I have a clone of *Rheum palmatum*, which has larger, redder leaves then *R. p.* 'Atrosanguineum' itself, but instead of producing fluffy spires of crimson-pink flowers, they are creamy-white. On looking it up in Graham Stuart Thomas's *Perennial Garden Plants* (what would we do without that mine of information?) I think my plant might be a good form of *R. p.* var. *tanguticum*, which he says produces white, pink or crimson flowers on different clones. I find one can get very muddled with rheums! I saw a form I much admired in the Munich

Botanic Gardens. Its leaves were still richly suffused red in July, while the leaf shape was not so palmate, but had far more indentations, scallop-shaped, along the edges. It was labelled *R. p.* var. *tanguticum*. I have since been sent something called *R. p.* var. *tanguticum* (not from Munich) which so far is a boring thing, with no red colouring at all and nothing like the plant I saw in Munich. One that I covet especially since seeing Roy Lancaster's slides of Nepal, in which he showed it growing in its natural habitat, is *R. australe*. It looks not unlike *Astilboides tabularis* in shape – a huge circular green leaf like a giant navelwort – and most desirable.

The ornamental rheums look their best from spring until about August, when they begin to look rather untidy and their colour fades. But by then other large herbaceous plants hide them from view. One which does this most successfully is *Inula magnifica*. A coarse great plant that stands easily 3m/10ft tall, it makes large piles of long, dock-like leaves. From them emerge stout stems topped with a spire of knobby green buds which open to smallish, yellow daisy flowers. The colour and size of the flowers are not really important, but the outline of the whole plant, from tipmost buds down the leafy stem to the lush pile on the ground, catches the eye and looks good in the setting.

It helps to remember that *Ligularia* is closely related to *Senecio*, and yet it is amusing to find a familiar relation is the common groundsel, *S. vulgaris*, which cowers like a mouse among its elephantine relations. *Ligularia* 'The Rocket' enjoys the wet clay, its black stems and narrow spires of clear yellow flowers outlined against the water. The shorter and bulkier *L. dentata* spreads its mahogany-backed leaves in the shade of *Salix elaeagnos*, where the huge heads of vivid orange daisies contrast with the fluttering grey and white leaves. Another 'groundsel', which produces quite sumptuous flowers is *L.* 'Gregynog Gold'. I like the large, heart-shaped green leaves, which make fine weed-smothering clumps. The inherited characteristics from its parents have produced a spire-like habit combined with large flowers, so the result is tall stems, 2m/6ft, set with large cone-shaped heads of bright yellow daisy flowers which have quite long drooping petals.

There are other interesting members of this varied family – some I have, some I covet. With them all it is vital to remember that slugs and snails dote on them, so make sure bait is laid immediately the leaves emerge in spring. It is miserable to face, for the rest of the year, those large prominent leaves riddled with holes.

Angelica archangelica creates an architectural feature, as well as being valued in the kitchen for its delicate flavour. I love to see its pale green heads supported well above its own foliage and the surrounding plants. When you scatter seed of huge plants haphazardly it is advisable to walk regularly among young trees and shrubs to remove anything (including seedling blackberries) which would, when mature, flop against the permanent plantings and spoil their shape.

Rheum palmatum var. *tanguticum*, an especially fine ornamental rhubarb, produces freshly coloured leaves in spring and continues well into late summer, providing a focal point in the wild garden or in a mixed border. It thrives in well-fed retentive soil, but will rot in boggy, ill-drained soil.

Kniphofias, or Red Hot Pokers, are also useful to break the comfortable monotony of too many rounded shapes. I have grown them from seed and selected those which made the tallest and biggest flowers, in shades of vivid red and orange, to group along the border, where it is not too wet in winter. For a background they have arching clumps of Pampas Grass.

It is interesting as you travel around to notice how variable are the flower heads of Pampas Grass. I have seen some so thin and skinny as to be worthless to my mind, especially when seen growing from a matted tangle of half-dead foliage. Neither can I say that I like the pink ones very much, in spite of seeing some magnificently grown specimens, the flower stems at least 4m/12ft, possibly 5m/15ft high. They had a dark, almost maroon-like depth of colouring, heavily overlaid with silky hairs which veiled and softened it. In the right place, with a light background, possibly a building, it might have looked very unusual and handsome.

I have a picture in my mind of Pampas Grass in November, on a silvery frosty morning, all colour gone, the reservoir sheeted with ice, the sky broken with horizontal bands of low cloud. A silver and white morning would be a dreamlike setting for the elegant plumes of the most beautiful of all Pampas grasses, *Cortaderia selloana* 'Sunningdale Silver'. The plumes are not solid dust-mops but open silky, feathery pennants, fluttering high on tall stems, sometimes 3m/10ft tall. I also planted *C. s.* 'Pumila'. It has close, compact and creamy-coloured heads on shorter stems about 1.5m/5ft high. I especially like its foliage, which makes a very attractive shimmering shape nearer the edge of the border. And I am glad to have discovered *C. s.* 'Aureolineata', whose leaves are yellow striped, making the plant a very light and important feature. It needs to be planted in an exposed position, either as a specimen in mown grass or as a focal point on the edge of a border.

Other great grasses for large water-sides must include *Miscanthus*, especially *M. sacchariflorus*, which can easily top 4m/12ft. But *M. sinensis* 'Zebrinus' and *M. s.* 'Silberfeder' grow almost as tall. All thrive with the minimum of attention once they have become established; merely cut down the tall canes before the new ones emerge in spring, preferably before winter gales have blown them into battered heaps. Many improved forms of *Miscanthus* have been introduced.

Arundo donax, the Giant Reed from southern Europe, must be the most imposing herbaceous grass that we can grow. From a great height it produces cascades of soft blue-grey ribbon-like leaves on tall, strong stems which shoot up from ground level each season. It deserves a choice situation in deep, rich soil, adequately watered. My plants of the rare and lovely variegated form, *A. d.* var. *versicolor*, will always remind me of my first visit to the nursery of the Countess von Stein Zeppelin in southern Germany. Her plant was growing in a large tub which could be carried to a sheltered place in winter. She showed me the little side shoots which grow in the axils of the leaves, and kindly gave me some. I brought them home, set them in pans and kept them in my frostproof but cool greenhouse where they rooted easily. Unfortunately this lovely plant is not reliably hardy in Great Britain, surviving outside in only the most favoured warm sites. I plant mine out in the summer, after the risk of late spring frosts has passed. By the autumn they have made large exotic-looking features planted among such treasures as *Actaea matsumurae* 'White Pearl', *Salvia uliginosa* and the lovely Japanese anemones. As insurance we keep our stock plants boxed up and covered with straw in a plastic tunnel, and still a few more in the frostproof greenhouse. Once planted they grow well and are so outstandingly good-looking that it is worth the trouble to keep them under cover in winter.

The yellow-flowered native water iris, *Iris pseudacorus*, makes huge clumps of handsome foliage which, together with its roots, protect the edge of the banks. I found that the wind-driven waves beat against the bare edges and started to wear them away. *Glyceria maxima* var. *variegata* has helped with this problem, being one of the few plants that can quickly colonize raw clay. It could be too invasive and is practically ineradicable, but I am counting on the natural development of large smothering shrubs, like the willows, to control it. Meanwhile its patches of green and white striped leaves look attractive from across the water. The Water Forget-me-not was brought in with the *Glyceria* and here and there floats out rafts of tiny blue flowers which are anchored among the grass roots.

A powerful invader, preferably planted by lakes or large reservoirs, is *Petasites japonicus* var. *giganteus*, the Giant Butter Burr, with huge round leaves that almost rival *Gunnera* when it is well established, more than 1m/3ft across. They look magnificent reflected in the water and I cannot help admiring their wickedly wandering shoots, thick as my thumb, which push through the clay like butter. We prise them out when we need to make new plants. The leaves disappear in winter revealing bare clay, where no weed can survive. In February this bare soil is suddenly decorated with Victorian posies. Round buds, large as tennis balls, open to layers of delicate green bracts which turn back to form an encircling frill for the centre, packed with tiny creamy-white flowers, faintly scented. So pretty they look, so desirable, especially to the flower arranger, but suitable only for landscape planting. We have, by tactful inquiry, saved several small rock gardens from being obliterated by this invasive giant because their owners fancied it on an early spring visit.

There are a few more great plants which provide flowers in late summer and autumn. Perhaps the finest is *Eupatorium purpureum*. We have a form which has extra-dark purple stems and deep coloured heads of cinnamon-pink fluffy flowers. They take several years to make imposing clumps, with dozens of flowering shoots which associate loftily with the large grasses at about 2.5m/8ft. They are so strong

OVERLEAF
The invasive roots of *Petasites japonicus* var. *giganteus* bind the steep clay bank of the farm reservoir. While we admire its Victorian posy-like clusters of flower in early spring, this plant can be contemplated only in large land-scaping projects where the huge round leaves, up to 1.2m/4ft across, make impenetrable ground cover.

they can push through rough grass, running buttercups and anything else that may have colonized the banks.

Fagopyrum dibotrys is a seldom-seen plant which has its place in the autumn scene. It is the American buckwheat, related to the *Persicaria* or *Fallopia*, and sends up quantities of elegant branched stems furnished with pretty leaves, triangular shaped, with veins and stems stained red. From late summer to November they are topped with lacy clusters of small creamy-white flowers.

In a rough corner, at one end of the reservoir, *Fallopia sachalinensis* creates a scene like a tropical jungle. Thick, jointed, bamboo-like canes rush up each year to about 5m/15ft, carrying huge oval green leaves. In late summer strings of little white flowers dangle from the leaf axils. In winter we cut them off at ground level and lug them to the bonfire, burning conveniently near.

MAINTENANCE OF LARGE, DAMP AREAS

At the start of this chapter I spoke lightly of maintenance with the minimum of upkeep. You may be wondering how it is done. At the beginning I started with clean ground because it was a newly remade stretch of water. That was an initial advantage. But the moment we started bringing in our garden compost we introduced weed seeds, and even the churned-up clay was not sterile; grasses, rushes, creeping buttercups and marsh thistles all appeared the first year.

We treat the farm side and the garden side of the reservoir differently. The farm side is a continuous rim of trees and bushes which look after themselves apart from a bit of pruning. And if that is not possible it is not a disaster. The bank is too steep and awkward to use a mulch of straw so we have allowed the natural weeds to cover it; they have also helped to bind it and prevent erosion by rainfall. The weeds are scythed down once a year, usually in July. This is not ideal for maximum growth and development but it is the best we can do and is probably as much as most people considering planting such a situation could manage. Satisfactory progress was made, after a slow start, with this low level of maintenance because, I think, only the toughest colonizers have survived and thrived.

Root competition from tightly packed weeds could be relieved by the careful use of a suitable weedkiller, but great care must be taken to see that it does not come in contact with the green bark of young trees. Weeds closest to the young stems should be removed by hand. We use baled straw to keep the area around newly planted trees and shrubs clear of weeds. Inspect them, in winter especially, to make sure that mice are not nibbling the tender bark.

If you are thinking of adding some interesting trees and shrubs to already established scrub or marshland then I would advise you to use a total weedkiller several weeks before planting around each individual site that you propose to plant.

Ideally, of course, you could scythe the brushwood and dig out a sufficiently large space for a newcomer to find breathing space, but for most people today that would mean the job would never get done. There is either not enough time or enough muscle to do the job.

I do not like using weedkillers, but there are times and situations where they are the practical best. Provided they are used infrequently, that the right ones are chosen and used with great care, then I find that I am able to reclothe and care for my soil and plants most of the time by natural means.

I have already said that the reservoir border on the garden side is much wider. It is also less steep and faces a broad grass walk which runs alongside it. It has become the mixed planting of trees, shrubs and large herbaceous plants which I have just been describing. Originally I promised myself that this garden must not demand any fussy handwork, and so it has remained, apart from pruning and cutting down. From the beginning of planting it has been mulched with straw. I buy several trailerloads of straw bales from a nearby farm every autumn. Straw saves months of work, helping to feed the soil as well as protect it. We put it down thickly all over, like a great eiderdown, usually before Christmas. It is a good job for raw cold weather.

The straw is inviting to walk on, to inspect plantings, without clay-covered boots, and the strong-growing herbaceous plants push up through it with no difficulty. Hardly a weed appears. If, as I usually do, I have afterthoughts and wish either to remove or add something, it is no trouble to push aside the straw, dig a hole, add gritty compost and then tidy the straw around the new introduction. We do not necessarily add straw every year. It depends how much is left at the end of the season. In the spring we lightly sprinkle, over newly laid straw, a straight nitrogenous fertilizer such as sulphate of ammonia to help break it down. It is necessary to do this otherwise the micro-organisms which actually do the work take nitrogen out of the soil and so, temporarily at least, the plants are losing nitrogen rather than gaining it.

We are using mulches more and more, rather than weedkillers. Both cost money, but with a mulch the results are all bonuses. The soil surface is protected from compaction, hardcapping in dry weather, erosion when it is too wet – as well as the germination of weeds. Beneath the surface moisture is conserved and over the years a good soil texture is gradually built up. With a mulch plants are not shocked – they do not have to pull themselves together as they do after even a mild dose of poison – but grow away well and themselves cover the ground more efficiently.

I use straw among our trees, shrubs and areas of coarse planting. Where the straw would look unsightly I use pulverized bark. As with the straw mulch a light dressing of nitrogenous fertilizer applied before the bark is spread is beneficial, although there have been seasons when I have omitted to provide it, with no ill-effect.

It is not cheap gardening to use mulches. But a crushed bark mulch looks so good, and is beneficial in every way. It enables me to grow thousands of plants which I could not possibly do if the same acreage had to be carefully hand-weeded many times a year. There is some hand-weeding to be done, especially in the early part of the year when really determined weed seedlings manage to struggle through the mulch. But it is a much quicker and more pleasant job than niggling fine grasses and weed seedlings out of every bare square metre or foot.

Annual meadow grass, once my worst weed, is of no consequence now. Those odd ones that appear are almost a pleasure to pull out, which they do so easily. Fat Hen and chickweed still tend to be too much in evidence the first year after the ground has been heavily mucked or I have rotavated in last year's compost heap.

But once we have pulled out these nuisances, and in some places have had to top up with a little more bark, the rest of the season remains fairly clean, the major part of our time in the garden being taken up with general tidying, such as cutting down finished plants and cutting grass edges, with only the odd bucketful of weeds to pick up as we pass by.

I am often asked how much bark to put on, how deep should it be. Not less than 2.5cm/1in, more if you can afford it. It is not an economy to put it on too thinly. The soil must be well covered and sufficiently deep so that strong-hearted seedlings cannot struggle to the light. Sometimes, with new plantings of small things, we have to make two attempts to cover the soil, otherwise the small plants are buried. I find too that I have to make sure that scratching blackbirds searching for worms do not bury tiny treasures.

The clay-based Reservoir Border consists mainly of mid- to late-summer perennials. Shrubs and bamboos behind them screen the view of our neighbour's reservoir in summer, when the water may drop to a low and unsightly level. In winter, when leaves have fallen and plants have been cut down, we appreciate the big expanse of water, which is brought to life by flocks of ducks.

7 | Garden Management

PLEASE DO NOT SKIP THIS CHAPTER. It is bound to be tempting to do so – all that boring stuff about soil structure and double digging. Besides, it usually takes all one's time to get new plants into the ground as quickly as possible before they have dried out and died. So one cannot take too long preparing the site. I know, I have thought and behaved in exactly the same way. But for the last four decades I have been involved almost daily with land that had been considered unusable by anyone within living memory, where I have a varied range of soil conditions. There is raw red gravel which would ideally make driveways or building material; elsewhere there is moist sour silt and beyond that solid brick-making clay. I have been forced again and again to study my soils, to see how I could improve them and maintain that improvement.

Soil is our most precious commodity, however bad it may, at times, appear to be. Oil and precious elements we could live without, but we were born originally out of the soil and must respect it. As a child I loved the feel and smell of soil and no doubt exasperated my mother by frequently being covered with it. Even today I am sometimes guilty of traipsing it over newly washed tiles, when it is understandably called 'dirt'. But I cannot bear to hear people speak of soil as dirt, although I believe that in the United States of America it is the generally accepted word. Perhaps there it is not so generally used in a derogatory sense.

When newly planted, the borders are well-mulched with crushed bark to help prevent the germination of weeds in the freshly disturbed and enriched soil. By mid-summer of the second year the area was crowded with strong plant-growth, leaving little room for invaders. Maintenance consists chiefly of grooming – deadheading and trimming back spent growth, but remembering to leave promising seed heads.

SOIL IMPROVEMENT AND BORDER RENOVATION

I spend a lot of time in this book describing plants and plant groupings which are suited to specialized conditions, primarily damp ones. But the right choice of plants is not the whole answer. We must begin, and end, with the type of soil.

I admit that I have become obsessed with my soils, with the challenge surrounding me in my varying types, situated in close proximity, in a comparatively small area (6.1 hectares/15½ acres) of land. Nothing gives me more pleasure than being able to push my hand into the soil with scarcely the need for a fork. Of course, I am far from achieving this everywhere and frankly will never do so, but it is the goal for which I aim. Like most of you reading this book, I had neither the experience nor the facilities at the beginning to cosset my soil as I am able to do now, but then, neither was Rome built in a day. I began as an innocent amateur, not having seen or touched such land before. In the *Gravel Garden* I describe how I established plants in free-draining gravel and sand and in the *Woodland Garden* explain the measures we took to improve dry, impoverished soil beneath trees. So in this chapter I focus on how I have dealt with my silt and clay soils.

Before I begin, however, I want to mention the management of lawns and grass walks on heavy soil, since the best-planned borders can be degraded by poorly kept or neglected grass. Since I first wrote *The Damp Garden*, we seem to have cured the problem of moss in our lawns, (vast mats of which needed to be raked out in springtime) by hiring a mechanically driven lawn aerator. This has alternate spikes and hollow tines that remove plugs of compacted soil. Then grit is brushed into the holes. Where many visitors' feet compact the grass, this treatment is needed in both spring and autumn.

Several chapters would be needed to do justice to the full story of lawn maintenance in damp gardens and I confess to being more interested in the plants. I rely on my staff to maintain our grass. I can tell you this, however: grass is not just a hard-wearing border-to-border carpeting material to be rolled out and then left to fend for itself, apart from savage attacks with a lawn mower. The rest is another writer's story.

THE SILT

Initially the silt seemed wonderful. Black and practically stoneless, it was so easy to dig and a great joy after years of sticky boulder clay in our previous garden, and then the stony gravelly soil we also have here. In places where there had been tall stands of bracken rising and falling for scores of years, the soil was soft and full of humus, and surely would grow anything. For several years, at the very beginning, we had little help in the garden. We often lined out our plants in temporary resting-places while we cleared and marked out new beds. I enjoyed digging the soft, damp soil. It was most satisfying to dig out the rope-like roots of bracken, long underground thongs of wild hop and remaining stumps of sloes and blackberries. (The mountainous tangles of blackberry bushes, wild sloe, elderberry and sapling willows had already been swept away by the bulldozer.)

The fine soil felt good in my hands and smelt sweet most of the time. But here and there as I was digging it smelt sour. I knew that meant bad drainage somewhere but I did not stop to consider what we should do about it. I pressed on, impatient to have the beds ready for planting as soon as possible. 'Plant in haste, repent at leisure' is an old saying, but like many wise words they are always more meaningful to me after I have burnt my fingers.

For the first year or two most of the plants did well in the virgin soil. The pleasurable digging had fluffed it up, making a nice crumbly texture for them to root about in. The dormant weed seedlings welcomed the improved conditions, and they shot up too. Before long we were continually weeding, carting off load upon load of topsoil attached to the weed roots. Then we had a typical long period without rain. There was no protecting layer of plant growth, whether weeds or accumulated leaf-litter. (I soon found that the autumn leaves are all blown away when there are not enough plants established to trap them.) Although there was moisture available, derived from springs not far below, the top spit became dry and the surface caked. When the rain eventually came it could not penetrate the dried silt but lay on the surface rather like mercury, or where there was a slope it ran off. In some places, at the end of winter, I could still dig and find dry, powdery soil. We used to wish in those days for a fall of snow, to lie like melting sugar on the surface and slowly soak into the parched soil beneath.

I found that shallow-rooting plants like *Tiarella*, *Tellima* and *Heuchera* spread their soft little roots like a web over the surface of the silt. Once it became panned, by treading or by rainfall, these carpeting plants could be lifted off the surface with their roots clinging to a few soil particles, unable to penetrate the compacted soil.

Something had to be done to improve the soil structure. We realized that although it had appeared to be laced with humus (we were largely taken in by the rich, dark colour), that was not the case in most places. So I began my policy of carting back the vast piles of rotting weeds, cut-down remains of summer and anything else I could find to improve the texture of the soil. We had noticed that where Percy, with his bulldozer, had made an enormous bonfire at the very beginning of the garden, the plants always looked well, where the ashes had been spread. I am sure that it was not only the potash and other nutrients that may have been provided by the ash, but also the opening of the soil by those sticks and particles of charcoal which were not consumed by the fire, and which probably took several years finally to break down.

OVERLEAF
The Damp Nursery stock beds are at their best from midsummer onwards when perennials and grasses needing retentive soil create an almost prairie-like effect. Here we can plant bolder, larger groups than in the garden, which resembles a painter's palette rather than the structured designs of a garden.

About seven years after we had begun the garden I decided to start my plant nursery. Slowly the two projects grew side by side. The growth of the nursery helped the development of the garden, not only by providing some help with maintenance, but also by forcing me to consider better methods and management.

I discovered the importance of using various mulches, including crushed bark and straw (see pages 62 and 147), for weed control and moisture conservation. Also, when they eventually rot down and become incorporated with the soil, they help to improve the soil texture.

For close-textured soil, the addition of humus was not enough. Perhaps it would be more accurate to say that, despite occasionally being able to buy muck to add to the compost, these dressings were not enough to prevent the soil settling down too firmly, making it difficult for fine roots to penetrate. It was too cold and sticky in spring when I wanted to plant. What could I do to open the soil? We were using fine grit, 6mm/¼in gravel, to mulch the tops of the nursery pots as a guard against excess evaporation and a similar grit in the mix inside the pot. Neither this grit nor sand, whether sharp or otherwise, proved adequate to open up dense textured soil.

The Shade Beds, which I have described in Chapter 3 were going downhill. Only the most strongly rooted plants, such as *Hosta*, *Eupatorium* and *Ligularia*, were giving their best. Even *Trollius* and the astilbes were dwindling. This was maddening because there was moisture, not too far below them, but there was no capillary action, no natural sucking up of water between the soil particles.

We decided to remake these beds, to dig everything out except the trees, shrubs and those plants not distressed. Keith did this, carefully lining out everything worth preserving in a reserve border. He also dug out pernicious weeds, such as running buttercup, Hedge Woundwort, *Stachys sylvatica*, which is easily recognized by its pungent, unpleasant smell, and plenty of 'Codlins and Cream', a kind of Willow-herb commonly found in damp soil. These and others were weeds which had invaded the beds and penetrated plants, undetected over the last few years. As much garden refuse as was available was spread over the beds, then a thick layer of 10mm/⅜in gravel, enough to make complete cover, was flung across the soil. The work was done in the autumn, when the soil was not wet and everything could be incorporated evenly and lightly.

The following spring I started replanting. What a difference there was in the soil! In April, often using only a hand fork to make the holes, I found it light and open, not wet, but damp enough to provide plenty of loose crumbs to press round the roots of the plants. In the same area, where such preparations had not been made, the soil came up solid and wet, and had to be beaten with a border fork to break the slabs into lumps, not fit for fresh plantings at all. As the soil slowly dried out it broke down quite finely – but that was at least six weeks, possibly two months later and I like my major planting done before June. But because of the quality of the soil, and the presence of underground springs, I do continue to add a few plants throughout the summer to these beds which remain damp, something I cannot possibly do in the dry gravel areas of my garden.

More recently we have felt the need to incorporate stones more deeply into areas of close-textured soil to provide better capillarity lower down in places where the soil has become compacted or is ill drained. Having removed plants from the area to be improved, we take out a trench one spit deep (i.e. the depth of the spade) and cart it to the opposite end. We loosen (with a pick if necessary) and also remove the compacted soil at the bottom of the trench. Then shovels full of 10mm/⅜in stone (the same as we use to top up the general paths) are flung across the sloping face of the trench to ensure drainage from top to bottom. The stones are not laid on the bottom of the trench in a solid layer. We add plenty of compost, bonfire waste or well-rotted manure before the next spit of soil is dug and thrown forward. We wait some time before replanting to allow the fluffed-up soil to settle, and then, when planting, the various additions become more mixed.

Sometimes we need to rejuvenate the soil in this way in only part of an area, perhaps following a period of excessive rainfall, where it would be impractical or indeed undesirable to remove established plants or shrubs. In this case we have learnt to retain the same surface level, not to create a lower level behind the improved drainage that could become waterlogged.

THE CLAY

I find the clay in my garden the most difficult, next-to-impossible stuff to deal with. I am not referring to heavy clay-based soil, which is bad enough, but to the dense plasticine-like substance which is my subsoil in the Damp Garden, and with which I only come into close contact in two very different situations.

The first is by the water-side. I have mentioned the problem briefly elsewhere, but as it is a problem that never goes away, it needs to be looked at, and dealt with, repetitively.

My original borders around the first ponds near the house were not very well prepared. It was partly impatience, partly that we had not enough additional good material to add – and, I must confess, we did not feel up to prising out any more of the wickedly heavy clay than we were obliged to do. Over the years the more vigorous plants – *Miscanthus*, *Gunnera*, *Iris* and *Phormium* – waxed bigger and taller in the solid clay, but the more delicate plants, like primulas and astilbes, waned. They hung on but did not flourish; neither were there the sheets of seedlings I had hoped for. The thin layer of vegetable waste which we had originally applied was soon used up, and several years of weeding in the pre-mulching era had removed much of the heavy meadow silt. In places we were down to the solid substratum.

One tends to lose interest in beds which are not functioning properly. I knew that something drastic would have to be done when I could make time to stop and think what that should be. Suddenly it came to me. The two narrow beds along the wettest edges must go. A time comes when I realize that I must cut down the work, especially when I have been busy making new and better beds elsewhere. So these rather fussy beds disappeared, and it was good to see the clean line of mown grass alongside the water, with just a few leafy plants like *Zantedeschia aethiopica*, Arum Lily, *Carex elata* 'Aurea', and several forms of *Iris laevigata*, planted in the water to soften the hard block edging.

Now I was left with two water-side beds each about 28m/90ft long and 3m/10ft wide; this is wide enough to plant balanced groups of medium-sized plants, like *Iris*, *Astilbe* and *Primula*; or just wide enough to fit a *Gunnera*, or a big group of *Rodgersia* or *Ligularia*. The soil is not saturated 3m/10ft away from the water's edge, but the water-table is not far below. I thought that if I could improve the quality of the top spit of soil, some of that moisture would rise through capillarity, and could be used by plants which needed damp conditions but would not tolerate drowning.

Once again the smaller plants were removed and heeled-in. The beds were virtually emptied – only the great gunneras were left with their lofty companions, *Miscanthus sacchariflorus* and *M. sinensis* 'Zebrinus'. (And, of course, the framework of *Taxodium distichum*, *Metasequoia glyptostroboides* and a few water-loving shrubs.) *Carex riparia* 'Variegata' was painstakingly removed, every wiry thong that could be seen. It is one of the loveliest waterside sedges, with its long, thin arching leaves which are striped white, many of them in spring being totally white. However, it does run about much too invasively if planted without fore-knowledge. In small tidy areas it should either be avoided altogether, or perhaps planted in an interred bucket with only the smallest of drainage holes. By lake-sides, or pond-sides, among coarse plantings of large bog-side plants, it will probably be subdued by other inhabitants just as demanding.

There are still two things vital to improving the soil in my bog beds. One is to have plenty of lightening material to add, the other is to have a strong and willing helper to do the adding. I am not so good now at heaving heavy weights. Thankfully, I have enthusiasts who enjoy tackling such jobs.

I have come to the conclusion that, wherever possible, we must leave the pure clay alone and try to build a soil on top of it. Several layers had already been removed over the years on the roots of weeds, so the level of the pond-side borders was below the level of the mown grass walks. I needed a large amount of gravelly soil to put on to them as a basic layer.

What is waste at one end of my property is a valuable commodity at the other. The nursery is sited on very stony soil. From time to time some of this is dug out to make way for plunging beds or covered tunnels. The top spit, although gravelly, is not worthless, having had generous dressings of some kind of vegetable waste over the years, and is piled into heaps until we need it. It is a lovely feeling to have plenty of the right material to hand. The old tractor, with its large three-sided metal box on the back, which we call a 'buck', made many trips to bring a fresh spit of topsoil to the pond-sides. (We now have two Gators, invaluable for carting, less damaging to lawns, having large, wide tyres.)

The next ingredient for my pond-side beds was a large heap of nursery and garden waste consisting of spent potting soil and rotted vegetable matter. This was spread all over the gravelly soil. Finally a layer of grit was spread over this, and the whole rotavated as deeply as we could.

This work was done in the autumn. On a cold but sparklingly sunny New Year's Day, I went out to examine these beds. With a long pronged fork I dug into the mixture and found a most satisfying depth, almost two spits deep, above the clay, and several wriggly pink worms in each hole. These will have been introduced no doubt with the additional soil which has included good topsoil saved when plants have been dug up to be divided. The soil which falls from the roots to the pack-house floor is always the best, including leaf-mould and decomposing bark from earlier dressings. All this good material is a bonus derived from the routine work of the garden and nursery. Whenever I feel a little anxious about the time we spend weeding, cutting down and tidying up, which is little enough, I remind myself that the large piles of waste will, in a year or two's time, be worth more than loads of muck to me. Rotted down they will be readily available to the plants whereas muck, unless very old, has to be broken down by soil organisms before it is available.

On the whole I tend to use farmyard manure as an additional mulch, where I think such plants as hostas and hellebores, both greedy feeders, need it, and keep it on top of heavy soil, letting the birds pull it about in winter, and then the worms drag it down. Some years it produces a crop of Fat Hen, a typical farm weed, which probably seeded over it as it lay in the farmer's yard, but that is easily pulled out. Otherwise I dig in muck, or rotavate it into my light land over a three-year rotation, if I can manage that.

FERTILIZERS

I have scarcely mentioned the use of concentrated fertilizers. That is not because I disapprove of them. In my own garden I have, from time to time, had the soil tested to see whether it were short of one particular mineral – magnesium perhaps, or potash. Then I would add what was needed.

Sometimes, when the soil is too acid, or out of balance for any other reason, plant nutrients become locked up and no amount of concentrated fertilizer poured on to it will be effective. Clay soils which have been farmed or gardened over a long period with only concentrates, with no bulky organic matter returned to feed the soil organisms (which play such a part in the health of plant life), become lifeless and eventually barren. Fertilizers can work well only when there is a proper balance, a good soil structure, organic matter and a healthy soil population. I personally look upon fertilizers as vitamin tablets, which are useful when necessary but do not take the place of the good square meal, which is what humus is to plants and the soil population. When that is present you rarely need concentrates.

For those who cannot make or obtain enough vegetable waste, a combination of well-pulverized bark, plus a little organic concentrate would be the next best thing. I use chemical concentrates rarely and sparingly when telltale signs of deficiency are seen.

SOIL TREATMENT SUMMARY
CHECK DRAINAGE
- Dig a trench through waterlogged soil to see the profile of soil beneath the surface. Sometimes you find a block of clay, which is causing the trouble.
- Digging a trench is not as bad as it sounds. Use as narrow a spade as you can find to keep the trench narrow.
- Fill the trench three parts with coarse stone, cover it with a sheet of polythene, and fill the remainder of the trench with soil.
- For those with large areas to drain, there are firms who specialize in laying perforated plastic pipes. They use quite a small machine, which makes a narrow slit trench. Make sure that the pipe is laid on a bed of coarse stone, with more laid over it, so that water can trickle to find the slits in the pipes and be carried away.

DIGGING
- Deep digging is helpful if soil has become very compacted, but try not to bring subsoil to the surface.
- In clay, or structureless soils where rain and air cannot easily penetrate, I find that gravels, about 10mm/⅜in, spread generously and forked in the top spit – or deeper if you can – will do much to improve soil texture.
- A heavy soil left rough dug in winter, will fall into a crumbly tilth in spring after frosting, if you catch it just right.
- When planting trees or shrubs in clay soil it can be detrimental to dig deep holes, as they can fill up with water. It is better to dig a wide, shallow hole,

spread the roots over and then mound up soil and compost over the roots to form a mound. This will allow roots to penetrate without being waterlogged.

- For general purposes, once shrubs and herbaceous plants have been planted on heavy soil, add improving materials to the surface. Most feeding roots are in the top few centimetres or inches of soil, so it is there they will be searching for organic matter. Too much forking about will damage them.

MULCHING

A mulch will protect those feeding roots. It will protect the surface of the soil from drying out, and check the germination of weed seeds. Once established many of the plants themselves will do all this.

Fine material to be used among small shrubs and plants, and where the appearance is important:

- Bark, available in various grades. Use a finer grade among small plants. If the pieces are not sufficiently crushed sturdy seedlings jostle their way among them, as the pieces slide on each other, rather like tiddlywinks. The bark needs to be shredded to a fibrous texture when it is more stifling. Untreated bark, obtainable in bulk, or smaller amounts from the source of supply (usually the Forestry Commission – or else they will advise) is usually fairly well pulverized. If the bark has been freshly pulverized it is best to let it lie in a heap for several months so that it becomes partially decomposed.
- Spent hops from breweries; available in some places.
- Grit – useful as a mulch on top of pots, sink gardens and raised beds of alpines.
- Cobble-like stones and slate – these can be used as a mulch and weed-deterrent where they are readily available. Soil always seems to be moist under stones.

Coarse material for use in large areas, chiefly among trees and shrubs:

- Bark – the coarse grade is ideal.
- Straw – obtainable ready baled from farms or contractors. Not expensive – a good dressing lasts two years. Remember to add a little nitrogen.
- Mushroom compost is pleasant and easy to handle but may result in too great a build-up of chalk, which could be washed down on to soils containing acid-loving plants.
- Black polythene and permeable black ground cover can be obtained in strips or sheets from horticultural suppliers. Both are useful, primarily in the vegetable garden or where plants are in rows.

8 | The Homes of Some Hardy Garden Plants

PERHAPS THE BEST PLACE to seek knowledge of plants is to go and see them growing in their native environment, but that is rarely possible. In this chapter I would like to share a little of the invaluable background knowledge which my late husband, Andrew, patiently collected over fifty years of reading and research, as it has been such a help to me. Of course, he did not, in every case, visit and study on the spot the flora, climate and geology of those distant lands, so relied for information from botanists who had published their findings in scientific books and papers in many languages. He translated much of his information from botanical works written in French, German and Russian.

I have done no serious plant collecting, but holidays abroad have been an inspiration for plantings made many years later. My first trip to the Swiss Alps resulted in unforgettable memories of seeing some of the plants we were struggling to grow flourishing in their native home. *Sedum, Sempervivum, Dianthus* and *Euphorbia, Potentilla* and thymes were no problem at home, and on the hot rocky slopes we saw them in profusion with achilleas, *Biscutella*, and linarias which we knew we could grow. But the rich, low-lying valley meadows were a different matter. Fed by melting snow from the glaciers at the head of the valley were many desirable flowers and grasses just about to be cut for hay. Snowy masses of *Leucanthemopsis alpina*, indigo-blue *Phyteuma*, large pink pokers of *Persicaria bistorta* (*Polygonum bistorta*) with occasional clumps of the pale yellow Globeflower, *Trollius*

Bowles' Golden Sedge, *Carex elata* 'Aurea', and the purple-leaved *Phormium* add sharp contrast of form to the cavalcade of flowering plants which comes and goes as summer progresses.

europaeus, in the really boggy places. Much higher, where the short turf is still watered from below though the sun may be hot in a clear blue sky, we found *Geum montanum*, several species of orchid and, of course, many kinds of gentians, including the stately *Gentiana lutea* whose roots are used to flavour the famous mountain liqueur. Here I saw for the first time the orange daisy-flowered *Arnica montana*. With memory prompting me I bent my head and put my nose into the sun-warmed petals, and in a moment the curious long-remembered smell carried me back to my childhood and a small, dark green bottle with faded label, 'Tincture of Arnica', kept inside the case of the mantelpiece clock, to soothe bumps and bruises. Before leaving that mountain village I had to buy a bottle to take home to treat my own small daughters' bruises.

Beside tumbling brooks we saw *Aruncus dioicus* and *Thalictrum aquilegiifolium* arching their feathery flower heads over the water. Although they do not need boggy soil in English gardens neither will they flourish in parched conditions. *Primula farinosa* was always to be found in the really wet soil at the edge of little runnels of water.

There were far, far more plants. But in those early days, although I saw them with my eyes, I did not have the knowledge to comprehend them.

The substance of this chapter, then, is written by my late husband, the scholar, linked here and there by comments from myself, the gardener. Andrew's lifetime's study has been my inspiration, to make my garden and write my books. We can none of us reproduce the dark, wood-scented shade of a mountain forest with its moss-covered boulders and cascading brooks, or suggest the rich meadows just before hay time, where we would recognize many of our well-loved garden plants. But I learnt from Andrew that where I have a rather dank shady place, for instance, I should look for plants whose natural home is woodland; or where I have a sun-scorched stretch of gravel to think of using plants from sunny Mediterranean hills.

Knowing where a plant comes from is not only interesting – it is helpful when planting to have an idea of its natural environment and associations. Our garden plants have been brought home from countries that lie in the temperate belts of the world, both north and south of the Equator, by brave and dedicated travellers and collectors over several hundred years. I am writing mainly of 'species plants', that is, plants found growing wild in their native homes, not cultivars that we have 'improved' by selection or hybridization, which bear little resemblance to their ancestors. Although I am addicted to species, it would be absurd to deny the value of cultivars to the garden. Roses and chrysanthemums are obvious examples and the enormous variety in shape, colour and form of these two genera alone adds greatly to our pleasure in the garden. Any visitor to my garden could not fail to notice the old-fashioned roses, and selected clones of variegated plants, none of which would survive for long in the wild.

Not all wild plants would be suitable for cultivation in gardens. Some that have been introduced have been greatly improved by the plant breeders, while others could still be enhanced by careful selection or hybridization. But although that is so, we are constantly amazed and enchanted by the vast numbers of plants that we grow which are just as they were when they were found in the wild. The study of the habitats of our garden plants is, of course, an enormous subject, and one in which continuing study will produce fresh information. There will, without doubt, be corrections made, both in nomenclature and statements, but also we hope new evidence to fit into the jigsaw of our knowledge and experience.

Plants have had to adapt themselves to the conditions in which nature has placed them – and they in turn, as the plant community has developed, have played a part in recreating that environment. Swamps have been colonized by tall reeds and grass-like plants, for example. In the course of time, as the roots have matted and rotted, as the silt has been held and built up around them, more plants have grown up on top of the lower layers until a substratum has been formed which provides a foothold for tree seeds, like poplar or willow, blown in by the wind. So a forest may eventually be formed with firm soil to walk upon where once a boat may have been punted through the still water. We can see this type of change in our gardens where, with careful use of colonising plants, we help to turn a previously windswept and empty site into a haven for plants that need more sheltered conditions. This is what is meant by creating a micro-climate.

Although most of our colourful shrubs and stately trees were also originally found growing wild, I do not have space to write much about them. It is the plants, which clothe the floor of the temperate world with which I am concerned, and of these I shall talk almost entirely of the herbaceous perennials.

Herbaceous perennials – those which make a long-lived rootstock, from which leaves and flowers grow up to produce seed, and which then die down again, to reappear next year – have evolved where there are regular seasons of good growing conditions long enough for them to develop their strong roots and underground resting buds. They are only overcome in such situations, in nature, by taller-growing bushes and trees; but even in forests many can make do with, or even prefer, half-light.

Annuals are plants which are adapted to take advantage of short periods of good growing conditions between long ones when growth is impossible. There are not many of them where perennials form communities, as there is no room for them to seed (so strong perennials make excellent ground-cover) but they are very common, as we know to our cost, on poorly cultivated land and disturbed ground, or in countries where winter cold and spring moisture are quickly followed by drought. They must rely on a sharp burst of growth producing blooms and setting seed by the thousand with all speed. Some can manage this in such a short time that they can complete their lifecycle more than once a year, and are called ephemerals.

Biennials are in a sense modified annuals, which take two years before completing their lifecycle. There are also some plants needing several years to build up enough strength to flower and set seed, after which they die, such as 'Century plants' and some bamboos. These, together with the annuals and biennials all of which flower only once in their lives, are known as mono-carpic plants.

Now to return to our specific subject, which is to look briefly at the natural homes of moisture-loving plants. I find that I have at least two main groups of plants that need moist growing conditions. First there are those that like sunlight, and come from open places, either in lowland water-meadows and swamps, or from damp mountain meadows. Second there are those that need shelter from strong sunlight and wind, and come from shady forests or open woods.

I can describe only a few of the regions from which our garden plants come, and only a very few of those plants which grow in them. Not all of the plants mentioned in these wild groupings are in my alphabetical descriptions, as I would not want to grow them in my garden, but they are included to paint the scene, for they help to form the background. For these associate plants, which many people might call weeds, I would substitute more decorative plants of similar growth from other regions of the world, or varieties of them selected and 'improved' in gardens. In place of the European Hemp Agrimony, *Eupatorium cannabinum*, for instance, I plant the double, *E. c.* 'Flore Pleno', and for *Thalictrum flavum* I might use *T. flavum* subsp. *glaucum* or even *T. aquilegiifolium*. There are so many fine plants from which to choose! Incidentally, I find it interesting to notice that where similar conditions occur in widely separated parts of the world, the same, or closely related plants, are to be found – for instance, the various species of *Trollius* or *Caltha* along the brooks in mountain meadows, or the different species of *Anemone* and *Viola* carpeting the summer-green forests in spring.

Most of the plants I mention are adaptable within limits, or we could not grow them in our gardens. For instance many plants which are typical of water-meadows may also be found in man-made grasslands if they are damp enough, or even in open moist places among trees where enough sunlight can reach them, and where rainfall is adequate.

FLOOD-MEADOWS, MARSHES AND SWAMPS

Before embankment or other control, rivers and streams, if they flowed through gently rolling lowlands and plains, meandered this way and that, thus more or less levelling their valley bottoms. As the snows melted in the spring, or after heavy rains, they broke through low places in their banks and spread over these plains.

As the floods subsided, the water flowed back to the main river, leaving a fresh layer of rich, fine silt on the flats and gentle rises, on which grew lush meadows; there were also undrained wet hollows and ponds. In the growing season the level of the water in the ground was (and is) never far down, even on the higher parts of flood-plains, and often stands just below the surface, causing marshy places.

As spring comes in Britain and the cooler parts of Europe and west Asia, the glistening yellow cups of the Marsh Marigold, *Caltha palustris* open, with pale lilac Lady's Smock, *Cardamine pratensis*, among fresh green grasses and the dark clumps of rushes. Very locally in Britain, but more common further south in Europe, the Snake's Head Fritillary, *Fritillaria meleagris*, hangs its maroon-chequered bells. Later, among yellow buttercups and pink Ragged Robin, the rusty plumes of sorrel, *Rumex acetosa*, the nodding brownish-pink heads of Water Avens, *Geum rivale*, and locally the rosy-lilac spikes of orchids, or the flat, white sprays of Sneezewort, *Achillea ptarmica*, come into flower. Contrasting with these colours are the black-red drumsticks of the Great Burnet, *Sanguisorba officinalis*.

Common further north are the heads of soft, blue cups of Jacob's Ladder, *Polemonium caeruleum*, and the fluffy pink spikes of bistort, *Persicaria bistorta*. Groups of the creamy-flowered meadowsweet, *Filipendula ulmaria*, stand along the waterways, where Creeping Jenny, *Lysimachia nummularia*, runs; here and there, colonies of the Marsh Violet, *Viola palustris*, show pale lilac flowers, and the Marsh Spurge, *Euphorbia palustris*, though not native to Britain, spreads its yellow heads on tall, leafy stems.

Where the meadows rise higher above the water-table are red and white clovers, the Common Daisy, *Bellis perennis*, the blue spikes of bugle, *Ajuga reptans*, the white plates of yarrow, *Achillea millefolium*, yellow potentillas and many more.

A jungle of taller plants, which are not often found in the open meadows, grows under the alders and other trees and bushes, along the banks of streams and lakes, especially where there is broken sunlight. Colonies of Yellow Loosestrife, *Lysimachia vulgaris*, tall plants of Hemp Agrimony, *Eupatorium cannabinum*, with fluffy heads of dusty pink, the purple or white crosiers of comfrey, *Symphytum officinale*, pale yellow Meadow Rue, *Thalictrum flavum*, and the rosy-white wild valerian, *Valeriana officinalis*, compete with nettle beds on soggy soil. Here and there are clumps of the Marsh Fern, *Thelypteris palustris*, or the Marsh Helleborine, *Epipactis palustris*, which sends up spikes of white orchid-flowers, lined with pink.

The water's edge is lined with the slender crimson-purple spikes of Purple Loosestrife, *Lythrum salicaria*, tucked among sedges, pink 'Codlins and Cream', *Epilobium hirsutum*, and locally the Great Spearwort, *Ranunculus lingua*, with its large yellow buttercups, both of which spread fast and can become bad weeds in gardens. Spreading into the water are the Yellow Flag, *Iris pseudacorus*, the Water Mint, *Mentha aquatica*, with its whorls of lilac, and tall grasses, one of which, the reedgrass, *Phalaris arundinacea*, has produced the white-striped 'Gardener's Garters'. Also rooting on the edge and in shallow water are the Water Forget-me-not, *Myosotis scorpioides*, watercress, *Nasturtium officinale*, and in the north of Britain, the creeping white arum, *Calla palustris*, and the Bog Bean, *Menyanthes trifoliata*, which reaches the Arctic. Only in more southern marshes grow clumps of the Summer Snowflake, *Leucojum aestivum*, hanging its green-tipped white bells.

In the quiet water itself, to a considerable depth, grow rustling beds of reeds, *Phragmites australis*, with their purple plumes, or the tall, grey leaves and brown pokers of bulrush, *Typha*, with water-lilies, *Nymphaea*, and *Nuphar*. Growing in shallow water not far from the edge are arrowhead, *Sagittaria sagittifolia*, the Water Plantain, *Alisma plantago-aquatica*, and the beautiful Flowering Rush, *Butomus umbellatus*.

Many plants of the flood-meadows, marshes and swamp, or closely related species and varieties, grow in such situations all over temperate Europe and Asia, and several grow in North America too. The Marsh Marigold is ubiquitous, and so is the reed and the Greater Bulrush, while a great many others are absent only from limited areas.

Growing among these widespread plants are others which are not ubiquitous. In Eurasia some are more common eastwards, or confined to the east, while others are found only in the west. The tall clumps of *Iris sibirica*, with their rich blue flowers, grow in damp or wet peaty meadows from central Europe to the River Lena in Siberia, often with the Great Burnet, and there is a closely related *Iris* as far as Japan. The long, slender, lilac spikes of *Veronica longifolia* appear in central Europe also, and spread as far east as the flood-meadows of the River Yerisey and beyond, among spires of dark blue *Delphinium elatum*. Stout plants of *Veratrum album* var. *lobelianum* (an eastern European variety) raise columns of greenish-white stars, above pale lavender flowers of the cranesbill, *Geranium sylvaticum*, and pink *Persicaria bistorta*. The yellow Daylily, *Hemerocallis lilioasphodelus*, opens new flowers every morning in drier meadows from south-eastern Europe to far eastern Asia. It is also found in the open, rich grassland of central Siberia, known as the steppes.

The Sweet Flag, *Acorus calamus*, grows wild in swamps and in shallow water along rivers from eastern Europe across Asia to Japan, and is also common in eastern North America, but not western Europe. This curious gap is probably due to its extermination in the last Ice Ages, when mountains and the Mediterranean blocked retreat southwards; and many other trees, shrubs and plants, or closely related ones, once widespread, are also found only in eastern Asia and eastern North America.

Quite different in their range are the two magnificent species of *Lysichiton*. The Asiatic one, *L. camtschatcensis*, pushes up its white, arum-like spathes, followed by vast

Our native Flag Iris, *Iris pseudacorus*, makes robust, leafy clumps which colonize marshy ground, shallow water, or the open border in heavy soil. I like especially the form *I. p.* var. *bastardii* which has pale, creamy-yellow flowers, while, in early spring I welcome the newly emerging fans of *I. p.* 'Variegata' whose young leaves are vividly striped with butter yellow.

leaves from the mud at the edges of ponds and rivers, from north Japan to Kamchatka and east Siberia. On the other side of the north Pacific, its American cousin *L. americanus*, with canary-yellow spathes, grows in similar situations from Alaska to northern California. Another plant of much the same range, though not strictly of water-meadows, but growing in damp, peaty, stony grassland, or in partially shady glades of peaty conifer forests, is the Black Sarana, *Fritillaria camschatcensis*, which hangs its black-maroon bells from Oregon to Alaska, and the north Pacific islands and Kamchatka to north Japan, always within the influence of the Pacific.

True water-meadow and swamp plants of eastern Asia are the two irises, *I. ensata*, which has given rise in Japanese gardens to many forms and varieties, and the beautiful soft blue *I. laevigata* which grows in wetter places, and even shallow water, from Japan and Manchuria to south-west China.

Growing among many plants which are also common in Eurasian water-meadows and marshes are some confined to North America, a few of which I mention here. Among the tall grasses of swamps and river banks of the eastern USA and Canada, as far west as the Rocky Mountains, stand the blazing scarlet spires of the Cardinal Flower, *Lobelia cardinalis*. It reappears, with a gap of hundreds of kilometres or miles between, in the mountains of southern California. Although it grows where the winter temperatures may drop many degrees below zero in the northern part of its range, it is liable to be damaged, or even killed by spring frosts in Britain, where it is usually unprotected by snow, and starts into growth too soon during mild periods. This is also true of a number of other plants from Canada and even the coldest parts of Siberia, where the intense frost is uninterrupted until summer warmth quickly comes and melts the snow once and finally. A plant of the eastern United States and Canada, which does well in Britain, if given the right conditions, is the Pickerel Weed, *Pontederia cordata*. In America it forms colonies in the shallow water of ponds, lakes and quiet streams, and is common everywhere. In British ponds, the water protects its roots from unseasonable changes in the weather.

North America is rich in tall members of the daisy family, many of which grow in the water-meadows and marshes and flower late in the season. The parent of many of our tall, large-flowered Michaelmas Daisies, the lilac-blue *Aster novi-belgii* is abundant in marshy places from Canada to Georgia, mostly not far inland from the Atlantic, while another commonly grown Michaelmas Daisy, the rosy-lavender *Aster novae-angliae* grows in less wet meadows and spreads further west. Contrasting with the rose-purples, blue-mauves and pale lilacs of the asters, of which there are many species, and colouring the damp meadows and marshes in the autumn sunshine, are the rich yellows of the Goldenrod, *Solidago*, *Helenium autumnale*, a few perennial sunflowers, *Helianthus*, the big plants of one of the Coneflowers,

Rudbeckia laciniata, which prefers damp river-side thickets, and other yellow-flowered daisies. *Solidago canadensis*, which extends west to damp valleys in the prairies, is the chief parent of our tall garden Goldenrod, and most of our garden sunflowers also come from among the tall grasses of such damp places in the prairies.

DAMP MOUNTAIN MEADOWS

I am going to talk about the meadows in the zone of the upper forests and just above the tree-line, not the short, high alpine turfs, where plants grow under harsher conditions, and often need special treatment in gardens.

The mountain meadows usually grow on the bottoms and more gently sloping sides of high valleys, where rich humus soil can collect among fragments of rock. Rain and melting snow keeps them damp all summer, water seeping through the soil and stones, or trickling in innumerable little runnels; but only where the water is held up are there boggy patches, especially along the smaller streams. On either side, on steeper slopes consisting mainly of broken rock with some leaf-litter soil, grow the forests, or at higher levels bushland, often of rhododendrons. The vegetation in these high valleys, with the snow peaks above, therefore, varies greatly within quite short distances, from lush, open, sunny meadows with marshy places, and partially shaded forest edges, to buttresses of rock, screes and cliffs, some also in full, hot sun, and very dry.

There is much discussion about the plants of limestone (calcareous) and non-limestone (siliceous) mountains. In this book I do not include many plants typical of limestone soils. Rainwater dissolves limestone, enlarging the cracks and sinking away quickly, in some districts forming caves and underground rivers. The soil therefore tends to be drier than on siliceous mountains, where most of the water runs off on or near the surface. I grow many plants from the calcareous mountains on my rather acid soil, but only in the well-drained, drier parts of the garden (see *The Gravel Garden*), while many plants from siliceous mountains are happy in the damper parts. There are certainly plants which are adapted to acid peat soils, and generally fail on chalky ones, especially members of the heather family, and those which, when wild, seem to be able to compete better, and are more abundant on calcareous soils and are absent on acid ones. But, in gardens, I have come to the conclusion that the amount and continuous availability of water, and the speed of drainage, are more important than the amount of lime initially present in the soil. Perhaps to bear out this theory, plants usually confined to acid soil, such as heathers, grow on hard limestone in the very wet climate of western Ireland, where their dead leaves and roots eventually form a surface layer of peat from which the lime is washed out. Also, the plant explorer, George Forrest, emphasizes that in Yunnan in south-west China, with a wet climate, the mountains are mostly of hard limestone, yet are covered with notoriously lime-hating rhododendrons.

So consider your annual rainfall, and your drainage, as well as the nature of the bedrock under your soil.

Grasses do not play such an important part in the mountain meadows as they do in the lowland ones, and in the height of the season the mountain meadows become sheets of varied colour. In the central European mountains, among the first plants to flower at the edge of the melting snow is *Crocus vernus*, varying from white to purple, and the parent of the big Dutch cultivated forms. The Pyrenees and north Spain seem to be the headquarters of the daffodils. Several yellow species flower early, and a little later whole meadows are covered with the white *Narcissus poeticus*, often standing above sprawling mounds of the Horned Pansy, *Viola cornuta*, their violet flowers carried on long stems. The taller meadow plants grow up quickly, and are soon in flower. The lavender *Geranium sylvaticum*, the blue bellflowers (members of the *Campanula* family) and Mountain Cornflower, *Centaurea montana*, the cream or purple of rampions (*Phyteuma*), one of which, *P. ovatum*, is nearly black, a pleasing contrast to the more vivid flowers, and the burnt orange of *Crepis aurea*, are set off by colonies of pink *Persicaria bistorta* in damp places, and yellow Globeflowers, *Trollius europaeus*, along the streams. Several other lowland plants ascend to these meadows – white yarrow and Ox-eye Daisy in great numbers on drier slopes, and buttercups. The Red Campion, *Silene dioica*, is rather unexpectedly common, being a woodland plant in the lowlands. Pink and rose-purple orchids add their colours. The season ends with the rosy-lilac cups of *Colchicum autumnale* and, in the Pyrenees, the lavender *Crocus nudiflorus*.

Taller plants grow at the edges of the woods, and in part-shaded torrent-fed gullies, where there is ample water trickling through the rich humus soil among rock fragments. The tall bellflower, *Campanula latifolia*, the yellow foxglove, *Digitalis grandiflora*, the beautiful fluffy lilac heads of *Thalictrum aquilegiifolium*, blue-purple and pale yellow monkshood (*Aconitum*) and the Fair Maids of France, *Ranunculus aconitifolius,* can all be found, while *Lilium martagon* raises its spotted mauve-pink turkscaps among the rocks and sometimes in the open meadows.

Many beautiful plants come from the high meadows of the Caucasus and Minor Caucasus mountains between the Black and Caspian Seas, especially in the west which receives more rain and melt-water from deeper snow. The soil of these meadows is always nearly black with humus, often deep, and where it is shallower, as in the drier east, the meadows are shorter and thinner, though most of the same plants are to be found. The meadows grow among the highest woods, and extend above them for some distance.

The large-flowered, soft blue *Scabiosa caucasica* is common in damp places, together with the sprawling *Gentiana septemfida* lifting rich blue trumpets, and the much paler blue spires of *Veronica gentianoides*, while *Tanacetum coccineum* adds its white to rosy-red daisies, with pincushion heads of *Astrantia maxima*, surrounded by their petal-like bracts, all of crushed-strawberry pink. There are big plants of *Geranium ibericum*, with rich mauve-blue flowers, the smaller mounds of beautifully crinkled leaves and white, violet-pencilled ones of *G. renardii*, yellow species of *Primula*, clovers, vetches and tall spires of *Digitalis ferruginea*, with tight-packed, small trumpets of golden-brown, which prefers the edges of the woods, as do the large spreading clumps of *Stachys macrantha* showing off big whorls of crimson-purple.

Where there is an even greater abundance of water always trickling through deep, humus-rich soil, such as in sheltered, steep gullies, huge plants crowd together. The big spreading leaves and pale straw-yellow flowers on tall stems of *Cephalaria gigantea* are characteristic, not only of these wet ravines, but all over the damper parts of the meadows. With them in the wet gullies grow the enormous umbellifer *Heracleum mantegazzianum*, blue and yellow Monkshoods (*Aconitum*), the dark blue *Delphinium elatum* and other tall larkspurs, the magnificent *Campanula lactiflora*, which can be a man's height, crowned by heads of soft, blue bells, while at the edges of these jungles stand the lemon-yellow turkscaps of *Lilium monadelphum*, which also often grow in part shade near the woods, and the rich yellow suns of *Inula orientalis* and *I. magnifica*. Half choking the mountain streams is the large and spreading Marsh Marigold, *Caltha palustris* var. *palustris*, while the sky-blue comfrey, *Symphytum caucasicum*, runs on the banks.

As the meadows fade in the autumn, and the surrounding woods shed their foliage, leaving only the dark conifers, the great lilac goblets of *Colchicum speciosum* appear, and in the east, especially on the Minor Caucasus, the nearly blue *Crocus speciosus* gives the last colour to the meadows.

The vast wall of the Himalayas is drier at its western end in Kashmir than on its eastern part, where it checks the full force of the south-west monsoon, the wettest place on earth being on the hills near its foot. As the mountain chains rise from a tropical climate to everlasting snow, the only plants hardy in Britain come from the upper forest zone and above. Many are unique to the Himalayas, mixed with more widely distributed plants, and to the east with ones also found in China. I mention here a few plants from the damp valley meadows of the central Himalayas, with their boulder-strewn torrents and side gullies, their marshy level places, and with their steep rocky slopes rising on either side, where woods of birch and conifers grow, or scrub of low rhododendrons.

The sloping or fairly level meadows are lush and very flowery. Growing among such widespread plants as *Caltha palustris* (in wet places), *Polemonium caeruleum* and *Aruncus dioicus*, are the white, blue-backed flowers of *Anemone rivularis*, other anemones, the slatey-blue violet-stained ones of *Delphinium brunonianum*, the purple-marked yellow lilies of *Lilium oxpetalum* and the purplish-blue ones of *L. nanum*. Also there are the straggling plants with silvery-silky leaves of *Potentilla atrosanguinea* var. *argyrophylla* sending up open sprays of rich yellow, orange-eyed blooms, with the blood-red ones of its close relative or variety *P. atrosanguinea*, and the spiky spires of *Morina longifolia* showing whorls of white trumpets which turn crimson as they age.

Sprawling plants of *Geranium wallichianum* show their purple-blue, white-eyed flowers with those of other geraniums, and the short *Trollius acaulis*, whose yellow saucers open wide. *Codonopsis rotundifolia* twines among the taller plants, hanging its large yellow-green bells veined with purple. (*Codonopsis clematidea* scrambles over rocks in the damp valleys further west, from the Himalayas to the Hindu Kush and the Tien Shan.) *Primula denticulata* lifts its lilac drumsticks in the meadows with other small primulas, and also in the birch woods. Where the streams fall steeply and the banks are of rocks, a few bushes find roothold, and silver-grey mounds of *Anaphalis nepalensis* var. *monocephala* and *A. triplinervis* with their papery-white heads spread over them, contrasting with the deep green carpets, studded with pink spikes, of *Persicaria affinis*, which also colours rocky hill-sides. *Persicaria vacciniifolia* is not a meadow plant, but forms wide mats over loose boulders in the light birch copses and among dwarf rhododendrons.

Accumulations of settled or lodged rocks and boulders at the foot of slopes and in small side gullies provide the damp, sheltered pockets which some plants prefer. The small *Bergenia stracheyi* is one of these, and also grows in damp grassy patches among the dwarf rhododendrons. The blue poppy, *Meconopsis aculeata*, which dies after flowering, also favours such pockets under boulders, and *Corydalis cashmeriana* spreads sheets of vivid blue among the rocks and low rhododendrons. Where the meadows have been broken up by grazing animals or other causes, and bare soil exposed, tall stands of *Impatiens glandulifera* spring up, hanging their large, curiously shaped pink flowers.

The mountains of west China in the Province of Sichuan on the border of Tibet rise abruptly in a broad series of fore-ranges from the Red Basin, which is subtropical, with palms and tall bamboos. Westward beyond these fore-mountains, an enormous wall, with peaks of 6000m/20,000ft and over, forms the border of high, rolling tablelands at 4500m/14,000–15,000ft, extending into northern Yunnan Province, covered by rather monotonous short mountain grassland. Other isolated, permanently snow-covered mountain massifs rise from the grassy tablelands, and the large rivers, including the Yangtze, have cut tremendous gorges through them. The bottoms of these river chasms are thousands of feet below the plateau, especially in north Yunnan, and the precipitous lower parts of their sides, being walled off from the rain, are hot and dry. The tributary streams also flow through steep, narrow rock defiles in their lower courses, but become wider with more gently sloping floors higher up. These upper valleys usually have damp meadows along their streams, with bushes where it is rocky, and on their sides grow fine conifer forests, interspersed with grassy slopes. It is in these upper valleys and mountain meadows, and in the higher meadows in the fore-mountains, that a large number of beautiful plants, hardy in Britain, have been found, though many are not yet common in gardens, and some, especially species of *Primula*, seem difficult to cultivate.

The fore-mountains receive much rain in summer from the south-east monsoon, except where shut off by mountains, as well as winter snow. On the high tablelands and their mountain ranges the winters are bitter, and the summer weather, in the thin atmosphere, is very changeable. Hot sun quickly changes to hail showers or cold misty rain, and there are almost daily monsoon thunderstorms in June and July. The mountains of western China and the eastern Himalayas, with its very varied conditions, have an extremely rich flora, and seem to be the central home of rhododendrons and primulas. I can mention only a very few plants which are common and easily grown in Britain, and first of all some which are not strictly meadow plants.

In bottom lands and along torrents in the fore-mountains, and spreading up the damp, rocky, once-forested sides, at comparatively low altitudes, are communities of tall herbaceous plants, most of which appreciate partial shade or some shelter, and before deforestation grew in open places in the summer-green woods. With *Aruncus dioicus* stand the tall green-leaved stems of *Artemisia lactiflora*, the large creamy-white plumes of *Astilbe rivularis*, and the slender rosy-purple ones on their red stems of *A. chinensis* var. *davidii*, the deep orange daisies of *Ligularia dentata*, and on more open rocky slopes the rosy-pink *Anemone tomentosa*. The big horse-chestnut leaves of *Rodgersia aesculifolia* with their tiered flower heads spread from the wood edges over damp rocky slopes, while *R. pinnata* grows in glades further south in Yunnan. *Bergenia purpurascens* prefers more open and drier rock slopes, often with lilies.

Lilies are most abundant on the steep sides of the dry, warm valleys, several of the species being confined to one valley. *Lilium regale* grows only on the sunny, rocky sides of the upper Min valley in deep, humus-rich crevices. Also growing in hot valleys and ravines in Yunnan is the beautiful, lilac-flowered *Thalictrum delavayi*, on stream-sides among bushes.

True mountain meadows occur at much greater altitudes, in valleys and high basins among the conifer forests. Here marshy stretches and stream-sides are coloured by species of *Primula*. These grow among more ordinary plants of damp meadows, such as a Marsh Marigold, *Trollius yunnanensis* and the smaller *T. pumilus*, both with large, wide-open, yellow flowers, the fringed pink *Dianthus superbus*, the pink spikes of *Persicaria bistorta* and *Anemone rivularis*. The tall stems of *Primula sikkimensis* hang their yellow bells from the eastern Himalayas to China, as do the mealy ones, topped by heads of the rosy-purple nodding flowers of *P. secundiflora*, often in the same meadows; but some seem more local, though abundant in their own district, such as some of the candelabra primulas, their flowers in whorls on tall stems. The soft orange *P. bulleyana* of north Yunnan, and the shorter but more brilliant red-orange *P. aurantiaca* of the same province, are two, and *P. pulverulenta* is another, its wine-purple whorls on white-mealy stalks being found only in a limited area in Sichuan. The bright yellow candelabra *P. prolifera* is more southern, on the Yunnan-north Burma border mountains, growing among irises and sedges. The plant explorer Kingdon-Ward found the Giant Cowslip, *P. florindae*, growing in groups along the mountain streams, nearly blocking their flow, and damp meadows full of *P. alpicola* of varying colours, in south-east Tibet, above the gorge of the Yarlung Zangbo (once spelt Tsangpo), which becomes the Brahmaputra on entering India. These high meadows have much the same character, with their conifer-forested sides, as those further east in China. They are also the home of the beautiful Blue Poppy, *Meconopsis betonicifolia*.

In the high mountains of Sichuan and Yunnan, where the streams flow swiftly, and their banks are stony and rocky, bushes grow, and the deep violet-purple *Iris chrysographes* with its yellow pencillings takes shelter, with violets and primulas, and at the edges, *Semiaquilegia ecalcarata* (which also grows all over the high grasslands) hangs its pale, brownish-lavender, spurless columbine flowers.

In high marshy basins, especially where manured by yaks, stand the pale pagodas of *Rheum alexandrae* above yellow Marsh Marigolds and sometimes with colonies of tall blue irises. Another rhubarb, the huge *R. palmatum*, prefers well-drained rocky places on the borders of mountain lakes and streams, sometimes among low bushes.

The mountains of north-east China and Manchuria have hard winters with bitterly cold, dry winds out of Siberia, and rather short rainy seasons in the hot summers. They were once forested with summer-green trees and pines at lower levels, passing to spruce and larch woods higher up, much of it now reduced to bush. In the meadows and openings among the woods grow such widespread Eurasian plants as the Great Burnet, *Sanguisorba officinalis*, Jacob's Ladder, *Polemonium caeruleum*, and the Meadow Cranesbill, *Geranium pratense*, while higher up where the conifers become scattered and grow mainly on the rocky sides of the valleys, appear the *Persicaria bistorta*, blue and yellow monkshoods (including *Aconitum lycoctonum* subsp. *vulparia*), and the dark blue columbine, *Aquilegia vulgaris*.

Growing with these are Asiatic plants, the orange-yellow, wide-open flowers of *Trollius asiaticus*, lemon-yellow Daylily, *Hemerocallis minor*, and the beautiful Lady's Slipper Orchid, *Cypripedium macranthos*, its large single bloom veined with crimson and with a crimson-purple pouch. *Anemone rivularis* grows along the brooks, with the white or rose plumes of *Astilbe chinensis*, while the leafy plants of *Nepeta sibirica* raise their whorls of lavender in the meadows.

These meadows pass into shorter, soft alpine turfs up to the craggy peak ridges and rock slides, with familiar Eurasiatic plants of high mountains, such as Edelweiss, gentians and forms of the Iceland Poppy, *Papaver nudicaule*. Sheltering among piled rocks, from the woods right up to the peak ridges, are big plants of the rhubarb, *Rheum australe*, while in light mountain woods of birch and oak, is the pure white *Paeonia lactiflora*, not a meadow plant, but a parent of many garden peonies, growing with *Lilium concolor* var. *pulchellum*, showing heads of upright, scarlet, saucer-shaped flowers, together with columbines, yellow daylilies and geraniums.

Japan is much more influenced by the surrounding seas, and has a wet climate with rain for most of the year, and with much snow in the north and on the Japan Sea side of the main island. Due to a warm Pacific current washing the south-west, and a cold one the north, the summers in the two are different – hot and muggy in the south, and cool and foggy in the north. Several huge plants, copiously watered by snow-melt and misty rain, grow along the streams in the mountains of the north, and some extend to Sakhalin and even south Kamchatka. Colonies of 3m/10ft, arching, bamboo-like stems of *Fallopia sachalinensis*, with their big leaves and rather small white flower-spikes, and the meadowsweet, *Filipendula camtschatica*, raising its white or pink-stained fluffy plumes to more than a man's height, are two of these which also colonizes brook banks in the mountain ravines.

Most of Japan's high mountains are in the centre and the north, and are of granite, hard metamorphic or volcanic rocks. They yield sandy soils, which become enriched with humus if not disturbed.

The sub-alpine conifer forests give way upwards in the north to thin woods of a birch, *Betula ermanii*, or bush thickets on the rocky slopes, with meadows in the valleys, and these in turn to dense elfinwood of Dwarf Pine, *Pinus pumila*. Growing only in north Japan and Sakhalin in the damp meadows is *Ligularia hodgsonii*, spreading heads of big yellow daisies, where the nodding deep rosy-red bottle-brushes of *Sanguisorba hakusanensis* also stand. Two rather small but beautiful day-lilies grow in the high meadows of the north, *Hemerocallis middendorffii*, its soft apricot-orange flowers overtopping its leaves, and *H. dumortieri*, with its orange-yellow ones which are brown-backed.

The mountain meadows and ravines of Japan share a number of plants with the mainland of Eurasia, but often as a Japanese variety. The Marsh Marigold has its Japanese and east Asiatic race, as does *Aruncus dioicus*, but the *Persicaria bistorta*, *Thalictrum aquilegiifolium*, and *Ligularia dentata* have not developed a local form. Growing with these in the damp meadows and along streams throughout Japan are more strictly Japanese or east Asiatic plants, of which I will mention only the purplish-crimson candelabra *Primula japonica* of wet stream-sides, and *Filipendula multijuga*, which raises flattened heads of fluffy rose-pink flowers, and which is a parent of the garden plant called *F. purpurea* or *F. palmata*.

The magnificent Golden-rayed Lily, *Lilium auratum*, grows in colonies in rocky, sometimes shady, lower mountain meadows, in the main island only, often with Tiger Lilies, *L. lancifolium*, which also are found in Manchuria and China.

Lastly I will talk of a few of the plants of damp mountain meadows among the upper conifer forests of western North America, the Cascades, the Rockies and the Sierra Nevada, but not of the alpine mats and rocks. Many plants are found on all these mountains, but others are confined to one system of ranges.

Beginning the season, and closely following the melting snow-banks, whole mountain-sides in the Rockies become coloured by the yellow Glacier Lily, *Erythronium grandiflorum*, often mixed in the north-west, though in separate colonies, with the white *E. montanum* with an orange throat, which is difficult to cultivate in Britain. As the summer advances, in both the Rockies and the Sierra Nevada, lining the stony mountain brooks through the meadows, is the deep rose-pink *Mimulus lewisii*. In the Rockies this is often growing with the narrow, sky-blue bells of *Mertensia sibirica*, or *M. ciliata*, white *Caltha leptosepala* in marshy places, and the pale creamy-yellow or white open flower of *Trollius laxus*. The spotted, yellow Monkey Musk, *Mimulus guttatus* also climbs to timber-line on marshy stream-sides on all the western mountains, sometimes spreading into the water, whereas the heads of pink flowers on tall stems of *Darmera peltata*, followed later by big umbrella-leaves, form their creeping colonies only along the brooks and torrents in the northern Sierra Nevada.

Growing in the open meadows of all the ranges are the heads of pale or dark rose, dart-shaped flowers on their tall stems, of several species of *Dodecatheon*, all rather alike, and each growing in its own mountains. The spikes of dark blue stars of *Camassia quamash* are seen in large colonies in damp places, the lavender or white daisies of different species of *Erigeron* colour the meadows, as do the deep yellow ones of *Arnica*, tall cluster-headed blue gentians, and the tall blue spikes of *Lupinus polyphyllus*, a parent of many garden lupins, and which is confined to the meadows of the Cascades and the Sierra Nevada.

Where the woods meet the meadows, and along half-shaded brooks, hang the vivid scarlet flowers of *Aquilegia formosa* var. *truncata*, among blue Monkshoods and larkspurs (*Aconitum* and *Delphinium*), and the tall stems of the Leopard Lily, *Lilium pardalinum*, topped by many scarlet turkscaps with yellow, spotted centres, standing in colonies on damp stream-banks, but only in the coastal mountains and the Sierras. The beautiful blue and white *Aquilegia coerulea* is confined to grassy meadows among the dark conifer forests of the central Rockies, where it is abundant.

SHADE PLANTS FROM SUMMER-GREEN FORESTS OF EUROPE, NORTH AMERICA AND JAPAN

Nearly all of shade-loving garden plants were found growing in deciduous or summer-green woods where they benefited not only from the comparatively still air, but also from its moisture, due to transpiration of the trees and bushes. Few can survive in permanent deep shade, such as under dense evergreens. Most require some light, some protection from the scorching midsummer sun and shelter from strong, dry winds.

Another class of plants, not strictly shade plants, grows on the margins of woods and in open glades and bushy places, such as hedges. They can flourish in sunlight, and die out in too much shade, but also need leaf-mould, protection from wind and a good water supply. I have already mentioned some of them, as they often grow on the borders of meadows. Some true woodland plants can also survive in such positions, even in open grassland in damp cloudy climates.

Brief descriptions of the different types of forest from which our garden plants come help us understand their needs away from their native environment.

All round the northern hemisphere is a broad forest zone of mainly coniferous trees. Similar woods also occupy the upper cloud belt on most mountain chains in the temperate parts of this hemisphere. The climate in which most of these coniferous forests grow is one of long, cold winters, often with much snow, and short, misty or rainy summers. There is little evaporation, and the movement of water is almost constantly downward in the soil, causing layers to form. The basic salts are washed down, the rotting of the needle carpet is therefore very slow, and these soils are acid and infertile. Many of the plants on the forest floor are specialized, and many occur nearly world-wide. Few garden plants for ordinary conditions come from these forests.

The conifer forests give way southward, through a region of mixed woods, to trees which drop their leaves in winter (summer-green trees), but only in those lands within reach of winds from across oceans, which bring them adequate water, spread throughout the year. The interiors of the continents are too dry for trees, and grasslands or deserts take the place of forest. The winters in the summer-green forest lands may be cold with deep snow, or rainy with little snow, but with periods of sharp frost. The summers are longer than in the coniferous forest zone, with spells of warm, dry, sunny weather between rainy times. Thus water moves up and down in the soil, bringing salts and enabling the leaf-litter to rot down to mild humus. These forest soils are usually rather acid, especially on top, but are fertile, and most of our best shade plants come from the woods growing on them.

Southward still, in warmer climates, the summer-green forests merge into woods of predominantly evergreen trees, but with broad leaves, not needles. These are of two main types, those of lands with fairly heavy rainfall throughout most of the year, such as Japan, central China, the eastern United States and New Zealand, and those with adequate rainfall in winter, but long, dry summers, typically round the Mediterranean, but also in southern California, parts of Chile and elsewhere. A number of shade-loving plants from these warm woods can be grown in Britain, mostly from cool, moist valleys in the mountains.

I would like to leave the conifer forests till later, and talk first of the familiar summer-green forests of Europe and their shade plants, and then discover how they differ from those of other parts of the world. The summer-green forests of Europe are predominantly either of various species of oak, or of beech. Other trees mingle with them, and locally may be numerous, especially in the south. On deep, moist soils of the lowlands (often clays or silts) the main oak is the Pedunculate Oak, *Quercus robur*, growing all over Europe to the Urals. Also widespread, but not so far east, is the Durmast Oak, *Q. petraea*, which needs a moister climate but can flourish on shallower, rockier or more sandy soils. Other oaks grow in the south. The beech can grow on fairly shallow soils, whether calcareous or not, but requires a damper, more equable climate than the oaks. It therefore becomes a mountain tree in the south and east, forming a zone in the cloud belt above the oaks, but below the conifers. In the central European mountains the beech often mixes with silver firs (*Abies*) and other trees. Where the beech woods are nearly pure and dense, there is very little underwood and the ground plants are also scanty.

Many shade plants grow in all the European summer-green forests, whether of oaks, mixed trees or beeches, wherever there is enough light and plenty of moist leaf-mould. The ground plants are more influenced by the dryness or wetness of the soil, and the amount of light which can reach them, than by the species of trees forming the canopy, but some plants are much more abundant, or confined to the wet Atlantic climate of the west, while others are found only in the woods of the more continental east, or the southern mountains.

Mature lowland oak woods, not thinned, coppiced, grazed or otherwise modified by humans (which are now very rare), do not cast such a deep shade as pure beech forests. They allow enough light for some bushes and many plants to grow on the forest floor. Most flower in the spring sunlight before the canopy is fully developed, to be pollinated by flying insects, and provide the beautiful woodland scenes we love.

Our own pale yellow primrose, *Primula vulgaris*, does not extend to north-east Europe, but carpets woods on heavy loams, being especially common in the west. Another western plant is the bluebell, *Hyacinthoides non-scripta*, which is most abundant on lighter, sandy loams, avoiding very damp soil, and reaches along the Mediterranean to Italy. Its place is taken in Russian oak woods by the smaller, purer blue *Scilla siberica*, which pushes up to flower through the melting snow, and by *S. bifolia* in south-east Europe. So we find bluebell woods, followed later in the season by open stands of bracken, *Pteridium aquilinum*; and primrose woods, usually with wood anemones, though they will sometimes all grow in the same wood, often in patches according to the texture and dampness of the soil. Much more widespread on both heavy and light though moist soils, is the Wood Anemone, *Anemone nemorosa*, carpeting the woods of both oaks and beeches, and even the northern conifers far into Siberia, with its delicate white cups; while from central Europe eastwards to Russia the yellow *Anemone ranunculoides* becomes common in well-lit oak woods.

The foliage of many spring plants disappears as the shade of the canopy deepens, such as that of the two similar, lilac-flowered *Corydalis* species, *C. cava* and *C. solida*. Also that of the Lesser Celandine, *Ranunculus ficaria*, which is abundant in damp places in the woods as well as in water meadows, as is the bugle, *Ajuga reptans*, whose mats remain green; and *Geranium sylvaticum*. Others keeping their foliage all summer are the lungwort, *Pulmonaria officinalis*, its white-spotted leaves not fully spread till its pink buds have opened to pale blue bells, while *Lamium maculatum* not only keeps its leaves but continues in bloom later. Both grow throughout Europe, as do the violets (*Viola odorata, V. riviniana* and others) which produce their showy flowers early, but their inconspicuous self-fertile ones later. Another method of securing pollination is that of the widespread Asarabacca, *Asarum europaeum*, which takes advantage of the beetles foraging in the leaf-litter by producing its liver-coloured, foul-smelling flowers beneath the foliage.

The Cuckoo Pint, *Arum maculatum*, sends up its green, or occasionally purple, spathes in moist woods all over Europe, while the delicate little Wood Sorrel, *Oxalis acetosella*, opens its pencilled white flowers and folds its shamrock-leaves every night, in all damp, shady forests whether of oaks, beeches, or northern conifers right round the northern hemisphere. Another plant of the northern woods, including those of the conifers, is the baneberry, *Actaea spicata*, which prefers damp soil. Lily-of-the-Valley, *Convallaria majalis*, is also mainly northern, in oak, beech and conifer forest, often in large colonies, but wide districts are without it.

In open glades in the woods, where the sun filters down more freely, grow the Wood Spurge, *Euphorbia amygdaloides*, the Red Campion, *Silene dioica*, and the scrambling Yellow Archangel, *Lamium galeobdolon*. When the oaks are in full leaf in midsummer, only a few, not very showy flowers bloom in the shade, most relying for pollination on the breezes, and including woodland grasses such as the Wood Millet, *Milium effusum*. The invasive bracken is now tall in open sandy woods. Other ferns are still green in damp places, though they are not very numerous, the Lady Fern, *Athyrium filix-femina*, the Male Fern, *Dryopteris filix-mas*, and *D. spinulosa* being the commonest. There is little autumn display in the woods.

Beeches often form nearly pure forests with very little under-wood between the tall grey trunks, which cast deep shade, but even when these are mature, and the stronger trees have killed out the weaker ones, there is a rather sparse growth of spring-flowering plants. In the deepest woods few plants grow among the slowly rotting leaf-litter; several of those that do are plants with no green chlorophyll that live on decayed vegetation. In the mature forests on good soil, especially if other trees share the canopy, many of the same spring plants as in the oak forests shoot up as the beeches come into leaf, such as the Wood Anemone, violets, Wood Spurge, Yellow Archangel and Wood Sorrel. There are others which are more abundant in beech forests, especially on calcareous soil, or which are not often found in other woods, and which give them a character of their own.

On the Balkan mountains the early-flowering Lungwort, *Pulmonaria rubra*, and toothworts (including the Coralroot, *Cardamine bulbifera*), some of which also grow in the oak woods, but not so abundantly, are characteristic, often with *Geranium macrorrhizum*. Growing among the widespread snowdrop, *Galanthus nivalis*, and Spring Snowflake, *Leucojum vernum*, is the blue *Scilla amoena*, a plant of the eastern beech woods, as is *Helleborus purpurascens*. The Perennial Honesty, *Lunaria rediviva*, grows in the central European beech woods, where *Lathyrus vernus* and *Cardamine trifolia* are common. The Christmas Rose, *Helleborus niger*, and *Cyclamen purpurascens* grow in the beech woods of the Alps, as well as in other types of forest, as does *Hepatica nobilis*.

Not common, but characteristic of British beech woods on thin soil over chalk are *Helleborus viridis* subsp. *occidentalis, Polygonatum multiflorum*, and here and there in open places *Aquilegia vulgaris*, which is widespread over Eurasia in semi-shady places. Several orchids (*Epipactis, Cephalanthera*) are almost confined to these woods. The ramsons or wild garlic, *Allium ursinum*, and the Lily-of-the-Valley form wide drifts locally.

The forests on the western Great and Minor Caucasus, within reach of winds off the Black Sea, differ from those of central Europe in having a milder and wetter climate. Hard frosts occur in winter but do not last long, and the summers are hot. The woods are of mixed summer-green trees, predominantly of various oaks, with the eastern beeches higher up the mountains and in damp gullies down to sea level, but much of the underwood is of evergreen bushes, such as the common Cherry Laurel, *Prunus laurocerasus,* the holly and *Rhododendron ponticum*. The summer-green forests give way to those of conifers on the wet heights above. Between the bushes, in this comparatively mild climate, several of the plants growing on the forest floor still have their old leaves when they flower in the early spring, such as the forms of *Helleborus × hybridus*, and *Epimedium pinnatum* subsp. *colchicum*, while *Cyclamen coum* subsp. *caucasicum* sends up its leaves before the winter is over, and also flowers very early. Even the Mediterranean *Arum italicum*, also in leaf all winter, grows in these woods. Some of the many ferns are evergreen too, the Hard Fern, *Blechnum spicant*, forms of the Prickly Shield Fern, *Polystichum aculeatum*, the Ribbon Fern, *Pteris cretica*, which is not hardy in Britain, and the Hart's Tongue Fern, *Asplenium scolopendrium*, both usually growing in rocky places.

Flowering before the canopy becomes too shady are leaf-losing plants with big, lush foliage not yet fully spread, including clumps of *Brunnera macrophylla* and quickly spreading colonies of the borage-like *Trachystemon orientalis*, both of which climb to the mountain woods. Mats of *Omphalodes cappadocica* hang over shady rocks in the south, where the evergreen *Iris lazica* covers banks. Among the eastern plants are woodland ones widespread in Europe, the pale yellow primrose, *Primula vulgaris*, but only in the north-west, its pink close-relative further south, the Wood Spurge, *Lathyrus vernus*, the pale yellow-flowered sage, *Salvia glutinosa*, and many more.

The upper, cooler, mountain forests show a spring display more like that of central Europe. Very early to flower are cyclamen, blue *Scilla cernua*, snowdrop, *Galanthus plicatus* and other snowdrops, soon followed by *Pachyphragma macrophyllum* blooming before its foliage has carpeted the forest floor, as does that of the low comfrey, *Symphytum ibericum*, which flowers later in damp places. The pink *Corydalis angustifolia*, and the larger, mauve-purple *C. caucasica* are early flowering Caucasian and Iranian plants, while the toothwort, *Cardamine bulbifera*, *Anemone ranunculoides*, the baneberry, *Actaea spicata*, the Creeping Gromwell, *Buglossoides purpurocaerulea*, and the Sweet Violet grow over much of Europe. The Lady Fern and the Ostrich Fern, *Matteuccia struthiopteris* inhabit damp places. The huge plants of *Telekia speciosa* are common, following the streams from the lowlands up to the sub-alpine meadows, as they do in the Balkan woods also. The Willow Gentian, *Gentiana asclepiadea*, the Calamint, *Calamintha grandiflora*, and *Lathyrus aureus* grow in half shade at the edges of the woods, where they open out to glades and meadows.

The summer-green woods of eastern North America contain more varied trees, climbers and underwood bushes than those of Europe. They once stretched from the Canadian conifer forests nearly to the Gulf of Mexico, and from the Atlantic westward to beyond the Great Lakes, where the climate becomes too dry, and they give way to the prairies. The leaves of many of them colour vividly before they fall, and the forests are very beautiful before the first winter blizzards. The colouring of some of them is not so reliable in Britain, perhaps because the climate of the eastern United States is less oceanic than that of west and central Europe, more influenced by hot air from the interior and the south in summer, and by arctic winds in the winter, especially in the north, where the winters are much colder, with deep snow. The annual rainfall is 100–150cm/40–60in or more, heaviest in the southern mountain forests.

The forests vary over such a vast area, but most of the main trees can grow over the whole range where soils and sites are suitable. On the best soils and in cool sites, both in the north-east and southward on the Appalachians, the predominant trees are the American Beech and the Sugar Maple, with Lime, Yellow Birch, various oaks and sometimes Canadian Hemlock growing among them. On drier sites and in drier climates the main forest trees are several oaks and hickories, again with many other trees. These oak-hickory forests form the general western forest limit. From Virginia southward the lower and mid slopes of the Appalachians are covered by forests of more southern oaks (and American Sweet Chestnuts before they were destroyed by imported disease), while tulip trees, magnolias and many others are common. These southern mountain forests are the richest and most varied summer-green woods in America.

Many ground plants grow throughout the whole range of the summer-green forests, from east to west, provided their needs for moisture, shade or drainage are satisfied. However, a number which grow in the forests of the south do not extend to those of the north. Very early to flower, as the trees are breaking their buds and coming into leaf, are the Adder's Tongues, the yellow *Erythronium americanum* of damp woods, and the white *E. albidum* of rather drier forests of the Mid West, neither of which are as easy to grow in gardens as the far western species. There are also blue *Hepatica nobilis*, white anemones very close to the European Wood Anemone, the pink Rue Anemone, *Anemonella thalictroides*, the Blood Root, *Sanguinaria canadensis*, and the pale pink or white Dutchman's Breeches, *Dicentra cucullaria*. Soon several Wake Robins, forms of *Trillium*, including the beautiful *T. grandiflorum*, open their white, deep brownish-purple or occasionally greenish-yellow flowers, with the bellwort, *Uvularia perfoliata*, and the running Jacob's Ladder, *Polemonium reptans*. The Jack-in-the-Pulpit, *Arisaema triphyllum*, sends up its striped and hooded spathes, and violets, of which there are many eastern American species, show their white, lilac, yellow or deep purple-blue flowers, some preferring open, damp places, others dry, sunny woods.

False Solomon's Seal, *Smilacina racemosa*, and true Solomon's Seal (*Polygonatum*) flower a little later in the spring, and some woods are carpeted by the lilac-blue *Phlox divaricata*, or in the Appalachians, by *P. stolonifera*. The beautiful cool lilac to rosy-purple *Geranium maculatum* blooms in rich moist woods, as does the Foam Flower, *Tiarella cordifolia*, and the May Apple, *Podophyllum peltatum*. Growing in boggy places in the woods are colonies of the tall, white and carmine-pink Lady's Slipper Orchid, *Cypripedium reginae*, while the Moccasin Flower, *C. acaule*, prefers damp sandy or rocky woods. The scarlet and yellow *Aquilegia canadensis* and *Heuchera americana* which grow mainly in the Mid West states both grow in rocky but somewhat drier woods.

In the deep shade of midsummer in the woods, few but coarse weedy plants with inconspicuous flowers are to be found, but where sunlight can reach the ground, such as along streams, the Bee Balm, *Monarda didyma*, the tall *Phlox maculata*,

P. paniculata, *Actaea simplex*, in cool places, and in the Appalachian woods the Indian Physic, *Gillenia trifoliata*, are all in bloom.

As the canopy begins to thin in the autumn, woodland species of Michaelmas Daisy (*Aster*) and Goldenrod (*Solidago*), with some other members of the daisy family, such as Boneset (*Eupatorium*), here and there, come into flower after all else is over, especially in more open oak forests.

Apart from nearly cosmopolitan ferns, eastern North America shares some with Japan and east Asia only, such as the Northern Maidenhair, *Adiantum pedatum*, of moist, usually hilly woods, the Sensitive Fern, *Onoclea sensibilis*, of damp, open places, and which will flourish with its roots in wet mud, the Cinnamon Fern and the Interrupted Fern, *Osmunda cinnamomea* and *O. claytoniana*, both of damp or even wet forests. The Eastern Lady Fern, *Athyrium filix-femina* var. *angustum*, and the Common Wood Fern, *Dryopteris intermedia*, take the place of their European relatives, while the Hay-scented Fern, *Dennstaedtia punctilobula*, is confined to America, where it runs in open woods. There are many more.

The summer-green forests of Japan resemble those of eastern North America more closely than they do those of Europe. They are of equally varied trees and bushes, and also show vivid colouring of their leaves in the warm, dry autumn, after the hot, wet and humid summer. The winters in the summer-green zone are cold, dry and frosty, except on the Japan Sea side of the central mountains, and in the north, where the snow lies very deeply. The yearly rainfall is everywhere high, averaging 150cm/60in over much of Japan.

The summer-green forests extend from the lowlands and hills of south-west Hokkaido (the northern island) and the northern part of the main island (Honshu) southward, becoming mountain woods further south and west, where they merge into those of evergreen oaks on the hills and lower mountain slopes. The lowlands of the south-west are subtropical. Above the summer-green forests on all the higher mountains, and in the north of Hokkaido, are forests of conifers. In the forests of the warmer lower slopes and hills, the main trees are oaks, chestnuts and magnolias, with many others, and on the central mountains, with cypresses, Umbrella Pine and other conifers growing among them, or forming groves. Higher in the mountains beeches become much more common, still mixed with many other trees.

As in other summer-green forests, many plants shoot up and flower quickly in the spring, before the shade becomes deep. Several east Asiatic anemones and violets, not often grown in Britain, Japanese forms of *Hepatica nobilis*, and Dog's Tooth Violet, *Erythronium japonicum*, and a winter aconite, *Eranthis pinnatifida* with yellow-eyed, white flowers, are all early, though the last is rather local and rare in south-west Honshu. Japan has many species of *Asarum*, most with beautifully marbled leaves and making attractive ground-cover, but many are southern and local, and perhaps not very hardy in Britain. There are also many species of Jack-in-the-Pulpit (*Arisaema*), few of which are grown in gardens. More well-known and cultivated are the barrenworts, especially the large-flowered lilac to white *Epimedium grandiflorum*, which is also a parent of beautiful garden hybrids. Others that flower in the early spring are *Disporum sessile* and *D. smilacinum*, Asiatic species of *Trillium*, the rosy-purple *Paeonia obovata*, usually grown in Britain in its pure white form, the low yellow poppy, *Hylomecon japonica,* and the evergreen, orchid-like *Iris japonica* of the centre and south-west. Another evergreen, which makes carpets, is *Pachysandra terminalis* which produces its fluffy white spikes in the spring. The posy-shaped flower heads of *Petasites japonicus* appear before its huge leaves, along shady mountain streams.

Late spring and early summer is the flowering season of the species of *Hosta*, of which Japan has nearly all. Many are very local, a few inhabiting boggy places, some of the smaller ones damp crevices and pockets in cliffs, and those with larger leaves, such as *H. sieboldiana* on the wet, western side of Honshu, are plants of rich woods. Growing only in the woods on the high mountains of central and north Japan, *Glaucidium palmatum* also opens its large lilac flowers now, while *Rodgersia podophylla* spreads its big, bronzed foliage in glades in the same districts, blooming a little later.

In high summer, when much monsoon rain falls, members of the nettle family, umbellifers and other coarse plants, and the many ferns, predominate in the shade, but in more open places species of *Smilacina* and the Giant Lily, *Cardiocrinum cordatum*, come into bloom. Two plants, native in Japan only, and rare even there, are the tall *Anemonopsis macrophylla* of the woods on the mountain ranges of central Honshu, and *Kirengeshoma palmata*, scattered here and there on a few mountains of the southern islands of Shikoku and Kyushu, and probably a relic of an earlier age. Several species of toad lily, *Tricyrtis*, some local and rare, though *T. hirta* is rather common except in the far north, produce their curious spotted white or pale yellow bells in late summer and on into autumn, with the White Rue, *Boenninghausenia japonica*, in the central and southern mountains. Last to flower in the woods are species of Michaelmas Daisy and other, mostly tall members of the daisy family, and the white fluffy spires of *Actaea* (formerly *Cimicifuga*).

CONIFER FORESTS

The northern conifer forests in rainier climates, and on damp, close-textured soils, often glacial clays, are mostly of spruces (*Picea*), mixed with Silver Fir (*Abies*) towards the south. Similar forests grow in the upper cloud belt of many mountain ranges all over the temperate northern hemisphere where there is enough rain. The forests on drier sandy or rocky soils (and even dried-out peat hillocks), and in rather warmer climates, are mainly of pines (*Pinus*). In central and eastern Siberia, which has the coldest and harshest winters in the world apart from Antarctica, and at the uppermost limit of tree growth on many mountains, leaf-losing larches (*Larix*) replace the evergreen conifers.

The spruce-fir forests, the typical 'taiga' of the Russians, cast a dense, year-long shade. There are practically no underwood bushes, and the ground is covered by a thick, silent carpet of spreading mosses among the fallen needles. Only a few low-flowering plants and ferns are scattered in these sombre woods, where the trees grow well. The Wood Sorrel, *Oxalis acetosella*, the running Beech Fern, *Phegopteris connectilis* (syn. *Dryopteris phegopteris*) and a few other ferns, the mats of *Linnaea borealis*, and May Lily, *Maianthemum bifolium*, *Trientalis europaea*, *T. borealis* in Canada, the Whortleberry, *Vaccinium myrtillus*, and several wintergreen *Pyrola*, including the One-flowered Wintergreen, *Pyrola uniflora*, are characteristic. Several plants without chlorophyll live on the rotting needles in the deepest shade.

In Canada (and east Siberia) the creeping *Cornus canadensis* is common. The thick moss carpet and most of these little plants are also characteristic of pine and larch forests on moist soil and in moist climates. Larger plants only find enough light along streams, or where the spruces grow poorly, and are not very typical, many being also found in water-meadows or summer-green forests.

Finally I cannot leave out the magnificent conifer forests of the coasts and coastal mountains of western North America, from British Columbia to northern California, as some fine shade plants come from them. They are of mixed, huge conifers, hemlocks (*Tsuga*), thujas, spruces, the Douglas Fir, cypresses (*Chamaecyparis*) and, in the south, the redwoods (*Sequoia*), tallest trees in the world.

Annual rainfall here averages 150cm/60in, reaching 200cm/80in in places most exposed to the Pacific winds, and dropping to 76cm/30in, falling mostly in winter, at the southern limit of the redwoods, but there are frequent sea fogs in the summer where they grow, which condense and drip from the trees. The temperatures are never very low in winter, even in the north where there is snow, and the summers are cool.

There is an abundant underwood of shrubs, between which, on the mossy ground, grow colonies of the tall Sword Fern, *Polystichum munitum*, and other ferns, creeping mats of the Wood Sorrel, *Oxalis oregana*, with rosy-white flowers and of *Asarum caudatum* with curious, spider-like blooms, *Dicentra formosa*, the Fringe Cup, *Tellima grandiflora*, the Coast Trillium, *Trillium ovatum* which is closely related to *T. grandiflorum* of the east, *Heuchera micrantha*, a parent of many garden hybrids, Fairy Lantern, *Disporum smithii* and its relatives, the delicate little *Vancouveria hexandra*, *Linnaea*, *Trientalis* and many others. The beautiful *Erythronium oregonum* grows in the lowland forests only, and *E. revolutum*, also of the lowland woods, often at the edges of bogs, is found further south, while the flesh-pink Jacob's Ladder, *Polemonium carneum*, is a rather rare plant in the woods of north California and Oregon.

9 | Garden Plans

THE ART OF GARDENING, I think, is to select plants from similar environments and group them so that they complement each other, not vie with each other for attention. We should consider scale, observe form and outline, be aware of textures and study nature's gentle colour harmonies. If we could practise all this we would have a dissolving and constantly re-forming tapestry emerging throughout the growing season and, in some cases, throughout the year.

There are endless possibilities for grouping plants. Sometimes it is enough to find just three or four which, put together, create a little scene, an atmosphere, a melodic line perhaps; these things I feel when my planting comes right – which is not always. There must be a theme, which you state firmly. It may be a shady corner where you will intensify the feeling of cool tranquillity, or a sun-drenched area where you use richly coloured flowers of the prairies, such as rudbeckias and sunflowers, or *Trollius* and persicarias from lowland meadows in the Alps.

A very useful lesson that was brought home to me by my old and much esteemed friend, the late Sir Cedric Morris, is the fact that we can use space in the soil both ways. Not only do we plant side by side, but also, in different depths, we can plant one plant on top of another, provided their seasons for leafing and flowering do not overlap too much. This applies particularly to combinations of plants and bulbs, but can also apply with plants which die down early in the year to be followed by those that are backward in making an appearance.

A simple plank bridge, covered with small-mesh wire netting to prevent slipping in wet weather, crosses the open ditch running alongside the Wood Garden. Here various forms of *Iris sibirica* mingle with candelabra primulas and the handsome Sensitive Fern, *Onoclea sensibilis*, while hostas provide bold relief.

Within each plan for damp sites I list and show plants in separate groups, hoping it will help in visualizing the effect. In small-scale planting these individual combinations might well be ample, or could even be reduced again. They are not the only or the best combinations that could be made; neither need they be kept in watertight compartments. Plants of similar habit could be selected from the other groups and all would look harmonious provided you are careful to blend the shapes. It is as important to have plant shapes contributing to the design as it is to take care with colour blending. For myself it is more important. Naturally one avoids horrible clashes of colour, but that rarely occurs when plants are grown with their natural associates.

As we all sometimes think that the grass on the other side of the fence is the greenest, so we in dry areas tend to look towards the moist West Country, to wet Wales, the cool northern counties of England and to areas with high rainfall in other countries and feel envious of the plants that grow there so well, which often we cannot grow and should not attempt. I am lucky to be able to grow some of them, but there are far, far more to be found, and endless permutations for grouping them within the basic structure of design; that is, you take account of scale, shape and season, so that not everything is in bloom at once and that quiet seasons are well furnished with good foliage.

PLAN FOR THE SWAMP GARDEN

The majority of plants used must have perpetually wet soil; those indicated around the edge will grow in a few centimetres or inches of water. *Gunnera* is one of the few which could be harmed by being waterlogged in winter. I like to plant the crown of *G. tinctoria* slightly above water level on a raised mound or bank. Its roots quickly find boggy soil but the resting buds are not drowned in winter if the level should rise.

The same applies to *Phormium*. In very cold districts phormiums may not be hardy, but our established plants, together with the milder winters survive undamaged.

It is worth repeating that the ornamental rhubarb, *Rheum palmatum*, will rot if it is planted in waterlogged soil. It needs deep soil, enriched with well-rotted vegetable waste, that does not dry out. Well suited it will stand full sun, but also looks well in dappled shade. Savage winds can damage such huge and tender leaves, whereas the leaves of *Gunnera* are hard and horny. *Rheum alexandrae* will tolerate wetter conditions, as it grows wild in mountain meadows with candelabra primulas, but it will not tolerate waterlogged soil.

I would hesitate to use so many different plants all together unless the planting were on a very large scale. But I have made groups of plants, which I consider look

SWAMP GARDEN

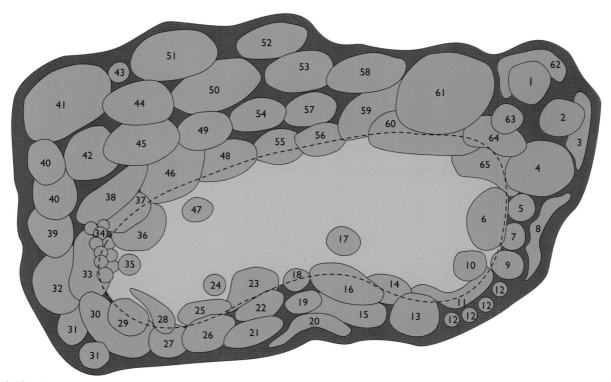

1 *Phormium tenax*
2 *Phormium tenax* 'Variegatum'
3 *Houttuynia cordata*
4 *Salix repens* var. *argentea*
5 *Senecio smithii*
6 *Zantedeschia aethiopica* 'Green Goddess'
7 *Iris versicolor*
8 *Lysimachia nummularia* 'Aurea'
9 *Lythrum salicaria*
10 *Schoenoplectus lacustris* subsp. *tabernaemontani* 'Zebrinus'
11 *Myosotis scorpioides*
12 *Primula bulleyana*
13 *Ligularia dentata*
14 *Lysichiton camtschatcensis*

15 *Verbena corymbosa*
16 *Darmera peltata*
17 *Aponogeton distachyos*
18 *Caltha palustris* var. *alba*
19 *Luzula sylvatica*
20 *Mimulus guttatus*
21 *Primula pulverulenta*

22 *Lythrum virgatum*
23 *Pontederia cordata*
24 *Butomus umbellatus*
25 *Iris laevigata*
26 *Persicaria milletii*
27 *Lysimachia ciliata*
28 *Calla palustris*
29 *Eriophorum angustifolium*
30 *Euphorbia palustris*
31 *Carex morrowii* 'Variegata'
32 *Iris ensata*
33 *Aruncus dioicus*
34 *Primula florindae*
35 *Typha angustifolia*
36 *Iris pseudacorus* 'Variegata'
37 *Cardamine raphanifolia*
38 *Astilbe* hybrids
39 *Rudbeckia fulgida* var. *fulgida*
40 *Rodgersia podophylla*
41 *Cornus alba* 'Spaethii'
42 *Rheum palmatum*
43 *Taxodium distichum*
44 *Miscanthus sinensis* 'Variegatus'

45 *Veratrum album*
46 *Osmunda regalis*
47 *Zantedeschia aethiopica*
48 *Onoclea sensibilis*
49 *Persicaria amplexicaulis*
50 *Miscanthus sinensis* 'Zebrinus'
51 *Salix elaeagnos*
52 *Miscanthus sinensis* 'Silberfeder'

53 *Eupatorium purpureum*
54 *Persicaria bistorta* 'Superba'
55 *Caltha palustris* var. *radicans* 'Flore Pleno'
56 *Carex elata* 'Aurea'
57 *Trollius europaeus*
58 *Ligularia* 'The Rocket'
59 *Persicaria campanulata*
60 *Menyanthes trifoliata*
61 *Gunnera tinctoria*
62 *Glyceria maxima* var. *variegata*
63 *Inula magnifica*
64 *Hemerocallis fulva* 'Green Kwanso'
65 *Caltha palustris* var. *palustris*

well together. There are, of course, endless permutations within this range, conditioned largely by the scale of planting.

I tend to think of natural pools with clay-based bottoms as I have had little experience with lined pools. The main problems with man-made pools are usually overall size – usually lack of size! – and depth of soil. However, small pools well maintained look infinitely more attractive than large, neglected, muddy ponds. A few well-displayed plants are much more effective than the confused tangle that can result when there is no shortage of room and enthusiasm but insufficient discipline meted out to plants and planters.

In designing my groups, whether large or small, I try to keep in mind the image of a main vertical line connected to the earth with strong and interesting foliage. This basic shape is emphasized and decorated throughout the growing season with a succession of flowering plants, until finally all together contribute to the warm glow of autumn with seed pods and flowering grasses, while the lush foliage, over many weeks, turns to rich shades of brown, copper and gold.

One last warning, when making an artificial pool. Unless you can arrange for irrigation, or some other artificial way to moisten the soil outside your pool, the natural state of the soil will probably be very dry, at least it will be when damp-loving plants are most in need of moisture. Possibly the best way to overcome this without irrigation is having the pool surrounded by paving and perhaps a rock garden, so leading more acceptably into plants associated with dry gardening.

PLANS FOR SUNNY DAMP BEDS

There are so many plants that could be selected for these beds, most well-known garden plants in fact, excluding those that could be called drought-resisting plants. I have chosen from among hundreds – if not thousands – about one hundred which would certainly suffer if planted in poor soil with low rainfall. They need a good moisture-retentive soil and adequate rainfall, but the soil must also be well drained, and in no case may it be waterlogged.

Having so many plants to choose from, I decided to divide the year in half and design two beds, one to flower from spring to midsummer, the other from midsummer until late autumn. Many of the plants which I have found look well together continue to provide flowers and foliage over several months, but to create a bed that is interesting for most of the year you can select groups from either plan, to your own choice, and match them together.

I have chosen some plants which are not reliably hardy, such as *Salvia uliginosa*, whose tall nodding heads of bright Cambridge-blue flowers are such a delight for weeks in autumn. It has survived here nine out of ten winters covered with some kind of litter, but we always keep a few roots potted and tucked under cover, in a

SUNNY DAMP BED FLOWERING FROM SPRING TO MIDSUMMER

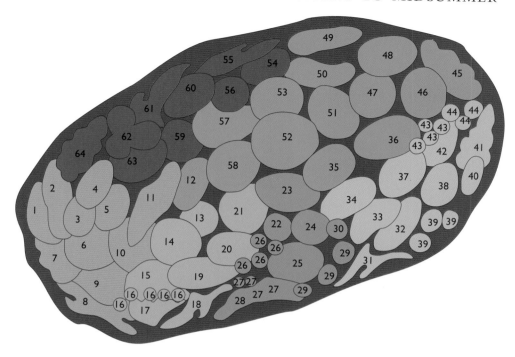

Group 1
1 *Campanula* 'Burghaltii'
2 *Aconitum* 'Ivorine'
3 *Aquilegia formosa*
4 *Valeriana phu* 'Aurea'
5 *Gentiana lutea*
6 *Achillea ageratum* 'W.B. Childs'
7 *Veronica gentianoides*
8 *Prunella grandiflora* 'Loveliness'
9 *Phlox pilosa*
10 *Monarda didyma* 'Beauty of Cobham'
11 *Nepeta sibirica*

Group 2
13 *Thalictrum flavum* subsp. *glaucum*
14 *Hemerocallis lilioasphodelus*
15 *Physostegia virginiana* 'Summer Snow'
16 *Zigadenus elegans*
17 *Primula denticulata*
18 *Ajuga reptans* 'Burgundy Glow'
19 *Persicaria bistorta* subsp. *carnea*
20 *Geranium* 'Johnson's Blue'
21 *Aruncus dioicus*

Group 3
22 *Camassia leichtlinii*

Group 4
23 *Filipendula purpurea*
24 *Delphinium* 'Alice Artindale'
25 *Morina longifolia*
26 *Lilium bulbiferum* var. *croceum*
27 *Fritillaria meleagris*
28 *Erigeron* 'Dimity'
29 *Geum* 'Lionel Cox'
30 *Leucojum aestivum*

Group 4
31 *Viola cornuta* Alba Group
32 *Aster tongolensis* 'Napsbury'
33 × *Heucherella alba* 'Bridget Bloom'
34 *Geranium clarkei* 'Kashmir White'
37 *Heuchera cylindrica* 'Greenfinch'
38 *Iris setosa*
39 *Bergenia* 'Abendglut'
40 *Dodecatheon meadia*
41 *Waldsteinia ternata*
42 *Astrantia maxima*
43 *Lilium monadelphum*
44 *Filipendula vulgaris* 'Multiplex'

Group 5
45 *Geranium sanguineum* 'Album'
46 *Stachys macrantha* 'Robusta'
47 *Leucanthemum maximum*
48 *Iris chrysographes*
49 *Alopecurus pratensis* 'Aureus'
50 *Campanula latifolia* var. *alba*

Group 6
35 *Campanula lactiflora*
36 *Cephalaria gigantea*
51 *Centaurea macrocephala*
52 *Phormium tenax* 'Variegatum'
53 *Miscanthus sinensis* 'Zebrinus'
54 *Euphorbia palustris*
55 *Rheum palmatum*
12 *Ligularia* 'The Rocket'

Group 7
54 *Symphytum* × *uplandicum* 'Variegatum'
55 *Ajuga reptans* 'Atropurpurea'
56 *Ligularia* 'Gregynog Gold'
59 *Hemerocallis fulva* 'Green Kwanso'
60 *Trollius chinensis*
61 *Verbena corymbosa*
62 *Rheum alexandrae*
63 *Geranium pratense* 'Striatum'
64 *Geranium himalayense*

covered plastic tunnel. In theory the same procedure goes for *Lobelia cardinalis*, but I must confess it has survived many years unprotected. However, it would be wiser to cover it.

The very large plants in the centres of the beds would probably be far too bulky for many people, but I would not ignore them altogether unless I had the tiniest of gardens.

I would not recommend *Cephalaria gigantea* (plan for Sunny Damp Bed Flowering from Spring to Midsummer on page 185) anywhere but in a large garden where, for much of the season, its displays of pale lemon scabious-like flowers perched on top of tall gawky stems can make unusual and interesting contrast, say on the edge of a shrubbery, or the back of a large border. I like to plant it with *Campanula lactiflora* because they are found growing wild together in well-watered and sheltered gullies at the head of mountain valleys where the forest ends, in the Caucasus.

Cephalaria alpina is similar, but smaller, and flowers more abundantly. *Campanula lactiflora* is one of the glories of the garden. Each plant sends up several strong stems 1.5m/5ft tall, each topped with a wide, airy bouquet packed with pale blue bells. Sometimes a white form occurs, sometimes a deeper blue. *C. l.* 'Loddon Anna' is soft amethyst. All are desirable, creating an atmosphere of lavish abundance, which should not be lacking in any garden. Just one or two good large plants can do that for you and remove any pinched feelings about having a small garden. I should not forget to tell you that if you cut off the main flower heads of the *Campanula* as soon as they have faded you will have a new crop almost as spectacular in the autumn.

In the plan for a Sunny Damp Bed Flowering from Midsummer to Late Autumn (opposite) I have used *Molinia caerulea* subsp. *arundinacea*, the purple-headed Moor Grass. All summer you hardly notice it among its colourful neighbours, where it eventually reaches about 2m/6ft. An upright column of stiffly held stems is topped in August with dark, purplish-green flower heads well worth looking at, but you still might not be very impressed – until late October and November, when almost all the flowers have gone and the leaves of the garden are having a ball, all to themselves, decked out in the final and most fiery colour scheme of the whole year. Then you can almost feel a glow from my clumps of *Molinia caerulea*. subsp. *arundinacea*. Every tall stem, thick and round as a knitting needle, every pennant-like leaf from tip to ground level, is ablaze with colour – making ripe corn look dull by comparison

I remember a cold, frosty day in November when I called the girls who worked with me then to come and stand among the glowing grasses, to see the light reflected from them – and there we stood, elated by the golden sheaves as tall as ourselves.

SUNNY DAMP BED FLOWERING FROM MIDSUMMER TO LATE AUTUMN

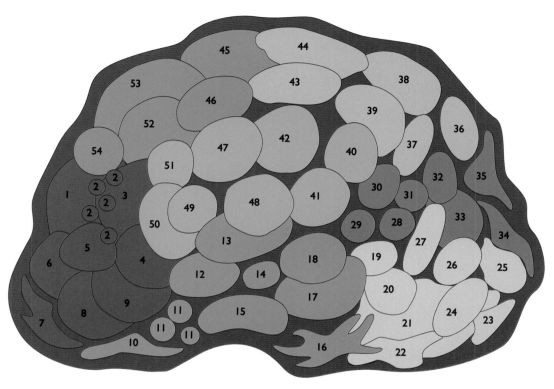

Group 1
1 *Liriope muscari*
2 *Lilium speciosum*
3 *Persicaria amplexicaulis*
4 *Leucanthemella serotina*
5 *Aconitum carmichaelii* 'Arendsii'
6 *Schizostylis coccinea*
7 *Viola cornuta* Lilacina Group
8 *Stokesia laevis*
9 *Astrantia major* subsp. *involucrata*
   'Shaggy'

Group 2
10 *Persicaria affinis*
11 *Molinia caerulea* subsp. *caerulea*
   'Variegata'
12 *Aster* × *frikartii* 'Mönch'
13 *Euphorbia sikkimensis*
14 *Artemisia lactiflora*
15 *Solidago* 'Queenie'
16 *Gentiana septemfida*
17 *Hosta ventricosa*
18 *Echinacea purpurea*

Group 3
19 *Salvia uliginosa*
20 *Stipa arundinacea*
21 *Epilobium glabellum*
22 *Ophiopogon planiscapus* 'Nigrescens'
23 *Nierembergia repens*
24 *Hosta undulata* var. *univittata*
25 *Mimulus* 'Wisley Red'
26 *Symphytum* 'Rubrum'
27 *Gentiana asclepiadea* 'Knightshayes'

Group 4
28 *Phlox*, border variety
29 *Veronicastrum virginicum* 'Album'
30 *Lythrum salicaria* 'Feuerkerze'
31 *Phlox*, border variety
32 *Lysimachia ephemerum*
33 *Lobelia cardinalis* 'Queen Victoria'
34 *Persicaria affinis*
35 *Pratia angulata* 'Treadwellii'

Group 5
36 *Astilbe* 'Sprite'

Group 6
37 *Chelone obliqua*
38 *Hemerocallis* 'Golden Chimes'
39 *Lysimachia ciliata*
43 *Astilbe chinensis* var. *taquetii*
   'Superba'
44 *Astilbe chinensis* var. *pumila*

Group 6
40 *Scrophularia auriculata* 'Variegata'
41 *Eupatorium purpureum*
42 *Phormium tenax* Purpureum Group
47 *Miscanthus* 'Silberfeder'
48 *Pleioblastus viridistriatus*
49 *Inula magnifica*
50 *Molinia caerulea* subsp. *arundinacea*
51 *Vernonia crinita*

Group 7
45 *Alopecurus pratensis* 'Aureus'
46 *Astilbe* 'Professor van der Wielen'
52 *Inula hookeri*
53 *Rudbeckia fulgida* var. *deamii*
54 *Lobelia* × *speciosa* 'Vedrariensis'

PLANS FOR SHADY DAMP BEDS

In making these plans I have tried to imagine gardens where light shade and damp conditions are constant. The shade could be provided by buildings or be overhead shade cast by trees. In all cases I am presuming there will be reasonable rainfall during the summer months as the plants I have chosen will not stand competition from the greedy roots of trees and shrubs close planted in the drier parts of the country. Neither am I imagining deep, dark shade.

In my own garden I have had to grow extra shelter, apart from my existing ancient oaks, to protect tender foliage not only from the glare of the sun but also to shield it from desiccating winds. I rarely imagine plants without trees and shrubs to provide a setting which will remain in winter, so I have indicated a few which I have used myself. If you already have a background established you could ignore my selection.

The plans started off as one border, but I decided it was becoming rather complicated to fit into a book, so it has become two plans which could be placed side by side, with perhaps a little modification at the seam, if you have room to expand and could manage them both.

Although called Summer Snowflake, *Leucojum aestivum* 'Gravetye Giant' flowers in spring, together with late daffodils. It makes large, free-flowering clumps in almost any soil except starved gravel, but thrives in boggy places, looking especially good among the leafless red-stemmed dogwoods.

They are not intended as plans to be reproduced faithfully, but to suggest groups of plants, which I have found grow and look well together in cool conditions. In cooler and damper regions, quite a few of the plants can be grown without shade. Others, like the *Rheum*, which I have chosen for dramatic effect, do not often need shade but certainly need shelter from damaging winds, and sometimes from sun scorch.

Primarily I hope my plans will be helpful to guide you as to approximately where in the border the plants could be put, whether for practical or aesthetic reasons. For example, plants which colonize freely, such as the modest *Geranium endressii*, have been relegated to positions under light trees or shrubs, where their spreading habit need not be for ever regretted.

Other plants, like *Aconitum* 'Ivorine', *Astrantia major* and heucheras, can be grown in sunny situations provided they are given deep, rich soil. But they harmonize with the real shade-demanders and add immeasurably to the design, as well as flowering satisfactorily in part shade.

Many more desirable plants that can be grown in cool shade are described and illustrated in my Woodland Garden.

From the deep, humus-rich soil of the Tall Grass American prairies come several handsome daisy flowers which extend the joy of summer, even though the days are shortening. *Rudbeckia fulgida* var. *deamii* has short, black central cones, so is known familiarly as Black-eyed Susan. In the foreground fading astilbes still look good, and will make long-lasting seed heads for winter effect.

SHADY DAMP BED (I)

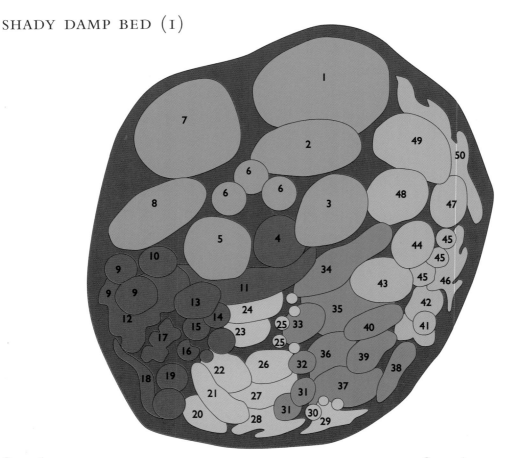

Group 1
4 *Polygonatum verticillatum*
9 *Hosta undulata* var. *albomarginata*
10 *Iris foetidissima* 'Variegata'
11 *Geranium macrorrhizum*
12 *Alchemilla mollis*
13 *Digitalis ciliata* or *D. grandiflora*
14 *Iris foetidissima* var. *citrina*
15 *Polystichum setiferum* Acutilobum
   Group
16 *Digitalis parviflora*
17 *Primula calderiana*
18 *Viola sororia* 'Freckles'
19 *Pulmonaria saccharata*

Group 2
20 *Arisaema candidissimum*
21 *Mertensia virginica*
22 *Dicentra spectabilis*
23 *Selinum wallichianum*
24 *Actaea matsumurae* 'White Pearl'
25 *Lilium speciosum*

26 *Aconitum* 'Ivorine'
27 *Actaea rubra*
28 *Viola sororia*
29 *Veronica prostrata* 'Trehane'
30 *Gentiana asclepiadea* 'Knightshayes'

Group 3
31 *Liriope muscari*
32 *Valeriana phu* 'Aurea'
33 *Persicaria virginiana* 'Variegata'
34 *Polygonatum* × *hybridum*
35 *Geranium endressii*
36 *Anemone* × *hybrida* 'Honorine
   Jobert'
37 *Hosta undulata* var. *univittata*
38 *Hakonechloa macra* 'Aureola'
39 *Geranium maculatum*
40 *Astrantia major* 'Sunningdale
   Variegated'

Group 4
41 *Pulmonaria longifolia*
42 *Heuchera cylindrica* 'Greenfinch'
43 *Hosta fortunei* var. *albopicta*
44 *Scrophularia auriculata* 'Variegata'
45 *Smilacina racemosa*
46 *Mitella breweri*
47 *Brunnera macrophylla*
48 *Aruncus dioicus*
49 *Rodgersia podophylla*
50 *Tiarella cordifolia*

Group 5: background
   shrubs and large plants
1 *Salix* × *sepulcralis* var. *chrysocoma*
2 *Pseudosasa japonica*
3 *Hydrangea paniculata* or
   H. macrophylla lace-cap varieties
5 *Weigela* 'Looymansii Aurea'
6 *Angelica archangelica*
7 *Salix alba* var. *sericea*
8 *Fargesia nitida*

SHADY DAMP BED (2)

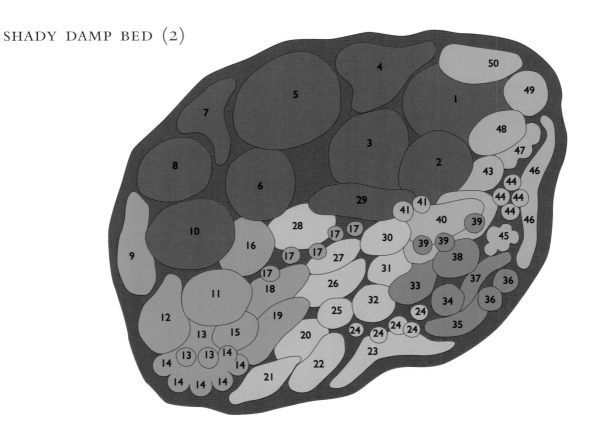

Group 1
9 *Epimedium × versicolor*
   'Sulphureum'
11 *Aconitum carmichaelii* 'Arendsii'
12 *Phlox paniculata*
13 *Milium effusum* 'Aureum'
14 *Primula vulgaris* 'Lilacina Plena'
15 *Paeonia mlokosewitschii*
16 *Hosta sieboldiana*
17 *Lilium speciosum*
18 *Anemone tomentosa*
19 *Geranium macrorrhizum*
   'Variegatum'

Group 2
20 *Cardamine pentaphylla*
21 *Blechnum penna-marina*
22 *Hosta lancifolia*
23 *Phlox stolonifera*
24 *Erythronium* 'Pagoda'
25 *Digitalis ferruginea*
26 *Fuchsia magellanica* 'Versicolor'
27 *Geranium phaeum*
28 *Euphorbia sikkimensis*

Group 3
30 *Gillenia trifoliata*
31 *Tricyrtis formosana*
32 *Brunnera macrophylla* 'Langtrees'
33 *Trillium grandiflorum*
34 *Lathyrus vernus* 'Alboroseus'
35 *Hepatica nobilis*
36 *Hosta fortunei* var. *albopicta* f. *aurea*
37 *Uvularia grandiflora*
38 *Euphorbia amygdaloides* 'Purpurea'
39 *Meconopsis betonicifolia*

Group 4
40 *Kirengeshoma palmata*
50 *Thalictrum delavayi*
51 *Tiarella cordifolia*
52 *Aconitum lycoctonum*
53 *Disporum sessile* 'Variegatum'
54 *Saxifraga fortunei* 'Rubrifolia'
55 *Ajuga reptans*
56 *Tellima grandiflora* Rubra Group
57 *Helleborus × hybridus*
58 *Polystichum munitum*
59 *Eomecon chionantha*

Group 5: background trees,
   shrubs and large plants
1 *Acer negundo* 'Elegans'
2 *Rheum palmatum* –
   for grand effect
3 *Eucryphia × nymansensis*
   'Nymansay'
4 *Trachystemon orientalis* –
   for ground-cover
5 *Liquidambar styraciflua*
6 *Mahonia japonica*
7 *Geranium endressii* –
   for ground-cover
8 *Ilex × altaclarensis* 'Camelliifolia'
9 *Physocarpus opulifolius* 'Luteus'
10 *Pleioblastus auricomus*

10 | Alphabetical List of Plants

Where ample moisture exists or can be contrived there need scarcely be a dull week from early spring until late autumn, as new growth and fresh flowers can be relied on without the interruption of damaging droughts. The following are the plants I grow and have come to know in my own garden around the ponds and in areas of retentive or spring-fed soil. I include some bog-loving plants, but the majority can be grown in any good moisture-retentive soil in areas where summer rainfall is adequate. While many, or most of them, do not need, and would not thrive in, really wet conditions, neither will any of them tolerate drought during the growing period. They require soil that does not dry out and, in some cases, a sheltered environment, providing some shade from direct hot sunlight and shelter from wind, which can cause immediate wilting of large soft foliage, even though there be ample moisture underfoot. The list includes some plants that I describe in my *Woodland Garden* which will thrive more easily in a damper climate with retentive soil. It is in no way intended to be a comprehensive list of all the good garden plants which one could grow given retentive soil and adequate rainfall. There are bound to be favourite plants missing.

A word of warning when planting aquatics. It is especially important in an ideal growing medium like tepid water *not* to plant things which will rapidly multiply so that the water vanishes. A frightening little surface smotherer is *Azolla filiculoides* (syn. *A. caroliniana*), Fairy Moss, looking like pink duckweed. It is the prettiest thing

I have seen these plants, *Valeriana officinalis* and *Deschampsia cespitosa* 'Goldschleier', growing wild in damp situations in the Swiss mountains. They add grace to a void in the wild garden, but here, isolated on the side of a mown-grass dam, they add elegance and style, looking decorative for weeks. The *Valeriana* needs deadheading before too many self-sown seedlings become troublesome.

for an indoor pool or aquarium, or perhaps a tiny outdoor pond where you can control it. But let one minute piece dangle its little roots below the surface of a large stretch of water and you will find it covering the entire surface in one season. Not only is this unattractive, it is dangerous. I have seen large stretches of the wide land-draining ditches in Holland covered with it, where perhaps a tiny piece has been flung away attached possibly to some discarded plant. It is always wise to examine carefully aquatics bought in from a nursery, where they may keep this charming menace for its proper use – in small, controlled tanks. A really hard winter may dispose of it. But I would not trust that some small piece does not survive, lurking in the frost-free muddy bottom of the pond, to float to the surface in spring.

Another charming invader that I came to rue the day I chose to plant it was *Villarsia* or *Limnanthemum peltatum* or, more correctly, *Nymphoides peltata*. A British native, the leaves make one think it is a miniature water-lily. Small, round and slightly mottled brown, they float up and lie flat on the surface, while the bright yellow flowers are pushed up 5 or 7.5 cm/2 or 3 in above the level of the water, shaped rather like convolvulus. Very pretty. But they have roots like bootlaces which interlace in the mud in shallow water, and before you know where you are the water is covered. A scattering of leaves on water is delightful, a carpet is a bore. But I have now planted it in a pond that quickly drops to 3m/9ft deep, and so far it is restricted to the shallow edge. One has to find out the most favourable depths in which to plant all water plants. Some will only stand a few centimetres or inches, others a metre or several feet.

Today there is a bewildering number of Daylilies, *Hemerocallis* hybrids, from palest cream, through shades of yellow, pink, scarlet and crimson to wine-purple, and in all sizes too. Here is *H.* 'Golden Chimes', which retains all the grace and lightness of its wild parents.

ACHILLEA. ASTERACEAE. Achilleas thrive in an open, sunny site in retentive soil. They perform best if lifted in spring every second year and young pieces are replanted in refreshed soil. Most of the following will have a second flowering if cut down after their first flush.

A. ageratum '**W. B. Childs**' is said to be of Swiss origin. In spring it forms neat, tidy, non-running clumps of fresh green finely cut leaves. By June it is a white bouquet swaying elegantly on the edge of a border. Each wide lace-like head is made of many flowers held in a flat loose cluster, poised on thin stalks, furnished with finely fretted leaves. 75cm/2½ft. Z3–8

A. chrysocoma '**Grandiflora**' is an imposing plant for the back of a large border, or in a wild garden. Tall stems, clothed from top to toe in handsome pale green divided leaves, are topped in midsummer with large domed heads of cream flowers. Z6–10

A. **Galaxy hybrids.** From parents *A. millefolium* and *A.* 'Taygetea' have come many named varieties, mostly from German horticulturists. They include *A.* 'Feuerland', which opens cherry-red fading to burnt orange, *A.* 'Inca Gold', terractotta orange fading to buff, while *A.* 'Lachsschönheit' opens coral-red and fades to soft peach. There are more! Z4–8

A. ptarmica is from the water-meadows of Eurasia. The Pearl Group, a garden variety, is also good for picking, and lasts well in the garden. Pure white, double, button-shaped flowers on 60cm/2ft branching stems in mid summer. It is invasive, but will grow in any good retentive border soil. Z4–9

ACONITUM. RANUNCULACEAE. Monkshood or Wolf's Bane. The flower shape strongly resembles a monk's cowled hood, but the tuberous roots are deadly poisonous if eaten. It does no harm to divide the crowded clumps occasionally, to encourage the production of strong flower stems.

A. × *commarum* '**Bicolor**'. A number of named garden plants shelter under this name, probably hybrids between *A. napellus* and *A. variegatum. A. napellus* (Eurasia) covers a number of allied species, including *A. napellus* itself, with finely cut leaves and almost unbranched spikes. Z4–8

A. variegatum (Eastern Alps and Central Europe) has tall branching spikes and large flowers. Both are found in partially shaded damp places. Hybrids include 'Blue Sceptre' and 'Bressingham Spire', with stiff straight spires of almost 1m/3ft carrying deep violet-blue flowers in July-August. 'Spark's Variety' grows tall, 1.5m/5ft, with open branching heads carrying darkest violet-blue flowers. Z4–8

A. carmichaelii is found in stands of large herbs on the borders of damp meadows and woods with *Filipendula, Veratrum* and huge umbellifers in Kamchatka and Amuria. *A. c.* 'Arendsii' is a fine form, superb in late September and October with large shadowed-blue flowers on 1.5m/5ft stems. Close inspection shows kinship with the buttercup family. If you lift the top petal, which looks like a hooded cowl, you will find it is sheltering the stigma while the rest of the petals form the familiar innocent face of the buttercup surrounding the central boss. Z4–8

A. lycoctonum subsp. *vulparia* is from woods and damp shady places in the mountains of Europe and north Asia to China. Tall, about 1.5m/5ft, the slender branching stems carry yellowish-green flowers, not unlike little delphiniums. It flowers for weeks in late summer. I have seen it massed in a grassy gulley in the Pyrenees, with the mauvy-rose fluffy heads of *Thalictrum aquilegiifolium.* Z4–8

A. '**Ivorine**' grows in rich meadows and on forest margins of north Europe from Norway to Russia. It is an exquisite plant for cool conditions with branching stems closely set with ivory-white hooded flowers. 75cm/2½ft. Z5–8

ACORUS. ARACEAE. The 'Sweet Flag' from east Asia and eastern North America; naturalized in Europe.

A. calamus grows in bog or shallow water, with long, narrow blade-like leaves attached to rhizomes, very like an Iris. The roots and leaves are spicily scented, valued when earth floors were strewn with sweet-scented rushes. They have been used medicinally and for their perfume and restorative qualities. Dried they are still used as flavouring, among other things in toothpaste, gargles and gin. Z4–10

A. c. '**Argenteostriatus**' makes a striking water-side plant: the handsome sword-like leaves are boldly variegated green and ivory-white, with rose-pink bases in spring. 1–1.2m/3–4ft. Z4–10

A. gramineus grows in wet places round ponds and along streams from India to China and Japan. It is much smaller and makes neat grass-like tufts, ideally suited for small ponds, sink gardens if kept moist, or even an aquarium. *A.g.* 'Variegatus' has leaves brightly variegated cream and green. 13cm/5in. Z5–10

ACTAEA. RANUNCULACEAE. The following plants we used to call *Cimicifuga,* but are now classed as *Actaea.* In my garden they are choosy, thriving only in areas of moist shade. The leaves, especially in full sun, will scorch. When well-suited, they are among the most elegant and beautiful of late summer–autumn plants.

A. matsumurae '**Elstead**' has finely divided dark green leaves. In September tall thin stems stained purple divide and carry spires of purplish-brown buds opening pure white flowers which are fixed close to the stem with tiny pink stalks giving just that touch of warmth which is missing in the icy purity of *A. m.* 'White Pearl'. 1.2m/4ft. Z4–8

A. m. '**White Pearl**'. Above a base of finely cut, light green leaves are held stiffly branching stems. In October each wand is set with seed-pearl buds of ivory tinted palest green. These burst open to form an elegant pure white bottle-brush carried on arching stems. The pale green seed pods, which form quickly once the flowers have gone, are attractive too. 1.2m/4ft. Z4–8

A. podocarpa. From the woods of eastern North America. One of the first to flower with broad cut leaves, rather like the Japanese Anemone, but lighter green. Tall stiff stems carry tapering spires of brown buds which open pale cream fluffy flowers in August. 1.5m/5ft. Z4–8

A. simplex 'Prichard's Giant'. Every part, except the foaming spire of flower, is deeply stained with dark purple. The upper surface of the large, handsome, divided leaves, the 2m/6ft column of slender branching stems and the round close-set buds all make a dramatic contrast to the narrow bottle-brushes of sweetly scented fluffy white flowers. This is a noble plant, flowering in late August–September. Z4–8

The following actaeas have poisonous berries, hence the common name Baneberry:

A. pachypoda. White Baneberry. From the forests of north-east America, this is a most extraordinary and beautiful plant when well grown. Elegant clumps of stiff slender stems are furnished with light green divided leaves. Spires of fluffy white flowers become spikes of pea-sized white berries in late summer. Each is fastened to the main stem by short stalks, which are thick and crimson-red. On the side opposite to the stem each white berry has a conspicuous black dot. 60–100cm/2–3ft. Z4–9

A. rubra. From the woods of north-east America, this makes far better plants and berries if grown in part shade, when it is the most showy *Actaea*, with large clusters of smallish berries. They are attractive in July when jade-green, and gradually turn to gleaming scarlet, remaining handsome for weeks into early autumn. 75cm/2½ft. Z4–8

A. spicata. The British and European species, from cool conifer forests, has clusters of small black berries at the tip of 45cm/18in leafy stems. Z3–8

ADONIS. RANUNCULACEAE. Choice plants for the early spring garden, with very superior buttercup-like flowers. Likes retentive soil in sun.

A. amurensis, from Manchuria and Amuria to Japan. Z4–7

A. 'Fukujukai'. The bent necks of this flower can be seen emerging in mild weather early in the New Year. The finely cut foliage and stems are purplish-brown at first but are green by the time the flower has opened its glistening yellow cup during February-March. 25cm/10in.

A. multiflora. 'Sandanzaki' (syn. *A. amurensis* 'Pleniflora'), among nests of ferny foliage crouch double, shining flowers with green centres. 15–25cm/6–10in.

A. vernalis. Found in the meadow steppes of Russia, with cowslips, the shining single saucer-like flowers are ruffed with fretted leaves. 23–30cm/9–12in. Z4–7

AJUGA. LAMIACEAE. Bugle. Sometimes classed as a rampant weed when well-suited among the wrong companions, it needs damp soil to show its best. The dark-leaved forms colour best in an open situation. All make good carpeters.

A. pyramidalis. From mountain meadows and open woods in central Europe to the Altai and China. It does not run invasively but makes dense, slowly spreading clumps of dark green smooth leaves. Spikes of small vivid gentian-blue flowers are held in whorls of navy-blue bracts, looking like little pagodas in spring. 15cm/6in. Z6–10

A. reptans. Found in water-meadows, damp spots in woods (mostly oak) in Europe and west Asia. All Z4–10

A. r. 'Atropurpurea' makes rosettes and runners of shining beetroot-coloured leaves with short spikes of blue flowers in spring. 13cm/5in. ·

A. r. 'Burgundy Glow'. The beautiful foliage is suffused rose and magenta, edged with cream. The light blue spikes of flowers are a bonus. 10cm/4in.

A. r. 'Catlin's Giant'. Tall stems bear 15cm/6in long spikes of rich blue flowers with purplish-brown calyces. After flowering new rosettes of large

glossy leaves assume this same dark hue. 30cm/1ft.

A. r. 'Multicolor' bronze foliage curiously splashed with pink and cream; only looks good when well suited in rich leaf-mould soil in semi-shade. 10cm/4in.

A. r. 'Variegata'. The least strong-growing, best in shade or on north-facing borders. Grey-green leaves are boldly edged with cream. 5cm/2in.

ALCHEMILLA. ROSACEAE. Found in France, Switzerland and a few spots in Scotland. Both *A. conjuncta* and *A. erythropoda* will grow in full sun if the soil remains damp. 15cm/6in.

A. conjuncta is closely related to *A. alpina*. It differs in that the individual leaflets, which compose the little parasol-shaped leaves, appear to be seamed half-way to the centre. The top side of each leaf is smooth dark green, the back appears to be lined with shimmering silk which just shows as a silver edge. Both leaves and small sprays of tiny green flowers are valued by flower arrangers, particularly for pressed flower pictures. In the garden the plant makes a neat low cushion, valued for its attractive foliage. Z5–9

A. erythropoda. My plant was discovered in a piece of mountain turf brought home from Turkey by J. R. Marr. Small scallop-shell leaves of soft blue-green are set off by sprays of tiny lime-green stars which turn coral-red as they age; a pretty foliage plant by the edge of a cool walk. Z4–9

A. mollis. Lady's Mantle is found in east European mountain meadows, making a far larger plant than the other two. The downy, rounded leaves may be 10–13cm/4–5in across, the radiating veins prolonged into gentle scallops whose fine serrated edges exude pearls of moisture on still humid mornings. All June and into July long sprays of frothy lime-green stars cool the wealth of colour that comes with mid summer. The flower stems are 46–60cm/1½–2ft. Z4–8

ALLIUM ursinum. ALLIACEAE. Ramsons. Comes from the moist woods of temperate Europe and far into Asia, often in wide drifts. This wild onion sends up flat heads of white, starry flowers, about 25cm/10in high, above two broad, shiny leaves, rather like those of Lily-of-the-Valley. As they seed and multiply readily, they soon form a carpet, and can be a nuisance in the garden, but are attractive in open woodland.

AMSONIA tabernaemontana. *APOCYNACEAE.* From north-east America. Will grow in half shade, or in full sun in moist soil. The charm of this plant lies in the curious colour of its flowers. At the top of many slender wands, set with narrow, willow-like leaves, sit dark-stemmed clusters of thin green and dark-blue pointed buds which open small slate-blue stars. The effect of greenish-blue in these modest heads is appealing. They flower from June to early July. 60cm/2ft. Z4–9

ANAPHALIS. *ASTERACEAE.* It comes as a surprise to learn that these grey-leaved plants come from damp places, but by experience I have found that they suffer where true drought lovers, like artemisias, flourish. They need a retentive soil to keep their foliage healthy until late summer when they produce their display of tiny white everlasting daisies. All these *Anaphalis* must be picked fresh for drying before the centres have browned. When dried they are lovely, massed alone, or used as filling material among other 'drieds'. *A. margaritacea* var. *yedoensis,* is a plant of warmer climates. I am familiar with the name *Anaphalis yedoensis,* which belongs to the form from Japan, where it is found in sunny places along rivers. Thin branched white-felted stems stand 75cm–1m/ 2½–3ft, bearing broad oval dark grey leaves with pale backs and white edges, topped with loose clusters of small chalk-white everlasting daisies. Stripped of leaves, hung upside down to dry they make excellent 'drieds'. *Anaphalis margaritacea*, in its other varieties from eastern North America and north-east Asia, is similar in habit with narrower green leaves. They both flower from August to October. Z3–8 *A. triplinervis* is found by rocky stream-sides in the Himalayas, sometimes with

mats of pink *Persicaria affinis.* Ideal for the edge of the border, it makes low, neat mounds of very white, felted leaves which are buried beneath white sprays of crisp white daisies, slightly larger than those of *A. m.* var. *yedoensis.* Flowers July to October. 30cm/1ft. Z4–9 *A. t.* **'Sommerschnee'** is a slightly smaller selection, which flowers a little earlier. 25cm/10in. Z4–9

ANEMONE. *RANUNCULACEAE.* There are many anemones, spring and autumn flowering, for dry and damp soils. I shall consider first the largest and stateliest, those known as Japanese anemones. This title includes some species and many cultivars, all providing long displays throughout late summer and early autumn. They thrive in well-worked garden soil, in sun or part shade, making colonising clumps when ideally suited. In light soil they must have sufficient moisture throughout the growing season. The following are the species from which the garden hybrids have been developed. *A. hupehensis.* This name is generally accepted as covering several varieties of Japanese anemone as well as the type. The type is a rare species from central and west China, with rounded pink petals, darker on the reverse; the leaves are divided into three deeply toothed leaflets, producing flowers in late summer. 60cm/2ft. Z5–9

Anemone × hybrida 'Honorine Jobert'

A. h. var. *japonica,* naturalized in Japan from China for hundreds of years. It differs from *A. hupehensis* in having many narrow, slightly quilled petals of uniform, soft magenta-pink. 60cm/2ft. Z5–9 *A. × hybrida.* I take refuge under this title with the many beautiful cultivars which have been produced from among these species. Some are larger, paler in colour, or deeper. Some are double. Personally I prefer the single forms with perfectly formed round cupped petals. *A. × h.* **'Honorine Jobert'** is the unsurpassed old-fashioned white, flowering for weeks in the autumn, elegant on tall stems up to 1.5m/5ft. There is a rose-pink form equally well-shaped. For smaller gardens or border edges there are dwarfer forms, including *A. × h.* 'September Charm'. 45cm/18in. Z5–8 *A. tomentosa.* The great plant collector, E. H. Wilson, mentions *A. vitifolia* as growing with *Artemisia lactiflora, Astilbe rivularis, Aruncus* and others in openings among woods in west Sichuan. This appears to be *A. tomentosa.* It is extremely vigorous, producing sheaves of shallow saucers, pale pink inside, with deeper reverse, and flowering earlier than garden hybrids. 1.2m/4ft. Z5–9 *A. vitifolia.* From the Himalayas. Although this name is usually applied to *A. tomentosa,* this rare plant is smaller and more compact. The flowers are usually white. 60cm/2ft. The following anemones are distinct from the Japanese anemones listed above. *A. narcissiflora* From damp mountain meadow slopes to the lowland Arctic meadows of Europe, to the Himalayas and Japan, and North America. The stems of this *Anemone* rise to a height of 20–60cm/8in–2ft, according to where it grows, from a clump of much-cut leaves. At the top, each bears a cluster of white flowers, usually with rosy backs, above a green ruff of leaves. Z5–8 *A. nemorosa.* Wood Anemone, of moist forests of Europe and north-west Asia. A very closely related plant is found in North America. They grow almost anywhere, preferably in part shade under trees or shrubs, in light or heavy soil but

Anemone nemorosa 'Royal Blue'

are best left undisturbed to colonize the floor of shrubbery or wood. There are several good named cultivars, which include 'Allenii', 'Blue Bonnet' and 'Robinsoniana'. They open to the sun large, shallow saucers of breathtaking blue, centred with yellow stamens, exquisite among the dark purple leaves of *Viola riviniana* Purpurea Group. 15cm/6in. Z4–8

A. ranunculoides. From damp open woods of Europe to the Caucasus. Has smaller flowers but creates a pretty effect with yellow pointed starry petals. 10cm/4in. There are paler versions, and a double form. All the wood anemones disappear by mid summer. Z4–8

A. rivularis. From the damp, rocky sub-alpine meadows of the Himalayas to the mountains of west China; a close relative of *A. narcissiflora.* The white petals are backed with metallic-blue, which is repeated in the blue anthers. 60cm/2ft. Z6–8

ANEMONELLA thalictroides. RANUNCULACEAE. The Rue Anemone is a delicate, Anemone-like little wood-lander, 15cm/6in, with heads of white or pale pink flowers in spring. I have yet to obtain it. Z4–8

ANEMONOPSIS macrophylla. RANUNCULACEAE. From mountain woods in central Japan only, and rare even there. This beautiful plant has leaves twice cut into threes, and its stems grow some

60–75cm/2–2½ft tall. They bear open heads of nodding, waxy flowers like those of an Anemone, purple outside and lilac within. It needs humus rich soil in a cool climate. Z5–8

ANGELICA archangelica. APIACEAE. From damp bushland of north and Arctic Europe and Greenland. A handsome Cow Parsley, whose smooth and tender stems are boiled and candied to make cake decorations. It needs deep moist soil to produce a large leafy plant with branching stems holding several large, domed heads of light green flowers. It looks very statuesque in the bog garden, overtopping most things. The seed heads should be removed before they have seeded into everything. Not a perennial, it may take two or three years to flower, seed and die. 1.8m/6ft. Z4–9

A. gigas is an intriguing Korean biennial that was sent to me from the USA. It produces domed, umbellifer flowerheads that are astonishingly beetroot-red. Save the seed for replacements. Z6–9

APONOGETON distachyos. APONOGETONACEAE. Water Hawthorn or Cape Pond Weed, from South Africa, is a very attractive aquatic. From a tuberous rootstock rise many green strap-shaped leaves which lie on the surface of the water creating a round, tray-like shape supporting a long succession of short spikes of tightly packed, sweet-smelling white flowers with jet-black anthers. It will grow in a few centimetres/inches of water or up to a depth of 1m/3ft. Z5–9

AQUILEGIA. RANUNCULACEAE. There are multitudes of aquilegias, both species and hybrids. Some enjoy sun, others prefer cool shade; most relish well-drained but not dried-out soil.

A. alpina. From the Alps and north Italian mountains, in rocky bushy places. Deep blue, sometimes blue and white. 60–100cm/2–3ft. Z4–7.

A. canadensis. From the north-eastern United States and Canada in rocky woods, this plant is similarly coloured

to *A. formosa* var. *truncata* but smaller, and with a larger central yellow bell of petals. 60cm/2ft. Z2–9

A. chrysantha. From the open woods of the southern Rockies. All soft yellow with long spurs, it is one of the species from which the long-spurred hybrids were raised, and is a vigorous plant, growing up to 90cm/3ft high. Z4–9

A. coerulea. From grassy openings in spruce woods and in aspen copses of the central Rocky Mountains. Blue and white flowers, long-spurred. 30–38cm/12–15in. Needs sheltered position, in sun or part shade. Z4–9

A. flabellata var. *pumila.* From alpine rocky turfs of north Japan, north Korea and Sakhalin. Z4–9

A. f. var. *pumila* f. *alba* has thick petalled creamy-white flowers. 25cm/10in. Z4–9

A. formosa var. *truncata* grows in the shade or part shade of wood openings in the Californian mountains and the Rockies south from Alaska. One of the daintiest, with multitudes of nodding flowers, brilliant scarlet and yellow on much-branched stems. The pistil and stamens extend well below the pointed scarlet sepals giving a sharp dart-like effect as the long spurs end in a very short circle of petals. May-August. 75cm–1m/ 30–40in. Z4–8

A. longissima, from partially shady rocky slopes on the last spur of the Rockies in west Texas. The flowers are almost white, with very long spurs. July-October. 75cm/2½ft. Z6–9

A. **Hybrid strains.** The long-spurred garden aquilegias are hybrids of the western American species. It is difficult to keep a particular strain pure from seed, as they cross very freely, but the progeny are nearly all beautiful. A few named hybrids have been inbred that are more reliably true from seed, for example the Star Series and the McKana Group.

A. vulgaris. Found in woods and thickets in the Alps, Europe, Siberia and the Himalayas. These crosses include many shades of blue, rich plum, soft pink and white. The blue-green foliage is as hand-

Aponogeton distachyos

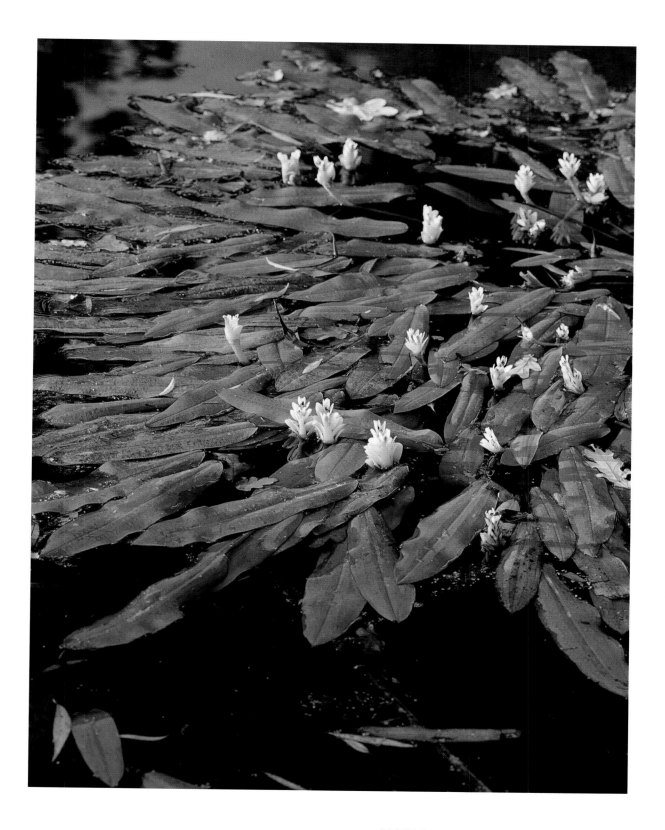

some as the flowers, especially late in the year when tinted with shades of purple. Excellent in shade or semi-shade, to follow spring bulbs. May-June. 75cm/2½ft. Z5–9

ARISAEMA. ARACEAE. Members of the *Arum* family, valued for foliage, flowers and berries. Most of them need plenty of humus in semi-shaded retentive soil.
A. candidissimum. From rocky slopes and cliff ledges in west China. The great plant collector, G. Forrest, first found it on the sides of the upper Yangtze gorge in Yunnan. One of the latest plants to appear through the soil. Not until June do the bare pink stems appear, opening into the narrow spathe which is white-veined and shadowed with pink and green on the outside, pink and white candy striped inside. The pointed tip overhangs the white spadix, sheltering it from the rain. Neatly wrapped round the base of the stem is a single leaf which unfolds surprisingly large, three-lobed, like a great clover leaf. A mound of them is very handsome, especially in autumn when they turn the colour of chamois leather. This plant will grow in an open situation, provided it is planted in good retentive soil, but is best sheltered from wind. Flowers 15cm/6in; leaves 8–23cm/3–9in long and wide. Z7–9
A. consanguineum. Found in moist wood openings and among bushes, from the Himalayas to the west and central Chinese mountains. Like a very elegant umbrella, supported on 45cm/18in long slender stems mottled green and brown. The green hooded flower, striped with brown, extends a long thin brown tail from the tip of the spathe to hang down in front. Does better in moist and warm gardens. Z6–10
A. tortuosum from woodland slopes of the lower Himalayas, has survived recent mild winters. It startles the unwary when they come face to face with its pale hooded flower standing about 1m/3ft tall above lower plantings. From a large underground tuber there rises a thick purple-stained stem; halfway up two pedate leaves appear, while above them is

Arisaema tortuosum

poised a snake-like hooded head, a narrow green spathe, and from the tip of the curved lid flickers the long, thin brown tail of the spadix. There are many of these strangely fascinating plants to be found; they need part-shade and deep retentive soil, well enriched. Z6–10
A. triphyllum. Jack in the Pulpit. From rich woods in the eastern United States north to Nova Scotia. For cool shady places. The markings on the spathe vary in intensity. Basically green, the stripes inside are light or dark purplish-brown, lit with palest green. Intensifying the colour is the dark spadix protected beneath the overhanging spathe tip. Orange-red berries seed themselves in favourable sites. June-July. 30cm/1ft. Z4–9

ARISARUM proboscideum. ARACEAE. From shady moist slopes in the Apennines. The Mouse-tailed Arum is well named: tiny tubers increase readily beneath humus-rich soil, sending up dense clusters of small shining green leaves. Hidden among them are tiny flowers, white inside with brown backs, the spathe tips extended into long thin tails which poke out among the leaves as though tiny mice had dived in, head first, to hide. Best in shade, near the edge of a path where you can stoop to see them. May. 10cm/4in. Z6–10

ARNICA montana. ASTERACEAE. From alpine and subalpine turf in the

mountains of central Europe and northern Asia, this plant produces handsome orange daisy flowers, long petalled and strangely scented. A distillation produces Tincture of Arnica, used to soothe bruises. June. 30cm/1ft. Z6–9

ARTEMISIA lactiflora. ASTERACEAE. Grows in moist meadows and forest clearings in the mountains of western China, often with tall anemones, *Aruncus, Astilbe rivularis* and others. It is the odd man out in a family, many of whom are adapted to drought conditions. Tall stems up to 1.5m/5ft carry jagged green leaves topped with large loose heads of small creamy-white flowers, effective among the autumn aconites or Japanese anemones. Z4–9

ARUNCUS dioicus. ROSACEAE. Goat's Beard. Grows in mountain woods and along shady stream-sides from central Europe to China and Japan; also in North America. Makes a superb garden plant from the moment its elegant sprays of light green pinnate leaves emerge in spring. I like it best just as the flowers are opening. Long tapering spires of tiny green buds become cream seed pearls, finally bursting into a plume of creamy frothy blossom towards the end of June. Male plants make superior flowers, but females produce graceful chestnut-brown seed heads. 1.5–2m/5–6ft. Z3–8
A. d. 'Kneiffii'. Flowers similar to *A. dioicus* but daintier, as is the whole

Aruncus dioicus

plant. The leaves look as though they have been eaten to the veins by some creature but perversely (perhaps because it is the natural state) these thread-like segments appear delicately attractive. Flowers slightly later. 60–75cm/2–2½ft. Z3–8

ASARUM. ARISTOLOCHIACEAE. Mostly hardy plants for shady places in leaf-mould soil, grown primarily for their foliage.
A. caudatum. Grows in deep conifer woods, often along streams, in the coastal mountains from central California to British Columbia. The leaves are some-what heart-shaped and matt green, while curious reddish-brown flowers with three tail-like tips lie flat on the ground, hidden among the leaves. 25cm/10in. Z6–9
A. europaeum. Covers the floor of central European, Scandinavian, Russian and west Siberian woods, as ivy does in British woods. Round kidney-shaped leaves of rich glossy green on slowly creeping surface shoots eventually make almost evergreen carpets. Dull brown flowers crouch unseen except by fertilizing flies and beetles. 13cm/5in. Z4–9

ASTER. ASTERACEAE. An enormous genus of daisy-like flowers, including many large and small perennial plants, including alpines. Michaelmas Daisies are among the large perennials. Most will only look their best in good deep soil with adequate moisture throughout the growing season. Some of the old-fashioned hybrids remain the healthiest, less prone to disease, with less floppy stems. Garden hybrids have been evolved from among the following species:
A. amellus. From open woods and rocky grasslands of central Europe to Asia Minor and the northern meadow-like steppes of Russia. The wild form is scarcely known, but many named selected forms exist, very varied in quality. The general habit is low growing with rough leaves and clusters of large flowers in many shades from lavender to violet, including various pinks. Some stand well, others flop untidily. A familiar named variety is 'King George'. It is

also one of the parents of the hybrid *A. × frikartii* 'Mönch'. 60cm/2ft. Z3–9
A. divaricatus found in open woodlands and thickets. Standing drier conditions than many other asters, this plant comes from southern Canada and the eastern United States. It has taken me some time and several plantings to appreciate this, one of the first Michaelmas Daisy-like plants to flower. It produces quantities of very thin, rather floppy branching stems which are almost black and make good contrast with clouds of tiny, white star-like flowers. But initially the flowers look just too small to be effective. However, gradually they expand a little more, and as they age they flush lilac-mauve, starting at their pointed tips until they are suffused to their central darkened hearts. I learnt from Gertrude Jekyll to group them among bergenias which they soften with pretty disarray, from mid August and into September. 60cm/2ft. Z4–9
A. ericoides. This Aster grows in rich soil in the eastern United States and Canada, and is also common in the prairies. There are many varieties, with almost no disadvantages. They make compact clumps of fine wiry stems covered with tiny leaves, branching into airy heads smothered with tiny starry flowers. They rarely need staking, and are seldom affected by disease. They come both short- and tall-flowering, late into the autumn. 90–120cm/3–4ft. Z3–9
A. e. f. prostratus **'Snow Flurry'.** I originally brought this home many years ago after a lecture tour of the eastern USA. Although I sent plants back for identification, no one could source it. Subsequently, by a consensus of opinion, it became 'Snow Flurry', since it produces ground-hugging stems, much-branched, to form a low sprawling cushion, smothered in autumn with tiny white daisies, resembling a snow drift. Z3–9
A. × frikartii **'Mönch'.** Each individual stem (90cm/3ft) produces seven or eight side branches starting from the base, all carrying further branching heads of flowers. An established clump will send up many such stems resulting in a wide-

Aster × frikartii 'Mönch'

spreading elegant bouquet of flowers which lasts for months (August–October), somehow never looking untidy with dead flowers. Individual flowers are 6cm/2½in across, warm lavender-blue with yellowish-green centres. Absolutely the best Michaelmas Daisy for long display and sheer beauty: does not need staking, and is not affected by mildew. Deserves the best soil and position in the garden. Z5–9
A. lateriflorus is found in damp or dry and rich meadows and prairies of the eastern and central United States and Canada.
A. l. **'Horizontalis'** is so stiffly twiggy it appears almost like a small shrub, covered all summer with small dark green leaves, the whole smothered by October with tiny starry flowers, silver-lilac petals centred with large bosses of clover-pink stamens. Good near autumn-flowering colchicums. 60cm/2ft. Z4–9
A. novae-angliae. From damp sunny meadows and along swamp edges in the north-eastern and north-central United States and Canada. This is the hairy-leaved parent of many garden hybrids, needing sunlight to open its incurved petals, but producing healthy disease-free offspring with tall stiff sturdy stems, up to 6ft/2m. The type has mauve flowers, but good clear pink shades include 'Harrington's Pink'. 'Andenken an Alma Pötschke' is compact and low growing, 75cm/2½ft, with startling cherry-pink flowers. Z4–9

A. novi-belgii. From swampy places where it is frequent near the Atlantic from Newfoundland to Georgia. Smooth green leaves on slender elegant stems (1.2m/4ft) are topped with large pyramidal sprays of cool blue flowers. Self-sown seedlings vary; some are rather wishy-washy. Modern named varieties tend to have developed the flower at the expense of the plant – too large double flowers proving overweighty for the stems which have to be supported. But the colours are often lovely, from white through shades of pink to lavenders and blue. Among the trouble-free old varieties are 'Climax', 1.5–2m/5–6ft with single mid-blue flowers, and 'Blue Gown' which flowers a little later. Z4–9

A. pilosus **var. demotus**. Growing in moist meadows in the eastern USA and Canada. It is very similar to *A. ericoides* but although larger overall the flowers and leaves are even smaller, large sprays of tiny white flowers lasting until the frosts. 1.25m/4ft. Z5–9

There are many different alpine asters. I select one of the best for general purposes, ideal to edge a border:

A. tongolensis from alpine grasslands of the south-west Chinese mountains. Tufts of hairy leaves produce many erect stems 23cm/9in, each bearing a solitary blue daisy flower. *A. t.* 'Napsbury' has large blue flowers lit with warm orange centres. Z5–8

ASTILBE. *SAXIFRAGACEAE*. Astilbes must have rich garden soil which remains moist (not waterlogged). Most look well and do better in partial shade. The species provides dwarfs as well as tall plants, so there is great choice among the many hybrids, for size as well as shades. Their rusty-brown seed heads in late summer and autumn are almost as effective as their tapering panicles of tiny flowers. The following are the few species I grow:

A. chinensis. From moist rocky slopes among woods in the northern Chinese mountains, north to Amuria, Manchuria and Korea. Z4–8

A. c. **var. davidii**. Found in moist, shady places in Sichuan with *Geranium*

napuligerum, Ligularia dentata, Adenophora, etc. It is similar to *A. chinensis* var. *taquetii*, but has slimmer spires of flower. Z4–8

A. c. **var. pumila** is a selected garden form, ideal for moist edges. Narrow branched spikes of densely set, rose flowers with blue anthers produce a mauve-pink effect. I like the narrow, stiffly upright silhouettes, which continue until winter as buff seed heads. Carpets of broadly spreading foliage make useful ground-cover. 38–45cm/15–18in. Z4–8

A. c. **var. taquetii**. From eastern China. *A. c.* var *t.* 'Superba' is the garden form. It flowers when other astilbes have finished. This *Astilbe*, and *A. chinensis* var. *davidii*, can do with less moisture (but not drought) and will take more sun than the others, but they will also flower and look superb in partial shade.

A. c. var. *t.* 'Superba' has smallish crinkled leaves tinged with bronze. The flower head, supported on a dark mahogany stem, held well above the leaves, elongates into a dense compound spire made up of thousands of deep mauve fluffy flowers. 1.2m/4ft. Z4–8

A. rivularis. Growing in lush valley meadows and wood edges from the Himalayas to the west Chinese mountains, this giant *Astilbe* is for the wild garden, or for large-scale water-side planting (not in the bog). Great stems of broad divided leaves, glossy above, bristly beneath, are so heavily veined they

produce a quilted effect. In August it is overtopped with huge arching plumes of small greenish-white flowers which last long as nut-brown seed heads. Underground shoots could be a nuisance in a restricted area. 1.8m/6ft. Z6–8

Hybrids

A. **× arendsii**. This group name, commemorating Georg Arends of Ronsdorf, Germany, covers many garden hybrids raised since 1907 between four species. These are the Chinese *A. chinensis* var. *davidii*, and three Japanese species, *A. astilboides, A. japonica* and *A. thunbergii*. Through these four, the differing characteristics have been introduced. Some, especially the dark red-flowered varieties, have beautiful, translucent, mahogany-tinted foliage which adds colour to the garden immediately it appears, remaining dark-tinted all summer. The flower colours range from white, through shell-pink, rose-pink and salmon to red and magenta. The shapes of the spires vary as well – some are short and stocky, some tall slender pyramids, others make graceful recurving panicles. The following hybrid is less frequently seen but suits my garden:

A. **'Professor van der Wielen'**. This large graceful plant is well provided with handsome leaves, topped with arching sprays of creamy-white flowers. August. 1.2m/4ft. Z4–8

A group of dwarf hybrids has *A. simplicifolia* among several parents.

Astilbe × *arendsii* 'Venus'

Astilbe 'Sprite'

A. simplicifolia comes from central Pacific Japan where it is rare. The group includes the following very popular plants:

A. 'Bronce Elegans'. Very attractive bronze-tinted, shining green leaves are topped with short arching sprays which open creamy-salmon flowers, fading to deep rose. 30cm/1ft. Z4–8

A. 'Sprite'. Much-divided leaves, chocolate-bronze when young, slowly changing to very dark green, the setting for wide triangular sprays of pale, shell-pink, fluffy flowers. They last for weeks, imperceptibly deepening to chestnut and finally reddish-brown seed heads – most welcome in the autumn border. August-November. 38–45cm/15–18in. Z4–8

ASTILBOIDES *tabularis* (syn. *Rodgersia tabularis*). SAXIFRAGACEAE. From China. This produces large, round, teatray-sized leaves, dimpled in the centre where they are attached to the stem which may be 60–90cm/2–3ft tall. The edges of the leaves are slightly scalloped. It is one of the most beautiful, large, simple leaves. A strong flower stem rises high above the leaves carrying heavy drooping clusters of white starry flowers. 90–120cm/3–4ft. Z5–7

ASTRANTIA. APIACEAE. Masterwort. The flowers of *Astrantia* are modestly charming at a distance, quite entrancing close-to: branching stems are topped with a continuous display of posy flowers, each consisting of a dry-textured ruff of petal-like bracts, the centre filled with tiny quivering fertile flowers. If you press your thumb into the centre it lies flat like the spokes of a wheel, making a perfect flat shape for dried pictures, not messily squashed. They will grow in part shade or open borders provided there is adequate moisture.

A. 'Buckland'. A fine selected hybrid has white outer ray 'petals', green tipped filled with a posy of tiny pink flowers, overall effect pale pink, flowering for weeks in summer. 75cm/2½ft. Attractive seedlings occur and are introduced in various shades of pink. Z4–8

Astrantia major subsp. *involucrata* 'Shaggy'

A. major. From subalpine meadows and open woods of the central European mountains.

A. m. alba. I collected my form from a roadside ditch in the Auvergne. Has many upturned, posy heads, each made of many, narrow ivory segments, green tipped filled with quivering green ovaries. It starts flowering in midsummer, continues until late autumn. 75cm/2½ft. Z4–8

A. m. subsp. *involucrata* 'Shaggy' can produce flowers more than 8cm/3in across with long narrow white 'petals', more widely separated with green pointed tips. 75cm/2½ft. Z4–8

A. m. 'Rubra' was one of the first wine-coloured forms, smaller than other astrantias, about 45cm/18in high. Sometimes I think it a dull plant until I look more closely. The flowers are a sombre burgundy-red with tufts of stamens the same shade tipping the jade-green seed cases which fill the centre. My plants often look best in autumn when moister soil and a little shade encourage a fresh crop of flowers, perfectly formed, the buds glowing ruby-red, and a low sun shining through the opened 'petals' like stained glass. In recent years improved forms introduced include *A. major* 'Claret' and *A.* 'Hadspen Blood'. Z4–8

A. m. 'Sunningdale Variegated'. One of the most handsome of variegated foliage plants: leaves shaped like deeply cut sycamore leaves. In spring, deep green floods the centres, washing out towards the edges and tips which are vividly pale green and cream, a striking feature for several weeks. Then, as the flower stems mature, in June, the leaves darken to green all over. Flowers similar of the type are produced continuously until late autumn, making two seasons of interest from this fine feature plant. 75cm/2½ft. Z4–8

A. maxima. From rich moist subalpine meadows and wood edges of the Caucasus, found growing in well-watered rocky gullies with giant *Heracleum*, *Cephalaria*, or in open meadows with *Scabiosa caucasica*, *Veronica gentianoides* and others. This plant has broader and fewer 'petals' of even rose-pink inside, bitter-green on reverse, filled with rose-pink fertile tufts. The leaves are smaller and rounder, divided into three parts. It increases by thin white underground shoots so making slowly invasive clumps in the right soil and conditions; it is hopeless in poor sandy soil. A very choice and beautiful plant. 75cm/2½ft. Z4–8

BERGENIA. *SAXIFRAGACEAE*. Megasea or Saxifrage. Although bergenias will tolerate drier conditions than hostas, the damp garden would be deprived without them. Where they come from indicates that they are not meant for really hot spots. Apart from the species there are many hybrids. The flowers are handsome but it is primarily the foliage, large, rounded and evergreen, that I value most. With the new hybrids much emphasis is on those which colour well in winter. For the best colouring they need full exposure and good drainage. While the crimson tones are superb on my light soils, they are also rich, but darker, where my soil is heavier. However, in cold ill-drained clay soil they can suffer winter damage. Early flowerers used sometimes to be spoilt by late frost, but with global warming we now have warmer winters and earlier springs, and massed *Bergenia* flowers are a beautiful and long-lasting sight.

B. ciliata. Comes from Nepal, Kashmir and west Pakistan, where it is found on damp rocky slopes among woods. The large rounded leaves are densely covered on both sides with short fine hairs, softly furry to touch, matt dark green to look at. Well-placed against a wall or warm corner they are distinctively good-looking all summer. But the first sharp frost destroys them, although the stout rhizomes are unharmed. Palest pink flowers are set off by cherry-red calyces, but too often are reduced to brown pulp by late frosts. 30cm/1ft. Z3–8

B. cordifolia. Comes from Siberia. One of the largest leaved species: rounded, leathery green leaves, slightly puckered with crinkled edges, and large heavy sprays of light pink flowers in April. 45cm/18in. Z3–8

B. c. '**Purpurea**'. Large smooth leaves, with wavy edges, are green all summer, except for the odd ones which turn bright red or yellow, usually in late summer, before they decide to die. The rest remain, to assume warm bronze and magenta tones as the weather grows colder. The tall flower stems 45cm/18in looking like sticks of rhubarb are topped in May with close-set heads of vivid magenta flowers which some find shocking and are, if scarlet tulips are nearby. Not so free flowering as some, but odd blooms appear again in late summer. Z3–8

B. crassifolia. From moist openings in larch-pine forests, up to the subalpine

Bergenia cordifolia 'Purpurea'

meadows of the Altai and Trans-Baikal mountains of Siberia. Large oval or spoon-shaped leaves produce even brighter winter colour. Leaves have surfaces ranging from cherry-red to rich plum, with reverse sides a glowing carmine-red, making vivid patches of colour against emerald winter grass. Flowers in May on slender stems, dainty sprays of pale lavender-pink. 38cm/15in. Z3–8

B. purpurascens. From moist rocky, bushy slopes in the Himalayas to the mountains of the China-Tibet borderlands. Most bergenias tend to hold their leaves horizontally in large rosettes which, closely packed, make useful ground-cover. In summer *B. purpurascens* has dark green, narrow tapering leaves held straight upright, quite useless as ground-cover, but perfectly designed to show off their superb winter colour. A slight twist to the leaves further aids the display of deep beetroot, almost liver-red on the polished surface, with lighter carmine-tinted backs for contrast. The flower stems are slender, cherry-red, topped with drooping clusters of brownish-pink flowers. 45cm/18in. Z3–8

B. stracheyi. From grassy, bouldery slopes, often among dwarf rhododendrons, in the Himalayas. This is a little thing by comparison. Small rounded leaves about 8cm/3in long make neat rosettes. Pure white or pink flowers with green eyes and calyces crouch low in tight clusters among the leaves. Z4–8

Well-known hybrids include:

B. 'Abendglut' (Evening Glow) makes smallish, flattened rosettes of rounded slightly crinkled leaves, very dark-toned in winter. Flowers appear intermittently in spring and early summer (a few more in autumn), arching sprays of wide open crimson-pink flowers. Z3–8

B. 'Beethoven' is an Eric Smith plant. Leaves and flower clusters are twice the size, a really first-rate pure white form, when the weather permits. Z3–8

B. 'Eric Smith' was a seedling given to me by Eric Smith, with *B. purpurascens* and *B. cordifolia* 'Purpurea' as parents. It has the colour of the former and the generous curvaceous shape of the latter. In a bed of many new hybrids it stands out easily as the best foliage form. Z3–8

B. × *schmidtii* is possibly the most generally known hybrid – not the most interesting. Flowers very early, often in February if the weather is right, tucked deep among the leaves, gradually emerging with quite large sprays of soft pink flowers if undamaged. It has rather flat oval green leaves which never change colour. 30cm/1ft. Z4–8

B. 'Silberlicht' (Silver Light). I think this plant varies from year to year. The flowers open white, enhanced by soft chocolate-brown calyces. As they age they become suffused with pink – sometimes. But other years the pink tinge comes much sooner. I suspect it may be caused by cold weather. The flat smooth leaves remain green in winter. 30cm/1ft. Z3–8

BOLTONIA asteroides. ASTERACEAE. From the north-eastern United States. When well grown, in full sun and fertile soil adequately watered, this plant is most attractive when it produces huge sheaves of small, white, Michaelmas Daisy-like flowers in October. It tends to be tall and leggy and may require staking. We prefer to reduce the plants by about a third in early summer to make more bushy self-supporting plants. *B. a.* 'Snowbank' is more compact. *B. a.* var. *latisquama* has larger flowers, tinted lilac, and 'Nana' is a dwarfer clone. Z4–9

BRUNNERA macrophylla. BORAGINACEAE. A woodland plant from the summer-green forest of the Caucasus mountains facing the Black Sea, and along its coast. In spring wide sprays of tiny forget-me-not-sized blue flowers are held above the heart-shaped leaves developing beneath them. As the flowers fade the leaves become a feature, large as tea plates, matt and dark green. Although they will do in comparatively dry shade they are finest where the soil does not dry out. Z4–8

B. m. 'Dawson's White'. The central zone is marbled greyish-dark green, irregularly bordered with ivory-white;

Brunnera macrophylla 'Dawson's White'

sometimes almost the whole leaf is white. It must have a sheltered shaded site with sufficient moisture. The variegation is delicate and browns easily. 45cm/18in.

B. m. 'Hadspen Cream'. Another good plant from Eric Smith. Light green leaves are irregularly bordered with deep cream which dissolves partly into the central zone. Easier to produce perfect leaves, and gentler in colouring than *B. m.* 'Dawson's White', but does need part shade and good soil. 45cm/18in.

B. m. 'Jack Frost'. This striking form has all over silver leaves finely netted with green, making stunning contrast among plain green leaves.

B. m. 'Langtrees' was given to me by Dr Tony Rogerson; the name commemorates his garden in Devon.

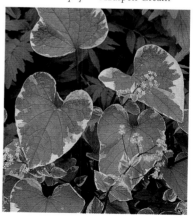
Brunnera macrophylla 'Hadspen Cream'

Large dark green leaves are evenly marked with a border of silvery-white spots which look as if they had been applied with a brushful of metallic paint. 45cm/18in.

BUGLOSSOIDES purpurocaerula. *BORAGINACEAE*. From open woods of central and southern Europe to the Caucasus. The Creeping Gromwell sends out long, arching stems which root at the tip and are covered with narrow, dark green leaves, so forming wide mats. The flower stems are upright and rise from the rooted centres to about 30cm/1ft, bearing forked clusters of quite large Forget-me-not flowers of an intense rich blue. Z6–9

BUTOMUS umbellatus. *BUTOMACEAE*. Flowering Rush of Europe and temperate western Asia. It prefers a free root run in shallow water, but in a small pool is best confined in a large pot. it needs to be broken up and replanted occasionally to induce flowering. Above narrow sword-shaped leaves stand tall 90–120cm/3–4ft flower stems. Shaped much like an *Allium* flower head, the green and maroon-stained buds open pale pink flowers, with dark centres, held upwards on irregular-length stems. They make good seed heads with upturned red-brown capsules. Z5–11

CALLA palustris. *ARACEAE*. Found around and in ponds and quiet water in northern Europe, Siberia, eastern

Butomus umbellatus

Canada and the north-east USA. Long rhizome-like stems float at the water's edge, anchoring themselves in the mud or bank-side by string-like roots which dangle from the undersides. Small, shiny, heart-shaped leaves clothe the stems which do not flower until the second year. Small greenish-white arum-like flowers in May are followed sometimes by small round clusters of red berries. A useful plant to mask the pond edge. 8–10cm/3–4in. Z2–8

CALTHA. *RANUNCULACEAE*. Buttercup-like plants for very wet soil. *C. leptosepala*, from wet subalpine and alpine stream-sides in the Rocky mountains – Alberta and Oregon to Arizona. Slow-growing and comparatively rare, it has white flowers and dark stems. 23–30cm/9–12in. Z5–9 *C. palustris*. The King Cup or Marsh Marigold, common in marshy meadows and sometimes wet woods throughout Europe, northern and central Asia and North America. One of our best native plants, it is still to be found in Britain along river banks, stream-sides through open woods or low-lying wet meadows. Best suited perhaps for the larger garden pond, it makes a large graceful mound of shining rounded leaves, with brownish branching stems covered with single flowers filled with rich yellow stamens. 45cm/18in. Z4–9 *C. p.* var. *alba*. From the Himalayas, this plant looks and behaves so differently one could imagine it belonged to a separate species. Early in February the first rounded buds are pushed through the mud to open green-centred white flowers of appealing purity. Whatever the weather the flowers keep coming, creating a dome of white blossoms by the water-side. By April seeds are already formed but there are still fresh flowers and many more buds to come, tucked down in the damp shadowed clumps of neat round leaves. 38cm/15in. Z2–9 *C. p.* var. *palustris*. (syn. *C. polypetala*). Found along brooks and by springs in the Caucasus mountains. Differs from *C. palustris* in being much larger and

more exuberant and flowering earlier. It is not a clump former but throws long rooting stems across wet ground or extends rafts of round shining saucer-sized leaves from the pond side to float over the water. A joy for large soggy areas, or by lake-sides, and invaluable for softening large areas of water's edge, not for the small garden pond. It never makes a brassy display, but individual stems hold out larger-than-usual flowers for your inspection, continuing this pleasing habit for many weeks, in spring and early summer. 60cm/2ft. Z4–9 *C. p.* var. *palustris* 'Plena'. Every single blossom has become a packed rosette of creamy-yellow, longer lasting than the single form, less delicate, but very impressive. They increase slowly, which makes them doubly desirable, being choice and beautiful. 75cm–1m/2½–3ft. Z4–9 *C. p.* var. *radicans* 'Flore Pleno', the very popular double form. I like to look closely at the individual flowers: five broad yellow sepals support a packed heart of crimped petals, green-centred when young. Although very compact, and much more suitable for small areas, it is almost too packed with colour for my taste, but the shining mounds of foliage make good ground-cover for the rest of the year. 30cm/1ft. Z4–9

CAMASSIA. *HYACINTHACEAE*. Bulbous plants which make handsome vertical features in early summer, either

Caltha palustris var. *palustris*

naturalized or in a border. They will not thrive in poor dry land.

C. cusickii. From damp meadows in Oregon. Very large bulbs produce long wavy leaves about 2.5cm/1in wide and 38cm/15in long. Smooth flower stems grow up to 90cm/3ft , topped with spires of ice-blue narrow-petalled star-shaped flowers. Z3–10

C. leichtlinii. Common in damp, rather sandy meadows near the coast of British Columbia, it seeds itself readily in damp soil. Tall slender spires of cream-coloured, almost waxen flowers can be allowed to raise themselves in gaps among low shrubs or rounded mounds of plants. 90–120cm/ 3–4ft. Z4–10

C. quamash. Grows in wet meadows and along stream banks in colonies, on the Rockies and mountains from British Columbia to Utah and central California. It has blue flowers varying in intensity, as has *C. cusickii,* and there is some confusion in gardens concerning the two. But the bulb of *C. quamash* is a staple article of diet for the Native Americans. The bulbs, about 2.5cm/1in in diameter, are placed in baskets in a kind of 'Dutch Oven' in which the leaves of *Lysichiton* are included. There they are cooked slowly in hot steam and left to cool, when they will have dissolved into a kind of flour from which bread is made. When boiled in water the bulbs also yield a kind of molasses. 30cm/1ft. Z4–10

CAMPANULA. *CAMPANULACEAE.*

Another huge genus containing species for moist conditions. The following are a few which would collapse in my gravel soil, but do well elsewhere, where the soil does not dry out.

C. 'Burghaltii', a hybrid, related to *C. punctata*. A tangle of underground shoots send up slender stems hung with long pale-washed grey-blue bells, 5–8cm–2–3in long which have unfolded themselves from dark purple-pleated buds. The gradations of subtle colour, together with the size of blooms, draw attention to this lovely plant. It will grow in sun, in well-fed soil. First flowers in

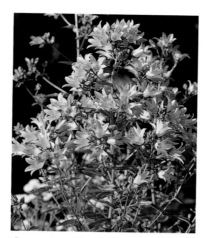

Campanula lactiflora 'Loddon Anna'

early summer, often a second crop in autumn. 60cm/2ft. Z4–8

C. lactiflora. From well-watered gullies between the upper forests on the Caucasus, with *Heracleum*, *Cephalaria*, *Telekia* and other large plants. Glorious in good soil, each stout leafy stem supports a huge bouquet of hundreds of open bell flowers, to be found in several shades of blue. *C. l.* 'Alba' is a white variety. *C. l.* 'Loddon Anna' has large heads of soft dusky pink flowers. Plants stopped in May will flower later, so the season can last from July to the end of September. For full sun or part shade. 1.2–1.5m/4–5ft. Z4–9

C. latifolia. Grows in moist woods in northern Europe to central Siberia, and in damp mountain gullies further south to the Caucasus. Strong basal clumps produce stiff upright stems with large, rather nettle-like leaves. They are smaller in the top half where long tubular flowers almost 8cm/3in long, in good forms, are set in the axils of the leaves. Variable from seed, there are selected forms, shades from violet-blue to palest mauve. My favourite is *C. l.* var. *macrantha* 'Alba' – white with extra large bells, placed against a dark background, or in cool shade. 90–120cm/3–4ft. Z4–8

C. latiloba is found in central Siberia in moist open or part-shaded places. It makes mats of rosettes on the ground of which the strongest send up flower

spikes. The only variety I have is 'Percy Piper', close set for more than half the length of stem, with rich blue, flat, saucer-shaped flowers, each containing a blue ovary, like a jewel, from which protrudes a three-branched blue stigma. 60–75cm/ 2–2½ft. There is a pale pink form too, but the one I covet is *C. l.* 'Alba'. Z4–8

C. punctata. Of grassy slopes in the hills and mountains of Japan and north China. I include this plant because, although seldom seen, it is thought to be a parent of *C.* 'Burghaltii'. It has large tubular flowers of creamy-white or mauve, spotted with red. 30cm/1ft. Z4–8

C. trachelium. Nettle-leaved Bellflower or Coventry Bells. A spreading plant, valued in the wild or where there is ample room for its leafy stems which carry wide bells in the top half. Double forms are good, in white and lilac – in summer – up to 90cm/3ft. Z4–8

CARDAMINE. *BRASSICACEAE.* Known

as Cuckoo Flowers, Lady's Smock, also Cress. There are several of these spring-flowering plants worth growing in half shade among shrubs, and in cool beds or borders. They like best a light soil well enriched.

C. bulbifera. Coralroot is similar to several of its close relatives, and is not the most decorative. But I have allowed it to colonize a rough area on the edge of my Wood Garden. Its heads of tiny pink flowers make an attractive haze in early summer. Z4–9

C. pentaphylla. From beechwoods of the Alps and Pyrenees. In early spring it unfolds fine-cut, purple-tinted leaves together with bowed flower buds. As they expand the leaves become fresh green and the flowers open into showy heads of soft lilac-pink, cuckoo flowers. The roots are curious – clusters of white scale or tooth-like shaped pieces – best divided in spring. 30–38cm/12–15in. Z5–9

C. pratensis. Common in wet meadows and other damp places of temperate and cold Eurasia and North America, it is usually found in gardens as the double form.

Cardamine quinquefolia

C. p. 'Flore Pleno'. Small, pinnate (cress-like) leaves form a flat rosette rather like a green paper doily. In May delicate stems carry a shower of tiny double pale lilac flowers, about 30cm/1ft high. It does not set seed, but leaves lying on the wet surface sprout roots and tiny shoots which form new plants. Z3–9

C. quinquefolia, spreads by means of underground shoots but is not to be avoided since it forms attractive mounds of overlapping, fresh green, pointed, finger-shaped leaves, welcome early in the year, while trusses of bright, mauvish-pink flowers are a surprising contrast among icy snowdrops. 20cm/8in. Z3–9

C. raphanifolia. From wet meadows and brook-sides in the Pyrenees and northern Spain. A larger plant than *C. pratensis.* Rich green foliage makes spreading mats in wet soil by the water-side. In spring long shaped heads of light mauve flowers (about the size and shape of Honesty) make cool contrast with pale spring foliage. 30–60cm/1–2ft. Z3–9

C. trifolia. From moist woods on the lower Alps and other southern mountains. A tiny charmer for the edge of a damp shady path, a damp raised bed or a cool spot in the rock garden. Roundish, three-part leaves are evergreen, becoming purple-tinted with winter cold. In early spring naked stems carrying heads of small chalk-white flowers stand above the slow spreading mat. 15cm/6in. Z3–9

CARDIOCRINUM *giganteum.* *LILIACEAE.* Found wild in open or part-shaded glades in woods in the Himalayas and south-west Chinese mountains. It must be the event of a lifetime to see these magnificent plants in flower. It takes several years for the bulbs to reach maturity and then hollow flower stems, as much as 8cm/3in across at the base, shoot up to about 3m/10ft or more. The base and lower part are clothed with large bright green glossy leaves, much like those of Arum Lily, but heart-shaped. In July the upper half of the stem is hung with many greenish-white, trumpet-shaped flowers, some 25cm/10in long. When the flowers are over the leaves remain fresh until autumn, supporting the large and handsome seed cases. Finally all collapses. The bulbs which have expanded this tremendous effort are exhausted and waste away, but offsets are to be found, and must be planted out in deeply prepared pits, filled with rich vegetable waste and good topsoil. Z7–9

CAUTLEYA *spicata* **'Robusta'.** *ZINGIBERACEAE.* Related to *Roscoea.* From the Himalayas. For deep rich soil, in sun, but sheltered from wind. In late summer spikes of light orange flowers make bold contrast with maroon-red bracts. They are held just above the long pointed leaves, set upright against stout red-tinted stems. The black seeds which follow are enclosed in almost white cases, on erect stems. 60cm/2ft. Z7–9

CENTAUREA. *ASTERACEAE.* Most knapweeds are valued for their ability to thrive in poor soil. The following prefers something better.

C. macrocephala. From subalpine meadows of the Caucasus. It makes robust clumps of coarse, tongue-shaped leaves. In July the stiff flower stems are topped with large, yellow knapweed flowers which emerge from shining-brown scaly buds. Strong enough for the wild garden, it is effective as a background for something lighter in a border. 90–120cm/3–4ft. Z3–8

CEPHALARIA. *DIPSACACEAE.* Widespread in rich, moist, subalpine meadows of the Caucasus.

C. alpina is similar to *C. gigantea* but more free-flowering and less gawky, making a tall upright shape crowded with primrose coloured scabious-like flowers, very effective in mid-summer. Up to 1.8m/6ft. Z4–9

C. gigantea is a great gawky plant but intriguing where room can be found for it. Stout enough for rough-cut grass, a tough rootstock produces a base of large, handsomely divided leaves. Branched stems are flung well above the final leaves ending in primrose-coloured, scabious-like flowers with green centres, occurring on and off until autumn. 1.8–2.25m/6–7ft. Z3–8

CHAEROPHYLLUM *hirsutum* **'Roseum'.** *APIACEAE.* From mountain meadows of the Caucasus, Soviet Armenia and Georgia; this lovely umbellifer is one of the joys of early summer. Over a base of feathery leaves stand branching stems each holding a flat-topped head of lilac-mauve tiny flowers. Likes sun or part shade in retentive soil. 60–75cm/2–2½ft. Z5–8

CHAMERION *angustifolium.* *ONAGRACEAE.* Found in moist open woods and banks of Northern Europe and Asia to Japan, and North America from east to west, spreading quickly after

Chaerophyllum hirsutum 'Roseum'

forest fires. The well-known Rosebay Willowherb (syn. *Epilobium angustifolium*) is much too invasive for the garden but I was given *C. a* 'Album' some years ago and it has not become a nuisance. It has not had the best of conditions, but it certainly deserves a good spot in the wild garden which it graces in late summer with tall spires of cool white flowers with green calyces. 1.2m/4ft. Z3–7

CHELONE *obliqua*.

SCROPHULARIACEAE. The name is derived from the Greek for turtle. From marshy places in eastern North America, sometimes in part shade. It adds rich colour – a warm cyclamen-pink – and an unusual shape to the autumn garden, provided the soil remains moist. Dark green leafy stems are topped with a tapering cluster of buds which, as they swell and open, resemble the wide gaping head of a turtle. When the terminal flowers have faded new buds open down the stem to prolong the season from mid August to October. By then the spikes of fat green seed pods remain, interesting in the garden or picked. 75cm–1m/2½–3ft. Z4–9

CHIASTOPHYLLUM *oppositifolium*.

CRASSULACEAE. In crevices of limestone cliffs, sometimes part shady, of the basal slopes of the Caucasus facing the Black Sea; often with ferns and *Sedum stoloniferum*. It is very attractive in a cool crevice on the rock garden, or a shaded raised bed which does not dry out in summer. Rounded fleshy leaves, scallop-edged, look healthy all the year round: 10–15cm/4–6in stems carry drooping sprays of bright yellow flowers in June. Z5–8

CHRYSOGONUM *virginianum*.

ASTERACEAE. From the USA where it grows in rich soil. This low-growing plant might be ignored if it did not flower so persistently. Slightly bristly, tooth-edged leaves on reddish stems carry star-like five-petalled flowers of bright canary-yellow with brown dots of stamens, for weeks, all summer – a modest edge to a border. 15cm/6in. Z5–9

CHRYSOSPLENIUM *davidianum*.

SAXIFRAGACEAE. At first glance resembles a bright carpet of Euphorbia heads. Round flat heads, 5cm/2in across, consist of small, saucer-shaped, bright yellow saxifrage flowers surrounded by scallop-edged bracts. Soft furry leaves on hairy reddish stems form a flat carpet on a damp shady bank. 5cm/2½in. Z6–9

CLINTONIA *andrewsiana*.

CONVALLARIACEAE. From the deep shade of conifer forests of the north Californian coast ranges. My knowledge of this plant is confined to the fresh green leaves, rather like Lily-of-the-Valley, which emerge from a basal crown. The flower stem is topped with pinkish-purple, bell-shaped flowers, followed by bluish-purple berries in autumn. It does best in light humus soil, in a damp shady position. 60cm/2ft. Z4–8

CODONOPSIS *rotundifolia*.

CAMPANULACEAE. A vigorous scrambler with greenish bells veined blue-purple. I do not grow this one, and have lost some of its relatives, but will try again. Z3–9

COLCHICUM. COLCHICACEAE.

Most make large bulbs so need a good diet to produce them. Although some are found in moist meadows, most of mine do best in well-drained soil that has been heavily enriched. A wet climate would not hurt the bulbs but waterlogged soil does not suit. They look right in rough-cut grass, or in drifts among shrubs coming up through a suitable ground-cover. There are many different species and forms. All Z4–9. These are just a few:
C. agrippinum – see under *C. variegatum*.
C. autumnale. Wild in Europe in mountain meadows, rarely seen in Britain. Misleadingly called Autumn Crocus and Meadow Saffron: it is neither. (*Crocus sativus* produces saffron.) *C. autumnale* has flowers of rosy-lilac, about 5cm/2in long, on perianth tubes of 10–20cm/4–8in, appearing in autumn without leaves (so they are also called Naked Ladies) which do not emerge until late winter to become a feature in spring.

C. a. 'Alboplenum' increases slowly. Double white flowers with pointed petals are held close to the soil on short stems. Flowers late in the autumn.
C. a. 'Album' produces clusters of small white goblets on long white stems. Very attractive, increases well.
C. cilicicum. Wild in central Turkey, in the Taurus Mountains; probably related to *C. autumnale*. Free flowering, on shorter stems than most, so stands up well, opening a month before *C. speciosum*. Leaves appear soon after the flowers have finished. (Flower segments 5–7cm/2–3in on short perianth tubes.)
C. speciosum. Wild in northern Turkey, northern Iran and the Caucasus, on mountain slopes up to 2000m/6000ft. Under this name are found some of the best and largest flowered forms found in gardens. Beautiful large goblet-shaped flowers have broad segments up to 3cm/1¼in broad, 9cm/3½in long, on sturdy perianth tubes. They range in colour through pinkish-lilac to strong reddish-purple. Some have a deep white throat. They are at their best in late autumn.
C. s. 'Album' is a treasure; large, pure, rounded petals form an almost closed goblet.
C. variegatum grows wild in the eastern Aegean Islands and western Turkey, but is unknown to me and rare in cultivation. *C. agrippinum*, which may be a hybrid of *C. variegatum*, has dark bluish-green leaves, with wavy edges, making a flattish rosette against the bare soil in spring. The flowers are not rounded but funnel-shaped, opening flat when the sun warms them. The very pointed segments, 4–5cm/1½–2in long and about 2.5cm/1in broad create a flower up to 8cm/3in across, on short perianth tubes. The flowers are pinkish-lilac in colour, chequered with a darker shade. In good soil they make up well, one bulb increasing to a dozen or more in time, all producing several flowers, so that an individual clump will carry a fine cluster of flowers. In poor thin soil, however, the offsets will be too small to flower.

Convallaria majalis in berry

C. 'Waterlily' is the popular double variety. They are all best grown through some kind of low ground-cover which supports their stems and keeps their petals free from rain-splashed mud. Their large glossy leaves are handsome in spring, dying away in mid summer.

CONVALLARIA *majalis.*
CONVALLARIACEAE. Lily-of-the-Valley. Native in the woods of Europe, from the Mediterranean to the Arctic Circle and across temperate Siberia. A well-prepared bed under a north- or east-facing wall is a good situation. Good drainage, plenty of humus, cool conditions and patience to see if they will settle where you have chosen are what they need. Once established they can become a menace so think several times before choosing your site. 15–23cm/6–9in. There are several different forms apart from the commonly grown native. Z4–9
C. *m.* 'Albostriata' produces leaves with narrow cream stripes. 15cm/6in.

COPTIS *trifolia. RANUNCULACEAE.*
From damp conifer woods and bogs of the colder parts of the northern hemisphere, a tiny plant for a choice cool place. Low mats of shiny green, deeply cut leaves are starred in March with single saucer-shaped flowers on 8cm/3in stems. The yellow roots produce a dye, and a valuable tonic medicine. Z2–7

CORNUS *canadensis. CORNACEAE.*
From the conifer forests of Canada, the northern USA and north-east Asia including Japan. Underground shoots revel in moist leaf-mould soil and send up whorls of rounded shiny leaves which form a low carpet in partial shade. Just above them, in June, stand the flowers, looking rather like large greenish-white buttercups, but in reality the 'petals' are four large bracts. The centres are supposed to set small scarlet berries; mine never do. But the leaves and stems change to lovely wine shades in autumn. 15cm/6in. Z2–8

CORYDALIS. *PAPAVERACEAE.* Most
have fragile-looking flowers and leaves, and some will stand surprisingly dry conditions. The following look and last better in partial shade with soft damp soil in the growing season:
C. *cashmeriana.* Found wild in the Himalayas from Kashmir to Bhutan and southern Tibet, up to 6000m/19,000ft on bouldery slopes, often in sheets. This exquisite plant needs cool peaty soil in a north-facing situation. Neat clusters of finely dissected light green leaves show off short dense clusters of vivid sky-blue flowers in early summer. 15cm/6in. Z6–8
C. *cava.* Widespread from northern Europe to the Balkans, in rich woods. There is confusion between this and C. *solida*, but the tuber of C. *cava* is often hollow on the upper surface and makes a larger plant, 15–20cm/6–8in, with soft spires of plum-purple flowers, and grey-green leaves, much dissected. They appear unaffected by the cold days and nights of early spring. I particularly like the creamy-white form, C. *c. albiflora.* Z6–8
C. *cheilanthifolia.* From China. It remains a feature almost all the year round with its pretty fern-like foliage of soft olive-green and long display of light yellow flowers. It will seed itself among primroses in partial shade. 25–30cm/10–12in. Z5–7
C. *flexuosa* 'China Blue'. This tantalizes all who fall for its exquisite sky-blue flowers, looking like shoals of little fishes swimming through a sea of finely cut blue-grey leaves. It needs humus-fed

Corydalis cava albiflora

loose soil, part shade and luck!, or possibly enough rain at the right time. Z5–9
C. *f.* 'Père David' has light-green leaves and sky-blue flowers. 30cm/1ft. Z5–9
C. *solida.* Widespread in Europe from Scandinavia to the Balkans, in open woods and bushy places. The unsuitable-sounding name refers to the tubers which are like little new potatoes, slightly flattened and yellow in colour. This pretty little plant suddenly appears among early spring flowers. Much-dissected pewter-coloured leaves are topped with soft clusters of bluish-lilac flowers which look so well with the purple-flowered *Erythronium* and snowdrops. When they have set seed their fine foliage quickly disintegrates and they disappear without trace. 8–10cm/3–4in. Z6–8

CREPIS *aurea. ASTERACEAE.* Found in
subalpine meadows from the Carpathians to the Alps and Apennines. This plant has rosettes of leaves much like the common dandelion, but more refined. The flowers are burnt-orange, lovely beside something blue. 10–30cm/4–12in. Z6–9

CROCOSMIA. *IRIDACEAE.* Montbretia.
These plants grow in any soil except heavy untreated clay or bog. They thrive best in humus-enriched soil that does not dry out, where their bulbous roots will increase and flower freely unless over-crowded. They may be divided in spring

and replanted in refreshed soil, in full sun or part shade. Their flowering season is August–September. The tough and indestructible montbretia, now called *Crocosmia* × *crocosmiiflora*, has been superseded by some very beautiful hybrids which are becoming more widely known and enjoyed. Most are bred from two species, *C. aurea* and *C. pottsii*, found wild in South Africa.

C. aurea is tender, but its clear light colouring and wide nodding flowers have contributed to some fine hybrids. Unfortunately it follows that some of the large-flowered varieties are less hardy than those with smaller flowers. 90cm/3ft. Z6–9

C. × *crocosmiiflora* has the hardy *C. pottsii* as one of its parents. This plant's vivid vermilion-red flowers are smaller than those of the other two species, and are borne on erect, not arching, 1m/3ft stems. *C. pottsii* and *C. aurea* have produced many hybrids, bred early in the 20th century, varying considerably in size of flower and hardiness. Many have been lost, but some have survived and been revived from old gardens in the milder and damper West Country. I grow the following (all Z6–9):

C. × *c.* 'Citronella'. I suspect this name, but as such I obtained it. It is much admired for the cool contrast between its light green leaves above which stand upright spires of soft orange-yellow flowers. 60cm/2ft.

C. × *c.* 'Emily McKenzie'. This is the only really large-flowered variety that I possess. Flowering later than the others, the large, widely expanded flowers are dark orange, strongly contrasted with dark maroon-red calyces and, as if that were not enough, there is a ring of blood-red around the pale throat from which flare out light orange stamens. 60cm/2ft.

C. × *c.* 'George Davison'. This name commemorates the head gardener at Westwick Hall, near Norwich, who was one of the first hybridizers of these plants. I like to have this plant of his, raised not so far away from me, in East Anglia. It flowers earlier than *C.* 'Citronella', with warmer flowers of soft orange, on slightly arching stems. 45cm/18in

C. × *c.* 'Solfatare'. I do not do well with this strangely lovely hybrid. Neither cold nor too dry conditions suit it, so it belongs more happily to warmer, wetter areas. There its sheaves of bronze-tinted leaves will not look as though they were on the point of dying, but only make you marvel how right they are to set off the soft apricot-yellow flowers in late August–September. 46–60cm/18–24in. Z7–9

C. masoniorum differs from the other species I list in holding its brilliant orange-red flowers upright on the top side of its arching flower stem which stands about 75cm/2½ft tall. The knobby seed heads which follow are a delight for flower arrangers, as are the dark green blade-shaped leaves which make beautiful curved shapes when dying to a soft warm beige colour. 90cm/3ft. Z7–9

C. m. 'Rowallane Yellow' has elegantly presented sprays of large, golden-yellow flowers flaunting yellow anthers. 90cm/3ft. Z7–9

C. paniculata. It is valued in garden design for its imposing sheaves of stiff, sword-like, pleated leaves which make strong contrast in mixed borders, and are particularly lovely in the autumn, when they turn to coppery shades. The flowers are less impressive, being rather small orange-red trumpets, but they are held in wide arching sprays and followed with an attractive seed head that adds interest to dried arrangements. 90–120cm/3–4ft. Z6–9

Alan Bloom has raised very fine hybrids. The most dramatic is perhaps 'Lucifer', which has the important architectural quality and is topped from July to August with wide purple-stemmed sprays of brilliant tomato-red trumpet-shaped flowers. 1.2m/4ft. Z5–9

There are others, varying in height and intensity of flower colour. 'Spitfire' forms a closer head of more widely opened brilliant orange-red flowers, the colour heightened by a yellow throat and protruding yellow stamens. Not so tall as 'Lucifer', it stands at about 75cm/2½ft and the blade-like foliage is also reduced in scale.

CYCLAMEN. *PRIMULACEAE*. I was uncertain whether to include cyclamens in this book as some will do in dry shade, and a few in full sun. They will not tolerate poor drainage, but as they are found wild in the shelter of low bushes in woods or among broken rocks and stones, watered by mountain storms, so in the garden they need open gritty soil well enriched with humus, sheltered from drying winds. The following are the hardy forms most generally grown.

C. coum has a wide distribution through eastern Europe, the Caucasus, Asia Minor and into Iran. The name covers a group of slightly varying forms. Some have leaves entirely green, others have silver marbling on green; sometimes they are round, or can be kidney-shaped. The flowers appear in winter to spring with short petals, ranging from white to rich carmine. All have a red stain at the base of the petals. 5cm/2in. Z5–9

C. hederifolium. The Ivy-leaved Cyclamen grows wild from Italy to western Turkey. This is the easiest *Cyclamen* to grow and makes large corms if left undisturbed. I have moved some in my garden almost 30cm/1ft across; they looked rather like dried cowpats. They have beautiful large leaves of varying patterns of silver and green, and are free flowering, in shades of pink and a fine pure white. We look for seedlings in early spring, and collect and box them up to give them a good start. But in more favoured sites, undisturbed under trees, they increase freely. 10cm/4in. Z5–9

C. purpurascens. Wild in the southern Alps, from Italy to Yugoslavia and Czechoslovakia. It flowers in autumn, all shades from white to pink, and is sweetly scented; best in semi-shade, not too dried out when dormant. The leaves remain for most of the year, rounded and varying from green to mottled silver. 5cm/2in. Z4–9

C. repandum is found wild from Italy to the Greek Islands. It does better in the warmer and damper south-west where I have seen it naturalised like bluebells under rhododendrons. The flowers are variable in shades of pink to white, and are scented. The leaves vary also, some dark marbled with pale green, others heavily silvered. 8–10cm/3–4in. Z7–10

CYPRIPEDIUM. ORCHIDACEAE. These are not easy plants but because of their unusual beauty they are much desired. They are comparatively rare in the wild so it is a debatable point whether we should leave them in peace in their native home, or try to preserve them in our gardens. Certainly we should not attempt them unless we have the right conditions. There have been more than a dozen different kinds introduced from northern countries around the temperate world. Here are some of the best known:
C. calceolus. Lady's Slipper. Found in rocky woods and clearings from central and northern Europe to Siberia; also in the Pyrenees and the Caucasus. It will grow in either chalk or acid conditions, though usually in limestone districts, provided there is good drainage combined with moisture-holding humus, in a cool sheltered position. Plants need to be left undisturbed for several years to produce many stems of slipper-shaped flowers. In spring one flower appears, sometimes two, consisting of a large pouch or slipper of yellow, netted with dark veins, balanced by twisted chocolate- brown 'petals'. 30–60cm/1–2ft. Z5–8
C. macranthos. From east Europe and Asia, has very large rosy-purple flowers. 30–60cm/1–2ft. Z5–8
C. reginae. Moccasin Flower. Grows in open boggy woods, moist meadows and peaty bogs in the northern United States and Canada, widely distributed from Manitoba to Georgia. This is the largest and most beautiful of them all, 38–75cm/ 15–30in. It must be planted in deep, rich peaty soil, with a little grit added. It will also do in turfy loam provided there is a moist bottom. Deep planting is necessary to keep the roots cool and moist in summer, safe from frost in winter. The whole plant is handsome. Deeply pleated leaves sprinkled with short white downy hairs are held upright on stiff stems. At the top are one or two flowers: each proudly held large pouch, about

4cm/1½in long, is rich rose-pink. The 'petals' are not twisted but are broad and snow-white, sometimes flushed rose. 60–90cm/2–3ft). Z5–8

DACTYLORHIZA. ORCHIDACEAE. Under this name are now found the following plants which formerly we called Orchis.
D. × braunii given to me years ago by the late Graham S. Thomas. It is a most handsome plant with heads of crimson-purplish flowers and spotted leaves. Z6–8
D. elata. Native in southern France, Spain and Algeria. This is one of the most striking terrestrial orchids we can grow in gardens. It needs deeply cultivated soil with plenty of humus. Heavy clay, dry sand or pure chalk will not do. It will grow in sun or part shade where the savage colour is enhanced by a dim background. Stout stems, growing up to 75cm/2½ft, are encircled towards the base with long fresh green leaves and topped with dense clustered heads of rich lilac-purple flowers. The flower head itself can be up to 23cm/9in. long. Z6–8
D. foliosa. The Madeira Orchid is often confused with D. elata, but the flower spike is less tall, more pyramidal in shape. The colour is redder, a rosy-purple, while the rich foliage is spotted with dark blotches. 46cm/18in. Z7–8
D. latifolia. This is the well-known Marsh Orchid, native to Britain and Europe. It has narrow leaves, often with maroon spots, and slender spikes of lilac and rosy-lilac flowers, with paler throats. Grown well, in deeply cultivated moist soil, it is well worth growing. 46cm/18in. Z5–8
D. maculata. This old name for the Spotted Orchid has been discarded as it seems to have covered more than one species. I cultivate one which I have not identified but which used to grow wild in the small wet meadow that is now my Damp Garden. Its leaves are covered with large maroon spots and it sends up spikes of white flowers faintly washed lilac, pencilled all over with darker lavender. 30–38cm/12–15in. Z5–8

DARMERA peltata. SAXIFRAGACEAE. From mountain streamsides of the northern Sierra Nevada in California. This is a plant for holding firm a muddy bank for its thick flattish rhizomes interweave over the surface of the clay. In early spring 60cm/2ft tall red-tinted, naked, hairy stems suddenly appear, topped with flat heads of pale pink flowers. As they fade scallop-edged parasol-shaped leaves, up to 30cm/1ft across on 60–90cm/2–3ft stems cover the area with eye-catching splendour. In some gardens they turn beautiful coppery shades in autumn; in mine they disintegrate into dreary shades of brown. Z5–9
D. p. 'Nana' is a smaller version. The leaf stems are 15–30cm/6–12in tall, the rounded leaves bronze-margined on their shining surfaces. I find it a handsome leaf to plant on a damp corner by the edge of a grass walk. Both these plants will grow away from water, provided the soil remains damp. Z5–9

DATISCA cannabina. DATISCACEAE. From Asia Minor to India, where it is found on rich alluvial soils of streams and riverbanks where prolonged frosts are rare. Each year it produces a clump of tall, stout unbranched stems, clothed in attractive pinnate leaves. They arch over gracefully at the tip, weighted by a fringe of tiny green flowers in late summer. It is a plant for large-scale planting, as a focal point, towering up to 2.4m/8ft if planted

Darmera peltata

Datisca cannabina

in deep, fertile moist soil. In winter protect with a deep mulch of leaf mould or well-rotted manure. It was a source of yellow dye, used for silk. Z8–9

DELPHINIUM. *RANUNCULACEAE.*
I make but brief mention of hybrid delphiniums, as I grow few. The following species include those which are parents of modern garden hybrids. They vary from dwarf plants which will stand fairly dry and sunny positions to tall forms which must have moisture throughout the growing season and shelter from damaging wind. Garden hybrids need well-prepared holes, using well-rotted farmyard manure, or vegetable compost, plus a mulch to keep the soil cool and moist.

D. cardinale is found among chaparral bushes or on stony stream-sides in sandy soil in mountains of southern California. It is not suitable for really damp soils in Britain, as they are too cold for it. It has long spikes of red flowers with yellowish inner petals, and is being used as a parent to introduce pink shades. Rarely seen in England, it needs full sun and rich moist soil. 1.2m/4ft. Z8–9

D. cheilanthum. Parent of many hybrids, this makes a dainty plant with wiry stems. 90cm/3ft. Z3–7

D. elatum. From well-watered rocky subalpine slopes in the mountains of central Europe, north and east to the Caucasus and Altai, and the flood-plain meadows of the Ob and Yenesei in

Siberia, reaching the Arctic. This is a tall blue species which has been the main parent of tall garden hybrids. 1.8m/6ft. Z2–9

D. grandiflorum. From lower mountain meadow-steppes to alpine turfs from Lake Baikal to north China. Also responsible for dwarf and dainty forms. 60cm/2ft. Z4–9

D. nudicaule. From the cool canyons of the coastal mountains of northern California. This is another Californian with soft orange-red blooms; not a good perennial as a garden plant, but being used for breeding. Z5–9

Hybrids
The hybrid delphiniums fall into two main groups. The tall, large-flowered hybrids. 1.2–2.5m/4–8ft need the richest soil, staking and every other care including slug bait. The others are the Belladonna Group which are smaller 1–1.5m/3–5ft, seldom need staking, are less heavy in effect, but still tasty to slugs. The only one which has survived the changes in my garden is 'Alice Artindale'. In deep enriched soil she makes a good 2m/6ft, and needs staking I regret to say. The tapering spires are close set with tightly double flowers which are remarkable. Not a formless muddle as you might expect, but even petals, tightly packed, of rich blue edged with green towards the centre, make perfect rosettes.

DICENTRA. *PAPAVERACEAE.* These
fragile-looking spring flowers are easy to grow in cool part shade with plenty of leaf-mould. All dicentras have a long flowering season, from late spring to mid summer.

D. cucullaria. Dutchman's Breeches is a little, early-spring plant, less than 15cm/6in high, its stem drooping with a few locket-shaped white or pale pink, yellow-tipped flowers, fancifully resembling a man's baggy trousers. It has several larger and more colourful relatives. Z3–7

D. eximia. From the woods of the USA. The type is similar to *D. formosa*, not well known in gardens. Z4–8

D. formosa. From forests and forest glades in the coast ranges and Sierra Nevada from central California to British Columbia. This I find the toughest, standing drier conditions than the others and making quite good ground-cover. Fern-like foliage, which remains good, is pewter-grey tinged with maroon, good contrast with bold leaves like *Hosta* or *Brunnera*. Nodding sprays of flowers, small rosy-red lockets, stand above the leaves. Named hybrids include 'Adrian Bloom' which has almost raspberry-red flowers, and 'Spring Morning', whose flowers are palest pink. 38–46cm/15–18in. Z4–8

D. f. alba forms low mounds of much divided fresh green leaves and carrying clusters of small greenish-white heart-shaped lockets held on jade-green stems. 30cm/1ft. Z4–8

D. 'Langtrees'. I was given this hybrid, which varies slightly, by the late Dr Tony Rogerson. The foliage forms dense colonies of an outstanding blue-green colour, as much commented upon as the cream- and pink-tinted flowers. It is a help to know that this plant runs vigorously in rich light soil, but in the right place that is no disadvantage. 46cm/18in. Z4–8

D. spectabilis. Bleeding Heart, Dutchman's Breeches and Lady's Locket: all these nicknames have been given to this well-loved plant. It comes from cool sheltered places in Korea, Manchuria and China. From top to toe it is good to

Dicentra spectabilis 'Alba'

look at. Standing about 60cm/2ft an established clump sends up many graceful stems, lightly set with greyish-green leaves. Sprays of comparatively large, heart-shaped lockets dangle beyond the foliage on rose-tinted stems, each flower a rich rose colour. If you are indiscreet and turn the heart upside down and open the petals you will see, sitting inside, the little white shape which suggests the name 'Lady in the Bath'. Z3–8

D. s. **'Alba'**. This exquisite plant has light green leaves with almost translucent green stems from which dangle large ivory-white lockets. 60cm/2ft. Z3–8

DIERAMA. IRIDACEAE. Angel's Fishing Rod. Bulbous plants from mountain-sides in rich moist soil, often part shaded, in eastern Cape Province, South Africa.

D. dracomontanum. This dwarf species, about 75cm/2½ft, flowers freely, with 'rods' more upright than those of *D. pulcherrimum*, their lines not cast so wide and taking up less space. The flowers are soft rose-pink. Hybrids between the two occur readily. Both these species of *Dierama* like full sun in a deep, retentive, but not wet, soil. Z8–9

D. pulcherrimum. Tall, grasslike clumps of tough broad leaves erupt like a fountain. High above them cascade sprays of large delicately formed bells which fall in showers from the tips of fine wire-like stems. They vary in colour from silvery-pink through deep rose to plum-purple. Attractive too are the bead-like seed cases, strings of small chestnut seeds enclosed in silvery paper cases. There is a pure white form. 1.5m/5ft. Z7–9

DIGITALIS. SCROPHULARIACEAE. I grow several perennial foxgloves in semi-shade with leaf-mould soil. Those I have seen in the Alps were always on dampish north-facing slopes, grassy verges or among low bushes. The following have a long flowering period during July and August:

D. ferruginea. From subalpine and woodland meadows of the Caucasus, this plant is quietly distinctive. It has dark green leaves and tall slender spires of round buds which open short, rounded, bronze-coloured flowers. 1.2m/4ft. Z4–9

D. grandiflora. From open mountain woods and rocky slopes of Europe to Siberia. This plant has broader, slightly hairy leaves. The good-sized flowers, 4–5cm/1½–2in long are primrose-yellow, netted inside with brown. 60cm/2ft. Z4–8

D. lutea has smooth green leaves and tall stems which branch a little, carrying one-sided racemes of very narrow creamy-yellow flowers. 1–1.2m/3–4ft. Z4–8

D. parviflora. On stonefalls and steep rocky grassland from hills to subalpine zone of the north Spanish mountains. I find this plant very distinctive; dingy from a distance, fascinating when seen close to. Its leaves are distinguished from the others by purplish-mauve shading at the base of the leaf stalk and a fine white rim which edges the leaves. The stout flower stem is short, about 60cm/2ft, crowded for the top two-thirds of its length with narrow copper-coloured flowers set all round the stem, which is unbranched. Close-set chestnut-coloured seed cases prolong the season of interest. Z5–8

There are others, but foxgloves have no scruples about intermarriage, so I am not at all certain of the purity of some of my plants.

DIPHYLLEIA cymosa. BERBERIDACEAE. Umbrella Leaf. From rich woods in the Appalachian mountains of the eastern USA. This is a woodland plant, to grow with blue *Meconopsis* in damp cool shade. Round, two-lobed leaves attract attention because they are large, almost 30cm/1ft across when well grown. Clustered heads of unremarkable flowers are followed by deep indigo berries held well above the leaves. 75cm/2½ft. Z7–9

DISPORUM. CONVALLARIACEAE. These are related to *Polygonatum* and *Tricyrtis*. They like moist peaty or woodland soil in partial shade.

D. sessile. From woods in hills of Japan, Sakhalin and Ryuku islands.

D. s. **'Variegatum'**. A very attractive foliage plant, like a dainty Solomon's Seal, about 46cm/18in high with oval leaves conspicuously striped pale green and white. The flowers in spring are creamy-green bells. Z4–9

D. smithii. From the northern conifer forests of the west coast of North America. This is a dubious name for a plant which makes low hummocks of rather wiry stems covered with shining green leaves. Hidden among the are small ivory bells which later turn into bright orange fruits. It must have moisture and shade. 30cm/1ft. Z4–9

DODECATHEON. PRIMULACEAE. These are North American plants of damp places ranging from moist valleys in the Prairies to high mountain meadows of the Rockies and western ranges, one extending to the Arctic. There are about thirty different species, much resembling one another, except that some, such as *D. meadia*, are taller. *D. m.* f. *album* is a lovely white form. The colour range is from white to rose and purple. Very beautiful on account of their downturned, dart-like flowers poised on short arching stalks which spring from the top of each stem, they make basal clumps of broad-bladed leaves, rather like primroses, but smooth and sometimes brownish-green. They like moist but well-drained soil with plenty of humus, and shelter from the sun.

D. meadia is hardy to Z5–7

Dodecatheon meadia f. *album*

Echinacea purpurea 'White Lustre'

ECHINACEA. ASTERACEAE. Wild in rich moist meadows of the eastern and south-eastern USA , this is a dignified, late summer daisy of unusual colouring. Several large daisy flowers produced at the top of stiff branching stems have widely separated clover-red petals. In startling contrast the hard central cone glistens orange-brown. It needs a sunny situation in deep retentive soil enriched with humus. 75cm/120cm/2½–4ft. In recent years deeper shades as well as white forms have been introduced.
E. purpurea **'White Lustre'**. These bold daisy flowers have greenish-white petals falling back from large central cones which look like tarnished brass as yellow stamens open and fade. 75cm/2½ft. Z4–9

EPILOBIUM *glabellum*. ONAGRACEAE. From wet, rocky subalpine and alpine mountain slopes in New Zealand. Tumbled masses of cream-coloured funnel-shaped flowers seem to continue from mid to late summer, followed by fluffy seed heads but no troublesome seedlings. Clumps of small shining light green leaves expand slowly but are never a nuisance. It grows easily in retentive soil, in sun or part shade. 30–46cm/12–15in. Z7–9

EPIMEDIUM. BERBERIDACEAE. Although some epimediums will tolerate dry shade, they make superb ground cover more quickly in rich, damp leaf mould. They are indispensable beneath trees and throughout my shady borders, so many species and cultivars are described in my *Woodland Garden*. They come into the story of the Damp garden (see Chapter 1), which would be deprived without them, but here I restrict myself to a few choice forms suitable for small areas (all Z4–9):
E. davidii. From west Sichuan. Above small, pointed, leathery leaves, stained bronze in spring, stand wire-thin, dark stems carrying flights of lemon-yellow, long-spurred flowers, backed with dark-red calyces. 30–38cm/12–15in. Z7–9
E. 'Enchantress'. Low mounds of long, leathery, pointed leaves are bright green in spring, when it carries sprays of pale-pink flowers, and purple-stained in winter. 25cm/10in. Z5–9
E. grandiflorum subsp. *koreanum*. From moist woods in the hills of Japan. Makes sprays of creamy-yellow, columbine-like flowers; long, shimmering spurs dangle among the clumps of emerging leaf stems, above light-green leaves, tinted bronze in spring. 30–45cm/12–18in. Z5–9

EPIPACTIS. ORCHIDACEAE. Marsh Helleborine. Quiet unusual plants for damp, not saturated, soil in part shade, valued for their shape as much as their subtly coloured flowers.
E. gigantea. The Brook Orchid. Found on the banks and streams and around springs along the Californian coast, east to Montana and Texas; sometimes called 'False Lady's Slipper'. It is related to the *Cypripedium*, and resembles it in the leafy stems although they are taller and more graceful, making an interesting vertical shape. The tip curves gracefully with the weight of several curiously formed, smallish flowers of sombre green and brown. The lower lip is not pouched but open and inviting, like a treacherous trap, lined with orange-red and leading to a dark purplish-crimson heart. 30cm–1.2m/1–4ft. Z4–8
E. palustris. The Marsh Helleborine. From wet woods and marshy stream-banks of Europe and temperate Asia, except in the extreme north. 20–50cm/ 8–20in. I do not have this plant but it looks attractive in a photograph I have of a piece of wet fenland, growing with the Marsh Fern, *Thelypteris palustris*, and *Lysimachia vulgaris*. Narrow leaves, ribbed and lance-shaped, stand upright on stems which grow 30–60cm/1–2ft. The slightly drooping flowers held in a loose spike have three pale greenish-purple sepals with three white petals tinged with pink at the base. Z4–8

ERANTHIS *hyemalis*. RANUNCULACEAE. The Winter Aconite. From woods and shady places of south-eastern Europe, and widely naturalized elsewhere. This little plant will grow in the open, as its cut parasol leaves and yellow buttercup flowers in their green frill appear and disappear again – so early in the year. It grows large and finer in moist shady places. 10–13cm/4–5in. Z4–7
Eranthis pinnatifida is a little white winter aconite with frilly leaves. Z4–8

ERIGERON. ASTERACEAE. A very large genus, including some North American species, which together have resulted in many named garden hybrids. They are sun-loving but will not give their best in thin starved soils. Reasonably retentive soil means a longer lasting display. Of the many hybrids my favourite is 'Dimity'. Tidy clumps of evergreen leaves produce a succession of pinky-mauve daisies with orange eyes and buds, a lovely combination throughout June and July. Short stems, 30–38cm/12–15in, prevent the plants becoming untidily floppy. Z5–8

ERYTHRONIUM. LILIACEAE. Dog's Tooth Violet, Adder's Tongue, Glacier Lily. All these names describe different parts of the plants or their habitat. They are choice and spring flowering, needing cool peaty or leaf-mould soil in light shade. There are about twenty different species, all but one from America. The hybrids look well coming through low ground cover such as *Tiarella cordifolia* or *Viola riviniana* Purpurea Group, protected from cold, spring winds which can damage the delicate lily-like blooms.

Erythronium californicum 'White Beauty'

E. californicum. Found wild in California from sea level to 1000m/3000ft under pines, redwoods and maples in humus-rich soil. Creamy-white lily-shaped flowers show orange-brown markings ringed round the base. Dark green leaves are strongly mottled with brown. 30cm/1ft. Z5–9

E. c. 'White Beauty'. The flower stems, 15–23cm/6–9in carry large pale cream flowers which reflex back to show creamy stamens and a ring of reddish stain at their base. Broad wavy shining leaves are slightly marbled. Z5–9

E. dens-canis. Dog's Tooth Violet. Grows wild in woods and grassy glades, sometimes in colonies in mountain meadows, as in the Pyrenees; widespread in Europe across Russia to Korea and Japan. Small corms, smooth, ivory-white and pointed are shaped like the canine teeth of a dog. The colour of the flowers varies from almost white through rose to deep cyclamen. Long petals on short (8–10cm/3–4in) stalks hang folded on dull days, but flare back like cyclamen petals when the sun warms them. The leaves are oval and matt, blotched with brown on bluish-green. High in the Pyrenees you can find them everywhere in short turf, but thunderstorms wet them most days while their leaves are up. They soon disappear after the flowers have faded. 15cm/6in. Z3–8

E. oregonum. Found wild in northern Oregon, Washington and Vancouver Island in fir woods. This is an easy species, with white or cream flowers with yellowish centres outlined with zig-zag markings of deep orange brown. 38cm/15in. Z5–9

E. 'Pagoda'. A cross with *E. tuolumnense*, it stands a little taller than *E. c.* 'White Beauty' with creamy yellow flowers, and stems and leaves a little more strongly tinted brown. Z4–9

E. revolutum. Widely distributed from central California north to southern Canada and Vancouver Island, near streams, swamps and in woods up to 1000m/3000ft. Its large drooping flowers are clear rose-pink, two or three to a 25cm/10in stem, held well above brown-tinted leaves. Among named forms is 'Pink Beauty'. 25–30cm/10–12in. Z5–9

E. tuolumnense. Grows wild in California, in Tuolumnense County, at 500m/1500ft in gritty clay soil, rich in humus, beneath oak and Yellow Pine. Its rather more upright leaves are shining yellow-green. Tallish stems, 38–46cm/15–18in carry several bright yellow flowers held well above the leaves. Z4–9

EUPATORIUM rugosum. *ASTERACEAE.* White Snakeroot from woods of eastern North America. It has nettle-shaped leaves but does not sting. It is well liked by those who know and grow it well, but needs moisture-retentive soil to keep health and vigour into September when the leafy stems are topped with loose flat heads of fuzzy, creamy-white flowers. It is not spectacular, but unusual and attractive. It does need a bit of support. 75cm–1m/2½–3ft. Z3–9

E. purpureum resembles Hemp Agrimony, but is bigger and brighter coloured. It is found in damp water-sides in south-east Canada and the eastern USA. This plant is handsome in a big way, standing 2–2.5m/6–8ft. It is a magnificent structural plant seen from a distance, impressive close-to and has a long flowering season in early autumn. Many stout purple-tinted stems are furnished from top to bottom with whorls of dark green pointed leaves. Large flat heads, more than 30cm/1ft across of mauve-

Eupatorium purpureum subsp. *maculatum* 'Atropurpureum'

pink upturned fluffy flowers on dark purple stalks are repeated on a dozen or so smaller side branches. *E. p.* subsp. *maculatum* 'Atropurpureum' has extra dark purple stems and purplish-rose coloured flowers. *E. p.* 'Purple Bush' is more compact. Z2–9

EUPHORBIA. *EUPHORBIACEAE.* Spurge or Milkweed. There are many species. Care needs to be taken with the milky white sap which can blister skin. The following prefer cool conditions and moisture-retentive soil.

E. amygdaloides. From the woods of central and southern Europe and western Asia to the Caucasus. Our native Wood Spurge is a relative of *E. a.* var. *robbiae*. It grows best in leaf-mould soil in part shade. The splendid form with young foliage and stems of rich mahogany-red, *E. a.* 'Purpurea', can be ruined by mildew, which is aggravated by drought conditions. The plants recover, but the display is spoilt. There is also a variegated form. I have yet to grow this really well – perhaps it never does, or perhaps I have not given it just the right place. Flowers in spring. 46cm/18in. Z5–9

E. a. var. robbiae. Found in woods, sometimes with *Hypericum calycinum*, from the southern Balkans to Turkey. It would be a shame to leave this one out, as although it will grow in dry shade, gardens with damper conditions would be deprived without it. It is invasive, so is not suitable for very small gardens, but is invaluable where there is room, in sun or shade. The dense colonies of large rosettes, darkest green lit by long heads of yellowish-green flowers which start in spring, continue through the summer and can look well, bronze-tinted, in autumn. It makes handsome evergreen ground-cover. 60–75cm/2–2½ft. Z6–9

E. griffithii. From the Himalayas. The selected form 'Fireglow' has almost tomato-red flowers, light olive-green foliage with red veins, and orange-brown stems. It will grow in full sun but likes heavy retentive soil. I have a form with darker flowers, stems and foliage which originated at the nursery of the late Hilda Davenport-Jones, who was succeeded by Elizabeth Strangman, selected by Christopher Lloyd and named *E. g.* 'Dixter'. The backs of the young leaves and veins are coral red, the flower stem intensifying in colour leading to flowers which are brilliant orange-red. The chaplet of leaflets beneath the clustered flowers are also stained and shaded with this fiery colour. Gives a long display – early to late summer. 90–120cm/3–4ft. Z4–9

E. palustris. Found in marshy places from France to the Balkans and western Asia. This plant does for the damp garden what *E. wulfenii* does for the dry garden. It makes a spectacular feature plant with many leafy stems, 90–120cm/3–4ft high,

Euphorbia griffithii 'Dixter'

creating a bushy shape that can be several feet across, topped for weeks in spring and early summer with wide flat heads of soft greenish-yellow flowers. Odd fresh flowers are produced later in the year, and in the autumn the dying foliage sometimes turns to brilliant shades of cream, orange and crimson. Z5–8

E. sikkimensis. From the Himalayas. In February and March, among pink and purple hellebores, the new low rosettes of leaves and stems are tinted glass-red. They elongate into tall willowy stems, 1.2–1.5m/4–5ft, when the leaves have become light green with a white vein and noticeable red leaf stalks, creating a very fresh effect at the end of July and on into September. The flowers, in wide flat clusters, commence in early July. By August the round blue-green seed capsules continue to be set off by yellowish-green collars. The central head is surrounded by two or three side branches which carry fresh flowers in autumn. Z6–9

FAGOPYRUM. POLYGONACEAE. The annual *F. sagittatum* is cultivated for its seeds, to make poultry food, and buckwheat flour for human consumption. Another of my mystery plants was given to me as *F. cymosum*, but I believe it now to be *F. dibotrys*. It makes an elegant leafy perennial for the wilder parts of the garden. A slowly increasing rootstock sends up 1.5–2m/ 5–6ft tall branching

Euphorbia palustris

stems which carry large ivy-shaped leaves marked with red veins. Large panicles of small, white, polygonum-like flowers appear by the end of August, continuing into October, lovely among tall miscanthus grasses and autumn flowering daisies. Z4–9

FALLOPIA. sachalinensis. POLYGONACEAE. Found along mountain streams and in damp mountain gorges of north-west Japan and Sakhalin. This is a giant, suitable only along river-sides, reservoirs or lake-sides with other great herbs such as *Petasites japonicus* var. *giganteus*; or isolated in grass and mown around. The thick, hollow, jointed stems which grow up and die down every year soar to some 3–4m/10–13ft. They are hung with large, oval, green leaves, at the base of which, in midsummer, dangle catkin-like sprays of small greenish-white flowers. They create a tropical effect but can be bitterly regretted in the wrong place. Z5–9

FILIPENDULA. ROSACEAE. Sometimes confused with *Astilbe,* having similar tiny fluffy flowers, but the meadowsweets are held in flattish heads instead of narrow spires. They are damp meadow plants so must have retentive soil. Some are tolerant of part shade, which prolongs the flowering. Their woody rootstocks are not far beneath the surface so a mulch is very beneficial. These plants used to be called *Spiraea,* and there is still some confusion in my mind over their exact identification.

F. camtschatica. From mountain ravines, often in colonies along streams, of north Japan, Sakhalin and Kamchatka. The Kamchatkan Meadowsweet stands 90–180cm/3–6ft high, with big leaves of a large, divided end leaflet and very small side ones, and spreading wide branching heads of little white to pale pink flowers, fluffy with stamens. Z5–9

F. palmata. From flood-meadows of eastern Siberia to Japan. (The garden plant may be a hybrid.) I think this is the plant I grow. It does not run, but forms tall (1.2–1.5m/4–5ft) elegant clumps of

Filipendula palmata

light green foliage topped with wide flat heads composed of hundreds of tiny pale pink flowers. Z3–9

F. purpurea 'Elegans' has rather darker, more finely cut leaves with brighter and darker pink flowers and glowing heads of bronze-red seed heads, as effective as the flowers. The meadowsweets I grow I value highly, my only regret is their susceptibility to mildew. Where I have planted them in damper soil this has not been such a problem. Z3–9

F. rubra 'Venusta'. Queen of the Prairies. From damp meadows of the north-eastern USA. We grew this originally as *Spiraea venusta* 'Magnifica'. It is magnificent where there is room. It sends out exploring roots and shoots seeking fresh soil, but being shallow-rooted is not difficult to dig up and replant. Tall,

Filipendula purpurea 'Elegans'

2–2.5m/6–8ft stems carry dark, green, vine-like leaves and are topped with wide feathery masses of deep rose flowers about 30cm/1ft across. Z3–9

F. ulmaria. Our native Meadowsweet; of wet meadows and water-sides in Europe and temperate western Siberia. There are two cultivated forms of this in gardens. Z3–9

F. u. 'Aurea' can be one of the choicest foliage plants, if you can grow it well. It needs enough light to produce rich yellow leaves but not direct sunlight which scorches them. It must have continuously damp soil. The quality of leaf deteriorates a little when the white flowers are freely produced, but I usually cut them off to encourage new foliage, which remains yellow through the entire season. 90cm/3ft. Z3–9

F. u. 'Variegata' can look well if it is regularly divided and planted in refreshed soil. The dark green vine-shaped leaves are centred with vivid yellow. It is inclined to revert, and is prone to mildew. 90cm/3ft. Z3–9

FRAGARIA × *ananassa* 'Variegata'. ROSACEAE. A variegated cultivated strawberry. It needs retentive soil when it will make handsome clusters of leaves broadly splashed with creamy-white. Young plants are produced at the end of runners so it will weave itself between other plants preferably in part shade. A few fruits are produced, usually malformed, but they taste like the real thing. 8–10cm/3–4in. Z3–9

F. vesca 'Semperflorens'. These are the alpine strawberries which flower and fruit from May to November, including named forms such as 'Baron Solemacher'. Part shade, a humus rich soil and a regular supply of moisture is what they need. 15–25cm/6–10in. Z2–9

FRITILLARIA. LILIACEAE. There are many species of these strangely attractive bulbs in cultivation. I describe some in *The Gravel Garden* and *The Woodland Garden*. Here are a few which need moist conditions, in humus-rich soil, with good drainage.

Fritillaria camschatchensis

F. camschatcensis. In damp peaty meadows, sometimes in part shade, all round the north Pacific, from Oregon to Alaska and Kamchatka to north Japan. This extraordinary fritillary likes a rich open soil in part shade where it will do well, making its curious bulb which looks rather like a small spoonful of cooked rice squeezed into a round ball. The bulblets can be pulled apart and grown for several years before they make a flowering stem. Fresh green, glossy leaves are set in whorls around the stems (30–38cm/12–15in). The flowers are open pendent bells. They are almost black, smooth outside, heavily corrugated inside where the colour is slightly lighter, dark chocolate-maroon. There is some colour variation: some bulbs produce less fine, not such dark-coloured flowers. There is also a green form. They flower in May. Z3–8

F. meleagris. Snake's Head Fritillary. Our native species, also found wild in most of central Europe to Scandinavia, in damp meadows. This lovely plant can still be seen in Britain, in a few protected water-meadows. It is easily grown provided the soil never becomes too dry. Standing 25–30cm/10–12in, the stems are lightly set with narrow blue-green leaves. The tapering chequered bells with angular 'shoulders' can be found in many shades. The white and palest pink ones are usually shaded and faintly chequered with green. The warm plum and sombre purple shades have darker chequering, and are sometimes overlaid with a greyish bloom. April-May. Z3–8

F. pallidiflora. Found wild in the central Siberian mountains, up to 3000m/9000ft. This is a treasure for the garden. On short thick stems, 30–46cm/12–18 in, broad, lance-shaped, grey-green leaves diminish in size towards the tip. The lovely flowers, several to a stem, are large and pale citron-yellow, overlaid with green and faint tan veining. They will grow in sun but need deep enriched soil. April-May. Z5–9

F. verticillata. Found wild in central Siberia and east to China, in grassy openings in woods. All shades of green are displayed in this modest plant. Slender stems, up to 60cm/2ft long, are set with whorls of narrow, blue-green leaves which become slimmer towards the top of the stem when their tips become tendrils, perhaps to ensure that in the wild the flowers are held well up among surrounding grasses. They can be exasperating to grow, making many bulbs but only a few flower at a time. We have a free-flowering form given to me by the late Sir Cedric Morris. The angular seed cases surrounded by dried tendrils are works of art and rare enough to be treasured among dried flowers. Z5–8

GALANTHUS. AMARYLLIDACEAE. There are listed more than five hundred forms, hybrids and species of snowdrop, a handful of which I describe in *The Gravel Garden* and *The Woodland Garden*. In general it helps to know that most do best in heavier soils and semi-shade, and that their bulbs should not be dried out or sun-baked. Most are woodland or mountain meadow plants of central and especially south-east Europe and west Asia to the Caucasus and north Iran, though a few (from the eastern Mediterranean lands), prefer drier, scrubby places, sometimes in full sun.

GALAX urceolata. DIAPENSIACEAE. Grows wild in open woodland in mountainous districts from Virginia to Kentucky. A beautiful foliage plant for cool moist conditions, the round heart-shaped leaves are of a leathery texture on fine wirelike stems. They are rich green and glossy with marked veins radiating from the centre. In winter they are edged and sometimes flushed with reddish tints. The size of the leaf varies according to the amount of moisture. Rarely 8cm/3in across in my garden, I have seen it described as twice that size in favourable circumstances. Slender spires (30cm/1ft) of tiny white flowers are produced in early summer. A lovely plant for a cool peaty garden. Z5–8

GENTIANA. GENTIANACEAE. It comes as a shock to learn that there are about four hundred species of *Gentiana*, including some which are yellow and scarlet as well as blue, purple, violet and mauve. Those we are concerned with are moisture-loving plants from high mountains where they are fully exposed to sun but have a continuous supply of underground water in summer. I can only describe those I grow, which must be the least difficult.

G. acaulis. The well-informed know of the myths and mystery surrounding this plant. Most of us are content to think of it as the large, intensely blue trumpet which sits close to the ground on absurdly small clusters of tiny leaves. It likes full sun in heavy soil that does not dry out. In some gardens it produces sheets of flower, in others green mats with no flowers. One is advised to move it, metre by metre or yard by yard, until, with luck, it arrives at the right place. 5–10cm/2–4in. Z3–8

G. asclepiadea. Grows in woods and damp meadows and rockfalls in the mountains of central Europe to the Caucasus. The Willow Gentian is so called because of its narrow leaves on long graceful stems which bow beneath the sheaves of rich blue flowers arranged around the upper half of the stem. Planted in deep moist soil (including chalky soils), well enriched with humus, in shade or part shade and left undisturbed, these plants grow larger and more impressive. The white form, *E. a.* var. *alba*, has slightly smaller flowers but, well placed, perhaps near *Euphorbia sikkimensis*, its arching stems crowded with green-throated white trumpets are very unusual in September. 60cm/2ft. Z5–9

G. a. 'Knightshayes' is distinguished by deep blue trumpets which have conspicuous white throats. 60cm–1m/2–3ft. Z5–9

G. farreri. Discovered by Reginald Farrer in alpine turfs in Kansu, north-west China. The plant we now grow may not be the original introduction but it is of a blue unlike any other, a light, glowing Cambridge blue, on narrow trumpets which have white throats, striped and spotted with green. They sit on low small-leaved cushions of fresh green. A sunny site that does not dry out, in lime-free soil, is what they need. 10cm/4in. Z4–8

G. lutea. Grows in subalpine and alpine stony grasslands of central and southern Europe to Asia Minor. It is a splendid sight to see great clumps of this unusual-looking gentian in sunny mountain meadows where the cows graze, leaving them isolated in short turf. It is easy to mistake them for *Veratrum*, which sometimes grow with them. Tall stout stems, 75–120cm/2½–4ft, are set with wide, upstanding ribbed leaves and topped with whorls of pale yellow trumpets. The pale fawn-coloured clusters of pointed seed cases are also worth having. Patience is needed to achieve several flowering stems as large plants cannot be transplanted, only young seedlings, preferably pot grown. July-August. Z5–8

G. sino-ornata. From high alpine turfs in south-west China or the borders of Tibet. These plants make wide-spreading mats of grassy foliage and will produce sheets of upturned blue trumpets streaked with green if your soil is lime-free and has remained moist (but not stagnant) throughout the summer until the end of September-October. A good mulch of crushed bark aids this, and also helps to ensure that you have a bed of gentians and not annual meadow grass, which surreptitiously germinates among them and is a great fiddle to weed out. 10cm/4in. Z4–8

GERANIUM. *GERANIACEAE*. Cranesbills. These hardy plants are among my most valued for furnishing the garden. They both mark and provide cover for bulbs such as lilies and *Camassia*. Their pretty foliage makes contrast between strong-leaved plants like *Hosta* and *Hemerocallis*, as well as providing modest charm between more spectacular subjects best separated. They quickly make practically weed-proof ground-cover. It is hard to imagine gardening without them. There are many which will grow in almost any soil, ranging in size from those suited to small gardens or the rock garden, to larger plants ideal for borders and shrubberies. I wrote about those that tolerate dry conditions in *The Dry Garden* and *Gravel Garden*. Many tolerate shade and are included in the *Woodland Garden*. A few of these last creep into this book since they respond well to something better, together with others I consider too choice to risk in my really dry areas.

G. clarkei **'Kashmir White'**. A beautiful plant making spreading clumps of fretted leaves above which rise 60cm/2ft branching stems crowded with saucer-shaped flowers more than 2.5cm/1in across. They are white, finely veined and capillaried with lilac. Z4–8

G. endressii. From the Pyrenees. In its several tonal shades, this is one of the best: light silvery-pink, salmon-pink and deeper rose-pink forms can be found, together with finely cut parasols of apple-green leaves which cover the soil in weed-proof mounds. Given time it can become invasive. Z4–8

G. himalayense. From the Himalayas. Under this title shelter several good plants. *G. h.* 'Gravetye' makes low, 30cm/1ft dense clumps of finely cut leaves which are tinted with bright shades of orange and scarlet in the autumn. The large single flowers are violet-blue with a warm reddish centre. It flowers throughout June and early July and increases well in any reasonable soil, in full sun. Z4–8

G. **'Johnson's Blue'**. This outstanding good garden plant is similar in habit to *G. himalayense*, but without the reddish

centre the blue of the petals seems more intense. 30cm/1ft. Z4–8

G. macrorrhizum. From shady rocky slopes of southern Europe. This *Geranium* will stand fairly dry conditions in sun or shade, but it is so useful in any area provided there is good drainage that I cannot leave it out. Its scented, scallop-edged leaves give dense weed-proof cover about 30cm/1ft high. Small, unrooted pieces of woody stem with just a tuft of leaves can be broken off and stuck into cool soil in spring. They will root quickly, and are invaluable where large areas need to be covered. Pale shell-pink flowers held in deep coral-coloured swollen calyces have long protruding stamens while thrust beyond them is the rapier-like pistil, the 'Cranesbill'. (In many members of this family the pistil is attached at the base to the seed case and when they are ripe the 'rapier' splits and projects the seeds far away from the parent plant.) There is also a form with magenta-pink flowers. They flower in May-June. Z4–8

G. m. **'Variegatum'**. The slightly felted leaves are splashed with cream and gold, sometimes with a dash of cherry-red

Geranium phaeum

around the scalloped edges. The flowers are magenta-pink, held just above the leaves. A cooler situation, in part shade, suits this plant best. 23–30cm/9–12in. Z5–8

G. maculatum. From rich woods of eastern and midwestern USA and southern Canada. This makes a choice feature plant, one of the earliest to flower in May. Clustered heads of soft lilac-blue flowers with pale centres stand on 60cm/2ft stems, pushed through a dome of large parasol-shaped leaves with frilly edges. They will stand full sun in an enriched retentive soil, but also look well in part shade with *Dicentra* and *Tellima*. The leaves are beautiful in autumn, suffused with fawn, orange and red. Z4–8

G. nodosum produces myriad light purple flowers whose pale centres are enlivened with thin crimson veins and pale blue stamens, all fluttering on their dark stems above glossy maple-shaped leaves. Good in sun or shade. 38cm/15in. Z5–8

G. × oxonanum **'Wargrave Pink'** is the name of the salmon-pink form, while *G. × o.* 'Claridge Druce' is a very vigorous hybrid, making larger mounds, 60–90cm/2–3ft high, with darker grey-green leaves and magenta-pink flowers. These plants produce flowers throughout summer and autumn. While invaluable as ground cover for large areas these delightful plants need restricting if they become too invasive. Z5–8

G. phaeum. From damp meadows and open woods of south-central Europe. Silk-textured flowers of blackish-maroon float on slender branching stems 60–75cm/2–2½ft in shade or part shade over light green foliage freckled with dark brown spots. The clumps divide easily, and seedlings occur, all making useful cover. Flowers of seedlings will vary; some will be light plum-coloured. There is also a white form. Z4–8

G. p. **'Samobor'**. Introduced by Elizabeth Strangman, this plant makes a striking feature since each leaf, marked with a central blotch of chocolate brown is handsome all summer long. Z4–8

G. pratense. The Meadow Cranesbill. In moist meadows from the Pyrenees and

Britain to north China. The single-flowered varieties have two faults. They seed too freely, and they tend to flop. But for many people these faults are redeemed by the sheaves of beautiful clear blue flowers. Among the best is *G. pratense* 'Striatum', whose flowers are striped blue and white. There is also a pink variety. Where there is ample room, or in the wilder parts of the garden, or in thin woodland, they are delightful. 75–90cm/ 2½–3ft. The old fashioned double forms do well in a sunny or part-shaded border in a retentive soil, and remain in flower over a long period throughout June and July (all Z4–8):

G. pratense 'Plenum Violaceum'. The colour and shape of these flowers remind me of some old fashioned roses. Fully double, the petals are ruched and puckered in shades of pinky-mauve, deepening to violet in the centre. They stand about 23–30cm/9–12in, and flower from mid June to August.

G. p. 'Plenum Caeruleum'. Light violet-blue flowers, making a fine display for weeks.

G. p. var *pratense* f. *albiflorum* 'Plenum Album' has greenish-white double flowers, rather smaller than the others.

G. psilostemon. Formerly known as *G. armenum.* From the mountain meadows of north-east Turkey and the minor Caucasus. Although it enjoys full sun, I have found that this grand plant does altogether better when not starved or allowed to get dry. It needs good drainage, but a little extra moisture means more luxurious plants which retain their flowers longer. From that moment in spring when pointed crimson-red buds appear at soil level, immediately identifying it, it calls for your attention. Gradually a handsome mound of wide, deeply cut parasol-shaped leaves is formed. Above them, in mid summer, comes a long succession of intense magenta-carmine flowers, dramatized by black centres. Lovely autumn tints in the foliage provide a final display. 60–75cm/2–2½ft. Z4–8

G. sylvaticum. From mountain meadows and open woods of Europe to Siberia,

reaching the Arctic. Another early feature plant, making a good companion for *G. maculatum.* The flowers are darker, violet-blue with a white eye, standing up to 90cm/3ft tall over clumps of dark green divided foliage. Z4–8

G. wallichianum. From the Himalayas in damp valley meadows and wood edges. *G. w.* 'Buxton's Variety' is a treasure among many good cranesbills, and since it saves itself for the late summer it needs and deserves a good retentive soil. It makes lax sprawling stems radiating from the centre of the clump. The pretty wedge-shaped leaves are deeply toothed and speckled, light on dark green. The perfect saucer-shaped flowers are blue streaked with fine red veins which run into a cool white centre filled with purple-black stamens set around the carmine stigma. It is just breathtaking, from August to the end of October. It looks wonderful draped like a shawl over a low wall, but on the edge of a border it is a joy to look down upon and its neighbours are not too smothered by the continually lengthening flower stems. 30cm/1ft. Z4–9

GEUM. *ROSACEAE.* The following are all single-flowered types which are ideal as border edging plants. They like sun, but will not stand drought at the root. A reasonably heavy soil with plenty of humus and adequate rainfall will suit them.

G. 'Borisii'. The neat clumps of dark green leaves make a perfect setting for bright tomato-coloured flowers on short stems about 30cm/1ft. They flower throughout May and June. Z5–8

G. 'Coppertone'. This seedling occurred in my garden. It makes a rather more refined plant, with slightly nodding flowers whose petals are the softest apricot-pink, or newly polished copper. 25cm/10in. Z5–8

G. 'Lionel Cox' has soft red-brown stems and dark calyces which hold greenish-yellow petals, sometimes flecked with red. It starts flowering in May, and where there is plenty of moisture will continue almost all summer, often giving

a good display in August–September. 30–38cm/12–15in. Z3–8

G. rivale. Water Avens. From the wet meadows and marshes of the lowlands and mountains of northern and central Europe and Asia, and most of North America to the Arctic. The following are attractive garden forms, all 30cm/1ft and needing damp soil. Z3–8

G. r. 'Album' has nodding heads of white flowers in green calyces; a modest plant for a cool spot. Z3–8

G. r. 'Leonard's Variety'. Above strong clumps of green divided foliage stand hairy red stems holding clusters of almost bell-shaped flowers. Mahogany-red calyces enclose coppery-pink petals with yellow stamens peeping below. Z3–8

GILLENIA trifoliata. *ROSACEAE.* From rich woods in the Appalachian mountains of the eastern USA. Seen as a single stem of flower I do not think this plant would turn many heads, but growing as a well-behaved clump in a suitable setting, in part shade, and deep rich soil, it is rarely passed by. Massed stems, 90–120cm/3–4ft high, are clothed with widely spaced trifoliate leaves. The colour of the russet stems intensifies towards the tips of the branchlets which are set with almost red buds from which flare ribbon-like white petals. The flowers are small but the general effect is distinctive and dainty. When the flowers have gone sprays of reddish-brown calyces remain. Z4–8

GLAUCIDIUM palmatum. *GLAUCIDIACEAE.* This beautiful Japanese semi-woodland plant is native to the islands of Honshu and Hokkaido, and is part of the woodland flora on the high mountain slopes. Regrettably I have not yet established a plant. More has to be done to create just the right micro-climate. Gardens where the air is moist as well as the soil, combined with plenty of rich leaf-mould, may perhaps see plants with many stout shoots, some up to 1.2m/4ft in height, carry two large palmate leaves just below the large, four-petalled, pinkish-mauve flowers. Z6–9

GUNNERA. *GUNNERACEAE*. The two gigantic species cultivated in gardens produce the largest leaves we can grow in the temperate zone. They can be grown without access to a pond or lake, but then a huge hole, 2 x 1m/6 x 3ft should be dug out, drainage material put in the bottom, and the hole filled up with a rich mixture of loam, manure and vegetable waste. In summer ample water must be given. By natural water a good hole must still be prepared, but the crown must rest well above the water level with no risk of flooding in winter. It is a waste of a good plant to press the roots into a slit made in raw clay. Once established, give generous dressings of manure every spring if you wish for the largest leaves, which have been recorded at 2.75m/9ft in diameter on stems 2.5m/8ft high. That is possible in the warm counties of the south-west, and no doubt in Ireland, but a foot or two less is still pretty impressive while leaves 1.2–1.5m/4–5ft across are adequate. The plants need to be sited where they are not tattered and torn by strong winds. Give the resting crowns some protection in winter .

G. manicata inhabits deep valleys and gulleys full of rich alluvial earth and decayed leaves in southern Brazil. It is the more tender of the two. It makes the largest leaves and is also distinguished by its fruiting body. It is rather absurd to talk of the flowering stem of these gunneras. They thrust up enormously heavy club-shaped stems covered with pointed knobs, or in the case of *G. manicata*, the knobs are more widely separated, are longer, and more flexible, like fingers. The whole thing is brownish-green to start with; one never sees anything that could be called a flower, but something must go on because minute round seed capsules are formed which turn orange as they mature. Z7–10

G. tinctoria is found further south than *G. manicata* (as far as the colder regions of Patagonia and Chile) so it is somwhat hardier. Its rounded leaves are rather more puckered and scalloped, but the stout stems never grow quite so tall. Z7–10

G. prorepens is one of the low-growing species which are so different from the giants that you would not imagine they could be gunneras. Clusters of heart-shaped, tooth-edged leathery leaves with a warm bronze tint are studded in late summer with spikes, 5cm/2in tall, of closely set, tiny red round fruitlets looking like sticks of sealing wax. Z8–10

HACQUETIA *epipactis*. *APIACEAE*. From bushy places in the eastern Alps. With its first flowers opening in late January or early February, this curious little plant eventually makes low cushions packed with yellowish-green flowers. In fact each 'flower' consists of six large, frilly, petal-like bracts which are olive-green, while the centre is packed with many tiny, fluffy, yellow flowers. Division of the black bootlace-like roots should be done just before growth commences in early spring. They prefer to be left undisturbed, in retentive soil and part shade, when they will reappear as reliably as winter aconites. 13cm/5in. Z4–9

HEDYCHIUM *densiflorum* *ZINGIBERACEAE*. Ginger Lily from the east Himalayas. Many strong stems are handsomely dressed in long tapered leaves topped with bottlebrush-like spikes of small apricot flowers. 1.4m/3½ft. Z7–9

HELENIUM *autumnale*. *ASTERACEAE*. Native of North America, growing in wet meadows. Will thrive in less wet, provided the soil does not dry out. Try it with damp-loving grasses. Among many hybrids I prefer the following:

H. **'Moerheim Beauty'**, an old favourite, unbeaten for effect and performance. Makes a compact, self-supporting plant, much branched, topped with rich, burnt orange-red flowers whose drooping petals surround a brown velvety central boss of stamens. With or without dead-heading new flowers are produced over several weeks in late summer – early autumn. 75cm/2½ft. Z4–8

H. **'Sonnenwunder'**. Taller stout stems are topped with large bouquet-like heads of clear yellow daisies. Z4–8

Gunnera tinctoria

Helianthus 'Lemon Queen'

HELIANTHUS *decapetalus*. ASTERACEAE. The wild perennial sunflower from North America, found in open woods, clearings and scrub. The following are well-known garden hybrids.

H. 'Capenoch Star'. This specially fine sunflower has medium sized flowers, its large dome-shaped yellow centre surrounded by broad yellow petals. It forms large, leafy, self supporting plants for mid-border, flowering late summer – autumn. 1.5–1.8m/5–6ft. Z5–8

H. 'Lemon Queen'. Stout branching stems form an imposing leafy shape, alight in September – October with myriads of pale-lemon daisy flower. Staking is avoided if this plant, and other late summer flowerers such as asters and heleniums are cut back in early summer to encourage fresh growth and bushier, stouter plants. Z4–9

HELLEBORUS. RANUNCULACEAE. These plants will grow in almost any soil and situation but do best in a retentive yet well-drained soil, in part shade or sun. They do not object to lime. Shading the roots with a mulch or dressing of manure helps to preserve moisture, and feed them; they are greedy feeders. Their large evergreen leaves are ornamental and make good ground-cover. Watch for aphid attack in early summer when the leaves are tender and juicy; it is wise to cut off the leaves of the Christmas Rose and Lenten Roses in late winter to lessen damage by leaf spot, which shows black or brown blotches on the leaves. This can be a nuisance in warm damp weather and if left spreads to the flowering shoots and destroys them. An insecticide copes with the aphis. A fungicide protects the newly emerging flower stems and young leaves.

This is a fascinating genus and I include just a few of the ones I grow:

H. argutifolins, from Corsica, Sardinia and the Balearic Islands. Stout stems form compact, shrub-like mounds all summer of handsome grey-green leaves, markedly veined. The great flower heads are made up of many pale-green cups. 60–75cm/2–2½ft. Z7–9

H. foetidus is found wild in Britain, and in Europe from Spain to Italy. It prefers damp woods and coppices on limestone or chalk. In the garden it grows perfectly well without chalk, in sun or shade, where not too dry. Drooping clusters of palest green bells stand above delicate mounds of holly-green leaves, fan-shaped and finely divided. It has a strange pungent winter smell. 46–60cm/1½–2ft. Z6–9

Helleborus × hybridus (*H. orientalis* of gardens). Lenten Rose. This group contains the most sumptuously beautiful of late-winter–early-spring flowers. Grown from seed few can be discarded, with colours which will include greenish-white, bronze-white, pale pink washed with green, soft reddish-plum, or deep smoky purple. In shape and size they will vary too – there will be round prim cups, dark purple outside, cool green inside; others will droop like round ripe plums; and some will hold open their large petals to show pale cream stamens in startling contrast. Z5–9

H. lividus, from Majorca, is similar to *H. argutifolins* but is tender, and suitable only for really sheltered gardens. It makes a smaller plant (46cm/18in). The beautiful leaves are dark glossy green with conspicuous cream veins, giving a marbled effect. The backs of the young leaves and the leaf stems are plum coloured. In March–April large clusters of pale green, cupped flowers heavily flushed with rosy-purple almost smother the plant. I have hybrids from these two where the vigour and hardiness of *H. argutifolius* are combined with the light plum tints of *H. lividus*. They vary in intensity of colouring, but none are pure green, and some have particularly good foliage in spring. Z8–9

H. niger. The Christmas Rose. Found wild in woods and coppices on limestone in southern Europe, from Germany to Yugoslavia and Italy. It likes a fairly heavy, preferably alkaline, well-drained soil with ample humus, and then to be left undisturbed apart from a mulch and the occasional gift of old manure. Seedlings seem to vary slightly. There are named clones which include 'Potter's Wheel', supposed to be the largest. All are beautiful with large flat-faced flowers held stiffly on short pink stems; some turn to quite deep shades of salmon-pink as they age. Up to 30cm/1ft. Z4–8

H. viridis. Growing wild in central and southern Europe and Britain, in coppices on limestone, this is a quiet plant with deciduous leaves. The saucer-shaped flowers have a distinctly bluish-green tone. 30cm/1ft. Z6–10

H. v. **subsp.** *occidentalis.* This seems to be the north European version of *H. viridis,* growing in similar situations, including Britain. Even among our native plants there is some variation. The flowers are smaller, but more cupped, and plain green without the bluish tinge. Z5–9

HELONIAS *bullata.* Liliaceae. The Swamp Pink. This grows in moist areas in eastern North America and flowers in May. I lost my plant before it became established. It makes an overwintering crown of strap-shaped leaves; from the centre a 30cm/1ft stem emerges, topped with a tightly-packed head of small, pink, starry flowers. Z4–9

HEMEROCALLIS. Hemerocallidaceae. Daylily. Tough and enduring, these plants will grow in sun or part shade in any good border soil, provided it is not too dry, in grass in moist soils, or by the water-side. They have long been grown in gardens, admired for their lily-shaped and sometimes fragrant flowers which, individually, last only one day, but are produced in long succession. The Chinese have considered them a delicacy in salads for some thousands of years. Their new foliage, pale yellowish-green, is welcome in early spring while later the large fountain-shaped clumps make contrast, or ground-cover, or trouble, if they are in the wrong place, and flop over something more precious.

The species are not generally seen in gardens, but they have contributed to the amazing range of hybrids that can now be found, both in colour and form. There are some lovely greenish shades, many yellows, orange, soft apricot, shades of rose and deep mahogany-red. The larger-sized plants, with tall flowering stems, tend to be in less demand now but are still magnificent massed where room can be found. The small ones, some less than 60cm/2ft high, give the owner of the smaller garden a chance to look down the throats of these exotic plants. Specialist catalogues can be found giving details of many hybrids. The following are a few of the species which have contributed to the great variety:

H. aurantiaca. From China. It may be a garden form or hybrid; the flowers are intense orange. 90cm/3ft. Z5–10

H. citrina. Of uncertain origin. In gardens it is called *H.* 'Baroni'. This plant opens in the evening scented, pale greenish-yellow flowers, rather stiff and narrow. August. 90cm/3ft. Z3–9

H. dumortieri. From mountain meadows of east Siberia, Manchuria, Korea and northern Japan. Early flowering, in May-June, the plant has deep yellow flowers with dark brown buds, and is very free flowering and scented. 60cm/2ft. Z3–9

H. fulva. From southern Europe to eastern Asia, found in moist meadows and along stream-banks. This plant introduces the tan shades: the flowers have a zone of brown around the throat, and an apricot line down the centre of each 'petal'. 1.2m/4ft. Z3–9

H. f. **'Green Kwanso'.** From Japan comes this very old plant, making large clumps of broad leaves. The flowers are large, of a rich orange colour, with a strong central V of deeper orange-red. Within it is another, smaller, slightly malformed flower. This lacks the purity of form to be seen in the single flowers, but the 'petals' do not shrivel so quickly, so providing effective colour in landscape planting. July-August. 1.2m/4ft. Z3–9

H. f. **'Kwanso Variegata'.** The leaves are boldly striped with green and white, very handsome when it is good. The plants need to be watched, and only the best pieces replanted as it is inclined to revert. 75cm–1m/2½–3ft. Z3–9

H. f. **var.** *rosea.* A natural variant from Kuling, China. It is soft coppery-rose, a forerunner of the pink varieties. 90cm/3ft. Z3–9

H. lilioasphodelus. From moist meadows and steppes of south-eastern Europe to far eastern Asia. This old garden plant I would not be without, with clear yellow, perfectly shaped lily flowers, deliciously scented. Flowers in June. 75cm/2½ft. Z3–9

H. middendorffii. From high mountain meadows of Sakhalin, Amuria, Korea, Manchuria, north China and north Japan. Similar to *H. dumortieri,* flowering a little

Hemerocallis lilioasphodelus

Hemerocallis 'Winsome Lady'

later. Makes a low compact plant topped with branching stems of bright orange-yellow flowers with brown buds; scented. 60cm/2ft. Z3–9

H. minor. This Day Lily produces dense clumps of narrow grassy leaves, and flower stems about 25cm/10in high. The large sweetly scented flowers are rather few, and lemon-yellow, opening wide from brownish buds borne well above the leaves. This species and others have been used to create dwarf hybrids for small gardens. Z3–9

H. multiflora. From the mountains of central China. The last to flower, possibly a parent, with *H. dumortieri*, of one of the very best Daylilies, *Hemerocallis* 'Golden Chimes'. Standing well above neat clumps of foliage, the flowers are soft orange-yellow with contrasting brown buds. *H.* 'Corky' is similar, with flowers of soft yellow. These two have a delicacy combined with wealth of blossom that makes them very desirable. They flower in mid summer, at 75–90cm/2½–3ft. *H. multiflora* itself grows up to 1.2m/4ft. Z5–9

H. 'Winsome Lady' has beautifully formed wide, pale plum-washed creamy flowers held well above neat foliage. 75cm/2½ft. Z4–9

HEUCHERA. SAXIFRAGACEAE. The most popular are probably the red and salmon-pink flowering varieties which are easily grown in full sun and on any reasonable garden soil. They do not thrive in starved sand or gravel soils. Where the soil tends to be dry plenty of humus and a little part shade will help. If left to themselves they deteriorate, making many woody stems with small leaf clusters. Dug up, and the best pieces replanted into refreshed soil, they will make large handsome clusters of fine foliage, with stronger flower stems. The two I grow for their quieter colouring are:

H. americana. Satin Leaf. From dry rocky woods of the eastern USA to the Mississippi. The young leaves are an exquisite blend of soft orange-tan and brown shades maturing to green with copper-brown shading. The top sides glisten like satin, while the backs are slightly bristly. They are somewhat heart-shaped, scallop-edged and slightly puckered between the radiating veins. The flower stems, 60cm/2ft, topped with wide spires of tiny green and brown flowers are of secondary interest in the garden, but can intrigue the flower arranger. A succession of new leaves enhances the edge of the border until autumn, staying in good condition all winter until new ones push them aside in spring. They will thrive in sun or part shade in good retentive soil. Z4–8

H. cylindrica 'Greenfinch'. Western North America. There is nothing colourful or really dainty about this plant, but I like it. I would grow it for its foliage alone. In its best form large rosettes of round scalloped leaves are dark green overlaid with a silvery sheen. The dark veins become chocolate-brown in winter. Stiff, uncompromising 90cm/3ft stems hold small, pale green open bells in darker green calyces. The flowers are held sternly upright. Among billowing masses of *Polemonium carneum* and *Geranium* 'Johnson's Blue' this plant provides welcome contrast in form. From seed the flowers vary in size and the leaves may be plain green. Z4–8

H. sanguinea. Coral Bells. Found in northern Mexico and Arizona. Short stems 23–30cm/9–12in high carry large bells of brilliant red shades, over dark, sometimes marbled leaves. Alan Bloom has introduced very good named forms, including 'Firebird', 75cm/2½ft, and 'Red Spangles', 46cm/18in. Z3–8 Many selected forms of *Heuchera* are being introduced, some for improved flowers, others for the sumptuous marbled effect of the leaves. Among them:

H. 'Chocolate Ruffles', produces a sucession of leaves variously flushed in shades of tan and bronze on the surface, light-beetroot purple on the reverse, while the deeply cut edges curl and ruffle to produce an attractive textured effect. Z4–8

H. 'Persian Carpet' has flat, smooth leaves that show off the sumptuous marbled effect of intricate pale veins over a dark purple background, slowly fading to silvery pewter. Z4–8

× *HEUCHERELLA alba* 'Bridget Bloom'. *SAXIFRAGACEAE.* This plant makes low clusters of pretty scallop-edged leaves, light green in colour, slightly rough and hairy with a dusting of brown spots and blotches along the veins. Spires of tiny pink blossoms in shades of pink, light and dark, are held on dark brownish-pink stems, throughout May and June, often with recurrent blooms. This plant must have good retentive soil, preferably in part shade. 50cm/20in. Z4–8 Many new Heucherellas are being introduced from America, selected for both foliage and flower.

HOSTA. HOSTACEAE. Funkia or Plaintain Lily. Most of the hostas we grow in gardens today are hybrids or sports. Some came originally from Japanese garden clones, some are still being introduced by hybridizers in America and Japan. The late Eric Smith in Britain devoted many years to this genus. I had been curious to know just what conditions are like where they are found wild, or whether any are still found in natural surroundings. I was especially pleased to have a letter from a correspondent in Japan (Don Elick) who knows the country and flora well. I quote from him:

Hostas are amazingly adaptable but in the wild they generally grow in rich, damp, shaded sites. Only a few true bog species grow in the open, and this in mountain sunlight with long days of storms and mists. Our mountains in summer are rainy and dark. Let no one fool you about rarity. Hostas are everywhere in this country, though the species are very local. Actually they can be grouped roughly by preference to site. A few grow in true bogs or snow-melt meadows, i.e. *Hosta lancifolia*, the smaller species such as *H. longipes* and the *venusta* group on wet cliffs or shaly slopes, and the big-leafed ones in rich woodland.

My local big species are not at all distinguished, with coarse leaves and spacy flowers the colour of dirty dishwater. A nice medium sized species which may be *H. tardiflora* grows about fifteen miles [24km] to the north of here on the wet cliffs of Tenryn river gorge. I have never seen a variegated *Hosta* in the wild, the fancy-leafed forms have arisen in cultivation or were collected out of existence years ago.

In my own garden I have found that while some hostas will do fairly well in drier situations provided the soil is well enriched with humus, and covered with a mulch, they all do infinitely better in part shade where the soil remains moist. The yellow-leaved forms particularly need shelter from direct sunlight which scorches their thin leaves, although they need enough indirect light else their leaves will turn green too quickly. The lovely 'blue'-leaved forms, whose dark green leaves are coated with a waxy bloom, thrive and look better in part shade. The late Eric Smith produced some lovely 'blue' hybrids, and new variegated ones also. Once planted in suitable conditions hostas should not be disturbed. It can take several years for a newly acquired *Hosta* to recover completely from the surgery that is necessary to remove it from the named clone. Often the first year or two the leaves are half the size they can be when properly established. Finally it must be remembered that snails and slugs thrive on a diet of *Hosta*, and nothing is more depressing than to see these lovely leaves riddled with holes. Slug deterrent must be used as soon as the buds swell preparatory to unrolling the first leaves, and not forgotten later. I find a mulch of pulverized bark seems to discourage slugs and snails. Since I first wrote this book named variegated and 'blue' hybrids have been (and are being) introduced in bewildering variety. I confess to have passed through my hosta phase and out the other side although I still love and grow those I first met. The following are well tried:

H. crispula. This especially fine *Hosta* differs from *H. fortunei* 'Albomarginata' ('Thomas Hogg') in having much larger leaves, of darker green, with the undulating edges broadly banded with white. It is much better when grown in shade. 75cm/2½ft. Z3–9

H. fortunei **'Albomarginata'**. Grown in open sunlight this can be quite boring – large sage-green leaves with very narrow, white margins. This also is the look of newly divided pieces. But, once established in rich soil and shade, the degree of variegation can be dramatic. In the most shaded leaves, often those shaded by others in the clump, half or more of the leaf surface will be ivory-white. In others the broad white margin penetrates from the edge down between the veins making longitudinal patterns of cream on the central green zone. This plant can be either a disappointment or a real delight. The leaves are moderately large and heavily corrugated, on tall stalks. 75cm/2½ft. Z3–9

H. f. **var.** *albopicta*. A great favourite, handsome when only half suited, but transformed when left undisturbed in deep moist soil in shade. The leaves will then be 23cm/9in long not counting the stalk, and 15cm/6in across, of a delicate, almost translucent texture, the centre in shades of yellow and cream, the outside border painted with a brushful of wet, dark green paint. By mid summer they will have become green. The leaves are slightly puckered between the wide-spaced veins. 75cm/2½ft. Z3–9

H. f. **var.** *albopicta* **f.** *aurea*. These delicate leaves are entirely butter-yellow for their first few weeks in spring. Strong sunlight will disfigure them with brown patches. By mid to end of June they will have become light green. 40–60cm/16–24in. Z3–9

H. f. **var.** *aureomarginata*. This is an excellent garden plant, taking more light without detriment provided the soil is not dry. It differs from *Hosta ventricosa* 'Aureomarginata' in having larger leaves, broader at the base and more rounded. The slightly puckered centre is dark green with a broad irregular greenish-

yellow edge which lasts through the season. It is vigorous 60cm/2ft and increases well. Z3–9

H. **'Frances Williams'** (*sieboldiana*). Medium-sized deep blue-green leaves, heavily veined and quilted, have a wide butter-yellow margin which runs irregularly towards the centre. There are others which are probably of the same origin (*sieboldiana*) which look similar, and to confuse matters are probably called 'Frances Williams' too! They are all interesting but not all are as good. 60–75cm/2–2½ft. Z3–9

H. **'Halcyon'** (Tardiana Group). Raised by the late Eric Smith of *The Plantsman*, this is still possibly the best blue-leafed hosta. Heart-shaped leaves are so coated with a fine wax film that they appear blue. Fine heads of lilac-blue flowers on purplish stems appear in late summer. 30cm/1ft. Z3–9

H. **'Honeybells'** has the blood of *H. plantaginea,* so inherits the perfume, but has very pale lilac flowers instead of white. The leaves look similar, light olive-green and pointed, with undulating edges, but they are stronger, retaining a fresh healthy look when some other hostas are past their best. 90cm/3ft. Z3–9

H. **'Gold Standard'**. Desirable throughout the growing season. Medium sized leaves strongly veined are a lovely shade of yellow, thinly rimmed with green. This colour remains rich yellow as the

Hosta 'Frances Williams' (*sieboldiana*)

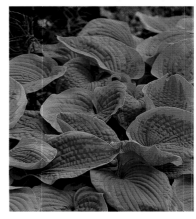

leaves mature, while pale lavender flowers appear in mid summer. 60cm/2ft. Z3–9

H. lancifolia. Although smaller than many and 'penny plain', this *Hosta* deserves to be more widely appreciated. The dark green, shining, narrow leaves make wide overlapping mounds, useful as ground-cover, attractive as a garden feature, or as leaves to pick. The flowers are good – large, deep lilac trumpets on tall slender stems – produced with such generosity as to make a welcome feature in late summer. 90cm/3ft. Z3–9

H. plantaginea. One of the few hostas which comes from China and not Japan. It is very choice and lovely to look at, but not the easiest to grow well, needing both moisture and warmth well into autumn. It is then, in October, that the surprising large lily-like flowers, marble-white in colour and texture, are usually produced. In cool counties the chill of winter usually overtakes them before the flower spike has had time to unfold. But the leaves are beautiful too, glossy, arching, heart-shaped leaves of yellowish-green tone. They are as fresh as the spring in late autumn. *H. p.* var. *japonica* is similar, but has longer narrower foliage. Both these hostas make good conservatory plants. Or they could be used (as all the hostas) in garden pots or tubs, sheltered from excessive sun, provided they are kept well fed and watered. 60cm/2ft. Z3–9

Hosta *fortunei* 'Albomarginata'

H. 'Royal Standard'. Here is a valued hybrid which, in good conditions, grows easily and robustly. Stout green buds open pure white, sweetly scented trumpet-shaped flowers held well above strong clumps of deeply veined, fresh green leaves. August–September. 75cm/2½ft. Z3–9

H. sieboldiana. This is generally recognized as a wild plant and not a garden cultivar. It grows in the woods on the west side of central Japan which receives much snow. Of all hostas this one produces the largest, most dramatic leaves. Grown from seed there will be slight variations in depth of colouring: some will be light grey-green, some more bluish. They may vary too in the amount of deep veining or puckering. But all, in ideal conditions, can make leaves up to 46cm/18in long from tip to base of the leaf, and 30cm/1ft across. It is usual to buy plants from a good clone which has been selected for division. The flowers, which are very pale lilac, set in rather stumpy heads, stand just above the mounds of leaves. In late autumn the dying of these leaves is breathtaking. Almost overnight, after the first frost, the colour changes to glowing shades of honey as the great piles slowly disintegrate. 75cm/2½ft. Z3–9

H. s. var. *elegans*. This selected variety has very large leaves with a deeper tone of grey-blue, deeply veined and puckered. 75cm/2½ft. Z3–9

H. 'Tall Boy'. A superior hybrid with large, heart-shaped and fresh green leaves

Hosta sieboldiana var. *elegans*

which make impressive clumps while above them on erect stems, sometimes more than 1.2m/4ft, tall hang rich lilac bells throughout August. A spectacular *Hosta* to place in bays among shrubs. Z3–9

H. tokudama. Said to be wild in south-west Honshu, Japan, this *Hosta* produces fewer leaves, rather cup-shaped and deep grey-blue. It is a parent of some of the new 'blue' forms. The colour is caused by a heavy wax coating over a firm textured, dark green leaf. This 'blue' colouring is a marvellous foil for orange and apricot-coloured primulas, and, strange as it may sound, is not killed by the true blue of *Meconopsis betonicifolia*, the lovely Blue Poppy from the cloud layers of the Himalayas. 30–46cm/ 1–1½ft. Z3–9

H. undulata. This is a small-growing *Hosta*, very good as edging to shaded borders. The leaves are almost spirally twisted, with centres totally cream and with dark green undulating margins. It is very good in early summer but new leaves with less marked variegation are produced later in the year. The leaves stand scarcely 30cm/1ft high, he lilac flowers on 46cm/18in stems, are produced in late summer. Z3–9

H. u. var. *albomarginata*. I have great affection for this *Hosta*. It is so reliable. Not so glamorous as some maybe, but never untidy or boring. The medium-sized fresh green leaves are not rounded, but narrowish with pointed tips. The wavy white margin extends partly down the leaf stalk, while there is a shading of light and dark green in the centre of the leaf. Fresh leaves continue to be produced until well into the autumn, while the smooth texture prevents dirty drips from overhead trees disfiguring them. 60cm/2ft. Z3–9

H. u. var. *univittata* is very similar to *H. undulata*; sometimes it is hard to tell the difference, but this one is a little taller, and more vigorous. 38–46cm/15–18in. Z3–9

H. ventricosa. This is perhaps the finest green-leaved *Hosta* with broad, heart-shaped leaves of rich dark green, evenly veined. Of all *Hosta* flowers, apart from the elusive white of *H. plantaginea*, this is the finest, with large, dark lilac bells, more rounded in outline, with internal veining. 75cm/2½ft. Z3–9

H. v. '**Aureomarginata**'. The variegation forms a butter-yellow border which partially seeps into the centre. As the leaf matures the variegation becomes pale cream, almost ivory, unlike some other hostas whose variegation turns to green. This make it one of the best variegated hostas but it is not the most vigorous, needing patience as well as good conditions, moisture and good feeding. 75cm/2½ft. Z3–9

HOUTTUYNIA cordata.

SAURURACEAE. Found in shady wet places from Japan, Taiwan (formerly Formosa) and China to the Himalayas. It can be grown in squelchy soil, even in several centimetres or a few inches of water, or in any cool but moist border. It has a creeping root-stock, not difficult to control provided you keep an eye on it. Lax stems carry bluish-green, heart-shaped leaves blotched and margined with rusty-tan. Little white flowers with cone-shaped centres stand up on short stems. In the double, *H. c.* 'Flore Pleno', the centres become a cone of white petals. The leaves smell of bitter Seville oranges – some people think it is vile. I like it! 46cm/18in. Z5–9

H. c. '**Chameleon**'. Vivid as a Turkish carpet, variegated in tones of yellow, green, amber and red, this has become widely available. Good, where space is limited, in low tubs. Z5–9

HUMULUS lupulus. CANNABACEAE.
From damp or wet woodlands of Europe and central Asia.

H. l. '**Aureus**'. The Golden Hop does best in deep rich loam. New shoots emerge in spring and rapidly make at least 3–4m/10–13ft of growth, decked with handsome yellow leaves. It can be trained over a wall, or allowed to run riot over an old tree or large shrubs; not a tidy plant but adds light and charm in suitable places. Z4–9

HYLOMECON japonica. PAPAVERACEAE.
From woods in Honshu, Korea and northern China. Spring can come and go, when there is so much to see, without you noticing this modest woodland plant, but it is very pretty, low growing with leaves cut into dainty leaflets over which hover clear yellow poppies. 30cm/1ft. Z5–8

Houttuynia cordata

IMPATIENS glandulifera.
BALSAMINACEAE. Found in the Himalayas, on damp disturbed ground. A wickedly self-seeding annual, only to be admitted to the wild garden, or stream-side. There its great juicy stems bearing wide heads of pale or rose-pink hinged and pouched flowers give out a strangely sweet perfume on late summer evenings1.5–2m/5–6½ft. White-flowered *I. g.* 'Candida' is irresistible.

INULA hookeri. ASTERACEAE. From the
eastern Himalayas. This is a lovely plant to fill up moist places in the sun. From a running rootstock come quantities of branching stems, 75cm/2½ft high, clothed with softly hairy leaves. Exquisite green woolly buds, like downy nests, are complete in themselves, especially filled with morning dew, but twists of yellow appear, unfolding as many fine-rayed pale-yellow daisy flowers. August-October. Z4–8

I. magnifica. This plant is undoubtedly magnificent where there is room to show it off from top to bottom, and where it will not be caught by strong winds which will leave it tattered, or toppled. The leaves are shaped like a dock, but four times as large, of a rough matt texture. They make a handsome pile at the base of stout branching stems which can soar 2–2.5m/6–8ft in rich moist soil. The leaves ascend the stems in diminishing size to the wide branching head of flowers. These are large, 13–15cm/5–6in across, fine rayed yellow daisies. Z4–8

I. racemosa, from the western Himalayas, grows tallest of all, forming stout but narrow spires of closely set nobbly buds which open quite small yellow daisies, not much more than 2.5cm/1in across. It makes quite the most dramatic outline, either in the wild garden or by the water-side. 2m/6½ft. Z4–8

IRIS. IRIDACEAE. The following are irises
which need varying degrees of moisture, from the merely damp to several inches of water.

I. chrysographes. Found among bushes on brook-banks and damp valley sides in the

Inula racemosa

high mountains of south-west China. It needs deep soil which does not dry out and makes clumps of light green leaves, with flowers in varying shades of rich violet-purple to velvety-black. 46–60cm/ 1½–2ft. The broad dropping falls are just touched with a few specks of gold. There are several selected and named varieties. The two I have are:

I. c. **'Black Knight'**. The flowers are well formed, of dark indigo-purple, slightly larger than 'Black Velvet'. Z4–9

I. c. **'Black Velvet'**. The buds and newly opened petals, before the sun has dried the dew off them, are almost totally black, the texture of velvet. Twisted standards emerge between the broad central guards whose texture is of fine matt silk, a delicious contrast with the velvet-black falls. They flower in June. 46–60cm/1½–2ft. Z4–9

I. cristata. From the eastern USA. A wee thing for a damp pocket in the rock garden, it is inclined to be lost by even a small pool. From a tangled mat of slender rhizomes appear small tufts of leaves followed by pale lilac flowers with deep yellow throats. 15cm/6in. There is a rare and lovely white variety called *I. c.* 'Alba'. 10cm/4in. (*I. lacustris* is very similar to *I. cristata* but smaller, 8cm/3in.) Z5–9

I. delavayi. From wet mountain meadows of south-west China (Yunnan). The flowers are purplish. 46–60cm/1½–2ft. Z5–9

I. douglasiana. Confined to the coastal areas of southern Oregon and California,

a stretch of more than 1100 kilometres or almost 700 miles, and usually found on grassy hillsides and clifftops within sight of the Pacific. The flowers are variable from reddish-purple through lavender and blue to cream, marked with gold, blue or purple. The evergreen leaves are dark and glossy. Making low, wide-spread tussocks, often with rose-red bases. Well suited in any reasonable garden soil, it flowers in June. 30cm/1ft. Z7–9

I. ensata. From Japan and eastern Asia. I have not yet become addicted to these although they are works of art, long hybridized, improved and enlarged, sometimes too much, over generations of gardeners in Japanese gardens and nurseries, and also in the USA. They make the most exotic-looking flower, which has predominantly enlarged falls with diminished standards. The colours range from white, pink, lavender, violet, purple and more, some plain, some splashed and striped. They like moist lime-free soil, or good rich border soil, and full sun. June-July. 90cm/3ft. I love my white form which I raised as a seedling years ago. I also value the variegated form. Z5–9

I. e. **'Rose Queen'** is a hybrid with *I. laevigata*, and prefers a less saturated soil. The flowers are a rare shade of soft brownish-rose. There are others, white mottled with purplish-blue, and a plum-purple whose name escapes me. Z5–9

Iris ensata 'Rose Queen'

I. e. **'Variegata'**. The foliage goes through a dull patch as the plant is coming up to flower, but afterwards it produces splendid new leaves, fresh and handsomely striped in grey-green and white. The dark purple flowers always seem too good for a variegated plant. 60cm/2ft. Z5–9

I. gracilipes. Comes from Japanese woodlands, in rich humus and light shade. This is another pretty dwarf, with pinkish-lilac flowers, with orange crests, held on 25cm/10in stems. It flowers in spring, and should only be transplanted then, never in autumn or winter. Z5–9

I. graminea. From moist meadows of southern Europe. Thick clumps of narrow, dark green, grassy leaves almost hide the small flowers tucked in among them. The blue falls are in turn almost hidden by the broad central 'shields' of soft amethyst. The wiry standards are somehow fitted in between these two. Most people do not bother with this, but bury their noses into the little flower and breathe deeply the perfume of sun-warmed plums, preferably old-fashioned greengages. 30cm/1ft. Z5–9

I. innominata. Found wild in the Roque river area of south-western Oregon on rich, well-drained and wooded slopes. The original form introduced was yellow, with narrow leaves. In the wild the colours range from pale creamy-buff through yellow to orange, from orchid-pink to deep purple. They have been hybridized with *I. douglasiana* and *I. tenax*, so that now in gardens it is impossible to distinguish them and they tend to be called Californian (Pacific Coast) Hybrids. They are all without exception exquisitely beautiful in many shades, including cream, yellow, greyish-lilac, sulphur-veined copper, rose-maroon, veined blue and various shades of blue. They are as fascinating as a butterfly's wing. They make spreading tussocks of narrow dark evergreen leaves which emerge from rose-pink bases. Above them stand the frilled and fluted orchid-like flowers, to be followed by wide-opened seed pods, shaped like a flower, with pale beige linings. They need good drainage, a

Iris laevigata

Iris laevigata var. *alba*

Iris pseudacorus var. *bastardii*

sunny aspect and a retentive soil. 25cm/10in. Z5–9

I. japonica. From hilly woods of the southern parts of Japan, and China. The Japanese Iris sends up fans of shiny evergreen sword-leaves from its creeping rhizomes, which sometimes rise from the ground like small trunks. Its rather small flowers are carried in branching sprays some 30–60cm/1–2ft tall. They are soft lilac-blue, the frilly falls marked with a white central band spotted with yellow, recalling those of an orchid. Though this *Iris* is a woodlander needing a humus-rich soil and some shelter, it is shy to flower in shade in East Anglia and prefers a warm position, even in the sun, but must not be allowed to dry out. Z8–9

I. kerneriana. Found wild in damp places along the Black Sea coast in Turkey. A restrained and elegant *Iris* for June, with pale creamy-yellow flowers freely produced, and narrow green leaves. It likes a sunny place, in retentive, not waterlogged soil. 38–46cm/15–18in. Z6–9

I. laevigata. From shallow water and marshes from Japan to south-west China. This *Iris* loves squelchy soil, so it is ideal to plant in the water, to mask the pond edge. Unlike *I. ensata* it does not object to lime. Tussocks of soft green leaves are a setting for quantities of rich soft blue flowers, with broad drooping falls, like dogs' ears, with small upright standards of the same blue. 46–60cm/1½–2ft. Z5–9

I. l. var. *alba* has wide petals held out boldly with a central cream vein. The small standards are marked with a narrow vein of purplish-blue. 46–60cm/1½–2ft. Z5–9

I. l. 'Variegata' has the very best of variegated leaves for the water-side, most sharply striped in green and ivory-white. It can be smothered in big water-garden plantings, but in smaller pools where it can be watched it makes spectacular clumps of foliage which remain fresh until autumn. 30–38cm/12–15in. Z5–9

Iris pseudacorus 'Variegata'

I. pseudacorus. Found in shallow water, marshy land and boggy woods of Europe to central Asia. This is the wild Yellow Flag of our river-sides and ponds. It makes huge clumps of luxuriant dark-green, broad-bladed leaves, either in the boggy edge, or in several centimetres or inches of water. It is adaptable and will grow in any retentive border soil in the garden. Some better selections have larger, deeper yellow flowers. There is also one which has very pale creamy-yellow flowers, called *I. p.* var. *bastardii*. They flower in June. 90–120cm/3–4ft. Z2–9

I. p. 'Variegatus' is one of the loveliest foliage plants in early spring. Pale cream and butter-yellow leaves last many weeks into summer before changing to green. These last two, and any good deep yellow form, should be propagated by division, and care taken that seedlings from them do not root down and overpower them since they will be the common type. This can happen unnoticed all too easily. 60–75cm/2–2½ft. Z4–9

I. × *robusta* 'Gerald Darby'. Valued for the purple-stained base to leaves and purple flower stems which carry blue flowers in midsummer. Flourishes in shallow water or heavy retentive soil. 90cm/3ft. Z4–9

I. setosa. Found in marshes and bogs which are often peaty, from the Aleutians to eastern Siberia and the mountains of

Iris × *robusta* 'Gerald Darby'

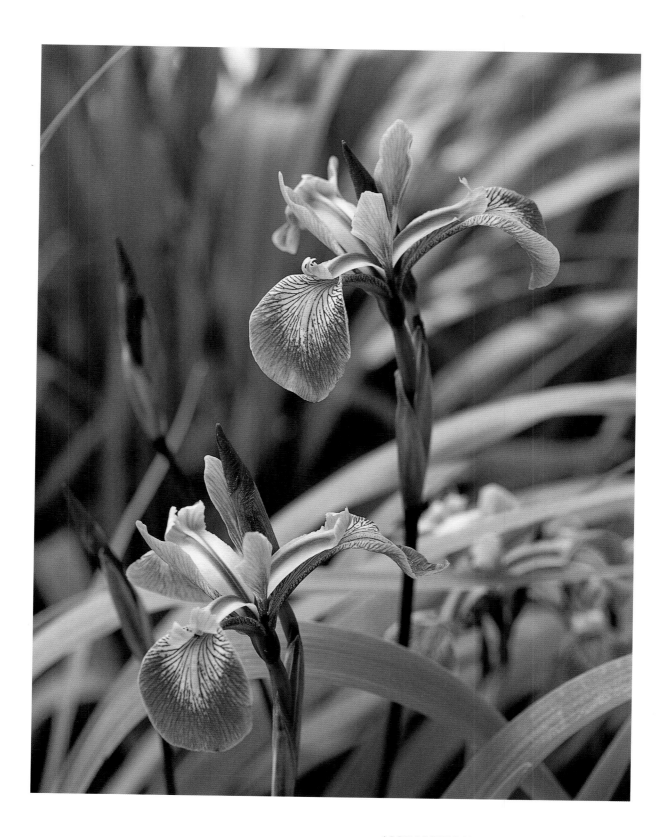

northern Japan. A free-flowering *Iris* for damp soil, in sun, in June. Above low arching clumps of grey-green leaves stand many branched stems crowded with flowers. From indigo-blue buds open wide drooping falls darkened with veins and shadows of deeper blue. Plenty of seed heads follow, rounded and pale brown in colour. 60cm/2ft. Z4–9

I. sibirica. From damp and often peaty meadows of central Europe to east-central Siberia. This *Iris* has been grown in gardens since the sixteenth century. It is most accommodating, growing in ordinary moist or dry, but not too dry, soil. It flourishes best in moist or retentive soil, in sun, producing healthy upright sheaves of narrow leaves above which stand slender branching heads of flowers. There are many selected forms. I prefer the ones with upright narrow standards and broadly flaring falls. The type is blue, but as well as many blues there are shades of plum, purple, cream and white. The narrow, polished, chestnut-brown seed heads are a joy to flower arrangers. 90cm/3ft. Z4–9

Much work has been done producing named forms of *I. sibirica* in shades of blue and cream. Among my favourites are 'Blue Burgee' (dark blue), 'Dreaming Yellow' (creamy white) and

Iris versicolor

'Sky Wings' (light blue). You have to see them – they are as beautiful as orchids.

I. versicolor. Both foliage and flower set each other off in this shorter, sturdy-looking *Iris*. The branched flower stems carry rich purple-blue flowers with strong clear veining on a white and pale gold centre. These stand just above tidy fans of short broad leaves of a rich, almost bluish-green colour. 60cm/2ft. Z4–9

I. v. 'Kermesina' has light wine-coloured flowers with a white and gold finely veined base to the petals. Both these irises like moist soil in sun, looking well with the orange-flowered *Primula bulleyana*. They flower in June. 60cm/2ft. Z4–9

JEFFERSONIA. *BERBERIDACEAE.* A cool shaded situation, sheltered from drying winds in rich leaf-mould soil is needed for these woodland treasures.

J. diphylla. A North American species found in woods on the eastern seaboard and in Tennessee. It is called 'Twinleaf' because each leaf is deeply divided into two halves. Pure white poppy-like flowers, about 2.5cm/1in across poised on 15cm/6in stems open in May. Z5–8

J. dubia comes from mixed conifer and summer-green woods in Manchuria and far eastern Siberia. Many tiny purple buds on thin wiry stems, about 10–13cm/4–5in tall open fragile-looking, pale lilac petals, commencing to flower before the foliage has unfolded, which finally forms low clumps of heart-shaped, blue-tinged leaves. Z5–8

KIRENGESHOMA. *HYDRANGEACEAE.* Wild in woodland on some of the Japanese islands, but rare even there.

K. palmata. This unique and lovely plant starts to flower about the end of August, until the end of September, later in cooler districts. Heavy clusters of fat, swelling buds cause the smooth purplish-maroon stems to bend low. The calyces are prominent, clasping the developing bud so that just before the petals open it looks not unlike a large hazelnut. When the petals are extended, the shuttlecock-shaped flower is about 5cm/2in long, pale buttery-yellow, of a thick waxen texture.

The flowers do not open very wide, but this does not detract from their beauty; it is the combination of buds and flowers, and the way they hang from the weighted purplish stems which is beautiful. Lush green leaves with irregularly cut edges clasp the stems in pairs. This plant must have deep moist soil, free of lime, and be sheltered from damaging winds. 1m/3ft. Z5–8

K. p. **Koreana Group,** from Korea, holds its stems more upright, while the flowers open a little wider. 60–75cm/2–2½ft. Z5–8

LAMIUM. *LAMIACEAE.* Dead Nettle. From open woods from France to west Asia. These plants can make very useful and pretty ground-cover. Like ajugas they sometimes tend to be dismissed as rampant weeds, but both are hard to fault in their natural setting – in cool humus soil which never thoroughly dries out, under trees or shrubs. They also make very attractive edgings to cool borders, both in leaf and flower.

L. galeobdolon. Yellow Dead Nettle or Yellow Archangel. From glades in woods, throughout Europe to the Caucasus. This plant can be bitterly regretted in the wrong place, where it will be smothering its neighbours, even climbing into shrubs or rose bushes. But under trees, or in rough hedge bottoms, its brilliantly frosted and evergreen leaves are much admired, as are the fine heads of lemon-yellow flowers. I have it as a carpet beneath bamboos, which seem to keep it in order. 25cm/10in. Z4–9

L. maculatum. The Spotted Dead Nettle has dark green crinkle-edged leaves with a broad silver stripe down the middle, rather like a badger's face. In flower there are three colour forms, a deep mauve-pink, a light rose-pink, 'Roseum' and white 'Album'. 15cm/6in. Z2–9

L. m. 'Aureum' is not nearly such a healthy plant, the leaves being totally warm tones of yellow. It needs rich leaf-mould soil which never dries out, and shelter from direct sunlight which scorches the delicate foliage. 10cm/4in. Z2–9

L. m. **'Beacon Silver'**. This form has almost totally silvered leaves, a bonus for the shade garden among the many shades of green. The leaves become speckled with purple blotching as quantities of deep rose-purple flowers are produced, but provided there is adequate moisture new growth completely refurnishes perfect carpets by the autumn. 15cm/6in. I have a charming white-flowered form sent to me by Philip Levesley, called 'White Nancy', in which the leaves are not disfigured by purple blotching. 15cm/6in. Z2–9

L. orvala. I first saw this beautiful Dead Nettle on a Chelsea exhibit of Messrs Blooms of Bressingham. Not at rest till I possessed it, it has taken several years to please it with a suitable position. It now thrives in part shade, in cool, well-drained but not too dry soil. The large heads of flowers are a rare shade of coppery-pink. The leafy plant, which is non-invasive, stands about 38cm/25in high and flowers in May. Z4–8

LATHYRUS. PAPILIONACEAE. Apart from the perennial climbing peas there are these little, low-growing, bushy plants which cover themselves in spring with small pea-shaped flowers. They are easily grown in retentive soil, preferably in part shade, although they will take some sun along the path edge.

L. aureus. Found at wood edges and in semi-shady places of Europe to the Caucasus. An unusual colour in the garden, it makes fresh, green, bushy plants about 46cm/18in high, carrying branched stems of orange flowers, held in loose clusters. It is a quiet plant, but distinctive. Z6–9

L. vernus. From forests, France to Russia and the Caucasus. It makes dwarf bushlets, not more than 30cm/1ft high, set with pairs of small, oval leaves. Tiny pea-shaped flowers, purple and blue with red veins, cover the plants in early summer. Z5–9

L. v. **'Alboroseus'**. In early May these low, bushy plants are smothered with dainty clusters of little pink and white pea flowers. 30cm/1ft. Z5–9

Leucojum aestivum 'Gravetye Giant'

LEUCANTHEMELLA serotina. ASTERACEAE. From Hungary. Another plant for damp places in the wild garden, or in the border with Michaelmas Daisies and *Aconitum*. Loose clusters of chalk-white, green-eyed daisies, each 5cm/2in or more across, are held on top of tall leafy 2.1m/7ft stems. Their freshness is welcome in the short days of October–November, provided they have been placed to face the sun: they will turn their backs to you if the sun is behind them. Z4–9

LEUCANTHEMUM. ASTERACEAE. Garden varieties have occurred between the original Shasta Daisy from Mount Shasta, USA and *L. maximum* of the Pyrenees. They include single flowers with either good broad petals or finely shredded ray-like petals, or they can be semi-double with interesting centres, or entirely double like pom-poms. Some are tall stemmed, some short. Naming can be hazardous. They flower July–August, all thriving in sun, in soil which does not dry out. 75cm–1m/2½–3ft. Z4–8

LEUCOJUM aestivum. AMARYLLIDACEAE. From wet meadows, stream-banks and open wet woods, from southern France to the Caucasus. This is generally known as Summer Snowflake, although it flowers in spring, April–May. It makes large bulbs and leaves not unlike a daffodil. The white bell-shaped flowers are very like snowdrops, but with out-turned green tips, and hang gracefully in a loose cluster from the top of tall 60cm/2ft stems. The best form is called 'Gravetye Giant'. It was selected by William Robinson, and named after his garden, Gravetye Manor. This bulb likes deep, rich soil, and will flourish by the water-side where a large clump makes a good feature. Z4–9

L. vernum. The Spring Snowflake from woods and meadows, France to the Caucasus. It appears earlier, in March, and is often mistaken for a snowdrop as it is much the same height. It opens white bells almost at ground level, gradually pushing them up on stems about 15cm/6in high. They look like tiny lampshades with a rounded, yet arched, shape to the open bells, with rims of yellowish-green tips. A good named form is *L. v.* var. *vagneri*. Z4–8

LIGULARIA. ASTERACEAE. Another race of imposing plants, all needing deep, well-fed, moist soil. They also need shelter from continuous strong sunlight and wind, both of which can wilt large soft leaves even if there is ample moisture. Slugs and snails too can ruin a fine display, so use deterrents early in spring and replenish them from time to time.

L. dentata. From damp mountain meadows of Japan to west China. Fine selected hybrids of this plant are sold under the names 'Desdemona' and 'Othello', but the seedlings from them produce good plants, varying in intensity of leaf colour and size of flower. Branched heads of daisy flowers are held well above the leaves on maroon-black stalks. The flowers are orange, with soft brown centres. Some have short, broad petals, others are longer and narrower; both are equally good. It is the impact of this rich orange colour held in large clustered heads which is so magnificent. The leaves, no less handsome, are large, roundly heart-shaped, almost beetroot-red when new, but becoming green on the surface, the undersides remaining purple, marked with heavy veins. July–August. 1.2m/4ft. Z3–9

L. 'Gregynog Gold'. This handsome hybrid has broadly heart-shaped leaves, richly veined, with neatly cut edges; 90–120cm/3–4ft stems carry close-set conical spires of large, bright yellow daisies. July–August. Z5–9

L. hodgsonii. From damp mountain meadows of north Japan and Sakhalin. This plant is similar but slightly smaller than *L. dentata*, and is usually seen with green kidney-shaped leaves, and heads of yellow daisies. 90cm/3ft. Z4–9

L. macrophylla. Of damp mountain meadows of the Altai, and northern Tienshan, in central Asia. I do not have it, but it sounds and looks good in Graham Thomas's book, *Perennial Garden Plants*. He says it is rare: 'the tall horseradish-like leaves are of grey-green, and the dense spikes of yellow daisies stand aloft like paint-brushes in the August landscape.' 1.5m/5ft. Z4–9

L. przewalskii. Found in damp mountain meadows among forests, in north-west China. It differs from the others in having its leaves cut into many pointed fingers. The tall stems are almost black, the top half making a spire of small, ragged-petalled, yellow daisies, effective against the black stems. 1.5–2m/5–6½ft. Z4–9

L. 'The Rocket' has large rounded leaves with neatly cut edges, and purple-black stems which set off the long narrow spikes of lemon-yellow, groundsel-shaped flowers. The total shape and colour produce a most handsome addition to the garden design. They flower throughout July, followed by attractive spire-shaped seed heads. 2m/6½ft. Z4–9

L. wilsoniana. From damp mountain meadows of west China. This makes a somewhat smaller plant, with roundish green leaves forming a comfortable mound about 60cm/2ft high and across, above which stand slender spikes of yellow flowers. It can easily be ruined by slugs or snails. 90–120cm/3–4ft. Z4–9

LILIUM. *LILIACEAE.* Most lilies need well-drained soil, so put plenty of grit into heavy soils, but add humus in lighter soils to conserve moisture during the growing season. Try to choose a site that gives shelter from damaging wind. Lilies suffer if they are dried out in summer, especially the stem-rooting ones, but they will also fail if their bulbs become waterlogged in winter. Though many flourish in the sun, some can tolerate shade and shelter from surrounding bushes; it is often helpful to check the wind. In recent years we have learnt to watch for and destroy the Red Lily Beetle which devastates all members of this family. From the vast field this species covers I select a few which like damp, but not water-logged, places.

L. concolor and its varieties. From mountain meadows of northern China and Mongolia to Japan. These lilies hold their star-shaped flowers upright in rounded heads on stems 30–60cm/1–2ft tall. They range in colour from scarlet to bright yellow, according to variety, some being spotted and some not. They have played a part in the breeding of the hybrid garden lilies now known as *L. × hollandicum*, which were once called *L. umbellatum*. Though I do not at present grow *L. concolor* or any of its varieties, I have some of its hybrids. Z4–9

L. lancifolium. Tiger Lily. From mountain meadows of Japan and Korea to west China. Although it may be considered

common this easy lily looks magnificent in late summer. Strong stems, 1.2–2m/4–6½ft, clothed with dark glossy leaves are topped with orange-red recurved petals, heavily dotted with black spots. Purplish-black bulbils are readily produced in the leaf axils. Z3–9

L. martagon. Turk's Cap Lily. From open rocky woods, wood-edges and rocky mountain meadows, central Europe to the Altai. High in the alpine meadows, tucked into a crevice between large boulders where the cows cannot reach them, you may find these lilies. In the garden they seem to like full sun or part shade provided the soil is deep. They make far taller stems, crowded with soft pinkish-purple flowers, than I have seen exposed in the wild. The white *L. m.* var. *album* is especially lovely in semi-shade. They flower in mid-summer, and stand 90–120cm/3–4ft. Z3–10

L. monadelphum. Wild in the Caucasus Mountains and into north Turkey, found in woods and sub-alpine meadows on very steep slopes, there can scarcely be a lovelier lily, in shape, colour and texture. It opens large nodding, recurved, bell-shaped flowers, of cool creamy-yellow with thick waxen-textured petals in June 90–120cm/3–4ft. Z3–9

L. pardalinum. From shady stream-banks and wet meadows in the mountains, from central California to British Columbia. This exception among lilies can be grown

Lilium monadelphum

Lilium speciosum var. *album*

in the bog garden, creating a stately feature as it rises above lush foliage plants and grasses. In July stout stems will carry up to thirty bright sealing-wax red flowers, with recurved petals showing large purple spots on the lower half. 1.5–2m/5–6½ft. Z5–9

L. speciosum. Rare in the mountain meadows of south Japan (Shikoku and Kyushu). Flowering in August–September, these well-known pink and white lilies vary considerably in depth of colour, from white, to almost totally stained deep rose-red. The type has white wavy-edged petals partially suffused with deep rose. In rich soil they make large grapefruit-sized bulbs, and the stout stems stand 1.2–1.5m/4–5ft, carrying many nodding flowers. They look lovely peeping through *Persicaria amplexicaulis* and *Salvia uliginosa*. Z4–9

L. superbum grows even taller, 2–2.5m/6–8ft, in really wet soil. Both these lilies have curious rhizomatous roots, making clusters of scaly off-shoots which can be split and replanted. Z6–9

LINNAEA. CAPRIFOLIACEAE. This name honours Carl Linnaeus, who originated classified plant names.

L. borealis. From shady conifer forests all round the northern hemisphere. This plant makes a dainty trailing evergreen over cool moist soil, ideal in partial shade, preferably in a peat bed. Tiny oval leaves are spaced along reddish prostrate stems. Small shell-pink bell-like flowers appear in mid summer at the end of short side shoots. 5cm/2in. Z2–7

L. b. subsp. *americana* is more robust than the European plant, and seems to do better in garden conditions. 5cm/2in. In the dry atmosphere of East Anglia I have been unable to grow either of these satisfactorily. Z2–7

LOBELIA. CAMPANULACEAE. The North American Cardinal flowers are among the most elegant for late summer, taking over from the candelabra primulas and needing the same deep, rich, moist soil. They are not averse to sunlight, but will flower in part shade.

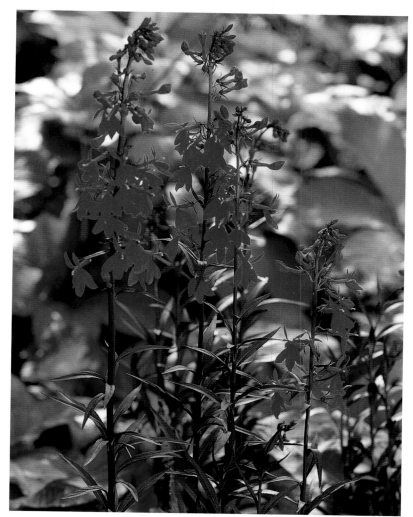

Lobelia cardinalis 'Queen Victoria'

L. cardinalis. From marshy meadows and shady brook-banks in all the eastern United States and Canada. This handsome plant makes a basal rosette of green leaves followed by large spires of scarlet, lipped flowers which last from mid August until well into September. 90cm/3ft. Z4–9

L. fulgens. From marshy places in Mexico, this plant much resembles *L. cardinalis* except that it has reddish stems and leaves and is not so hardy. Z8–10

The well-known garden plants 'Queen Victoria' and 'Bees' Flame' have large, velvety, scarlet flowers and dark, maroon-red leaves. They should be covered with a mulch put down by mid November, and left until about mid March. This will protect the fat buds which are just beneath the soil surface. They flower throughout August and September, standing 1–1.2m/3–4ft tall. Z4–9

L. siphilitica. Found in damp or wet meadows of the eastern United States. Looking very different from the scarlet lobelias this plant is more prim, with very erect stems clothed on the lower half with whorls of crinkled, light green leaves. The top half carries a narrow spire of small but intensely coloured tubular flowers, a combination of light blue flaring lips and darker shadowed throats. There is a white selection, *L. s.* 'Alba'. They need to be divided and replanted in fresh soil every few years. 75cm/2½ft. Z3–9

L. **×** *speciosa* **'Vedrariensis'** is a hybrid of *L. cardinalis* and *L. siphilitica*. It flowers later into September–October with long-lasting large spires of rich violet-purple flowers. This is a vigorous and reliable perennial, valuable in the autumn as a contrast to the many daisy-shaped flowers. 75cm–1m/2½–3ft. Z4–8

LYCHNIS chalcedonica. CARYOPHYLLACEAE. Maltese Cross or Jerusalem Cross, on account of the shape of the flowers; known since the time of the Crusades. This flat-topped Scarlet Campion does best in rich moist soil in full sun and looks very good by the water-side, flowering in July–August, dramatic with *Phormium tenax*, especially the purple-leaved form. 90–120cm/3–4ft. Z2–9

LYSICHITON americanus. ARACEAE. Bog Arum. From peaty marshes of central California to Alaska. Large, rich butter-yellow arum flowers appear through bare mud in early spring, followed by clumps of huge smooth, spinach-shaped leaves which grow 1.2–1.5m/4–5ft in my garden, making dramatic features by the water-side all summer long. (I measured them!) Z7–9

L. camtschatcensis. From swampy places of north Japan and far eastern Siberia

to Kamtchatka. This has pure white flowers. Neither these nor the foliage (75cm–1m/30–40in) attain quite such large dimensions as *L. americanus*. Hybrids occur between the two, producing much larger white flowers. They must all have very deep, wet soil. Z7–9

LYSIMACHIA. PRIMULACEAE. Yellow Loosestrife. All these plants will grow in full sun if the soil remains moist. They wilt and look miserable if the soil dries too much.

L. ciliata. From damp bushy thickets, by streams and damp open woods, in the eastern and central United States and Canada. I value this plant highly in my bog garden. Although it spreads by underground shoots it is not dangerously invasive. In spring the new shoots produce a carpet of pale brown rosettes turning to light green as many stems rise, 90–120cm/3–4ft. Half their length is topped with continuously flowering open heads of fresh yellow nodding flowers, each with a deep orange eye. They are not large, but are produced abundantly from July to September. Z3–9

L. c. **'Firecracker'** has leaves tinted beetroot purple, paling as they ascend the stems: good contrast for pale lemon flowers. Z3–9

L. clethroides. Found on sunny hills, from Japan and Manchuria to China and Indochina. This plant also produces dense colonies of flowering stems 1m/3ft from

underground shoots. The flower spikes, rather like curved, miniature *Buddleja* heads, are packed with tiny chalk-white flowers in late summer. Sometimes the foliage is tinted rich bronze and red in autumn. It will not tolerate drought. Z3–8

L. ephemerum. From rich, damp river-banks and marshy places of Spain and south-western Europe. This also has white flowers but looks very different. It does not run, but makes a tidy clump of basal foliage which sends up 1m/40in slender stems close set with leaves arranged in pairs. Seen *en masse* they are very distinctive, being long and narrow with wax-coated grey backs and a marked central vein. The general effect is grey, topped with long spires of tiny, round buds set close against the stem, opening to small, starry, white flowers with lilac centres which finally become dainty spikes of round brown seed capsules. Shorter, upright side shoots carry on the display which begins in early August and continues well into September. Z6–8

L. nummularia. Creeping Jenny. From wet meadows and wet woods throughout Europe to the Caucasus. This makes a pretty carpeting plant for the water's edge, or along any damp cool border. It has small, rounded, dark green leaves set in opposite pairs along the prostrate, trailing stems. In early summer they carry bright yellow cup-shaped flowers. It can be too invasive in small gardens. 5cm/2in. Z3–8

Lysichiton americanus

Lysichiton camtschatcensis

Lysimachia ciliata 'Firecracker' with *Rodgersia*

L. n. '**Aurea**' has golden foliage, exquisite as a flower among blue *Meconopsis* or blue-leaved hostas. It needs protection from scorching sunlight and is less vigorous. 5cm/2in. Z3–8

L. punctata. From shady damp places and along streams, often growing with *L. vulgaris,* from Scotland and Germany to south-east Europe. This plant is similar to *L. vulgaris*, whose place it takes in gardens, being more densely flowered with spires of bright yellow. In the wild garden, or around a lake-side or large pond, its invasive habit can be tolerated: it will establish broad sheets of bright yellow flowers with little or no maintenance. In smaller areas it is very enjoyable for a long while in mid summer, but the running clumps must be reduced. 1m/40in. Z4–8

L. p. 'Alexander', the variegated form, brings a touch of glamour in contrast to the type. New leaves have broad cream margins, suffused with pink. If pruned after flowering the variegated effect is retained. Z4–8

LYTHRUM. LYTHRACEAE. Purple Loosestrife. These plants are remarkably adaptable – they will grow in saturated soil by the water's edge, even underwater, or in an ordinary border – but they grow finer, and the flowers last longer, where the soil does not dry out.

L. salicaria. From Britain to China and Japan, and North America. In its natural state, along most stream-banks, it is a rather strong magenta-pink, which I choose to avoid. I prefer the softer and brighter shades of rosy-pink which have been selected and named. They make tall, leafy plants topped with long, flaming tapers which glow for weeks in late summer. They are great seeders, and the young plants quickly make tough deep roots, so beware – cut off the flower heads in time. 1.2–1.5m/4–5ft. Z3–9

L. s. '**Blush**' is especially attractive with slender spires of pale rose-pink flowers. Z3–9

L. virgatum. From western Asia. There are selected and named forms of this *Lythrum* which make much smaller, daintier plants

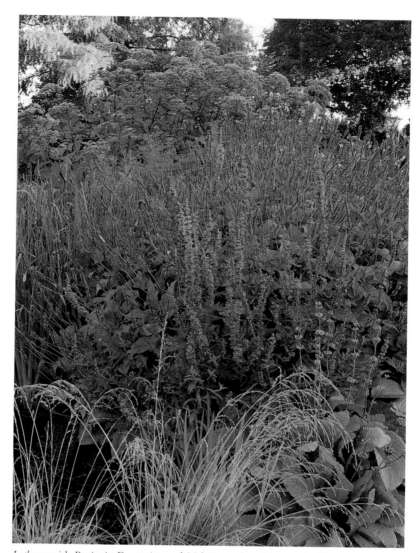

Lythrum with *Persicaria, Eupatorium* and *Molinia caerulea* subsp. *caerulea* 'Variegata'

60–75cm/2–2½ft. They are ideal for the smaller garden, and could easily be lost in large areas where *L. salicaria* would naturalize. The leaves are much smaller and less dense on the much-branched stems, which carry close spires of rosy colour. Among these *L. v.* 'Rose Queen' is ablaze in late summer with rosy-pink flowers which practically hide the small narrow leaves. They make very pretty plants, continuing to flower for many weeks, from July to September. Z3–9

MACLEAYA. PAPAVERACEAE. Plume Poppy. These stately plants have the advantage of lightweight flower heads so they need not be disfigured by staking. They are handsome from top to toe so need to be planted where other plants do not hide them, preferably not at the back of a border, although that is generally where they are placed! They need deep, retentive but drained soil.

M. cordata. From open meadows in the hills of Japan and China. It makes a compact, scarcely running root. The

Macleaya microcarpa 'Kelway's Coral Plume'

foliage is similar to that of *M. microcarpa*, but the creamy-white flowers are of better quality. 1.5–2.25m/5–7ft. Z3–10

M. microcarpa. From open scrubby hill slopes in China. It makes underground shoots which appear in unexpected places in spring, sending up a tall colony of 2.25m/7ft stems. The base and stem leaves are large, round and deeply indented, light olive-green above, with blue-grey backs. Slender panicles of creamy-white buds open to small fluffy white flowers which form tiny orange seed capsules. Although slight, the remaining seed heads are delicately colourful. Z3–9

M. m. 'Kelway's Coral Plume'. In this selected form the upper leaf surfaces are bronzed, and the dainty plumes of drooping flower buds are warmly tinted coral-pink, making a very pretty feature in August–September. 1.5–2m/5–6ft. Z3–9

MAIANTHEMUM bifolium. CONVALLARIACEAE. From moist shady woods, especially those of conifers, of Eurasia and North America. The little May Lily forms spreading colonies of slender stems up to 23cm/9in high, carrying glossy, heart-shaped leaves, and at their tops fluffy spikes of little white star-shaped flowers in early summer. Z3–6

MECONOPSIS. PAPAVERACEAE. To most of us this name calls to mind the exquisite Blue Poppy, but there are other coloured poppies in this genus.

M. betonicifolia. From moist mountain meadows among forests of south-east Tibet, upper Burma and Yunnan. Like crumpled pieces of sky caught up on tall slender stems, 1.2–1.5m/4–5ft, the petals expand to show a heart filled with yellow stamens. The leaves are covered with soft bristles. If allowed to flower too soon the plant usually dies; it must be well established, with several crowns, to be truly perennial. Plants grown from seed will vary in colour from sky-blue to rosy-lavender shades. Drying winds are death to these plants, whose home is in mist-drenched mountains. In gardens they must have deep, rich soil, moist but not stagnant, in a cool, sheltered position. In northern counties of Britain they can probably take more sun. In the south, light woodland creates both the right setting and micro-climate. But the north side of a wall, or a group of shrubs, might suit equally well. They flower in June. Z7–8

M. cambrica. From rocky woods and open rocks slopes in the mountains of west Britain to Spain. The prolific but lovely little Welsh Poppy with tissue-paper petals, in pale lemon or orange, hovers above dainty, ferny-green foliage. The only drawback is its birthrate, but that is an advantage in the right place, naturalized in semi-wild shrubbery or open woodland. There is a double form which curiously does set true seed, but not nearly so abundantly. They all flower for many weeks, from April to June, about 46cm/18in high – exquisite above a carpet of the Foam Flower, *Tiarella cordifolia*. Z5–9

M. grandis. From moist, rocky meadows of the eastern Himalayas. Another Blue Poppy which varies from shades of blue to a purplish tint. It is larger than *M. betonicifolia,* but since it hybridizes freely with that poppy it is not often seen in its true form. 90–150cm/3–5ft. Z6–8

M. napaulensis. From rocky, half-shady places in the eastern Himalayas to China. This is a monocarpic species, that is, it may live for several years but once it flowers it dies. The large rosettes of deeply cut evergreen leaves are covered with reddish bristles. The flower stem, thick as a walking stick, may be over 2m/6ft high. The flowers range in colour from white, light blue and pink to dusky purple. Z5–9

M. quintuplinervia. The Harebell Poppy. From alpine turves of the north-west Chinese mountains. Perched on thin, leafless stalks are drooping bells of soft lilac-blue, hiding inside their silky petals pale cream stamens. They spread by underground shoots which form low mats of slightly hairy grey-green leaves, and are not nearly invasive enough in my unfavoured garden. They flower from May to June, on 38–46cm/15–18in stems. Z7–8

M. regia. From the Himalayas of Nepal. A well-grown plant of this poppy allows no one to pass by without a second glance, and it is not blue, nor yet in flower. The huge bunched rosette, looking like some gigantic flower itself (it can become almost 1m/3ft across) lies flat against the dark, leaf-mould soil, every leaf covered with fine, golden hairs, which catch the light or hold the dew. All its strength and beauty fade as the strong flower stem ascends finally to display a great head of fifty or more, downturned, pale lemon, sometimes pink, saucer-shaped flowers. They set seed, and the plant is dead. Up to 1.5m/5ft. Z7–8

M. × sheldonii. (*M. grandis × M. grandiflora*). Progeny from this alliance has a great reputation for size of flower, brilliant colour and perennial habit. It makes strong leafy clumps in moist soil, but must be sheltered from too much drying air and screened from hot sun. 90–120cm/3–4ft. Z7–8

M. villosa. From the Himalayas, from Nepal to Bhutan. This is a perennial with beautiful leaf rosettes in winter. The leaves are deeply lobed, covered with bronze-golden hairs which can be rotted by excessive winter wet so should not be immediately under the drip from trees, although they do need partial shade. The flowers are yellow, wide and nodding. 60cm/2ft. Z7–8

MELITTIS melissophyllum. *LAMIACEAE*. Bastard Balm. From open woods of central and southern Europe to west Asia. I like this curious Dead Nettle. In the upper half of its slightly bristly, green-leaved stems are whorls of large, white-lipped flowers with a difference. Each lower lip is stained pinkish-purple. It likes a little shade and leaf-mould, in a retentive soil. 46cm/18in. Z7–10

MENTHA. *LAMIACEAE*. Mint. All mints prefer damp soil, but with their invasive habit they can make trouble if they are unwisely sited. One of my mistakes was to plant Water Mint, which has pretty mauve flowers, in my bog garden. It took a lot of moving; every small bit left undetected made feet of new shoots. Perversely it is possible to lose mints that you value. I had to move my 'Eau de Cologne'-scented mint from where it was contentedly confined and have not yet established it in a suitable home. The following mints are garden worthy, but could be dangerous nuisances in very small gardens, unless confined, perhaps in a bucket with the odd hole knocked in it for drainage.
M. × gracilis **'Variegata'** has dark green leaves striped with gold, on reddish-purple stems. It needs sun to produce the best colour and can be useful and decorative on the edge of a shrub border that is not too dry. *Arum italicum* grows well through it, marking its position when the mint is dormant in winter, while the stems of juicy red *Arum* fruits show up well among the green and gold of the mint foliage. 46cm/18in. Z3–8
M. longifolia. Horse Mint. From wet meadows and along water courses of central and southern Europe to central Asia. An attractive mint in leaf and flower: woolly, cylindrical heads of soft grey-blue flowers are offset by downy, grey leaves. 1.2m/4ft. Z6–9
M. pulegium. Pennyroyal. From marshes and wet meadows of mainly southern Europe to west Asia. This is used to make Oil of Pennyroyal. On damp soil it quickly makes flat-pressed mats of small shining green leaves, neat and useful as ground-cover. The whorls of lavender-

blue flowers, 15–23cm/6–9in high, are attractive. Z6–9
M. × villosa. Rounded, crinkly and very woolly leaves are edged and irregularly blotched with pale creamy-white. Sometimes whole shoots are entirely white. 60cm/2ft. Z3–7
M. suaveolens. I think this is better-looking than *M. × villosa*. The leaves are more evenly marked cream and green. 46cm/18in. Z5–9

MENYANTHES trifoliata. *MENYANTHACEAE*. Bog Bean. From peaty bogs, marshes and shallow water all round the northern hemisphere into the Arctic regions. This is another plant to unite water and land, ideal to soften the hard edges of a large, lined pool. It is a spreading plant, and will cover metres or yards when suited. Prostrate, branching stems are covered with smooth, grey-green, divided leaves, not unlike those of the vegetable Broad Bean. These stems

float like rafts on to the water from the moist pond-edge. Clustered heads of white, fringed flowers stand just above the leaves on 15cm/6in stems, in May. Z3–10

MERTENSIA. *BORAGINACEAE*. Valued for their delicate blue, bell-shaped flowers, these woodlanders are sometimes called 'Smooth Lungwort' to distinguish them from the bristly-leaved *Pulmonaria*. They need a little shade, in well-drained, cool, leaf-mould soil.
M. ciliata. Mountain Bluebell, or Languid Ladies. Found wild in subalpine meadows among spruce, or along mountain stream-banks in the Rockies from Montana-Oregon-Nevada to New Mexico. It is at its best in June, making 60cm/2ft high branched leafy stems dangling with small sky-blue bells which open from pink buds. In the wild it is found growing with the rosy-mauve musk, *Mimulus lewisii*. Z3–6

Menyanthes trifoliata

M. virginica. Virginian Cowslip. From moist meadows and along streams, sometimes in open damp woods, of eastern and central United States. This is one of the gems of the spring woodland garden. Arching stems, 30cm/1ft high, carry clusters of pink buds opening to cool violet-blue flowers. They droop, cowslip-like, over smooth. blue-green leaves. The new shoots, as they appear through the soil, are purple. 46cm/18in. Z3–9

MIMULUS. *SCROPHULARIACEAE.* Monkey Musk. Most of the musks quickly cover metres or yards of wet soil, if allowed, with carpets of green rosettes and vivid flowers. They will grow in the squelchy mud at the pond margins, or on the edge of a damp border. The coarse ones are suitable only for large areas. The smaller ones are for the really small pool edge, or damp cool spots in the rock garden, where they can be cherished.

M. × burnettii. A hybrid between *M. cupreus* and *M. luteus*. I find this neater growing than some. Low rosettes are smothered with pretty coppery-orange flowers in mid summer. 25–30cm/10–12in. Z6–9

M. cardinalis. Found along streams and in swamps of Oregon and California. This is an upright-growing musk which can take less-saturated soil, merely damp will do, provided it does not dry out. The light green leaves are downy, soft contrast for brilliant orange-red snapdragon-like flowers which come in long succession from mid summer onwards. Sometimes a seedling produces rich red flowers with dark centres showing sulphur-yellow stamens and throat. They stand 75cm–1m/30–39in. Z6–9

M. cupreus. From swampy mountain meadows in the Andes of central Chile. This is similar to *M. luteus*, but more compact in habit. Many named clones have arisen from it, one of the best being *M. c.* 'Whitecroft Scarlet', which makes very small-leaved rosettes which are lost beneath bright scarlet flowers. It is best in a choice, moist corner on the rock garden, where it can be cherished and

where it will stand not more than 15–20cm/6–8in high. Z6–10

M. guttatus. From stream-banks of California to Alaska, eastward to the Rockies. This is the familiar yellow musk spotted with brownish-red. Seedlings vary; some are more richly coloured than others. It is very rampant, lovely at the water's edge where its long trailers float out, full of flower, together with the Water Forget-me-not, *Myosotis scorpioides*. Included in this group would be the form 'hose-in-hose' in which one lipped flower sits comfortably inside another. There have been many hybrids bred from this plant, *M. cupreus* and *M. variegatus*, producing a variety of colours, but not all are reliably hardy. Z6–9

M. lewisii. Of damp mountain meadows and stream-banks in the Rockies and Sierra Nevada, from British Columbia to California and Utah. This is not one of the hardiest of musks but survives most winters, reappearing as a seedling or two if the parent has been killed. It makes low bushy little plants covered with flowers. They are such a pretty colour, warm rosy-mauve with yellow throats, continuing to blossom for several weeks in mid summer. Cool soil and part shade suit it well. It is lovely with *Persicaria macrophylla*, and *Mertensia ciliata*, with which it grows wild. 38–46cm/15–18in. Z5–10

M. ringens. From swamps and along streams of eastern and central United States and eastern Canada. This needs a small-scale design to show it off. Dark green, narrow leaves ascend erect square stems, ending with a spire of narrow snapdragon-like flowers, soft lavender-mauve. 75cm–1m/2½–3ft. Z6–9

M. 'Wisley Red'. This good hybrid makes compact plants with rich crimson flowers in mid summer. 20–25cm/8–10. Z6–9

MITELLA. *SAXIFRAGACEAE.* I have long grown this plant under the name *M. breweri*, which comes from conifer woods in British Columbia. I have learnt that my plant is not *M. breweri*, but may be *M. caulescens*. In cool leafy soil, in part shade, this is one of my favourite trailing

plants. It runs like *Tiarella cordifolia*, but is much smaller and daintier, its clumps and trailers covered with small heart-shaped lobed leaves. In May short stems carry inconspicuous flowers, creating a pale haze of green. When picked they are seen to be tiny green discs surrounded with whiskery fringes – such delicacy is too good to be overlooked in the garden. With choice woodlanders this little plant creates just the right floor for a miniature 'forest'. 15–23cm/6–9in. Z5–8

MONARDA *didyma*. *LAMIACEAE.* Bee Balm or Oswego Tea. From moist woods and along streams of the eastern and central United States and Canada. The pleasantly aromatic leaves can be infused in boiling water to make a refreshing drink. These plants need a rich moist soil; they are much more prone to mildew if the soil becomes dry. They make running clumps which send up many tall, 90–150cm/3–5ft leafy, branching stems topped with curiously constructed flowers. Each has a central boss of closely packed tubes from which emerge rings of curving, claw-shaped flowers. Among the hybrids are:

M. 'Beauty of Cobham'. Cyclamen-pink flowers spring from a deep purple centre while the surrounding and supporting large leafy bracts are also shaded purple – an altogether spectacular mixture. 75cm–1m/30–39in. Z4–8

M. 'Cambridge Scarlet'. Brilliant scarlet flowers emerge from a soft maroon centre. Large bushy masses of flower are formed by late summer. 1.2–1.5m/4–5ft. Z4–8

M. 'Croftway Pink'. The packed centre is pale, in keeping with the delicate shell-pink flowers. 90–120cm/3–4ft. Z4–8

M. 'Schneewittchen' is pure white. Up to 1.2m/4ft. Z4–8

MORINA *longifolia*. *MORINACEAE.* From mountain meadows of the Himalayas. This is a plant of character. It makes clumps of thistle-like leaves, narrow, dark green and softly prickly. If you back into them when weeding you are not hurt, but are aware of the pleasant spicy smell which comes from the bruised leaves. In mid summer several tall stems, 60–75cm/2–2½ft appear, carrying at intervals upturned, cup-shaped calyces which are filled with pale green narrow tubes. From these come hooded, tubular flowers, first white, deepening to rose and finally crimson, all colours being seen at once on the same stem. When they have gone the best part is left, the green stem with its upturned spiny seed heads, reminiscent of the roof of a pagoda. They make a supremely decorative shape, green or dried. They need well-drained but deep retentive soil. Z6–9

MYOSOTIS scorpioides. BORAGINACEAE. From stream-sides, marshes and sometimes wet woods of the northern hemisphere. The Water Forget-me-not of our ditches is happy along the muddy edge of the pond, even growing out into the water. In May and June it is smothered with branching stems of small blue flowers, delightful to trail among bog primulas and water irises. Once there were various varieties available, with larger or darker flowers. Someone may have them still. *M. s.* 'Mermaid' is an improved plant for smaller areas, being less invasive. 15–20cm/6–8in. Z5–9

NARCISSUS. AMARYLLIDACEAE. Most of the larger *Narcissus* species and hybrids, and several of the smaller wild ones, appreciate good moist soil. They have been much interbred, selected, enlarged and altered, and the resulting highly cultivated strains are out of the scope of this book. However, our own Wild Daffodil, *Narcissus pseudonarcissus,* is beautiful and has yielded some delightful forms of its own, and there are some hybrids of other wild species which retain much of the grace of their ancestors, especially those of *N. cyclamineus* and *N. triandrus.* These are larger and more robust than the wild plants, and I value them and grow them in drifts, where they flourish in retentive soil, or in part shade. I also grow forms of the Pheasant's Eye, *N. poeticus,* with its white perianth segments and little yellow and scarlet cups,

Narcissus cyclamineus

and a few other less altered hybrids and also species, which I cannot describe here. Z4–8

NEPETA govaniana. LAMIACEAE. From Kashmir. This is a surprising catmint which does best in cool, moist conditions. The lower half of the plant provides a setting of light green, scented foliage, while above it the erect branched flower stems are a-dangle with widely spaced clusters of lemon-yellow buds which open to paler, wide-mouthed, tubular flowers. The delicate display continues for weeks from late August into September. 75cm–1m/30–39in. Z5–9

NIEREMBERGIA repens. SOLANACEAE. From stream-sides and lake-shores of central Chile, Argentina and Uruguay. This is a choice and lovely little plant when grown well in sunny, well-drained but damp soil on the edge of a border, small pool or rock garden. It slowly makes close-spreading mats by means of underground stems. Surprisingly large, fluted, cup-shaped flowers – white with a yellow centre – nestle just above the leaves. 5–8cm/2–3in. Z7–10

Omphalodes cappadocica

OMPHALODES. BORAGINACEAE. These plants are valued for their lovely spring flowers, but also make good ground-cover in cool soil with ample humus. *O. cappadocica.* Grows over damp rocks in woodlands of the south Caucasus and Turkey. This plant will grow in sun where there remains enough moisture or in part shade. It does not increase as readily as *O. verna* but makes slowly creeping clumps of grey-green oval leaves which are prettily ribbed and pointed. In spring they are smothered with dainty sprays of rich blue flowers, larger than Forget-me-nots, and finer. 15cm/6in. Good selections are *O. c.* 'Cherry Ingram' and *O. c.* 'Starry Eyes'. Z6–8 *O. verna.* From open woods of southern Europe. Blue-eyed Mary is fine for naturalizing in light woodland or shrubberies where there is ample humus and rainfall. It rapidly increases by runners when established, making dense carpets of heart-shaped leaves. Throughout spring it is decorated with waves of tiny blue flowers. 10cm/4in. There is a white selection called *O. v.* 'Alba'. Z4–8

ORONTIUM aquaticum. ARACEAE. The Golden Club. For the edge of a pond, in water 30–45cm/1–1½ft deep.

From around the edge of the cluster of bluish-green, wax-coated leaves in early summer appear long white stems bearing upturned tips of minute yellow blossoms, making me think of the glowing end of a cigarette. They are the naked spadices most usually seen in arums protected by a showy spathe. Z6–10

OURISIA. SCROPHULARIACEAE. Choice plants for damp, well-drained sites, either in the rock garden or on a raised north-facing bed. In nature they grow in the open, in moist areas by stream-sides, so in the garden provide shelter from scorching sun or drying wind. They make close carpets of foliage from creeping rhizomes, and are best in lime-free soil. Z7–9

O. coccinea. From the Andes of Chile. This plant makes low tufts of bright green lobed and toothed leaves. Above them stand 20cm/8in stems of brilliant scarlet tubular flowers, not unlike tiny penstemons. They flower intermittently from mid to late summer.

O. macrocarpa. From moist, peaty, tussocky mountain grassland of western South Island, New Zealand, often with *Ranunculus lyallii*. This looks very different from *O. coccinea*. It has large, thick, leathery leaves with finely cut edges. Above them are held large clusters of pure white flowers, rather like those of *Bergenia*, with yellow eyes, on stems 15–20cm/6–8in tall.

O. macrophylla. From tussocky mountain grassland of southern North Island, New Zealand. This plant is similar but smaller: the same exquisite flowers are carried in whorls on stems up to 30cm/1ft high.

OXALIS acetosella. OXALIDACEAE. From moist shady woods, including the northern conifer forests, of Eurasia and North America. The Common Wood Sorrel makes low carpets of clover-like leaves, but they are softer and of a fresher green, and fold down each night. It sends up large, frail, white flowers pencilled with pink, each on a slender stem about 8cm/3in tall. It is thought to be the original Shamrock. Z5–11

O. oregana. From the coastal forests of northern California to Washington, the Redwood Sorrel is a rather larger plant, its flower stems reaching 15cm/6in high, and its leaflets often having lighter green marks. The flowers are pale to rose-pink, veined with a darker shade. This is a superior plant to our native Wood Sorrel. Z6–11

Orontium acquaticum

PACHYPHRAGMA macrophyllum.
BRASSICACEAE. From the deciduous
forests of the Caucasus. This useful and
pretty plant will grow and flower in quite
deep shade. Bunched heads of small white
cruciform flowers standing about
30cm/1ft high appear in early spring like
patches of snow among the first daffodils.
They are followed by large, round, shiny
green leaves, their overlapping mounds
making handsome ground-cover. Z5–9

PACHYSANDRA terminalis.
BUXACEAE. From the hill and lowland
forests of Japan and China. This plant
will make carpets of evergreen foliage in
densest shade provided it is not too dry.
In moist leaf-mould soil the underground
stems support evergreen rosettes of
toothed, leathery leaves which makes
dense but attractive ground-cover,
topped in spring with loose spikes of
creamy-green flowers. 30cm/1ft. Z5–9
P. t. '**Variegata**' has the toothed edges
of its leaves painted creamy-white. It is
a little less vigorous. 25cm/10in. Z5–9

PAEONIA. PAEONIACEAE. Whether
species or cultivars, Peonies need to be
planted in deeply dug holes, in a rich
mixture of decayed vegetable matter.
They last longer in flower if sited with
some shelter from direct sunlight and
damaging wind. A good mulch is
beneficial and the occasional dressing of
farmyard manure for feeding. I describe
only some of the species from which the
double-flowered garden hybrids have
been developed.
P. delavayi. From openings in pine and
evergreen oak forests of Yunnan and east
Tibet. This makes a woody shrub, up to
1.5m/5ft. Its chief beauty lies in the
foliage, which is finely cut, stained and
veined with maroon. The downturned
flowers are of wax-like texture, dark
crimson in colour, sometimes blackish-
crimson, lit with golden anthers. Z5–8
P. d. **var.** *lutea.* From openings in pine and
evergreen oak woods of the mountains of
Yunnan and east Tibet. Z5–8
P. d. **var.** *ludlowii.* This is another peony
I value more for its foliage and form than

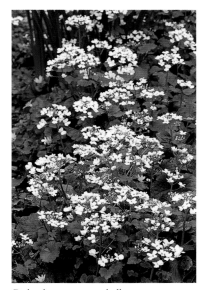
Pachyphragma macrophyllum

its flowers – which I often miss in the
spring, being smallish, drooping, saucer-
shaped blooms, clear yellow in colour,
already concealed in the imposing foliage
which clothes the large woody stems, up
to 2m/6½ft in height. I value it as a
background shrub, while in autumn large
fat seed pods dangle beneath the leaves,
filled with shining black seeds, large as
marbles. Z5–8
P. emodi. Grows in openings in mixed
forests of an evergreen oak, spruce and
tree rhododendrons, in high mountain
forests of the central and western
Himalayas. In spring the new leaves are
bronze and shining, each deeply cut to
the vein. Thin, red-tinted stems carry two
or three nodding white flowers. They are
flat-faced, about 5cm/2in across, ivory-
white petals centred with a golden circle
of stamens. 90cm/3ft. Z5–8
P. '**Late Windflower**' (*P. emodi* × *P. veitchii*)
is more generally known. It differs from
P. emodi in being somewhat larger overall,
yet remaining exquisitely beautiful.
Z5–8
P. lactiflora. From north-east Asia. This
beautiful and unsurpassed peony is the
forerunner of the large-flowered Chinese
hybrids. Easily grown in reasonably fertile
soil its huge, white, single flowers with

their central boss of yellow stamens are
well contrasted with healthy bronze-
tinted foliage and stems. 90cm/3ft.
Z3–8
P. mlokosewitschii. From the rocky sides
of gorges in deciduous mountain woods,
in two limited areas of the Caucasus,
and west Elburz. It is true that the pale,
lemon-yellow globular flowers are
fleeting but the whole plant contributes
colour to the garden for months. By the
end of February fat, cherry-red buds are
breaking through the soil, slowly
unfolding pleated leaves of warm
brownish-maroon, which only slowly
fade to soft grey-green as the flower buds
swell in May. It is worth the whole year
of waiting to see the large, rounded petals
open to filtered sunlight, sheltering in
their hearts golden stamens surrounding
a cherry centre. In the autumn tight seed
pods split open to show blue-black
'pearls' nestling against a crinkled
crimson lining. 60–75cm/2–2½ft. Z5–8
P. obovata **var.** *alba.* From glades in
mountain woods, from Japan and far
eastern Siberia to western China. You
need to be in the garden every day in
spring to make sure you do not miss such
fleeting but memorable beauty. Perfectly
round petals form translucent globes of
alabaster-white, parting just enough to
show a ring of yellow stamens enclosing
a crimson stigma. The stems and leaves
are lovely too, tinted with soft cherry and
copper tones. Surrounded by soft spring
colours it needs shelter from sudden cold
winds, even though it be May. Late in the
autumn there will be large satiny-blue
seeds. 60–75cm/2–2½ft. Z4–8
P. veitchii. From openings in forest and
bush on the mountains of south-west
China. This pretty peony is far removed
from the heavy-headed double cultivars.
It has dainty, finely cut, branched stems of
foliage, dark green in colour, above which
are carried flat-faced single flowers with
slightly fluted edges. Their colour ranges
from deep magenta to palest shell-pink,
the centres filled with cream anthers on
pink filaments. Grown from seed they
vary in size and colour. All are pretty but
it is worth selecting the larger flowered

forms. They flower freely, followed by copious seed heads which are also attractive to pick – not too large and filled with dark blue seeds. 30cm/1ft. Z6–8

PATRINIA scabiosifolia. VALERIANACEAE. I value the bright, fresh effect of this plant in late-summer–autumn. Above clumps of coarsely cut green leaves stand thin branching stems carrying sprays of clear yellow tiny flowers. 1.2m/4ft. Z5–9
P. triloba. From mountain meadows of Japan. A plant that flowers in July, in part shade, is worth knowing. Provided the soil has remained damp enough this little plant will produce cool sprays of lemon-yellow flowers above fresh green, deeply cut leaves. It spreads in a modest fashion, too nice to be a nuisance, not more than 30cm/1ft tall. Z5–9

PERSICARIA. POLYGONACEAE. The Knotweeds. The following plants provide some of our most attractive plants in the damp garden. They all need retentive soil, some needing more moisture than others, especially those with large leaves.
P. affinis. From the Himalayas, where it grows on rocky river-banks and meadows, and hangs in rosy clumps from moist precipices, often with *Anaphalis triplinervis,* which surprises me since the *Anaphalis* is a grey-foliaged plant, yet is affected by drought. In gardens it will stand less wet soil, but must not dry out. The type has short thick spikes of salmon-pink flowers. 25cm/10in. Z4–8
P. a. '**Darjeeling Red**' starts with thin rat-tail spikes, white at first, deepening to pink and finally filling out and deepening to dark crimson-red, all shades seen at the same time. The warm, reddish tints of the winter foliage are especially good. 25cm/10in. Z3–9
P. a. '**Donald Lowndes**' has short, thick pokers of seemingly double salmon-pink flowers. They flower from mid summer until the autumn frosts, and then the low carpeting foliage turns bright reddish-brown, remaining a feature all winter. 20–25cm/8–10in. Z4–8
P. amplexicaulis. From the Himalayas. This makes both a feature and a fine

Persicaria amplexicaulis 'Rosea'

background plant. Although it will grow in any good border soil, in rich, damp soil it makes huge leafy plants, 1.5m/5ft high and across. From midsummer until the first frosts it is alight with slim, vivid, crimson tapers. 'Rosea' is pale pink, 'Alba' white. Lovely behind *Aster × frikartii, Aconitum carmichaelii* 'Arendsii' or *Lilium speciosum.* Z3–9
P. bistorta. From damp meadows of northern Eurasia far into the Arctic. It has become a mountain plant further south. Z3–8
P. b. **subsp.** *carnea.* This plant belongs to the *P. bistorta* group, but is much more suitable for small gardens. It does not invade but makes tidy clumps of long, narrow leaves which are both undulating and curving. The almost bare flower stems

are topped with fluffy bottle-brushes of coral-pink. It flowers prolifically, at its best in early summer, but can make a fine show in autumn. It will stand less moist soil than *P. bistorta.* 46–60cm/1½–2ft. Z3–8
P. b. '**Superba**'. This selected form produces in May–June fat pokers of densely packed flowers 9cm/3½in long, more than 2.5cm/1in across, of soft mauve-pink. Large dock-like leaves are almost 25cm/10in long and 15cm/6in wide. It must have ample moisture, and loves to grow by the water's edge; slowly invasive. 75cm–90cm/2½–3ft. Z3–8
P. campanulata. From damp places in the Himalayas. This has lovely foliage as well as pretty flowers. It starts at ground level in spring, covering damp land with

clusters of crinkled, dark green leaves. As the colonies of flower stems grow, up to 1m/39in , one admires the ribbed leaves with pale buff-coloured backs set along the entire stem. Finally they are smothered with drooping panicles of tiny, pale pink bell-flowers which open from buds of deep rose. Although this plant spreads by surface shoots it is easily dislodged, never a nuisance. Its frothy heads of colour are a pleasure for weeks in late summer, early autumn. It will flower in sun or part shade. Z5–9

P. macrophylla. From moist stony alpine turf in the west Chinese mountains and Tibet borderlands to the Himalayas. Here is another late-flowering and lovely *P. bistorta* type. In moist soils, in sun, it flowers continuously throughout late summer and autumn. It makes neat compact clumps of narrow, wavy, dark green leaves. The flowers are small pokers on 46–60cm/1½–2ft stems, made of smooth buds which do not open to show their stamens, the waxy texture adding to the almost luminous shade of amethyst-pink. Z5–9

P. milletii. From moist stony alpine turf in the west Chinese mountains and Tibet borderlands. Another plant in the *P. bistorta* class, but I find it one of the less easy ones. It needs really moist soil, and can be overlaid by large calthas or ligularias in late summer and autumn. It makes slowly increasing clumps of dark green, narrow, undulating leaves,

producing on almost bare stems flower heads the size and shape of rich, ripe loganberries, a dark crimson-red. 46cm/18in. Z5–9

P. polymorpha. Sent to me by the famous landscaping team of Wolfgang Oehme and James van Sweden. I do not as yet know its native habitat. It forms a tall, columnar plant composed of stout stems handsomely clothed in large, pointed green leaves, crowned in midsummer with wide, branching heads of small, creamy-white flowers. By September, the flower heads become stained bronze pink and green. This plant makes an important statement towering above lower plants, such as hostas, dicentras, ferns and ajugas. Needs deep rich soil, sun or part shade, sheltered from wind. It dies down in winter. 1.8m/6ft. Z5–9

P. vacciniifolia. From bouldery slopes among birches and dwarf rhododendrons in the Himalayas. This is one of the smallest and prettiest of the persicarias. Completely prostrate reddish-brown stems will spread flat mats across paving or flow down a rock face, covered with tiny oval green leaves. In late summer the little flowers begin to appear, carried in upright tiny spikes, covering the plants with glowing pink; they flower from August to November. 8–10cm/3–4in. Z6–9

P. v. **Variegata Group** has branching stems covered with large, oval leaves, slightly ruched and wrinkled, irregularly

marbled in all shades of cream and green. Individual plants may be about 60cm/2ft high and across, clothed with leaves to the ground. It makes a beautiful light feature, against a plain green background, in soil that does not dry out, and sheltered from sun and wind which can damage the delicate foliage. Z5–10

P. virginiana. From woods and thickets of the eastern and central United States, eastern Canada and Japan.

P. v. **(Variegata Group) 'Painter's Palette'**. This is similar to *P. v.* Variegata Group, but the centre of each leaf is marked across with a distinct V-sign which runs parallel to the end tip. This V is almost brick-red when fresh, but darkens to blackish-bronze. The newest leaves are sometimes almost entirely cream, just faintly brushed with delicate touches of pink and pale green. Tiny rat-tail wisps of little brown flowers appear in late summer. 60cm/2ft. Z5–10

P. wallichii. From the Himalayas. Forms a great shrub-like plant, best suited to landscape planting, or areas of wild garden, since it spreads by underground stems. In spring it throws up many stout stems clothed in large, ovate leaves on red leaf stalks, crowned in autumn with airy sprays of tiny, white, honey-scented flowers, scenting the air far and wide. The effect is handsome and dramatic. Good near water with other giants, such as *Gunnera*, *Eupatorium* and *Miscanthus*. 2m/6½ft. Z5–9

Persicaria bistorta 'Superba'

Persicaria campanulata

Persicaria polymorpha

P. weyrichii. From gravelly mountain slopes of north Japan and Sakhalin; also on shingly sea-shores. This plant makes handsome rosettes of large, dark green, pointed leaves, and produces branching spires of tiny creamy flowers very like those of rhubarb, followed by flat, transparent, brownish-red seed cases. Its habit of growth and size of leaf make this a useful buffer between one type of plant and another. 60–75cm/2–2½ft. Z5–8

PETASITES. *ASTERACEAE*. These plants should be used only with careful forethought, as they are very invasive. Where there is room, around large lake-sides, farm reservoirs or heavy clay banks that need binding and covering, they can be dramatic and handsome.
P. fragrans. From southern Europe and north Africa. On a mild day towards the end of January or in early February, you may suddenly catch a sweet smell of almonds. It comes from this plant, Winter Heliotrope: 15cm/6in stems carrying up to ten little clusters of flower emerge before the leaves appear. Because there is little else to admire you look closely and see that the tiny starry flowers are white, with buds and calyces stained dull purple. Inside the flowers are little streaks and dots of purple. Rushing up to smother them are round, light green, heart-shaped leaves which will be from 15–20cm/6–8in across, making impenetrable carpets, well sited in hedge bottoms or waste land. This plant can be a pestiferous nuisance in the wrong place but I thought it looked beautiful along the road sides in Ireland. Z4–9
P. japonicus. From along streams in the woods of Japan, Korea and China. The variety *P. j.* var. *giganteus* is from north Japan or Sakhalin, and makes overlapping mounds of enormous round leaves, almost as impressive as *Gunnera*, up to 1.2m/4ft across. They disappear in winter, leaving totally bare soil which is dotted in February with round green buds the size of cricket balls. Rows of pale green bracts turn back like a ruff to leave a central posy of tiny, white, close-packed daisy

Petasites japonicus var. *giganteus*

flowers. The effect is enchanting, in the right place. Z5–9

PHLOX. *POLEMONIACEAE*. The United States of America is the home of our garden phloxes, which vary from creeping mats and cushions to the tall border varieties. There are many species and cultivars. The following are a few that prefer a cool and rather damp situation:
P. adsurgens. From shady rocky slopes and cliffs of the coast ranges of north California and Oregon. Too often thrust on to a hot rock garden, this lovely *Phlox* prefers a little shade and plenty of humus in soil that does not dry out. It makes a scrambling patch of lax stems covered with small, shining, evergreen leaves. Twisted buds open to shallow saucers of bright salmon-pink. *P. a.* 'Wagon Wheel' is the same colour, but the petals are narrower. Z4–8
P. divaricata. This creeping *Phlox* carpets some American woods with its lilac flowers as do bluebells in England. I grow two named selections, *P. d.* 'Blue Dreams' and *P. d.* 'May Breeze'. Z4–8
P. divaricata subsp. *laphamii* 'Chattahoochee' is an outstanding plant. Lax stems 15–23cm/6–9in long are clothed in narrow, slightly hairy, dark green leaves. They are topped with wide heads of silky flowers. The petals are

widely spaced, joined at the centre by a wine-red patch. The soft rich-blue bleaches to very pale blue as they fade, while the central zone deepens to purple, the whole making a striking harmony of blues on the same plant. I find it does best in cool shaded soil; tucked against a taller plant is sometimes enough shelter. It starts to flower in May, continuing until early July. Z4–8
P. paniculata. From woods of the eastern and central United States. This is a parent of the well-known garden border phloxes. It makes a tall, willowy plant, up to 1.2m/4ft, and when well grown into a substantial clump the delicate lilac-mauve heads are very attractive. It is not often seen in gardens, but its offspring need deep rich soil with adequate moisture all summer. A border which does not stand in sun all day is preferable. Such conditions help the plants to resist attacks of eelworm, to which they are martyrs. There is also a white variety, *P. paniculata* var. *alba*. Z4–8 There are many named cultivars. I grow the following variegated forms:
P. p. 'Harlequin', produced by Alan Bloom, has rather less cream variegation than *P. p.* 'Norah Leigh', but grows more strongly. The long narrow leaves have a shadowed central zone surrounded by an irregular border of cream which becomes wider and more conspicuous on leaves nearest the top of the stems. Heads of suffused purple-violet flowers in August seem surprisingly good for a variegated plant. They smell delicious. 75cm/2½ft. Z4–8
P. p. 'Norah Leigh' has almost totally cream leaves, with only a thin central zone of green. The result is a plant of little vigour, but it grows surprisingly well and manages to produce pale pink (or mauve pink) flowers. 46–60cm/1½–2ft. Z4–8
P. pilosa. From the prairies of the central United States and Canada, and also in the east. This *Phlox* runs about, sending up quantities of fine stems, 38cm–46cm/15–18in high, from underground shoots. Quite large loose pyramidal heads of soft pinky-mauve flowers, sweetly scented, provide colour for most of the summer, continuing on a succession of side shoots.

Phlox paniculata 'Norah Leigh'

This is a really good plant in retentive soil, and where it cannot engulf tiny neighbours. In drier soil it survives and flowers well in part shade. Z4–9

P. × *procumbens* **'Variegata'** is a carpeting plant which grows surprisingly well for a variegated plant. It excels itself by bearing strong heads of silky pink flowers which actually add something to the already colourful foliage. 15cm/6in. Z3–8

Phormium tenax

PHORMIUM. *PHORMIACEAE.* These plants provide a sharp, architectural feature, as yuccas do in the hot dry garden. They like heavy, enriched soil in full sun. In cold districts it is wise to protect them in winter with straw or bracken and possibly a sheet of polythene tied around. Continuous freezing wet can kill them to ground level, if not outright. Winter inspection is necessary by water-sides to ensure that water voles are not making their larder in the succulent leaf bases.

P. cookianum. From damp mountain scrub and grassland, and on wet rocks and cliffs in New Zealand. This makes a much smaller plant than *P. tenax*, with stiff sword-like leaves, valued in smaller settings as contrast among soft rounded shapes. It flowers more regularly. Wide-spread stems about 1.2–1.5m/4–5ft high carry rather dingy green and orange tubular flowers, but the almost black spikes of twisted seed heads are very decorative. There are several variegated forms to be had, imported from New Zealand, where they have been developed. They need protection from cruel north-east wind and frosts. Z8–10

P. tenax. New Zealand Flax. From river banks and marshes, damp sandy or

Phormium tenax Purpureum Group

gravelly places of lowland New Zealand. While the smaller, colourful, variegated forms are very admirable this one, huge and imposing, beats them all for form and dignity. Sword-like leaves, 1.5–2.5m/5–8ft high of smooth grey-green, edged with a dark brown line, can make a clump many feet round and across, like a gigantic, stiffly upright Iris. The curious flower spike towers up to 3m/12ft, carrying clusters of dull red flowers which later become black bunches of short banana-shaped seed pods. Z8–10

P. t. **Purpureum Group.** There are variations in size and tone of this variety. The best have large, dark purplish-brown leaves and are propagated by division. Seedlings produce some purple-leaved varieties, not necessarily as good – or they might be better. 1.2–1.5m/4–5ft. Z9–10

P. t. **'Variegatum'.** There are now several different clones available; the best have bright yellow leaves thinly striped with green, others commence with cream-streaked leaves maturing to grey-green edged with cream. In frost-free districts they are breathtaking, looking like great bursts of sunlight, 2–2.5m/6–8ft high and across. In less favoured districts they are still impressive, but it is wise to protect them. Z9–10

PHYSOSTEGIA virginiana. LAMIACEAE. The Obedient Plant. From damp places in the east-central United States and Canada. Running shoots send up many tall, slender stems, 75cm–1m/30–39in high, alternately set with pairs of narrow green leaves. Tapering spires, sometimes branched, of close-set, narrow, tubular flowers in glowing pinky-mauve make a display for weeks in mid summer. The flowers stand out from the stem on rows of hinged 'ratchets', so that you can push them to face another way. I wonder why such a complicated mechanism evolved? Z3–9

P. v. 'Alba' produces white flowers. It is not quite so adept at being pushed around, but I like the stems of close-set, upturned green calyces which remain to make interesting green spikes when the flowers have gone. 75cm–1m/2½–3ft. Z3–9

P. v. var. *speciosa* 'Bouquet Rose' produces long-lasting spires of pale lilac-pink flowers. 90cm/3ft. Z4–9

P. v. 'Vivid'. This flowers later, in early autumn, and makes shorter, denser spikes of light purple flowers, good on the edge of the border, among colchicums, or in front of Japanese anemones. 30cm/1ft. Z3–9

PHYTEUMA ovatum. CAMPANULACEAE. From mountain meadows and open woods of the central and southern European mountains. This is a tall strong rampion, growing to 60cm/2ft or even 1m/3ft, with heart-shaped leaves, and long columns of black-purple, curiously-shaped flowers which open halfway up but not at the tip. It seems to prefer damper meadows than most of its relatives. Z4–9

PHYTOLACCA. PHYTOLACCACEAE. These completely herbaceous plants take up a lot of room when well grown in deep, retentive soil. They make a huge woody rootstock which sends up thick, branching stems set with large, oval leaves up to 15cm/6in long. The foliage effect alone can be interesting as contrast among smaller-leaved shrubs, or at the

Physostegia virginiana
var. *speciosa* 'Bouquet Rose'

back of herbaceous plants. All parts of these plants are poisonous.

P. americana. The Virginia Poke Weed. From river-banks, open woods and bushy wood edges of the eastern and central United States. Every branch holds an upturned spike densely set with small, starry, white flowers. Slowly they develop as small green fruits. Gradually the tiny stalks and calyces turn carmine-pink as each fruit, still showing itself to be made up of a cluster of seeds, turns purple and then shining black. 1.2–1.5m/4–5ft. Z6–10

Phytolacca americana

P. polyandra. From Yunnan, south-west China. This species starts with pokes of vivid pink flowers but the final heads of evil-looking black fruits are made as much rounder, simpler berries containing a cluster of seeds inside. The contrast of black fruits with their crimson-stained stems and the surrounding yellows of autumn foliage can be very dramatic. 1.2–1.5m/4–5ft. Z6–9

PLATYCODON grandiflorus. CAMPANULACEAE. Balloon Flower. Widely scattered through the mountains of the Japanese islands, also in China, Korea and Manchuria. I find these lovely plants, being a relative of the campanulas, do best in deep, fertile soil. They flower late, from July to September, so need some moisture in mid summer. Neat clumps made up of many short stems, up to 30cm/1ft, are set with small, blue-green leaves. They are topped with a spire of large buds which slowly inflate like a balloon, until the petals split open to show large, flat-faced flowers with pointed petals in shades of blue, pale pink mother-of-pearl, and pure white. Z3–9

PODOPHYLLUM. BERBERIDACEAE. These plants when suited make slowly creeping rootstocks in cool, shady places in damp leaf-mould soil. They are curious, elegant specimen plants to be watched from the moment they unfold their pleated umbrella-like leaves, poised on the top of single stems.

P. hexandrum. From woods and among bushes in Sichuan, south-west China, to the Himalayas. Round, deeply lobed leaves are mottled brown when they first appear. On top of the leaf sits a solitary white-cupped flower. Later in the year, as the leaves begin to deteriorate, you will be astonished to see a large red fruit, as big as a bantam's egg, hanging just below the leaf. 46cm/18in. *P. h.* 'Majus' is an extra-large form; *P. h.* 'Chinense' has rose-pink flowers. Z5–8

P. peltatum. Mayapple. From moist woods of the eastern and central United States and Canada. This is similar, with rose-coloured fruits. They say it is a good colonizer, but I don't seem to have just what it needs. 46cm/18in. Z3–9

POLEMONIUM. POLEMONIACEAE. These plants will grow in sun, or part shade, in retentive soil. Their pretty, divided foliage and silky cup-shaped flowers will not stand very drying conditions.

P. caeruleum. Jacob's Ladder. From damp meadows of northern Eurasia and in mountains further south and in North America. At its base this plant makes a tidy mound of long, arching stems of narrow leaflets arranged in pairs. At the top of upright, branched stems, 75cm–1m/30–39in, are clusters of innocent-faced flowers, wide-open, sky-blue, the unmarked centre fading to white, holding out orange-tipped stamens. They are produced for weeks, even months on end, especially if not allowed to set early seed. *P. c.* subsp. *caeruleum* f. *album* is a fine white form, and there are varieties in varying shades of blue. *P. reptans* is shorter, 60cm/2ft, with a more open, spreading head of flowers and less finely cut foliage. Z3–8

P. carneum. From woods in the coast ranges of north California and Oregon. This makes tumbled stems smothered in loose heads of large, shell-pink saucers which open from cream buds and fade to soft mauve, about 46cm/18in high and wide spreading. Z4–9

P. foliosissimum. From the Rocky Mountains. This lovely plant produces throughout the summer a succession of rich purplish-blue cups, lit by orange stamens. It still looks good in late August with *Geranium wallichianum* 'Buxton's Variety' at its feet while *Ajuga reptans* 'Burgundy Glow' spreads its warm pink-toned carpet beyond them. 75cm–1m/2½–3ft. Z4–8

POLYGONATUM. CONVALLARIACEAE. Solomon's Seal. These are woodland plants that need to be left undisturbed in cool positions in humus-rich, retentive soil. They slowly make fat, white rhizomes which lie just beneath the soil surface. Polygonatums are indispensable

among ferns and hostas for creating a lush, leafy background, and are much appreciated by flower arrangers, whether for their arching stems of fresh green leaves, or for the little cream-green tipped bells which appear in spring. With hostas they die beautifully in autumn, glowing honey-gold before they become transparent and collapse.

P. curvistylum. From the Himalayas. Slender, arching stems flushed with purple are clothed in whorls of narrow, purple-tinted leaves from whose axils dangle clusters of little mauve, bell-like flowers. A dainty feature above tiarellas and *Viola riviniana* Purpurea Group. 60cm/2ft. Z6–9

P. × *hybridum* (*P. multiflorum* × *P. odoratum*). From woods and glades of Europe and northern Asia. This plant makes widely arching stems, 1–1.2m/3–4ft in length, with large, shining, ribbed leaves flaring to left and right on the upper side of the stem. As the stems unroll in spring, beneath them hang clusters of four or five small, green-tipped ivory bells, about 2cm/½in long, and narrow. Z4–9

P. × *h.* 'Betburg'. Collected in the Blackforest Mountains and named after the site, near Laufen, Sulzberg, by Isbert Preussler, head propagator for the late Helène von Stein Zeppelin, who gave the plant to me. Emerging stems and leaves stained chocolate-brown, slowly fading as the leaves mature. Produces purple berries in autumn. 75–90cm/2½–3ft. Z4–9

P. × *h.* 'Striatum'. This plant, with leaves strongly striped creamy-white and slightly twisted, is slow to increase. 46–60cm/1½–2ft. Z4–9

P. multiflorum. This produces more upright stems than *P.* × *hybridum*, with smaller, more close-set leaves with wax-blue undersides. Beneath hang small cream bells followed by a fine crop of berries. First they are dark bloomy-green, finally almost black: lovely for autumn arrangements. 46–60cm/1½–2ft. Z4–9

P. odoratum 'Flore Pleno'. This rare double flowered form has strongly scented, tubular flowers, cream with green tips, one inside the other. 30cm/1ft. Z4–8

P. o. var. *pluriflorum* 'Variegatum'. Pink-tinted stems with smaller oval leaves narrowly edged with ivory-white. 60–75cm/2–2½ft. Z4–8

P. verticillatum. Distributed over the temperate Himalayas and pretty general in the northern hemisphere in woods and rocky glades in woods, mostly in the mountains. This plant was found in Perthshire in 1792, and cultivated by John Tradescant as early as 1656. It is not showy, but I like its vertical form. Tall, slender stems, 1.2–1.5m/4–5ft, in rich soil, make graceful columns set with whorls of long, narrow, pointed leaves. They diminish towards the top of the stems where, at the nodes, are clusters of tiny, drooping, greenish-white bells, followed by little red berries. Z5–9

PONTEDERIA cordata. PONTEDERIACEAE. Pickerel Weed. From the shallow water of ponds and streams in the eastern and central United States and east Canada. Here is a handsome plant for shallow water, ideal to break the hard line of the pond edge. Standing above the water on 46–60cm/1½–2ft stems are clumps of beautiful leaves of an elongated heart shape, very smooth, almost wax-like, with a swirling pencilled pattern of light and dark green covering the surface. They are not veins – you can scarcely see a vein at all, just feel a thickening along the centre. In August there appear, just above the leaves, narrow spikes of closely

Pontederia cordata

set deep blue flowers, something like a small hyacinth, but much smaller, and softer textured. Z3–9

P. c. var. *lancifolia* has much longer, spear-shaped leaves on smooth green stems standing proud (1.5m/5ft) above the water surface. A valuable contrasting vertical among sedges, water iris or water-lilies. Z3–9

POTENTILLA. *ROSACEAE.* These are easy herbaceous plants in almost any soil in full sun or part shade. Poor dry gravels do not suit them but a retentive soil ensures a long display of bloom.

P. atrosanguinea. From a base of handsome divided leaves, come branching stems carrying intensely red, velvet-textured flowers. 46cm/18in. Z5–8

P. a. var. *argyrophylla.* From valley meadows or grassy mountain sides of the Himalayas, Kashmir to Nepal. Neat clumps of strawberry-shaped leaves heavily silvered with silky hairs are the setting for free-flowering, wide-flung sprays of yellow flowers, each with an orange heart. 46cm/18in. Z6–9

P. 'Gibson's Scarlet'. This plant produces a long succession of brilliant scarlet, velvety flowers with black centres, throughout late summer and autumn. The wide-sprayed branching stems are held rather flat. 46cm/18in. Z5–8

P. × *hopwoodiana* is an old variety that has come back into cultivation. It is much admired for its wide-flung sprays of pink and cream flowers, from midsummer to early autumn. Z5–8

P. nepalensis. From Himalayan meadows. There are several named forms or hybrids from this source. The two I have are:

P. n. 'Miss Willmott', which produces delicious raspberry-pink flowers over a long season, mid to late summer. 46cm/18in. Z5–8

P. n. 'Roxana' has warm orange flowers with brick-red centres. 46cm/18in. Z5–8

P. rupestris. From wooded rocky slopes in rock clefts in the mountains of central Europe and Asia. This pretty thing is a joy among unfolding *Hosta* leaves and primroses in late spring. Neat clusters of finely cut pinnate leaves are followed by

slightly hairy, pink-tinted stems topped with branching heads of pure white saucer-shaped flowers, each with a yellow eye. 46cm/18in. Z5–8

P. × *tonguei.* Too good to leave out, this little *Potentilla* will thrive almost any-where, but in good retentive soil scarcely stops flowering from early summer until autumn. It makes flat clusters of small dark green leaves, touched with copper. Low, wide-spreading stems carry a long succession of small apricot-coloured flowers suffused with dark red. 38cm–46cm/15–18in. Z5–8

PRATIA. *CAMPANULACEAE.* These creeping plants come mostly from Australasia, also from Asia and South America.

P. angulata comes from New Zealand, where it is found on shingly river plains in the west of South Island, growing with *Acaena anserinifolia, Leptinella squalida* and *Mazus radicans.* In the far south of South Island it is found with *Blechnum penna-marina, Astelia montana* and *Celmisia longifolia.* 5cm/2in. Z6–10

P. a. 'Treadwellii' is the form well known in gardens. It is a charming mat-forming plant on soil that does not dry out. Creeping stems carry small, rounded leaves, thick textured with prettily pointed edges. By June it is covered with starry white flowers, continuing for weeks. By the autumn they have become small rose-madder berries; the low green carpets are strewn with them. 5cm/2in. Z6–10

P. pedunculata. Forms dense green mats sprinkled in summer with small, sky-blue stemless flowers. *P. p.* 'County Park' has dark, gentian-blue starry flowers. Z5–8

PRIMULA. *PRIMULACEAE.* Certainly in areas of low rainfall you need moist retentive soil for the following species. Heavy soil, well enriched with humus, and shelter from too much sun and drying winds, are essential. In areas of heavier rainfall they might be treated with less reverence. Of all plants they are among the most desirable, whether planted in drifts along the water-side, or

as groups of two or three caught in a shaft of light beneath the shade of trees. There are hundreds of different species, many of them just the thing to torment those who pride themselves on growing difficult plants. The following I have learnt to know and grow without too much pain.

P. bulleyana. From wet valley meadows in the mountains of north Yunnan, south-west China. It was named in honour of Mr Bulley, the owner of the firm of Bees, who did much to finance plant collecting in China at the beginning of the 20th century. It is one of the easiest of bog primulas, provided you have continuously damp soil. Set in whorls around the stem are bright orange-peel-coloured flowers, maintaining a vivid display for weeks, and followed by tiers of round green seed capsules which finally dry pale brown. Given the right conditions they seed easily, making good ground-cover with their large oval leaves. 60–75cm/2–2½ft. Z4–9

P. calderiana. Widespread in high alpine meadows in west China, Bhutan, Tibet and Nepal. I am proud to grow this lovely plant in one of my few choice damp and sheltered spots. It dies back in winter to fat, ground-level buds. In spring the leaves emerge, pale green and upright, dusted with gold specks. The tall strong flower stems, 38–46cm/15–18in, carry drooping gold-dusted bells in deep purple or pale creamy-yellow, all with yellow eyes. They look like an extra-large form of *P. alpicola* which I have not succeeded in keeping long. (Over the years I lost or mislaid *P. calderiana,* but will try it again.) Z4–9

P. denticulata. From open birchwoods and meadows in the Himalayas. These hardy warriors thrive in sticky soil enriched with humus. With snowdrops still in flower, round fat buds emerge at ground level and immediately open a mauve eye or two, while the thick short stems, 23–30cm/9–12in, slowly push up the round, tightly packed balls of flower which have suggested the name, Drumstick Primula. *P. d.* var. *alba* has beautiful white flowers with yellow eyes. There are several

Primula bulleyana

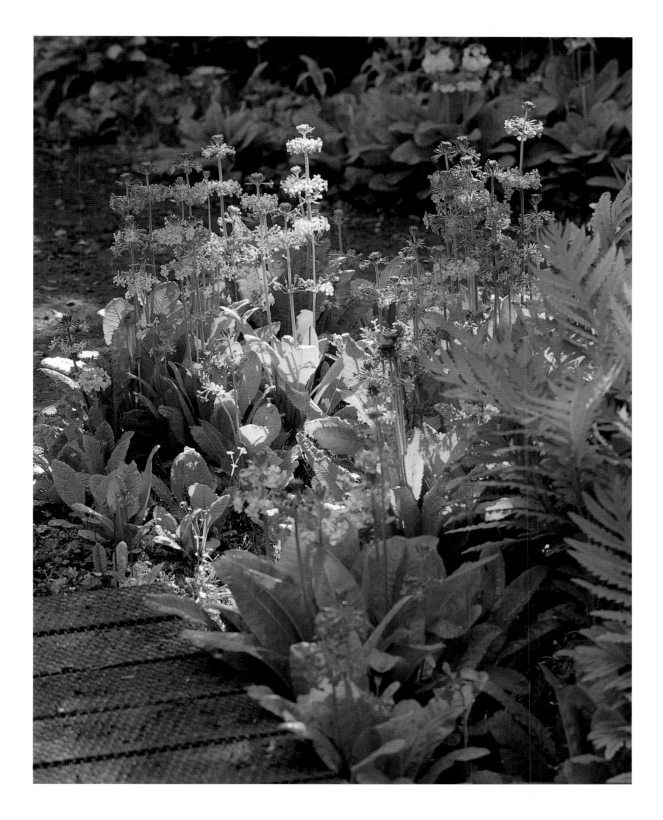

colour forms, shades of lavender, and rich carmine-red to purple. Not all are good; in some the individual flowers are small or washy-coloured. If grown from seed, select the best and propagate these from root cuttings taken when the plants are in flower. Pot the trimmed cuttings and keep in cool shade. Replace the parent plant with flowers removed and leaves reduced, also in a sheltered spot. Z3–9

P. elatior. From woods and moist meadows of Europe to the Caucasus and Iran. This is the true Oxlip, differing from the Cowslip in having a cluster of creamy-yellow primrose-like flowers nodding from the top of each stem. It prefers part shade and damp leaf-mould. 20–25cm/8–10in. Z4–9

P. farinosa. Bird's-eye Primrose. From wet meadows of the northern hemisphere, far into the Arctic; a mountain plant further south in all the great mountain ranges. Small leaf rosettes are dusted with meal, so they appear pale whitish-green. Above them short stems carry dainty heads of pinky-mauve flowers, yellow-eyed. 8–10cm/3–4in. It really does need wet conditions where it is not overwhelmed by its neighbours. Z4–8

P. florindae. From wet mountain meadows in south-east Tibet. The Giant Himalayan Cowslip, described by Kingdon-Ward when he found it in stream-beds with its bright red roots showing under water. It does well enough in heavy damp soil, but my plants are pygmies compared with what they can do in Scottish gardens. Flowering July–August, it prolongs the primula season with its large cowslip-shaped heads of sulphur-yellow, bell-like flowers. The flowers and stems are powdered with pale greenish powder, or farina, as are the handsome seed heads. There are selected forms in which the outside of the bells is red, the inside pale primrose. Sometimes a seedling has copper-tinted flowers. These used to be known as 'art shades', but they are neither better, nor worse, than the type. Stems 60cm–1.2m/2–4ft, according to condition. Z5–9

P. japonica. From wet stream-sides of Japan and Taiwan. Possibly the best-

Primula japonica

known of the candelabra primulas, and the first to flower in May. Large, broad, crinkled leaves are pale green, harmonizing with other soft spring greens, complementing the glowing crimson or rich pink tiers of flowers. Named forms include 'Miller's Crimson', which is dark red without any trace of mauve, and 'Postford White', both illuminated with yellow eyes. 46–60cm/1½–2ft. Z4–9

P. polyneura. From shady bouldery slopes among grass. Discovered by E. H. Wilson in west Sichuan around the beginning of the 20th century, this plant is good in damp soil and part shade. Downy, scallop-edged leaves nestle among the leaf-litter, producing in late May large, pink, primrose-like flowers. Grown from seed you may have other shades, from pale rose to deep purple, all with yellow eyes. Good forms can be increased by division in early spring, their soft foliage making good ground-cover. 13–15cm/5–6in. Z5–9

P. prolifera. From marshy meadows and stream-sides of the Yunnan-upper Burma mountains. This is a lovely buttercup-yellow, candelabra primula, with no farina (mealy powdering). The large flowers are set in as many as six whorls around the tall stems which can be up to 1m/39in high. An easy plant in moist soil. Z4–9

P. pulverulenta. From damp, part-shaded meadows of a limited area in the

mountains of west Sichuan, China. This is a favourite among the bog primulas; its flowers follow *P. japonica*. The leaves are smaller, narrower and heavily wrinkled. The 60cm/2ft flower stems are white with meal, and so are the buds which open deep, wine-coloured flowers with purple eyes. Among its most famous offspring is a group called *P. pulverulenta* Bartley hybrids. These enchanting hybrids have palest pink flowers, as many as five and seven whorls to a stem, enhanced with orange eyes, dancing like ballerinas in white tights among the floating balls of Cotton Grass, *Eriophorum angustifolium*. 60–75cm/2–2½ft. Z4–9

P. rosea. From the north-west Himalayas. I include this because it is so good in early spring, but I have lost it among my large water-side groupings. Situated in a moist, cool pocket of the rock garden many people could enjoy its low clusters of large bright rose flowers, 10–23cm/4–9in high. Z5–9

P. secundiflora. From damp mountain meadows, often with *P. sikkimensis* in north-west Yunnan and Sichuan. This primula has rather narrow leaves, and mealy stems from which the flower clusters tend to droop rather one-sidedly. The downturned bells are a rich wine-purple while the calyces are striped with black; a very elegant primula, flowering in June. 30cm/1ft. Z4–8

P. sieboldii. From wet, grassy river-sides in Japan, Korea and Manchuria. This delicate-looking primula manages well in shady leaf-mould, provided it does not dry out. It increases by creeping shoots which lie just beneath the surface, and so pop up unexpectedly, making spreading clumps of small clustered leaves. In spring, just above them, float fragile-looking flowers in pale shades of pink, lilac and white, several on dainty branching heads. 10–15cm/4–6in. Z4–9

P. sikkimensis. From wet meadows, with a wide range, including Nepal, Burma, Sikkim, Tibet and Bhutan to Yunnan and Sichuan in west China. Plants grown from seed may vary, some larger or deeper than others. A smaller plant than *P. florindae*, with bright yellow flowers, no farina, but a sweet scent, it needs wet soil. 46cm/18in. Z5–8

P. vialii. From moist grassy openings in pine forests on the mountains of Yunnan and west Sichuan in south-west China. Although not one of the easiest, most people who see this primula crave to grow it. At a quick glance (apart from its leaves) it looks like a weird little Red Hot Poker. The 30cm/1ft stem is topped with a narrowly pyramidal head of bright scarlet buds. Some time in June the bottom row of buds opens small, mauve primula flowers. Gradually all open, disposing of the wildly contrasting red tip. It is a worrying plant, its leaves not appearing through the soil until late May. Although supposed to be perennial, flowered plants often die unaccountably, so it is wise to collect seed to maintain young plants. It will grow in sun, but prefers part shade, in damp, humus-enriched soil. Z6–8

P. vulgaris. From woods, usually on heavy soil, and shady places of west-central Europe and the mountains of southern Europe to the northern Caucasus. This is our native Primrose, to be treasured, for it is every bit as lovely as any of the foregoing exotics. It loves heavy soil, well enriched with humus, preferably in a cool, shady position, not dried out by shrub roots. This applies to all the many cultivated hybrids and forms. There are primroses to be had in almost every colour of the rainbow, as well as doubles, hose-in-hose, polyanthus, etc. They are all fascinating, but none better than the perfect, cool, pale yellow *P. vulgaris*. Z4–9

Of the many forms and varieties I can describe only a few, including some of the genuine double, old-fashioned primroses with romantic names, delicate flowers and miffy constitutions. Among them I have *P. v.* 'Lilacina Plena', also known as 'Quakeress' or 'Quaker's Bonnet', whose flowers are pale lavender-lilac. *P. v.* 'Alba Plena' has perfectly formed double white flowers, also on lax stems; and *P.* 'Marie Crousse', a rich mauve-red, has petals edged with silver. Alas, they are not very robust. Given the best of treatment, rich moist soil in part shade,

Primula vulgaris

sheltered from wind, they can make astonishing growth, and be crowded with hundreds of flowers. But after two or three years they begin to deteriorate unless you dig them up, separate the crowns and cut away the ugly warty bases, just leaving the newly forming roots to each piece. Do this early in the season, cut off all the flowers and reduce the foliage. Pot up or box the pieces, growing them in a sheltered frame until strong enough to plant out in damp conditions.

P. Barnhaven hybrids. The Barnhaven primroses originated in America with Mrs Florence Bellis, who began in 1934 with Sutton's Seed Catalogue. After much cross-fertilizing, endless patience and the passage of many years, Mr and Mrs Jared Sinclair continued with her strains in Cumbria, adding their own little bits of magic and writing seductive descriptions and titles for their offspring. Their own double primroses, selected from hundreds of thousands that are discarded, had to be seen to be believed, not only for their perfect shape but also the infinite range of colours. After several years of seed sowing and rejection I had a few passable new doubles. Having obtained any kind of double primrose, there are still problems. If the leaves suddenly look drained and yellow, it is more than likely they are having the life sucked out of them by red spider mites – minute, red, dot-like creatures, almost invisible on the backs of the leaves. Just as likely, they

might have an aphis attack. But sometimes you can find no obvious reason for their discontent and can only suppose they disapprove of their situation. (Since first writing these notes more double primroses are available commercially, but although more robust they lack the finesse of the Barnhaven strains.)

The gold-laced polyanthus primroses As unlike the modern, large-flowered, bedding polyanthus primroses as could be, the hallmark of these little antiquities is the small size of their flowers. Small, neat petals of deep velvety-maroon, sometimes almost black, are edged with a fine gold or silver edging. There used to be named varieties; I have none of those, but have selected those I thought best from seedlings. Again I find they need regular division to keep them strong and healthy in stiff, humus-fed soil.

P. × *pruhoniciana*. This is a collective name for hybrids which are crosses between *P. juliae* (small purple-crimson flowers from moist mountain meadows in a limited district on the southern slopes of the Great Caucasus, often with *Gentiana septemfida* var. *lagodechiana*) and *P. vulgaris* 'Caerulea'. Well known in this section are the following:

P. 'Guinevere' is one of the best-known, with its polyanthus head on a very short stalk, making crowded bunches of light amethyst-pink flowers, intensified with maroon calyces and stems. The leaves, neat and narrow are shaded and veined maroon. 15–20cm/6–8in. Z4–9

P. 'Kinlough Beauty' may perhaps be included in this group. Neat, small flowers in light and dark shades of rosy-pink, each petal marked with a cream slash down the centre, leads to a bright yellow eye, making clustered heads of old world charm. This plant has a healthy constitution. 15–20cm/6–8in. I am not certain of this plant, as I was once sent something with the same name with larger, clumsier flowers. I prefer my form with its small, very neat flowers. Z4–9

P. 'Wanda' with vivid crimson-purple flowers over dark purple leaves is well known. I am pleased to have a rather more fragile-looking *P.* 'Wanda Hose-in-hose', which has two little flowers sitting inside one another. *P.* 'White Wanda' has generous posies of white primrose flowers set off by maroon buds, stems and calyces. 10cm/4in. Z4–9

P. 'Wanda Jack in the Green'. In the old-fashioned Jack in Green Group the calyces have developed into conspicuous green ruffs behind the flowers, which are still decorative when the flowers have dropped. Z4–9

PRUNELLA grandiflora. LAMIACEAE. Large Self-heal. From rather dry mountain meadows and open woods of south-central Europe. It makes a splendid edging plant, or good ground-cover, in damp soil, not too sun-scorched. It creeps over the soil with prostrate stems covered with small, dark, rough-surfaced leaves. Just above them stand crowded spikes of nettle-like flowers. The type is rich purple, but in gardens one usually sees *P.g.* 'Loveliness', which is pale lilac. There is also *P.g.* 'Pink Loveliness', with warm rose-pink flowers, and a white form too, 'White Loveliness'. 15cm/6in. Z4–9

PULMONARIA. BORAGINACEAE. There are several distinct species. They tend to interbreed, so the best forms are propagated by division, some from root cuttings. They provide two seasons of interest. In spring they are among the first to flower, and continue to do so for several months. Later in the year their robust clumps of fresh basal leaves, which are produced after the flowering season, make both a feature and ground-cover until the following spring. Their large leaves tend to wilt in sun; they need shade or part shade, in humus-rich, retentive soil. There is a tendency to mildew if they suffer dry conditions; work is being done to improve their resistance, but growing conditions affect that primarily. Since pulmonarias interbreed and seed readily, there are available many named intro-ductions, some with superior flowers, others with improved basal foliage. I include very few here. (You will find many more in *The Woodland Garden.*)

P. angustifolia subsp. *azurea.* From woods and moist meadows of the hills and mountains of central and southern Europe. This is the one which has totally plain, unspotted leaves, slightly bristly to touch. Z3–8

P. a. 'Munstead Blue'. This charming plant opens pink-tinted buds just as its small, oval green leaves are unfolding, often in February if it is mild. Soft clusters of pure blue flowers smother the low carpet of leaves, creating long-lasting pools of blue beneath early-flowering shrubs. 15cm/6in. Z3–8

P. longifolia. From woods and shady meadows of west and south-west Europe. Flattish rosettes of long, narrow, pointed leaves, dark green but heavily spotted with silvery-white, lie like sharp petalled flowers against the dark soil. In spring and early summer they produce quaint heads of small, deep blue flowers, held well above the leaves. 20–25cm/8–10in.

P. l. 'Ankum', from the nursery of Coen Jansen in Holland, produces clustered heads of small, violet-blue flowers followed by large, eye-catching clumps of long, narrow, almost entirely silvered leaves, striking contrasts among ferns, grasses and tiarellas. Z4–8

P. officinalis. From rather moist open woods of central and eastern Europe to Russia. This is the most commonly known form, with many local names, including Lungwort. (The even spotting on the leaves suggested the Latin name to the old botanists.) Soldiers and Sailors and Spotted Dog are among others. This plant has smallish, heart-shaped leaves, heavily spotted with silvery white. The flowers open in early spring, first rosy-pink, changing to purplish-blue. There are white-flowered forms. 25–30cm/10–12in.

P. o. Cambridge Blue Group opens rose-pink buds which quickly change to a clear lighter blue, one of the earliest to make a show. 15–20cm/6–8in. Z4–8

P. rubra. From openings in the beechwoods on the mountains of south-eastern Europe. While searching for snowdrops in January you may well see a glowing eye looking at you from the leafy depths of this plant. Its flowers are bright

coral-red with no hint of blue. They are at their best in March and April. The leaves are large and long, in plain apple-green, their hefty clumps very useful as contrast among the spotted types, extremely good ground-cover in shade. 30cm/1ft. A fine form with wide, white margins is *P.r.* 'David Ward', selected here and raised by David. Z4–8

P. saccharata. From south-east France and the Appenines. Plants under this name vary slightly in foliage and flower. All make large clumpy plants with very handsome basal rosettes of leaves. Some may be dark green with large, paler green spots, others will be smothered with bright silvery-white spots. In yet another the spots have joined together to make almost totally silvered leaves, and this we call *P. saccharata* Argentea Group. These plants are outstanding in the shade garden, in late summer and autumn, when their fresh, new basal leaves variously spotted or silvered, make eye-catching clumps in green shade. In early spring they all open pink buds from conspicuous dark purplish calyces, the flowers passing through mauve to rich blue as they age. Seedlings will vary in quality of flower. There is very fine white *P. saccharata* 'Alba', with flowers twice as large as those of *P. officinalis* 'Alba', vying with snowdrops for attention. 30cm/1ft. Z4–9

PULSATILLA. RANUNCULACEAE. I would not include the Pasque Flower, *Pulsatilla vulgaris* among damp-loving plants, but the yellow-flowered 'Shockheaded Peter' of high alpine meadows will tolerate neither drought nor starvation, and is one of the most covetable gems for growers of alpine plants.

P. alpina. From steep mountain grasslands of central and southern Europe to the Caucasus, and North America. This plant has white flowers with exquisite blue backs to the petals. 38cm/15in. Z3–9

P. a. subsp. *apiifolia* has light, lemon-yellow, shallow bowls filled with stamens, wonderful when sunlight slants through hundreds and thousands as they bow just above the short turf. It is almost as lovely when the flowers have become silky, silver seed-heads. A well-grown clump with finely cut woolly green leaves standing in full flower, in May and June, is one of the loveliest things we can grow. 46cm/18in. Z3–9

RANUNCULUS. *RANUNCULACEAE.*
All will grow in sun with retentive soil.
R. aconitifolius. From rocky stream-sides and wet, shady places in the mountains of central and southern Europe. Z5–10
R. a. **'Flore Pleno'.** This centuries-old garden plant has the lovely name Fair Maids of France. When well grown it makes quantities of wide-spreading branches, which divide and subdivide, and so can carry a huge bouquet of small, double-white flowers, exquisitely perfect, tinted green in the centre. The dark green pointed foliage remains discreetly in the background, doing nothing to detract from the sense of lightness and space in which these enchanting blossoms float. 60–75cm/2–2½ft.
R. acris. The Common Buttercup. From moist meadows of temperate Eurasia.
R. a. **'Flore Pleno'.** Another historical plant found in Lancashire in the sixteenth century and called Bachelor's Buttons. Long lasting and lovely, and much easier to grow than Fair Maids, it does not run but makes well-behaved tidy clumps which produce slender-stemmed bouquets crowded with glistening, densely double,

green-centred, yellow buttercups. It flowers in June, standing at 60–75cm/ 2–2½ft. Z4–8
R. a. **'Stevenii'.** I particularly like this tall handsome form of ordinary buttercup. It makes tall, 1.2m/4ft branching stems glowing in midsummer with multitudes of glistening, yellow saucers, sometimes semi-double, lovely among grasses, or overhanging water in a natural setting. Needs a bit of support: a few pea sticks. Z4–8
R. a. **'Sulphureus'**, makes clumps of much divided leaves, freckled brown, supporting branched stems of creamy-yellow buttercups. 38cm/15in. Z4–8
R. constantinopolitanus **'Plenus'.** From mountain meadows of the Pyrenees to the western Alps. It needs moist soil in sun to produce a long display of flowers, 5cm/2in across, densely double with row upon row of shining enamelled petals with bitter-green centres. It has rough bristly leaves, rounded with cut edges, not so divided as most. 45cm/18in. Z6–10
R. ficaria var. *aurantiacus.* This attractive celandine had mottled green and grey leaves, with glistening orange single flowers. It flowers in February–March. 8–10cm/3–4in. Z4–9
R. f. flore-pleno. A double-flowered celandine – such a clean shade of yellow with a tight centre of green which opens layer upon layer of shadowed petals. 8cm/3in. Z4–9

R. f. **'Brazen Hussy'.** Clusters of rich, bronze-brown leaves are a good foil for large single yellow celandines. 8cm/3in. Christopher Lloyd found this splendid form in his wood. *R. f.* 'Coppernob' has similar foliage, set off by shining orange flowers. Z4–9
R. lingua. Greater Spearwort. From marshes and water-edges of temperate Eurasia. This is an invasive bog-loving buttercup, only to be used where it cannot become a nuisance, or else strictly confined in a container. It will colonize in shallow water, where its long, spear-shaped leaves piercing the flat surface and large shining yellow buttercup flowers provide a tempting scene. There is a selected form called *R. l.* 'Grandiflorus'. 60cm–1m/24–39in. Z4–8

RHEUM. *POLYGONACEAE.* The ornamental rhubarbs are among the most statuesque and handsome of foliage plants, invaluable for creating a grand, lush atmosphere, even when space is limited. They like deep humus-enriched soil, and some shelter from both wind and scorching sun. Part shade suits them well. Ill-drained soil will cause the great woody crowns to rot.
R. **'Ace of Hearts'.** (*R. kialense* × *R. palmatum*). This small, ornamental rhubarb, suitable for small-scale planting was introduced by Jim Archibald. Dark, heart-shaped leaves, handsomely veined and backed with crimson creates a focal

Ranunculus aconitifolius 'Flore Pleno'

Ranunculus acris 'Flore Pleno' (enlarged)

Ranunculus acris 'Stevenii'

Rheum 'Ace of Hearts'

Rheum palmatum var. *tanguticum*

point. Tall flower spires of palest grey-pink make light and dainty verticals in early summer. 1.2m/4ft. Z5–9

R. alexandrae. From rich, boggy, high mountain meadows, or among scrub in north Yunnan and Sichuan, west China. This is quite different from the rest. It has much smaller leaves, shaped like overgrown Greater Plantain leaves, strongly veined – pale veins against dark shining green – and makes vigorous clumps in moist soil. In June a 75cm–1m/ 30–39in flower spike is set from top to bottom with large, pale cream, overlapping, papery bracts, beneath which are hidden little clusters of typical rhubarb-like flowers, sheltering from the wild rainstorms which they are expecting in their native home. In cultivation it seldom produces many flower heads, but one alone is sensational. Z6–8

R. palmatum. From west Sichuan, China, at great heights, by streams in rocky ravines, among alpine plants in rocky turf, or round alpine lakes in scrub. The type is not generally overpraised, but I think it could have wider recognition and use. In many gardens where *Gunnera* cannot be accommodated this plant provides those huge, cool, simple leaves that are needed to give style and atmosphere. Each apple-green leaf, up to 1m/39in across, is less cut than the red-leaved forms, and produces a more tranquil effect as it stands in a great overlapping pile. The towering stems, 1.8–2.1m/6–7ft, of

creamy-white flowers are softly harmonious. Z4–9

R. p. '**Atrosanguineum**'. The tall flower spike, 2m/6½ft, carries large leaves, 75cm–1m/30–39in across, which are deeply cut. As they unfold in March–April, from fist-sized, shining scarlet buds, crumpled and creased, they are stained deep mahogany-red, but as the leaves quickly expand, the colour fades from the surface, remaining on the undersides, so that a rustle of wind will reveal them as carmine-pink underskirts. In May the tall flower spike carries a froth of tiny crimson-pink flowers, which later become transparent brown seed cases. There are several other varieties, one called 'Bowles' Crimson', another,

Rodgersia pinnata

R. p. var. *tanguticum* produces larger, more richly coloured leaves, continuing to do so for longer, with tall spires of tiny white flowers. Z5–9

RODGERSIA. SAXIFRAGACEAE. These are among the finest of foliage plants for the water-side, or for cool, damp soil. They will grow in sun if the soil is very moist, or in shade in soil which does not dry out. They can suffer from sun-scorch and damage by wind. The roots are thick, slowly spreading rhizomes which can be divided.

R. aesculifolia. From openings and clearings in forest on moist slopes of west Chinese mountains. This makes handsome clumps, 90–120cm/3–4ft high, according to the amount of moisture. The leaves are shaped and arranged like those of the horse chestnut. Z5–9

R. pinnata. From openings in forests, stream-sides and moist meadows of south-west Sichuan and north Yunnan, China. This plant arranges its leaves in pairs, on either side of a central stem. The foliage is not quite so handsome as some of the others, but it flowers more freely, with flower spikes similar to *Astilbe* but more substantial. It can be found with white or pale pink flowers. 1m/39in. Z5–8

R. p. '**Superba**' is a very fine form with brilliant pink flowers, and copper-tinted leaves. 1m/39in. Z5–8

Rodgersia pinnata 'Superba'

Rodgersia podophylla

Rudbeckia fulgida var. *deamii*

Rudbeckia laciniata 'Herbstsonne'

R. podophylla. From mountain woods of Japan and Korea. The young leaves have wonderful rich bronze tones in spring, turning to green as they expand, but often copper-tinted when mature. Usually five leaves, broadly triangular in outline with jagged tips, are arranged at the top of each stem. 1m/39in. Z5–8

ROSCOEA. *ZINGIBERACEAE*. These are exotic-looking plants as well they might be, related to the root we call candy ginger. Their flowers may be described as halfway between an orchid and an *Iris*. The roots are fleshy, liking deep soil that does not dry out. They will grow in sun or part shade, in retentive soil.

R. cautleyoides. From turfy glades in mountain pine-oak forests of Yunnan, south-west China. This plant has long, light green leaves, ribbed and curving, which clasp the stem alternately. The light yellow flowers, of which there may be several in a close spike, emerge just above the leaves. There are purple cultivars. 46cm/ 18in. Z6–9

R. purpurea. From openings in woods of the Himalayas. The flowers have an upright purple petal. Below are two white, beak-like petals which enfold the precious stamens and stigma, while below them falls a broad and inviting flared petal which probably acts as an alighting board for some pollinating insect. 30–38cm/12–15in. Z6–9

RUDBECKIA. *ASTERACEAE*. Coneflower. These North American daisies, flowering in late summer and autumn, are distinguished by their hard, cone-like centres and somewhat drooping broad petals. They are happy in full sun, so long as the soil is retentive, which also means the flowering period will be longer.

R. fulgida var. fulgida. From damp meadows of the eastern and central United States. The problem of naming is multiplied since there are several selected forms found in gardens. Basically they all make tidy clumps of very dark green leaves which, in late summer, produce compact, branching heads set with bright-yellow daisies with dark-brown central cones, hence their common name Black-eyed Susan. Among the named varieties are *R. f.* var. *deamii* and *R. f.* var. *sullivantii* 'Goldsturm'. They may have slightly longer (or narrower) petals. Or they may flower a week sooner or later. All are a joy to have. 60–75cm/2–2½ft. Z3–9

R. laciniata. From brook-banks and damp thickets of the east and midwest United States and Canada. This and *R. nitida* are closely related. They too can be found in named selected forms. The main characteristic is the height, from 1.5–2.25m /5–7ft tall. *R. laciniata* has more deeply dissected leaves than *R. nitida*. Both produce sheaves of clear yellow daisies, enhanced by slender green central knobs. They are good in large gardens not troubled by wind. Z3–9

R. l. 'Herbstsonne'. A beautiful tall daisy for the back of a large border, sheltered from strong wind. In early autumn, strong leafy branching stems carry a long display of large lemon-yellow daisies, the broad petals reflexed from narrow green cones. If cut back in early June it will become sturdier. 2m/6½ft. Z3–9

SAGITTARIA sagittifolia. *ALISMATACEAE*. From the quiet water at the edges of ponds and rivers of Europe and Asia. The Common Arrowhead sends up shiny leaves of perfect arrow-head shape above the water on juicy stems. From among these rise flowering stems bearing whorls of a few rather large white flowers with conspicuous black-purple

Sagittaria sagittifolia

centres. If growing in faster running water, the leaves become strap-shaped and do not emerge into the air. It needs to be kept under control, as it spreads fast. 46cm/18in. The showier, double flowered form, *S. s.* 'Flore Pleno', is usually grown. Z6–11

SALVIA. *LAMIACEAE*. Most salvias need sunny positions and well-drained soil; some will tolerate quite dry conditions. The following flower late in the year and need a reasonable amount of moisture to keep their foliage healthy to the end of the season.

S. glutinosa. Jupiter's Distaff. From open mountain woods of south-central Europe to the Caucasus and Himalayas. A coarse plant for the wild garden, making branching stems set with rough, crinkled leaves, heart-shaped and pointed, as much as 18–20cm/7–8in long, so making quite a foliage feature. The chrome-yellow flowers, which appear in late summer, are arranged in a broad spike above the leaves. 75cm–1m/2½–3ft. Z8–9

S. guaranitica. From moist places in Paraguay. This plant is not reliably hardy in very cold soils, but it is worth covering the roots with a mulch, when it usually sprouts again in the spring. Stems 1.2–1.5m/4–5ft high carry scented matt-green leaves. At the tip of every branch are short spikes of indigo-blue buds which open in September deep blue, lipped and hooded flowers. They are larger than those of *S. uliginosa*, but in a less dense spike. Z9–10

S. uliginosa. From moist places of southern Brazil and Uruguay. Another slightly tender plant, but it is well worth protecting the roots in winter. Graceful, branching 1.5–2m/ 5–6ft stems are set with narrow, toothed leaves. They are topped with a continuous display of pure sky-blue and white flowers held in drooping, clustered heads until the first frosts destroy them. September–November. Both this plant and *S. guaranitica* need a warm, sheltered position in soil that does not dry out. Z8–9

SANGUINARIA *canadensis*. *PAPAVERACEAE*. From rich woods of the eastern and central United States and Canada. The common name Blood Root refers to the red sap which oozes from the thick rhizome if wounded. This choice woodland plant needs a shady site in damp leaf-mould. Some time in April fat flower buds push through the soft earth, their short, waxy, purple stems wrapped around in a frilled, glaucous leaf, like a shawl, for protection. The single, cupped flowers look not unlike large white celandines, but the very full, double form, *S. c.* f. *multiplex* 'Plena', with many narrower incurved petals, has you down on your knees to gasp and marvel. Each exquisite flower lasts several days. When they have gone the leaves expand to become quite large and round, with deeply indented margins, like small versions of *Macleaya* leaves. But the rhizomes spread slowly. When large enough they should be divided in August. 10–15cm/4–6in. Z4–9

SANGUISORBA. *ROSACEAE*. These plants are valued for their elegant pinnate foliage and long fluffy flowers. They increase fairly vigorously in moist soil, thriving in full sun. They are not tiresome invaders.

S. canadensis. From swamps and wet meadows of eastern Canada and the United States, becoming less common inland. Sometimes the green pinnate foliage turns to vivid autumn tints. Above it stand stiffly upright stems whose branching heads are topped with narrow white bottle-brushes. When the multitudes of fluffy stamens and petals have disintegrated the remaining green tapers are interesting, and useful for flower arranging. August–September. 1.5–2m/5–6½ft. Z3–8

S. hakusanensis. Above a base of pinnate leaves stands a crowd of upright stems bearing many drooping, catkin-like flower heads. This dwarf, compact form has great potential in retentive soil. August. 75cm/2½ft. Z5–8

S. obtusa. From certain high mountain meadows of north Japan, where it is rare.

Beautiful light blue-grey leaves set off larger, fluffier, deep rose bottle-brushes which nod and quiver at the end of long, slender, branching stems, in mid to late summer. 1.2–1.5m/4–5ft. Z4–9

SAXIFRAGA. *SAXIFRAGACEAE*. From this enormous and important genus of alpines I select only a few which are large enough to be associated with general garden plants. They all like a cool situation, a little shade and humus-enriched soil.

S. cuneifolia. From damp rocks in mountain woods of central and southern Europe and Spain to the Carpathians. This is a very easy plant, looking like a miniature London Pride. Small, neat, evergreen rosettes gradually spread into ground-covering mats. There is a variegated form, slightly speckled and spotted with creamy-yellow spots. In June 15cm/6in sprays of creamy-white flowers are more generously produced from rosettes planted in fresh soil. Z5–7

S. fortunei. From wet shady mountain rocks and ravines of Japan and Sakhalin to Manchuria and China. Round, veined leaves of wax-like texture are green above, pinkish-tan on the undersides. A late spring frost sometimes dissolves them, but new ones appear. In gardens the red-leaved forms *S. f.* 'Wada' and

Saxifraga fortunei

S. f. 'Rubrifolia' are bronze-red above, shining crimson-pink on the reverse. It is lovely to come upon these beautiful plants on an October evening when the wide, airy sprays of dainty white flowers appear to float over richly coloured leaves. Looking closer you see they have cherry-red stems, and the little flowers have yellow centres which become green pointed pods. One petal of each tiny star becomes an elongated ribbon 2cm/½in long. 30cm/1ft. Z5–9

S. stolonifera. Mother of Thousands. From damp rocks and wet places of south Japan to west China. Although not reliably hardy this will stand most winters tucked in among leaf-litter. Rounded leaves are veined and marbled with pale green. Young plants are produced on the ends of long trailing runners; and 30cm/1ft stems carry dainty sprays of white flowers, the lower petals several times as long as the upper ones. Z7–10

From the mossy saxifrages I have selected these three which I enjoy on the edge of a cool, shaded bed. They would be among the first plants to go on my north-facing raised bed – or a cool, shady pocket in the rock garden.

S. 'Bob Hawkins' makes neat low cushions of finely cut leaves held in fairly large rosettes. The new young growth is strongly variegated cream and green, while around the edges the tips of the old leaves are crimson. The flowers, on 15cm/6in stems, are white, making a long lasting display in May-June. Z4–9

S. 'Cloth of Gold' makes beautiful mossy carpets of light yellow rosettes which are vivid all the year round. In May they are studded with white flowers on short stems. There must be enough light to maintain the colour, but not direct sunlight which will cause scorching. 8–10cm/3–4in. Z4–8

S. 'Schwefelblüte' (Flowers of Sulphur) has creamy-green flowers over low compact green carpets, in April. 5–8cm/2–3in. Z4–9

SCABIOSA *caucasica.* DIPSACACEAE. From rich subalpine meadows of the Caucasus. I include this plant because

although it needs full sun and good drainage it has taken me a long time to learn to grow it successfully, and I have concluded that it likes a reasonably fertile soil with enough moisture in its busy flowering season. The addition of lime in acid soils may be helpful. It does not do well in poor dry soils. When suited it is one of the most beautiful flowering plants. The best known is probably *S. c.* 'Clive Greaves'; there are also several with white flowers. *S. c.* 'Miss Willmott' is a creamy-white form which starts flowering in early summer, and continues on and off throughout the summer. *S. c.* 'Moerheim Blue' has deep blue frilly petals with paler centres. All are beautiful, poised on long, scarcely leaved stalks. 60–75cm/2–2½ft. Z4–8

SCHIZOSTYLIS *coccinea.* IRIDACEAE. From South Africa. This is another plant needing far more moisture than you might imagine. It needs a warm, sunny situation in continuously damp soil if it is to flower well. The plants increase readily, sending up quantities of light green, blade-shaped leaves. Slender spires of buds appear in September, continuing to flower into the winter if it is mild enough. Autumn frosts damage the open flowers, but do not harm the unopened buds. Although likened to a miniature

Scrophularia auriculata 'Variegata'

Gladiolus, it has evenly shaped, beautifully rounded petals, satin-textured, which open flat in warm autumn sunshine. 46–60cm/1½–2ft. Z8–10

There are many named varieties. *S. c.* 'Major' has extra-large flowers which are ripe cherry-red. There are also some good pink ones, including 'Mrs Hegarty', 'Viscountess Byng', and Alan Bloom's 'November Cheer', which has especially fine pink blooms. I particularly like Eric Smith's 'Sunrise', which has flowers over 5cm/2in across in bright salmon-pink.

SCROPHULARIA *auriculata.* SCROPHULARIACEAE. From stream-sides and wet places in Europe.

S. a. 'Variegata'. This can be one of the most spectacular variegated plants when well grown. Square stems, much branched, form a stiff frame set with clusters of leaves. Each leaf is a narrow oval, of crêpe texture, with finely cut edges; a central zone of rich green is surrounded by an irregular border of startling cream. As the leaves get smaller towards the tips of the branches, they are almost totally cream. Finally they produce funny little spires of small, fig-shaped, brown flowers. It needs rich, damp soil, and shelter from wind and too much sunlight; enough shade may be achieved by other great herbs, perhaps ligularias, or a tall grass such as *Miscanthus*. 90–120cm/3–4ft. Z6–9

SELINUM. *APIACEAE*. There seems to be confusion between the following handsome umbellifers. My two plants are distinctly different.
S. tenuifolium. From the Himalayas. This is a kind of Cow Parsley, but so delicately lovely no one passes it by. Light overlapping fronds of finely cut, almost fern-like leaves are stiffly held out, like elegant filigree fans. Above them rise maroon-red, branching stems 1m/39in high which support delicate white parasols. The struts which carry the flat heads of multitudinous little white flowers are ghostly white. It is in flower in July. It must be increased by root-division. Z6–9
S. wallichianum makes a larger plant, up to 1.5m/5ft tall and wide, bearing handsome heads of creamy-white flowers, standing unaided in late summer among tall grasses. It is a valuable plant, but the foliage does not have the style and presence of *S. tenuifolium*. It sets seed freely which *S. tenuifolium* does not. Z7–9

SEMIAQUILEGIA *ecalcarata*. *RANUNCULACEAE*. From high mountain meadows and grasslands, and among bushes, of the China-Tibet borderlands. This plant is related to and closely resembles an *Aquilegia* in growth and foliage, and stands about 38cm/15in high. It does not make a vivid show but its open sprays of spurless flowers are a soft, pale purplish-brown, and have quiet charm. Z6–9

SENECIO *smithii*. *ASTERACEAE*. From southern Chile, Tierra del Fuego and the Falkland Islands, on the banks of pools and streams, often with *Gunnera magellanica* and marsh marigolds. This unusual plant likes to have its roots in rich, moist soil, even in soggy mud. It makes a coarse plant with huge basal leaves, broadly spear-shaped, 46cm/18in long and 23cm/9in across. They are rich, glossy green, somewhat puckered and tooth edged. A thick stem, 1.2–1.5m/4–5ft tall, supports a densely clustered flower head, sometimes 30cm/1ft across, made of many yellow-eyed white daisies, each over 2.5cm/1in across. Fluffy seed heads follow. Z7–9

SILENE. *CARYOPHYLLACEAE*. From open woods and shady mountain meadows of Europe to west Asia.
S. alpestris **'Flore Pleno'** is the double form of Pink Campion. It is an ancient cultivar, attractive with its rather loosely double flowers, easily grown in retentive soil and part shade. May–June. 60cm/2ft. Z5–8

SMILACINA *racemosa*. *CONVALLARIACEAE*. From woods all across the eastern and central United States and Canada to the Rockies. In good, deep soil, sheltered from sun and wind, this plant can grow to over 1m/39in. Slightly arching stems carry upturned leaves, more deeply veined than Solomon's Seal, to which it is related. They clasp the stem alternately to left and right, stopping before the tip, which carries a soft spike of fluffy, creamy flowers. Mine give every promise that later I shall see little berries, like 'vitrified drops of blood' but the promises drop off. Perhaps they need a moister atmosphere? I do enjoy the heady, lemon perfume. Z4–9

Smilacina racemosa

SOLIDAGO. *ASTERACEAE*. Goldenrod. I have to confess that these are not my favourite plants. The tall, gawky ones I have not left space for, but I do like some of the low-growing, late summer-flowering varieties which seem to have less awkward-shaped heads. Among the named forms I grow 'Queenie', which is a very nice little plant for a damp edge. × *Solidaster luteus* 'Lemore', very like *Solidago*, has longer individual florets in massed flower heads, a lovely shade of creamy-yellow. 60–75cm/2–2½ft. Z4–9
S. caesia produces many dark-tinted stems set with tiny pointed leaves, carrying small bundles of fluffy yellow flowers, like mimosa, almost the entire length of the stems, in late summer – autumn, for sun or part-shade. 75cm/2½ft. Z3–9
S. rugosa. From north east USA. Sturdy stems, up to 1.5m/5ft carry arching lateral branches which subdivide to form huge airy sprays of tiny yellow flowers, creating a most elegant fountain-like effect in late autumn. A super plant! Z4–9

SPEIRANTHA *convallarioides*. *CONVALLARIACEAE*. From China. This plant is related to Lily-of-the-Valley (*Convallaria majalis*), but is not nearly so invasive. The light green, broad-bladed leaves slowly spread into good clumps. Sprays of pure white, fragrant, starry blossoms appear in spring. It likes cool shady places in humus-rich soil, at home in limy or acid soil. 30cm/1ft. Z6–8

STACHYS *macrantha*. *LAMIACEAE*. From wood edges and mountain meadows of the Caucasus. Most members of this genus grow happily in dry, free-draining gravel, but *S. macrantha* needs retentive soil. It used to be called The King of Splendour. Regal and splendid it is in mid summer when its 60cm/2ft stems are set with whorls of large, lipped flowers in rich mauve-purple. For the rest of the year it covers the soil with thick mats of dark crinkled evergreen leaves. *S. m.* 'Alba' has pure white flowers on shorter stems. Z4–8

STOKESIA laevis. ASTERACEAE. From eastern North America. Not just another daisy, but a very distinctive one, with its own special character for late summer and early autumn. It is ideal for the front edge of a sunny border, in retentive soil, where it may spend the summer creating a healthy clump of long, narrow, soap-smooth leaves, slightly toothed at the base, capable of sending up 46–60cm/1½–2ft branched, flowering stems. By August curious buds are enclosed in rows of narrow, bristle-edged calyces which almost give the effect of a green flower themselves. But gradually they open to expose a pale, round bud which in turn opens lilac-blue with fine-cut petals surrounding a creamy-white centre. New flowers continue to open well into the autumn. There are purple, pink, and white forms. Z5–9

STYLOPHORUM diphyllum. PAPAVERACEAE. From shady woods of eastern North America. Sometimes called the Celandine Poppy, this plant likes cool, humus-rich soil in part shade. Its blue-grey divided leaves catch the eye as they appear through the soil in early spring, enhanced by purplish stems and veins. In April nodding yellow poppies make just the right contrast, followed by large seed pods. 38–46cm/15–18in. Z4–9

SYMPHYTUM. BORAGINACEAE. These plants will grow in part or full shade, flowering and making total cover among shrubs or under trees where few other plants would flourish. They can be too successful; it helps to know which are dangerously invasive.

S. asperum. A stately plant carrying leafy branched stems each weighted with drooping clusters of dark ruby-red buds opening gentian-blue bell-like flowers. 1m/39in. Z4–9

S. caucasicum. From along water courses in damp soil in the Caucasus. When in flower in spring, this plant is irresistible, with graceful sprays of forget-me-not-blue tubular flowers drooping over mats of well-shaped grey-green leaves. The danger is that it colonizes by means of strong underground shoots, eventually covering a wide area. Every small piece left in the ground produces a new healthy plant. It is confined to my heaviest clay banks, and invaluable where little else would grow. 60cm/2ft. Z4–8

S. 'Hidcote Pink' and *S. 'Hidcote Blue'*. These two hybrid comfreys make large, ground covering clusters of dark green, hairy leaves while the flowers stand well above them throughout May, held in conspicuous and very attractive sprays. 'Hidcote Pink' has flowers in shades of pale and rosy-pink. 'Hidcote Blue' contains shades of red, white and blue among its uncurling crozier-shaped flower-heads. They make ideal filler plants among shrubs or clothing the shady banks of a stream. 46cm/18in. Z4–9

S. ibericum. From mountain forests of the Caucasus. Invaluable as ground-cover in large shrubberies where it colonizes by means of underground shoots. It makes close carpets of slightly bristly, dark green leaves which remain until new ones replace them in spring. Very early in the year little croziers of orange-red buds unfold themselves to become small primrose-yellow tubular flowers. 20cm/8in. Z6–10

S. i. 'All Gold'. Large dock-shaped leaves (45cm/18in long) are entirely suffused yellow when young, gradually maturing green. Branched stems carry lilac tubular flowers in early summer. Z6–9

S. 'Goldsmith'. This is another good plant selected by the late Eric Smith. Low,

Symphytum ibericum 'All Gold'

neat clumps of matt, oval leaves have dark green centres surrounded by broad, bright yellow margins. The flowers are similar to those of 'Hidcote Blue'. It makes much less invasive plants. 20–25cm/8–10in. Z5–9

S. 'Rubrum'. Probably a garden hybrid. This is not nearly such an invasive spreader, but makes clumps of long, narrow, bristly, dark green leaves. Crozier-heads of vivid garnet-red flowers hang just above the leaves, lasting for weeks in early summer, with another show of welcome colour in the autumn. 38–46cm/15–18in. Z3–8

S. × uplandicum. A hybrid of uncertain name and origin. Z4–9

S. × u. 'Variegatum'. This foliage plant stands out above all else in the later summer and autumn border. During the early part of the year nothing will stop it doing its duty and sending up tall, leafy stems topped with indifferent pink and blue flowers. They are fussy compared to the grandeur of the basal foliage to come. By the end of July, with the flowering over, they start to create a huge cluster of large, overlapping leaves, like giant-sized dock leaves in shape, with a matt texture, shadowed greyish-green down the centre, surrounded by a broad irregular margin of cream. Occasionally a leaf is almost entirely creamy-white. Deep retentive soil in part shade is essential for this plant. 75cm/2½ft. Z4–9

TELEKIA speciosa. ASTERACEAE. Also known as *Buphthalmum speciosum*. Common in moist woods and along streams in south-east Europe to the Caucasus. A grand plant for large-scale planting, creating wide mounds of large, heart-shaped, aromatic leaves. Large, fine-rayed yellow daisies are displayed for weeks in mid summer. It is handsome as a grand feature plant in rough-cut grass, and is grown like this at Great Dixter. 1.5m/5ft. Z5–8

TELLIMA grandiflora. SAXIFRAGACEAE. From shady leafmould-rich woods, central California to Alaska.

Tellima grandiflora Rubra Group

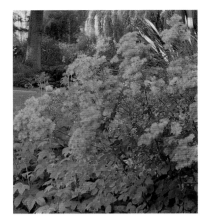

Thalictrum aquilegiifolium

T. g. **Rubra Group** is the best form usually seen in gardens. (The type is not so well coloured in winter.) Although it will survive in dryish soil in shade, it certainly does better where the soil does not dry out. One of our most valued winter-foliage plants; tidy clumps of scallop-edged leaves are, with the first frosts, flooded with rich carmine-red shades, brighter on the undersides. In spring multitudes of tall, slender wands carry tiny, pale green bells edged with rolled-up pink fringes, delicately pretty in a shady setting. 46cm/18in. Z4–7

T. g. **'Purpurteppich'** differs from Rubra Group in that the leaves become veined and stained with maroon in summer, while the flowers have dark stems and pink-stained rims to the slightly larger green bells. Z4–7

THALICTRUM *aquilegiifolium*.

RANUNCULACEAE. Meadow Rue. From moist mountain meadows, wood edges and rocky ravines of the mountains of Europe and Asia to Japan. This is beautiful in every part. The leaves, not unlike those of *Aquilegia* but smaller and greyish-green, ascend with diminishing size purple-stained stems and side branches. In June and July the tips erupt into wide heads of amethyst-pink fluff, rather like giant powder puffs. Later there are loose clusters of flat green seed cases, still good to look at. The white variety, *T. a.* var. *album*, is also very good. 90–150cm/3–5ft. Z3–9

T. delavayi. From valley stream-sides, often among bushes, at comparatively low levels in the mountains of Yunnan. Wide airy sprays, held 1.5m/5ft or so above the ground, consist of tiny lilac flowers filled with dangling, greenish-yellow stamens; star-shaped seed capsules mature before the petals have dropped. There is also a white form. The tall slender stems carrying more finely segmented leaves need some support and shelter from wind damage, preferably among other plants rather than clumsy staking. August–September. Z4–9

T. d. **'Hewitt's Double'** does not have quite such delicate charm, but the tiny pom-poms of deep lilac are very attractive and last well. 1.5m/5ft. Both these plants need rich, deep soil, in sun or part shade. Z4–9

T. diffusiflorum. From south-east Tibet, in moist, part-shady places. This treasure needs well-drained but damp leaf-mould soil in a cool, sheltered spot. In my garden it struggles, obviously needing a damper climate. Delicate stems about 1m/3ft tall, are set with sprays of very tiny greyish-green leaves, topped with drooping heads of surprisingly large lilac blossoms. Z5–9

T. flavum. The Common Meadow Rue is quite handsome, with graceful, much-cut foliage and pyramidal heads of fluffy pale yellow flowers in dense clusters, standing 1m/39in high. I do not grow it, but substitute *T. f.* subsp. *glaucum*. From stream-sides and wet places in the lowlands and mountains of Spain, Portugal and north-west Africa. This has perhaps the most handsome foliage of all thalictrums. Large fans of blue-green leaves, finely divided, are held stiffly from the central stem. The clustered heads of small, greenish-yellow flowers seem exactly right for the tall, waxy-grey stems and bluish leaves. This plant will grow almost anywhere, from the back of an ordinary border to the pond-side, where it will thrive among *Lythrum* and *Lysimachia*. 1.5m/5ft. Z4–9

T. kiusianum. From the mountains of south Japan (Shikoku and Kyushu). This little plant is about 8cm/3in high. It is difficult to distinguish petals from stamens, all so narrow giving the effect of tiny balls of lilac fluff floating on purple wiry stems over sparsely leaved plants. It runs a little if well suited, in moist humus soil. Z5–9

TIARELLA. *SAXIFRAGACEAE.*

With masses of fluffy white flowers and especially pretty leaves these are perfect for the woodland garden, among shrubs, or in cool pockets of the rock garden. They need light, humus-rich soil, with sufficient rainfall, not too dried out by tree roots. Many named hybrids are available, selected for free flowering or for interestingly marked foliage. The species include:

T. cordifolia. The Foam Flower. From rich moist woods of the eastern and central United States and eastern Canada. Running trails of pretty, heart-shaped, pointed leaves make attractive ground-cover, copper-tinted in winter; in spring covered with creamy-white flower spires. 23cm/9in. Z3–8

T. wherryi. From woods of the south-east United States. Tiny mounds of exquisite foliage, shaped like ivy, are velvety-textured in shades of moss-green with dark brown accents along the central vein. Spikes of pink buds followed by creamy-white starry flowers are produced throughout the summer. 25cm/10in. Z4–8

TRADESCANTIA *virginiana*.

COMMELINACEAE. Named in honour of John Tradescant, gardener to Charles I. Common Spiderwort. From the rich prairies of the central United States and in meadows further east. 46cm/ 18in. Z4–9

T. Andersoniana Group are the forms commonly seen in gardens. They are easily grown in full sun and any reasonably fertile soil. Their shape provides useful contrast of form among round-leaved plants; they make large clumps of long, narrow leaves deeply grooved to form cradles at the top of the flower stems, out of which tumble many buds, opening three-petalled flowers, each with a conspicuous fluffy centre. They have a very long season, from the end of May until the autumn. The flowers close in the afternoon. They can be found in several shades of blue, also white, purple and pink. 60cm/2ft. Z5–9

TRICYRTIS. CONVALLARIACEAE. Commonly called Toad Lily on account of the spotted leaves and flowers. These curious flowers are welcome in September and October as a change from the wealth of daisy flowers. They need moist retentive soil, in sun or part shade, and are lovely among hostas. They make slowly spreading clumps which produce many slender, branching stems. From a distance their colour is dingy, but close-to they are fascinating.

T. formosana. From the forests of Taiwan. Shining green leaves, alternately clasping 90cm/3ft stems are deeply veined and spotted with dark green freckles. Dark maroon flower stems emerge from the axils of the leaves along the upper half of the stems, producing a fine, open head of flowers which last many weeks. The buds are dark purple-maroon, opening upturned lily-shaped flowers with petals so densely spotted with reddish-purple they appear purple overall. The complicated arrangement of stamens and stigma, protruding from a gold-ringed centre, adds to the weird charm. 75cm–1m/30–39in. Z5–9

T. f. **Stolonifera Group** is similar, but grows taller, up to 1.1m/3½ft, and increases somewhat faster. The flowers appear paler, having fewer spots on cream petals. Z5–9

T. hirta. From the woods of Japan, where it is quite common. This plant has softly-hairy, matt-looking leaves, with mauve flowers held more closely to the stem, forming a spire rather than a branching head. The petals are white, finely peppered with purple. 75cm–1m/30–39in. Z5–9

T. h. **'Alba'**. Green-washed buds open to show white, wax-like flowers, with the important central heart of stigma and stamens in cream. It needs a warm site to encourage the flowers, which come rather late in the season. 75cm–1m/30–39in. Z5–9

T. ohsumiensis has pairs of pointed leaves wrapped round the stem, forming cradles for butter-yellow flowers faintly peppered red. Lovely with *Adiantum aleuticum* 'Imbricatum', the prettiest low-growing, lacy fern. 60cm/2ft. Z6–9

T. **'White Towers'**. Green matt leaves are set alternately along 75cm/2½ft stems. Each leaf base holds short-stemmed buds opening unspotted creamy-white flowers. Z5–9

TRIFOLIUM repens. PAPILIONACEAE. Commonly called shamrock. From the meadows of Europe and western Asia, from the Mediterranean to the Arctic.

T. r. **'Purpurascens'**. Clovers like heavy, retentive soil where they make handsome ground-cover in sun or part shade. This one has leaves of rich chocolate-brown, with faint green edges, which close up in the evening, and white flowers. 8cm/3in. Z4–10

T. r. **'Variegatum'** has green velvety leaves strongly veined with creamy-yellow. The leaves are larger, the flowers are pink. 15cm/6in. Z4–10

TRILLIUM. TRILLIACEAE. These are woodland treasures needing cool conditions in rich, leaf-mould soil that does not dry out. Patience also is needed to establish handsome clumps which are slowly formed by underground rhizomes. There are several species and forms; all are distinguished by the division of three – three leaves, three calyces and three petals. I have selected only the most popular.

T. chloropetalum. From low woods of the coast ranges from central California to Washington. Large maroon-red or (rarely) white petals emerge from the sheath-like calyces, standing stiffly upright, and attached directly to the large, flat 'collar' of three mottled broad leaves which are poised on 46cm/18in stems. Z4–9

T. grandiflorum. The Wake Robin. Found in woods, from Quebec to Florida and west to the Great Lakes. The best-known and possibly the loveliest *Trillium*. It makes a dome-shaped plant of veined and shining leaves which set off the pure white, open, funnel-shaped flowers. The pale pink form, *T. g.* f. *roseum*, is a great treasure with foliage warmly tinted also. 38cm/15in. Z3–9

T. g. **'Flore Pleno'**. It is breathtaking, in April, to see these perfectly formed, double white flowers, as lovely as little camellias. 25cm/10in. I had, but am ashamed and sad to say have lost, a form of *T. grandiflorum* which had white flowers splashed with green. Z3–9

T. rivale is a very dwarf member of the genus, found in damp, shady places in Oregon and California, plentifully watered by rain from the Pacific. It holds pale, pink-washed petals above small, pointed green leaves. I struggle to grow it in a sheltered shade house, knowing it would prefer a damper climate. 15cm/6in. Z5–9

T. sessile. From woods of the mid and eastern United States and Canada. Three

Trillium grandiflorum 'Flore Pleno'

large leaves, strongly marbled chocolate and green, are held at the top of a 25–30cm/10–12in stem, centred by the flower whose dark maroon petals are held stiffly upright. By July the colouring in the leaves has faded to shades of silvery-green. Z4–8

TRITONIA disticha subsp. *rubrolucens*. IRIDACEAE. Although related to *Crocosmia* this plant has a more delicate, less flamboyant character. Fresh green, narrow, blade-like leaves form the base for 90–120cm/3–4ft slender stems of flower which are held close on branching spires, gently curved. Each lily-shaped flower is 12mm/½in long, in a peculiarly attractive shade of pink. It is soft rose with a hint of brown about it, so thin petalled the light shines through. They produce new flowers for many weeks during August and September, if planted in full sun in deeply fertile soil. Z8–11

TROLLIUS asiaticus. RANUNCULACEAE. Globeflower. From wet mountain meadows of central and northern Asia. This Globeflower has leaves resembling those of the European one, but rather smaller and often somewhat brown-coloured. Its flowers are carried on stems

Trollius stenopetalus

30–46cm/1–1½ft high, and are open not globe-shaped) and deep yellow. It has produced beautiful orange varieties, and has been used in breeding some fine garden hybrids. I do not grow the wild plant, but have some of its progeny. Z4–8
T. chinensis. (syn. *T. ledebourii*). From damp meadows of the Amur, in far eastern Siberia, this flowers after *T. europaeus*. The flowers are the colour of orange peel, consisting of an outer cup of broad petals, with the central ones slashed to ribbons and held upright to form a palisade around the precious boss of orange stamens and stigma. 75cm–1m/30–39in. Z5–9
T. × *cultorum*. This name covers numerous varieties, derived from *T. europaeus* × *T. asiaticus* × *T. chinensis*, varying slightly in size and shades of yellow and orange. Their main display is in June–July, but they often give a second display in autumn, if in rich moist soil, in full sun. Robust cultivars include 'Superbus' with flowers of soft, light lemon-yellow, like a very large buttercup, and petals so rounded they form a globe, slightly translucent, 'Feuertroll' (warm orange) and 'Helios' (clear yellow). 75cm–1m/30–39in. Z3–8
T. europaeus. From damp meadows and damp woods of north and central Europe to the Caucasus, mostly on mountains.

This wild form can scarcely be improved upon, in colour or form. Z4–9
T. pumilus. From damp meadows and stream-sides of the mountains of west Sichuan, China. This little plant stands about 23cm/9in high, so you must kneel down to look into an enamelled buttercup-like flower with vivid orange stamens. They stand above a tiny clump of crinkled, cut leaves speckled with curious white spots. It is free flowering and lovely for a cool pocket in the rock garden, or on a damp raised bed. Z3–8
T. stenopetalus I particularly value it for its large, semi-double, clear, shining yellow flowers over a long period. Closely related to *T. yunnanensis*. Z3–8
T. yunnanensis. From high, wet mountain-meadows of west China and the Tibet borderlands. This has long-stalked leaves cut into threes or fives, and stems reaching 60cm/2ft bearing large, rich yellow, buttercup-like flowers, one to each stem. Z4–8

UVULARIA. CONVALLARIACEAE. Related to Solomon's Seal, these strange little plants like cool leaf-mould or peaty soils, in part shade.
U. grandiflora. From rich woods of the eastern and central United States and eastern Canada. In spring succulent-looking, olive-green stems, about 46cm/18in high, partially unroll narrow, pointed leaves along the stem. Between them, at the upper end, hang slightly twisted yellow petals, forming open bell-flowers. When they have faded the leaves straighten out and remain fresh for the rest of the summer. Z4–9
U. perfoliata. From moist woods of the east and central United States and Canada. This is similar to *U. grandiflora* but not quite so robust. The flowers are pale creamy-yellow, and open wider. 25–30cm/10–12in. Z4–9

VALERIANA pyrenaica. VALERIANACEAE. From the Pyrenees in France and Spain and the Cantabrian Mountains growing in damp woods and sub-alpine meadows. Above clumps of large, heart-shaped leaves stand maroon-

Uvularia grandiflora

Valeriana pyrenaica

Veratrum album

stained stems carrying lacy heads of tiny lilac flowers which produce clouds of fluffy seed heads. 90–120cm/3–4ft. Z4–9 *V. officinalis* forms a delicate column of branching stems, 1.5m/5ft tall, crowned with panicles of tiny, white, star-like flowers above finely cut foliage (see page 187).

VANCOUVERIA. BERBERIDACEAE.
These plants closely resemble the epimediums of Eurasia, but are found along the west coast of North America, in the deep shade of redwood, Douglas fir and other conifer forests, from central California to Oregon.
V. hexandra flowers later than epimediums, in June. Suddenly you find in a cool shaded spot fairy sprays, 25cm/10in tall of stiffly held, tiny white flowers, on wire-thin stalks. Dainty leaves, lobed like small ivy leaves are light green, held in clusters of three, on red-tinted wiry stalks. Z5–8

VERATRUM. MELANTHIACEAE.
Beautiful, large, deeply pleated leaves slowly expand in spring to make arching mounds of foliage. Later they send up statuesque flower spikes, 1.5–2m/5–6ft tall. They must have deep, damp soil, with generous dressings of farmyard manure. Slug deterrent or a prickly mulch must be put down as soon as they emerge. All these plants tend to be scarce because of the time it takes to raise them from seed, and then several more years to establish them as handsome clumps in the garden.

But they are worth the time and patience needed, there being nothing like them for shape and style. The seed heads are good in autumn.
V. album. From moist or wet mountain pastures, from central Europe to the Caucasus. Related forms are found in boggy places in Siberia and Japan. At the top of a stout stem is a large, branched spike of densely set, greenish-white, star-shaped flowers. 1.2m/4ft. Z4–7
V. nigrum. Found in mountain pastures, from central Europe to Siberia and China. It is similar in shape to *V. album* but can be taller, over 2m/6½ft, with short, branched spikes of darkest maroon stars. Z4–8
V. viride. From marshes and damp woods, across Canada to Alaska, south to the eastern United States. This plant has totally green flowers. 1.2m/4ft. Z3–8

VERBENA corymbosa. VERBENACEAE.
From Chile and southern South America. Most verbenas require well-drained soil in sunny situations, but this plant spreads freely in moist soil, and makes an attractive tangle around the edge of the golden-leaved *Cornus alba* 'Spaethii' or small shrubby willows. Its dense, branched heads of violet-blue flowers are produced for most of the summer. 46cm/18in. Z7–9

VERNONIA crinita. ASTERACEAE. From the south-central United States, in moist places. This makes a large, columnar plant of narrow, dark green leaves which clothe

stiff 2m/6½ft tall stems topped with flat clusters of small, tightly double, daisy-like flowers of bright reddish-purple. At a different time of year they might be considered small for such a leafy plant, but the intensity of colour makes an interesting companion for *Leucanthemella serotina, Aconitum carmichaelii* 'Arendsii', or even colchicums planted at the base. Z5–9

VERONICA. SCROPHULARIACEAE.
The following all prefer soil which does not dry out.
V. austriaca subsp. *teucrium.* From central and southern Europe to the Caucasus and northern Asia in dry grassland, open woods and wood edges. *V. a.* subsp. *t.* 'Crater Lake Blue' makes low tuffets of small, bright green leaves topped with 30cm/1ft spires of vivid blue flowers; a lovely edging pant with *Erigeron* 'Dimity'. Z3–8
V. gentianoides. From mountain meadows of the Caucasus. This low-growing plant makes neat clumps of broad, shining green leaves. In May, delicate 60cm/2ft spires of pale-washed blue flowers look charming on the edge of a border, in sun or part shade. There is a variegated form, with smaller leaves heavily splashed with cream, which is less vigorous. 46cm/18in. Z4–9
V. prostrata **'Trehane'**. From central and southern Europe in dry grassland. This garden form is a pretty carpeting plant for the edge of cool-facing borders. Bright

golden foliage makes contrast among neighbouring plants all summer. In June it is startling, covered with short spires of deep blue flowers. 15cm/6in. Z5–8

VERONICASTRUM virginicum. SCROPHULARIACEAE. From meadows, moist woods and thickets of the central and north-eastern United States and Canada. An elegant plant: tall, strong but slender stems, clothed in whorls of narrow, dark green leaves are topped with fine spires of tiny flowers, in pale blue, lilac-pink, or white (*V.v.* 'Album'), which is the best of all. Slowly making imposing clumps, they are ideal companions for border *Phlox*, flowering during August and September. Z4–8

VIOLA. VIOLACEAE. The following violas, especially in warmer, drier regions, need cool-facing borders with plenty of moisture-holding humus.
V. cornuta. From the Pyrenees, and elsewhere, sparingly in the Alps, in mountain meadows. It is easily grown in sun, in soil that does not dry out, or in part shade. It makes spreading carpets of small, neat, light green leaves, smothered with tall-stemmed, violet-shaped flowers, backed by a long spur or horn. Violas come in white, lilac-blue and deep blue, and are in flower for months in summer. If cut back as they begin to look shabby, and the soil remains damp, they will refurnish themselves and flower again in autumn. 15cm/6in. Z5–9
V. cucullata. Marsh Blue Violet. From damp, shady places of the eastern and central United States. The plant I have under the name *V. cucullata* 'Bicolor' has tall-stemmed white flowers marked with thin purple veins. It flowers in April and May. 15cm/6in. Z4–8
V. gracilis. From eastern Europe and the Balkans. Mine may not be the true species, but whatever it is I treasure my plant from the late Sir Cedric Morris's garden. It makes low mats of dark green, finely toothed leaves and in spring and early summer carries quantities of medium sized *Viola* flowers, of deep velvety purple-blue, the petals slightly

Veronicastrum virginicum

twisted, giving them butterfly grace. 10–13cm/4–5in. Z4–9
V. sororia. From moist open woods, especially of conifers, of eastern Canada and the north-east United States. This plant increases like *V. cucullata*, both by seed and by thick scaly rhizomes which can easily be pulled apart for propagation. Towards the end of April until mid May low clusters of fresh, round leaves are lost beneath generous bunches of large, white violet-shaped flowers. They are so lovely it scarcely matters they are not scented. The leaves continue to expand, to make weed-smothering clumps for the rest of the season. 15cm/6in. Z4–8
V. s. 'Freckles'. The base colour of these large violet-shaped flowers is pale blue, covered with dark blue freckles. This plant makes thick, scaly rhizomes, and after flowering continues to produce quantities of large, healthy green leaves, which make effective ground-cover. 15cm/6in. Z4–8

WALDSTEINIA ternata. ROSACEAE. Found in eastern Europe, Siberia and Japan in mountain woods. Much valued for its glossy, dark green, strawberry-like leaves, it makes thick-spreading carpets in sun or shade, in almost any soil, but will not stand drought. Sprays of bright yellow strawberry-like flowers are more abundant in sun, produced chiefly round the edges of the mats. 8cm/3in. Z3–8

Zantedeschia aethiopica 'Green Goddess'

ZANTEDESCHIA aethiopica. ARACEAE. From stream-sides and damp low places of South Africa. The well-known Arum Lily, handsome in leaf and flower, grows well in deeply prepared soil kept moist in summer. In winter the leaves collapse but the crowns must be protected with heavy mulching. They will survive in deep mud in natural clay-based ponds. 90–120cm/ 3–4ft. All Z8–11
Z. a. 'Crowborough'. This form was found established in an open sunny border in Sussex. Slightly smaller in flower and leaf than some of the florists' forms, it is an excellent plant, and grows vigorously in well-prepared holes. 1m/39in.
Z. a. 'Green Goddess' grows equally well in water or in a deeply prepared pit in a cool border. It has enormous, broadly spear-shaped leaves, and green flowers with white throats and will stand well over 1.2m/4ft when established in damp soil. In flower from July to September.

ZIGADENUS elegans. MELANTHIACEAE. From moist meadows and woods in most of the USA, except for the south-east, north-east and California. This unusual bulb sends up firm, grass-like foliage, above which stand elegant spires, 46–60cm/ 1½–2ft tall, of creamy-green, star-shaped flowers in July–August. Retentive, well-enriched soil produces the best results. Z4–9

A FEW BAMBOOS

I used to dislike bamboos, perhaps because too often they are not tidied up. Congested clumps are improved by thinning, to show off attractive canes. By cutting out some of the oldest shoots to ground level you allow room for young canes, and also remove tattered-looking pieces which have suffered from an extra-cold winter, or been much buffeted by wind.

There are many kinds to choose from. Some become much too large and overpowering for small gardens. Others may be low-growing, but are much too invasive, quite unsuitable for mixed groupings. Both these kinds are ideal where there is plenty of room, and are particularly valuable, I find, around the edges of farm reservoirs or private lakes that cover hectares or several acres and need variation from endless reeds and sedges. Their great charm is that they remain live and shining in winter, the very large ones looking particularly graceful when partnered by fine willows, alders and coloured-stemmed dogwoods.

CHUSQUEA culeou. POACEAE. This unusual bamboo from Chile has tall, stiff stems densely set with clusters of narrow, dark-green leaves creating a feathered effect. It needs time to develop and an open space in which to appreciate its architectural effect as a focal point throughout the year. 6m/20ft. Z8–11

FARGESIA murielae. POACEAE. This bamboo was introduced from China by Ernest Wilson and named after his daughter. Not so invasive, this is medium-sized, 2–3m/6½–9ft. The foliage is a light shade of green. The young canes are bright green, aging to dull yellowish-green. Making slowly increasing, rounded clumps, this bamboo can be used as a specimen or in tubs. Z5–9
F. nitida. From the wooded mountains of west Sichuan, west China, where the Giant Panda lives. The most beautiful of the tall bamboos. Although it may be 3–4m/10–13ft high, and a wide, dense

Sasa veitchii

clump, the effect is of delicate grace and elegance. The slender canes, stained dark purple, carry very narrow leaves, green above and grey on the reverse, so creating a light effect. It is ideal as a specimen plant in grass, or in a large tub. Z5–9

PHYLLOSTACHYS bambusoides 'Castillonii'. POACEAE. This tall bamboo has conspicuous orange-tinted stems, some of which develop a zig-zag pattern of growth at the base. Because it spreads it is suitable only for large-scale plantings. 3–4.5m/10–15ft. Z7–11

PLEIOBLASTUS viridistriatus (syn. *P. auricomus*). POACEAE. The Golden-Leaved Bamboo. As a feature this is perhaps the loveliest bamboo, safe in any garden, in good retentive soil. The leaflets are about 13cm/5in long, 2.5cm/1in wide, of soft, warm yellow, varyingly striped and shaded with light green, as though they were hand painted. I cut the canes down in spring so that the new canes shoot up with bright new foliage, unspoilt by tattered remains. In very sheltered gardens they could be left to create a taller feature. This bamboo looks well in a tub. 90–180cm/3–6ft. Z5–10

PSEUDOSASA japonica. POACEAE. From central and southern Japan and south Korea. This is the largest, heaviest-looking bamboo, best in large gardens. In good

moist soil it makes dense, invading thickets of olive-green canes which can reach up to 4.5m/15ft, heavily clothed with dark green, glossy, ribbon-shaped leaves. It is the better for being tidied up occasionally, to remove wind-bedraggled canes. Z7–10

SASA veitchii. POACEAE. From southern Japan. This bamboo makes low thickets (60cm–1m/24–39in) of purplish-green canes, furnished all summer with rich green leaves, about 15cm/6in long, almost 5cm/2in wide. In the autumn the colour is withdrawn from the edges, leaving a central zone of green, with creamy-white margins of varying widths. This variegated effect, seen in a low-growing mass, remains handsome all winter. However, it is very invasive: suitable only for large landscaping effect. Z5–10

Phyllostachys bambusoides 'Castillonii'

SOME GRASSES, AND GRASS–LIKE PLANTS

ALOPECURUS pratensis. POACEAE. From moist meadows of Europe and central Asia.

A. p. 'Aureus'. The Golden Foxtail Grass makes vivid clumps of low-growing foliage, 30cm/1ft, brightly striped with strong yellow and green. It is much stronger than *Milium effusum* 'Aureum', Bowles' Golden Grass, and useful as an edging plant where its form and colour make good contrast among such plants as *Geranium* and *Hosta*. It will stand sun provided it is in retentive soil. Z4–8

ARUNDO donax. POACEAE. From damp sandy places, often among river and sea dunes of southern Europe to Iran, India, China and Japan. The Giant Reed is the most stately of all grass-like plants. Tall, thick-jointed stems form a slender column from which cascade, evenly spaced, long blue-grey leaves. In warmer countries the stems tower 3.5–4.5m/12–15ft, but in the southern counties of England it is usually about 2.5m/8ft. It is wise to take a little trouble with winter protection around the base, while all the stems need to be cut to the ground in spring to make way for new shoots. Z7–10

A. d. var. *versicolor*. This lovely form has leaves broadly striped with ivory-white. It cannot be called hardy. I keep some plants boxed up, protected with straw in a plastic tunnel. Planted out in May in a border or in tubs, they make handsome features by late summer and autumn. 1.2m/4ft. Z8–10

CAREX. CYPERACEAE. Sedge. All these plants need fairly moist soil, when they will grow in full sun.

C. buchananii. From stream edges of South Island, New Zealand. As it is not reliably hardy, we used to tuck bracken or straw around our plants for the winter but with milder winters this has not been necessary. We cut off the weather-beaten tops in spring to make way for fresh new growth. This springs up to make a fountain shape: hundreds of shining, rounded stems in shades of buff and bright pinky-copper are curved with slender flower spikes meshed in curling wisps of leaf. There is not a hint of green. 60–75cm/2–2½ft. Z7–9

C. elata 'Aurea'. Bowles' Golden Sedge is lovely in shallow water or in a sunny place in damp soil. It makes graceful clumps of bright yellow, grass-like foliage with pointed clusters of brown flowers held stiffly upright in June. 60cm/2ft. Z5–9

C. oshimensis 'Evergold'. This eye-catching sedge makes a focal point, winter and summer, on the edge of a damp border. The narrow, grass-like foliage is bright yellow with narrow green margins. Spiralling out from the centre of the plant it makes spider-shaped clumps, showing off each leaf against the dark soil. 30cm/1ft. Z5–9

C. pendula. Good by the pond, from large grassy tufts, long graceful stems end in drooping fox-tails. 1m/39in. Z5–9

C. petriei. Forms eye catching clumps of pinkish-brown, grass-like leaves, effective as a dot plant, dramatic in drifts. Will tolerate acid or alkaline soil provided it never dries out. 30cm/1ft. Z6–9

C. riparia 'Variegata'. Narrow arching leaves are dramatically variegated white and green. Invasive. 60cm/2ft. Z4–8

CORTADERIA. POACEAE. The well-known Pampas Grass is sometimes devalued, either by being planted in unsuitable positions, or by the use of inferior varieties. Grown from seed both good and bad forms may be obtained, the bad ones having poor, skimpy flower heads, often of a dirty colour.

C. fulvida is found wild in damp places in New Zealand, along river-sides and in dune hollows, often with *Phormium tenax*. It is slightly tender so succeeds best in southern and western counties of the British Isles. It looks like a refined version of the South American Pampas Grass, starting to flower early, towards the end of June, with more delicate, less bulky plumes which hang gracefully to one side from the tips of tall 2.2m/7ft slender stems. When the flowers are young there is a hint of pink in the silvery-beige colour which changes to ivory with age. Z8–10

C. selloana. Found wild along water-courses and in moist places in Argentina and Chile. There are many forms, so it is worthwhile to check both the eventual size of the plant and the shape of the plume. Z7–10

C. s. 'Pumila'. This name means dwarf but do not be misled. By comparison it is a valuable, more compact plant with shorter, beautifully arching foliage which makes an all-year-round feature. But in good deep soil the flower stems stand 1.5–2m/5–6½ft tall. The flower heads are dense and upright, of a soft creamy-beige colour. They look best seen with the sun directly on them, not through them. Z6–10

Carex pendula

Carex petriei

Cortaderia selloana 'Pumila'

Hakonechloa macra 'Aureola'

C. s. **'Sunningdale Silver'**. Where there is room for a giant, this is my favourite. Huge mounds of wickedly sharp-edged leaves form a base for the flower stems which soar 2.5–3m/8–10ft tall. The drooping plumes are open and delicate, gleaming like silvery-white pennants among the rich copper and gold of autumn-tinted trees and shrubs which form a frame around them. They are equally beautiful with the light behind or in front of them. Z8–10

There are other named varieties of *C. selloana* which I have not grown. 'Monstrosa' has immense creamy-white plumes. 'Rendatleri' is also a giant, with pink-tinted plumes. I am not yet enamoured of the so-called Pink Pampas Grass. In those I have seen the colour tends to be a dark purplish shade hidden among the silvery silkiness of the flower and can, in the wrong light, look dingy. Well-placed it may look magnificent. *C .s.* 'Aureolineata' is variegated with leaves striped yellow and pale green; 'Albolineata' is a white-striped version.

CYPERUS *eragrostis.* CYPERACEAE. From South America. A plant enjoyed by flower arrangers: fresh green clumps of rushy foliage are topped in late summer by flower heads of curious green spikelets. 46–60cm/1½–2ft. Z8–10
C. longus. From wet meadows and stream-sides of southern Europe and south-central Asia. The Galingale is a graceful, tall, grassy plant for the water's edge – where there is room, for it is invasive – ideal to bind the banks of large ponds or reservoirs. The drooping clusters of chestnut-brown flowers and seed heads are attractive. 90–120cm/3–4ft. Z5–8

DESCHAMPSIA *cespitosa.* POACEAE. Tussock Grass. From damp meadows of Europe, central and northern Asia to Japan and northern USA and Canada. One of the prettiest of our native grasses, it forms dense tussocks of narrow, arching leaves which send up a shower of needle-thin flower stems topped with foaming sprays of tiny flowers. *D. c.* 'Goldschleier' (Golden Veil), with conspicuous pale sulphur-yellow stems, is a pretty specimen plant in retentive soil. 90–120cm/3–4ft. Z4–9

ERIOPHORUM *angustifolium.* CYPERACEAE. The Cotton Grass of bogs produces multitudes of fluffy, snow-white seed heads. Plant in boggy soil or at the water's edge. It spreads by underground stolons, so best planted in water in a large pot. *E. latifolium* is clump-forming and a safer plant for gardens. 50cm/20in. Z5–8

GLYCERIA *maxima.* POACEAE. From stream-sides and shallow water of Europe, temperate Asia and North America. *G. m.* **var.** *variegata.* In spring the young leaves are flushed deep pink as they push through the mud at the water-side. They quickly change to rich creamy-yellow stripes on green as the leaves lengthen, eventually making stems 90–120cm/3–4ft. This plant will climb the bank out of the water, and can be grown in any heavy retentive soil. It is very handsome, making bright patches from a distance, but it is invasive. Z5–9

HAKONECHLOA *macra.* POACEAE. From wet mountain rocks and cliffs of Pacific central Japan, where it is rather rare. *H. m.* **'Aureola'**. A pity it has such an offputting name, but few people pass by a well-grown clump of this lovely grass. It needs a cool-facing site, in deep moist soil. The ribbon-shaped leaves, set alternately along a red-tinted stem, create a light, arching effect. They are warm golden-yellow, finely striped with green, sometimes stained pink or bronze, and this fine colour lasts throughout the summer. This grass is slow to reappear and get going again, not usually until warmer weather in early summer. 30cm/1ft. Z5–9

LUZULA *nivea.* JUNCACEAE. From sunny openings in mountain woods of the Pyrenees to the Alps. This Woodrush is suitable to combine with plants, as it is not invasive. It makes neat, low tuffets of slender, slightly hairy leaves. Above them stand 46cm/18in stems topped with graceful panicles of parchment-coloured buds which open beige-white fluffy flowers. They look quietly elegant behind a foreground of the richly tinted foliage of *Astilbe* 'Sprite', or among small ferns and violets. Will grow in sun or part shade, in retentive soil. May–June. Z5–9

L. sylvatica. Great Woodrush. From moist woods, mostly in the hills of western, southern and central Europe. Z4–9

L. s. **'Aurea'**. Broad bladed leaves, totally golden-yellow form, dense arching clumps, catching the eye even in winter provided conditions are not too harsh. 30cm/1ft. Z4–9

L. s. **'Marginata'** is handsome when used as a contrast of form, and valuable as ground-cover in rough places, in damp shade, or to stabilize steep banks of heavy soil. Its clusters of broad, grassy leaves form dense creeping carpets. The leaves are narrowly edged with creamy-white, while bare stems hold airy sprays of little brown and yellow flowers in May. 46cm/18in. Z4–9

MILIUM effusum. POACEAE. Wood Millet. From moist woods of Europe, across Asia to Japan, also in the northern United States and southern Canada.

M. e. **'Aureum'**. Bowles' Golden Grass s much more delicate, its thin-textured foliage brightest in spring when it competes with the daffodils, fading to yellowish-green when its dainty sprays of tiny bead-like seeds shimmer in the cool shade of the damp woodland garden.

Seedlings come true, never too many to be a nuisance. 46–60cm/1½–2ft. Z5–8

MISCANTHUS. POACEAE. This race of noble grasses will grow in moist or dryish soils. I would not consider them to be drought-lovers, but they will grow in sandy soils providing there is sufficient rainfall. They grow best in deep, retentive soil.

M. sacchariflorus. From river-sides and wet places of Japan, Korea, Manchuria and north China. This grass is as grand and imposing as bamboo. Slowly increasing clumps of strong, jointed stems shoot up annually to 2.5m/8ft, clad from top to bottom with fluttering, ribbon-shaped leaves. It makes ideal contrast for *Gunnera*, or Ornamental Rhubarb (*Rheum*), and can be used as wind protection or shading for the late summer. It seldom flowers. Z5–9

M. sinensis. From drier, often sandy slopes, or on river sands of Japan and Korea to south-west China and Indo-China. I am proud to know the great plantsman, Ernst Pagels whose nursery is in Leer, North Germany. He has spent a lifetime selecting good plants for gardens without destroying their original character. He has become legendry for his work with *Miscanthus*, breeding new forms which flower regularly in our northern summers. (The species do well in hotter summers in the USA.) There are many named cultivars available, ranging from giants 2–2.5m/6–8ft tall to smaller versions ideal for small gardens. It is not easy to differentiate

between them, much better to see them *in situ*, but among the most distinctive I grow are the following. All Z5–9

M. s. **'Gracillimus'**. This plant is more suited to the smaller garden where it can be used as a superbly elegant specimen grass. The narrower leaves help to create a more delicate effect, curling gracefully round the narrow columnar shape as they lengthen. As the colour is withdrawn in late autumn, the stems and leaves become palest straw colour, too lovely to cut down until winter gales destroy them. 1.5–2m/5–6½ft.

M. s. **'Malepartus'**. Imposing columns of arching, broad, ribbon-like leaves, with conspicuous central silver vein. Large feathery plumes, silky and mahogany red when fresh, drying to pinkish-buff. From early Sept – Dec. 2m/6½ft.

M. s. **'Morning Light'**. This is of my favourites. It makes a graceful vertical, best isolated in a position where low autumn sunlight catches it from top to toe. It forms a column of stems clothed in very narrow leaves lit with conspicuous silver central veins, creating overall a delicate hazy effect. Perfect for small gardens. 90–120cm/3–4ft.

M. s. **'Silberfeder'**. This fine form flowers regularly in September – upturned feathery shuttlecocks, pale pinky-fawn in colour, fluffed out when it is dry, tight closed when it is wet. It can be used as an isolated specimen, or as background to late summer flowers. 2m/6½ft or more.

Miscanthus sacchariflorus 'Malepartus'

Miscanthus sacchariflorus 'Zebrinus'

Molinia caerulea subsp. *caerulea* 'Variegata'

Pennisetum alopecuroides 'Hameln' with *Calamagrostis* × *acutiflora* 'Karl Foerster'

M. s. 'Yaku-jima'. Quite safe for small gardens although it does increase slowly. Each clump is quite dumpy, yet attractive, reminding me of a crinoline, as it consists of layers and layers of ribbon-shaped leaves, while above them wave multitudes of flowering stems. In late autumn the whole plant bleaches to warm caramel colours. 1m/39in.

M. s. 'Variegatus'. The strap-shaped leaves, striped green and white, falling from rigidly upright stems, create a fountain of light all summer, in moist soil surrounded by lower plants, or isolated as a feature. 1.2–1.5m/4–5ft. Z6–9

M. s. 'Zebrinus'. Throughout the early summer one feels cheated by the healthy columns of plain green leaves, but in July cross bands of gold begin to show along the rich green foliage. From then until the frosts it catches the eye, as do the feathery flower heads which are regularly produced in October. 2m/6½ft or more.

MOLINIA *caerulea* **subsp.** *arundinacea*. POACEAE From wet heathy grasslands, and wet woods of Europe and temperate Asia. This grass is grown for its strong flower stems, up to 2m/6½ft tall, which are topped in August and September with heavy heads of dark greenish-purple flowers. They may be overlooked, because not until the oaks are russet-brown does this grass really play its part in the scene, and then it can dominate the garden. Every leaf and stiff, rounded stem becomes transformed, gilded to glowing honey-gold. Z5–9

M. c. subsp. *a.* **'Transparent'.** Above low neat clumps of narrow leaves stand tall, knitting-needle-like flower stems topped in autumn with tiny, rice-like seed cases set on hair-thin stems creating a gauzy effect. It makes an exquisite screen when still, or when bowing and dancing in the windy November the whole plant glows in shades of honey. 1.5–2m/5–6½ft. Z5–9

M. c. subsp. *caerulea* **'Variegata'.** Wherever there is retentive soil, or reasonable rainfall, no garden should be without this exquisite small grass. On the edge of a damp border it makes neat, dense tufts of narrowly arching leaves, conspicuously striped with cream. n autumn the pale colour is intensified as thin cream flower stems appear like a fountain. Finally the whole plant fades to parchment, beautiful to the last dead days of winter. Foliage: 46cm/18in; flower stem: 1m/39in. Z5–9

PANICUM *virgatum*. POACEAE. Switch Grass, grows orginally in the deep rich soils of the Tall Grass Prairies, which once covered the vast interiors of the USA. Many good forms have been introduced. *P. v.* **'Rubrum'** is a clump-forming grass with wide, airy panicles of tiny, chestnut-brown seedheads and narrow, ribbon-like leaves that are tinted red in autumn. This grass prefers deep retentive soil, will not thrive in starved gravel. 1.2m/4ft. Z5–9

PENNISETUM. POACEAE.
Fountain Grasses are widely distributed in tropical and temperate regions, including Eastern Asia and Australia, found in open meadows, openings in woods and stream-sides. They need warm summers toflower well but must have retentive soil. The following selected forms flower reliably.

P. alopecuroides **'Hameln'.** Above tidy clumps of glossy, bright-green foliage stand many thin, wiry stems carrying caterpillar-like heads in autumn: green at first, fuzzy with fine, dark hairs, fading to pale brown in winter. 60cm–1m/24–39in. Z5–9

P. a. **f.** *viridescens*. Has the largest, most handsome bottle-brush-like flower heads, dark green, shadowed with black, softened with long, fine hairs. Forms a much admired feature when every hair is caught in low sunlight. 60–90cm/2–3ft. Z6–9 *P. orientale* from central Asia to the Caucasus Mountains, and North India will tolerate drier conditions but not weeks of drought. Dense hummocks of fine, narrow leaves are crowned with thin wiry stems carrying hairy, caterpillar-like flower heads in soft hades of pale pinkish-mauve. 46cm/1½ft. Z7–9

PHALARIS arundinacea. POACEAE. From river banks and marshes of Europe and north-central Asia to Japan; also northern United States and southern Canada. *P. a.* var. *picta* 'Feesey'. Selected by Mr Feesey, this form of Gardener's Garters is covetable on sight since it makes only slowly increasing clumps of white or green stems carrying vividly striped, ribbon-shaped leaves . More white than green, so a dramatic feature plant. 75cm/2½ft. Z4–9 *P. a.* var. *picta* 'Picta'. Ribbon Grass or Gardener's Garters. This differs from *Glyceria maxima* var. *variegata* in that its variegation is sharply green and white. It too is very invasive, will grow in wet or surprisingly dry soil, usually about 60cm–1m/2–3ft tall, but can be taller in rich wet soil. Z4–9

SCHOENOPLECTUS lacustris (syn. *Scirpus lacustris*). *CYPERACEAE.* From usually quite deep water of lakes and quiet rivers over most of the world. The green, nearly leafless stems of the Bulrush rising out of the water, and up to 2.5m/ 8ft tall, with their heads of large red-brown spikelets, are handsome but suitable only for large sheets of water. The stems of *S. l.* subsp. *tabernaemontani* 'Zebrinus' have horizontal bands of pale yellow, while those of *S. l.* 'Albescens' are vertically and broadly lined with greenish-white, giving an attractive pale effect. Both these varieties seem to spread more slowly than the wild plant, but need a fairly large pond. Z7–10

SPARTINA pectinata. POACEAE. From marshy hollows in the prairies of the midwestern United States. *S. p.* 'Aureomarginata' makes tall graceful stems from which hang long,

narrow, ribbon-like leaves, edged with yellow. This grass likes moist soil. It is invasive but handsome in large landscapes. 2m/6½ft. Z4–9

STIPA arundinacea. POACEAE. From New Zealand. This draws attention when looking its best. It makes dense clumps of fine, arching leaves which become tinted bronze, red and orange in late summer, remaining so all winter, looking like mini-bonfires when caught in the sunlight. No less lovely are the long sprays, up to 1m/3ft long, of soft, silky bronze-brown seed heads which make one think of newly washed hair. It needs a retentive soil, and can be killed by very hard winters, but seedlings usually appear. Foliage: 75cm/2½ft. Z5–10

TYPHA angustifolia. TYPHACEAE. From shallow water or mud at the edge of ponds and quiet rivers of Eurasia and North and South America. The Lesser Bulrush has stiffer, narrower leaves which are less grey than those of *T. latifolia*, and narrower brown 'pokers', with a gap between the lower (female) and upper (male) parts. It stands some 1.2m/4ft or more high, and spreads rapidly, so is not suitable for small ponds unless confined in a container where it remains in scale. Z3–11 *T. latifolia.* From generally rather deeper water than *T. angustifolia*, round lakes and slow-flowing rivers of Eurasia and North America. The Great Reedmace or Cat's-tail stands 2–2.5m/6½–8ft tall, its strap-shaped, upright leaves are grey-green, and its thick 'pokers' are dark brown. It is rampant and will soon fill a small pond, but is a handsome plant for the margins of lakes. Does not invade deep water. Z4–11 *T. minima.* From shallow water and mud around ponds and along slow rivers of eastern Europe to the deltas on the Caspian and Aral Seas, and eastward, sometimes in brackish mud. This little Reedmace only grows from 30–75cm/1–2½ft high, with narrow grassy leaves, though there are none on the flowering stems, which are topped by oval or very short rusty-brown 'pokers'. In the wild it sometimes grows with the Flowering Rush, *Butomus*. Z4–9

FERNS

Most ferns need a cool, damp site sheltered from drying winds, especially in spring. Some of those listed here, including *Dryopteris filix-mas, D. goldieana, Cystopteris, Dennstaedtia, Hypolepis, Polypodium* and *Polystichum* will survive in surprisingly dry (if shaded) sites, but they will grow twice as large where there is more moisture.

For soil which never dries out (that is, has ample rainfall), there are: *Adiantum, Asplenium, Athyrium filix-femina, A. nipponicum, Blechnum penna-marina, B. spicant, B. tabulare* and *D. erythrosora*.

Species for bog or water-side include: *Matteuccia, Onoclea, Osmunda.* I am not an authority on ferns, gardening as I do in the least favourable part of the British Isles. There are many more forms available. On the whole I prefer the species as found generally in the wild to the excessively feathered and crested ones which were sought and treasured in Victorian times, the heyday of the fern collector. The following I grow in the limited areas that have evolved in making the garden. All are lime tolerant, except *Blechnum*.

ADIANTUM. ADIANTACEAE. Maidenhair Fern. This fern and the one following particularly need shelter from drying winds in my garden. *A. pedatum.* From rich, moist, hilly woods of most of the United States and Canada; also Japan, eastern Siberia, Manchuria and China. This choice fern is unusually shaped. From a slowly increasing rootstock it produces shining, purplish-black wiry stems which hold elegant divided fans composed of bright green rounded leaflets. 30–38cm/12–15in. Z3–8 *A. venustum.* From woods in the Himalayas. This increases more readily, especially in warm, damp regions. In my garden it makes small, lace-like fronds which remain all winter when they become bronzed. This fern deeply resents being buried, even shallowly. To propagate it, it is best to detach a rhizome carefully,

Asplenium scolopendrium 'Angustatum'

keeping its roots intact, place it on leaf-mould soil, and cover with pieces of flat stone. 23cm/9in. Z4–8

ASPLENIUM *scolopendrium*.
ASPLENIACEAE. Spleenwort. The Hart's Tongue Fern. From shady, rocky slopes and banks of central and southern Europe to the Caucasus, also Japan and North America (rare and local in the east). So common in the damper counties of the British Isles, so valuable in the garden, where there is not another leaf to take its place, it has long, undulating ribbon-shaped leaves arranged in open shuttlecock form. It will grow in any soil, including chalk, but will not tolerate drought. It can be grown by water, provided the crowns are not waterlogged, or in cool rocky crevices. There are forms with names such as Crispum Group and Undulatum Group, whose edges are gently or intricately fluted. There are others with crested tips to the fronds which, to my mind, do not improve them, but are quaint. They vary in height, but are usually about 30cm/1ft. Z4–9

ATHYRIUM *filix-femina*.
WOODSIACEAE. From moist woods of Europe, central and northern Asia and west North America. This species includes a large number of very varied ferns, collectively known as the Lady Fern, because of their slender, graceful appearance. They range from fronds standing 1.2m/4ft high to only a few inches. They all need shelter from drying wind. They can be found under a variety of names, suggesting that they also come in crested, tasselled, plumed and congested forms. Z3–9
A. niponicum. From hilly woods of southern Japan. The selected form, *A. n.* var. *pictum*, has delicate fronds which look as though they were washed over with pale grey paint, while the purple-tinted stems seem to cast a shadow down the central frond. To do well this fern needs the most sheltered position, in moist leaf-mould and in a moist atmosphere. 15–23cm/6–9in. Z4–9

BLECHNUM. BLECHNACEAE.
These ferns need lime-free soil.
B. chilense. From damp woods of central Chile. A magnificent evergreen fern for a cool, damp site in rich soil or by the waterside. The great fronds look as though they were stamped out of leather. Each pinna, set in pairs along the centre stem, is single and entire with undulating edges. They look like rows of little Hart's Tongues, making together one huge arching leaf of dark, matt green. The roots are slowly but steadily invasive. It needs a little protection in winter in very cold districts. 75cm–1m/30–39in. Z8–10
B. penna-marina. From damp woods, thickets and tussocky moors of southern New Zealand to southern Chile. *B. p. m.* subsp. *alpinum* looks charming in rock crevices, or can make effective ground-cover in moist shade, with its crowded colonies of small evergreen fronds, each a single stem set on either side with simple pinnae, dark leather-green surfaces with rusty backs. 20–25cm/8–10in. Z6–9
B. spicant. Common Hard Fern. Deer Fern. From forests and damp moors of Europe, north-east Asia and north-west America. This makes dense clumps of longer, larger fronds. The infertile bright evergreen fronds, shaped like ladders, spread outward from the centre which is filled with taller, upright fertile fronds. These are green at first with much narrower pinnae. When they have matured and scattered their spores they wither, standing in winter as curling, light brown skeletons. Size depends on moisture: 30–60cm/1–2ft or more. This fern does well in retentive soil under trees and shrubs, or in damp, shady rock-work. Z4–8

CYSTOPTERIS *bulbifera*.
WOODSIACEAE. From moist, rocky woodland banks of eastern and central North America. It differs from *C. fragilis* in bearing bulbils under the leaves which sow themselves in cool areas where the plant grows well. 46cm/18in. Z3–9
C. fragilis. From shaded moist rock and banks in the mountains of the cooler parts of the northern and southern hemispheres. This is so pretty and fragile-looking in spring: delicate sprays of tiny lace-like leaves, very light green when they first appear in spring, are held on wiry stems. It must be sheltered from wind and strong sunlight, in light leaf-mould or peaty soil through which its creeping stems can wander. 23–30cm/9–12in. Z2–9

DENNSTAEDTIA *punctilobula*.
DENNSTAEDTIACEAE. From open sunny woods of eastern and central North America. This can be a menace in the wrong place, among shade-loving treasures, but it is very pretty in woodland, or among shrubs. It runs underground, like bracken, sending up very finely divided bright green leaves, about 30cm/1ft high. Z3–8

DRYOPTERIS *affinis* (syn. *D. pseudomas*). DRYOPTERIDACEAE. Golden green when young, this beautiful fern stands out early in the year. Later the great fronds, richly green remain a striking feature until severe frost. Although vigorous it varies in height according to conditions. 60cm–1.5m/2–5ft. Z4–9
D. dilatata. The Broad Buckler Fern. A robust fern for naturalizing in woodland. Beautiful, graceful, wide spreading fronds on bright green stalks. 1m/3ft. Z4–8
D. erythrosora. From hilly woods of southern Japan to the Philippines, Korea

Matteuccia struthiopteris

Onoclea sensibilis

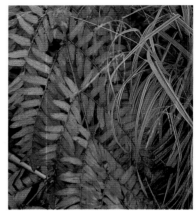

Osmunda regalis in autumn

and China. The most remarkable thing about this fern is the young foliage which is a warm brownish-red in spring, remaining so for a while, then fading to light glossy green as the fronds mature. In moist, shaded conditions, it will continue to produce fresh fronds until autumn with great effect.
46–60cm/1½–2ft. Z5–8

D. filix-mas. From woods and shady places of Europe to central Asia, also the Andes and in Africa. This is the most widely distributed of British ferns and includes a large range of variations, including crested, congested and other aberrations. Some are beautiful, but hard to beat is this, our Common Wild Fern, the Male or Buckler Fern. It will put up with almost any situation (except boggy soil), and is the only fern I know for quite dry shade. It never fails to unroll elegant sheafs of typical fern-like fronds, light green deepening to dark green, remaining well into the winter, but not really evergreen. Fronds: 90–120cm/3–4ft. Z2–9

D. goldieana. From rich woods of the north-east and central United States and north-east Canada. There is a distinctly yellowish tinge to the extra-large, boldly divided leaves when they first appear in spring. This is not always apparent when first planted. 90–120cm/3–4ft. Z4–8

D. wallichiana. Found in much of Asia, from the Himalayas to Japan. It is the grandest, most handsome, and yet hardy enough to be grown in all but the coldest

districts. It commands attention from the moment it emerges in late spring. The tightly rolled 'buds', covered in soft, dark brown scales lie huddled together for protection. As they slowly unfurl, tall green stems clothed in almost black scaly hairs are in marked contrast to the golden-green tone of the expanding fronds. When well pleased, in cool, damp shade, in acid or neutral soil, the fronds can stand 1.2–1.5m/4–5ft tall. Z5–8

HYPOLEPIS millefolium. DENNSTAEDTIACEAE. From mountain woods and scrub and wet tussocky moors of New Zealand. This is another invasive ground-covering fern, similar to *Dennstaedtia*, welcome where its foraging roots can do no harm, and where the finely cut, dark green, woolly leaves will be an enchantment. 30cm/1ft. Z7–9

MATTEUCCIA struthiopteris. WOODSIACEAE. Ostrich Plume Fern. From moist, shady places, especially along streams of the north-east and central United States and Canada, also Europe to Siberia, China and Japan. One of the most beautiful ferns for damp, even boggy conditions, sheltered from drying winds and sun. The fronds emerge from the top of a short trunk to form an open, pale-green shuttlecock of breathtaking, lacy design. In winter dark brown fruiting fronds are left behind. However this is a stoloniferus fern, capable of making large

colonies in cool, moist situations, where it needs watching, and curtailing. Z2–8

ONOCLEA sensibilis. WOODSIACEAE. From damp or wet, shady places in the east and central United States and Canada; also Japan, Korea, eastern Siberia and Manchuria. This is a firm-textured fern, but not quite so leathery as *Blechnum*. Broadly segmented, light green leaves make an arching mass in damp or wet soil. An accommodating fern, it will grow in fairly dry soil in shade or, if allowed, will spread in dense carpets over the surface of water. It makes a lovely contrast to water irises and bog primulas. 46cm/18in. Z4–8

OSMUNDA. OSMUNDACAE. Named after Osmund, a Saxon chieftain who hid his daughter in a clump of this fern to protect her from the Danes.
O. cinnamomea. The Cinnamon Fern sends up large, barren fronds, reaching 60cm–90cm/2–3ft long on stems 30cm/1ft in length. Its fertile fronds are distinct and much smaller. The whole plant is thick with rusty wool when young. Z3–9
O. claytoniana. The Interrupted Fern forms an outer circle of once-divided, arching barren fronds 30–60cm/1–2ft and ones bearing fertile divisions standing upright in the centre of the clumps to a height of 90–120cm/3–4ft. The fertile pinnae (divisions) are halfway up these fronds and are small, cylindrical, and velvety brownish-green. Z3–8

Polypodium interjectum. 'Cornubiense'

O. regalis. The Royal Fern. From marshy woods and wet places of Europe to the Caucasus, the Himalayas to Japan, eastern North America to the West Indies, South America and South Africa. This is the largest, most handsome fern we can grow out of doors in the British Isles. It revels in wet, boggy soil, making an ideal feature by still water where its elegance can be reflected. Large elegant fronds tower above bog irises, stand up to ligularias, and finally outshine them all in autumn, as they assume glowing tints, from orange-copper to russet-brown. They tolerate sun, provided their roots can reach water, and wax larger on a diet of, fibrous loam and vegetable compost. 1.2m/4ft. Z4–9

POLYPODIUM POLYPODIACEAE. Polypody.

P. interjectum 'Cornubiense. I value this lovely Cornish variant which has beautiful, much divided fronds that create a lacy effect that lasts all winter. By spring the overwintered foliage looks tired and rusty, and should be removed before there is any sign of emerging buds. These are late to wake up, in time to freshen the garden in August with lovely fresh spring-green fronds. Z5–9

P. vulgare. From steep, shady banks and rocks, often on tree trunks, of Europe and Asia to Japan, eastern and central North America and South Africa. This is the one fern which may be seen in hedge bottoms in dry East Anglia, most often

where there is chalk in the soil. But that is not to say that it cannot be enjoyed in damper places together with its many variants – fronds broader, much divided, fringed, feathered, etc. It is often seen on tree branches in the moister West Country. It is a colonizing fern, making effective ground cover. 30cm/1ft. Z5–8

POLYSTICHUM. DRYOPTERIDACIEAE. This family includes some of the most beautiful and varied ferns.

P. aculeatum. Hard Shield Fern. Native of Europe, including the British Isles and much of Asia, in deciduous woodland, often on limey soil. This is a strong, stout fern, distinctive to look at but slow to increase. In spring the unfurling fronds curl over backwards, like reversed crosiers, then form a perfect shuttlecock shape of fresh, glossy daintily cut plumes emerging from the centre of the previous year's ruff of overwintered, leathery fronds. 75cm/2½ft. Z4–8

P. lonchitis. Holly Fern. From shady, rocky mountain slopes of Europe and Asia to Japan. It looks as though one had taken the scissors to the Hart's Tongue Fern and cut it across to the vein, into many fine segments; similar in shape but smaller than *P. munitum.* Both ferns do best in cool moist districts. 46cm/18in. Z2–8

P. munitum. Christmas Fern. Sword Fern. From conifer woods of Alaska to California, common under the giant

Polystichum aculeatum

redwoods. This is the finest evergreen fern, perfect in the shade garden as background for hellebores and snowdrops. With large, curving, dark green leaves, simple in shape, but with narrowly divided pinnae as *P. lonchitis,* it creates an imposing feature. 1m/3ft. Z3–8

P. setiferum. The Soft Shield Fern. From woods; nearly cosmopolitan. Z5–8. There are many variations, among them:

P. s. Acutilobum Group. One of the very best of delicate-looking ferns, yet it will grow in comparatively dry shade. However, it grows twice as tall in damper gardens. From among the old leaves, which do not collapse until late spring, unroll new fronds of exquisite lace-like delicacy. Fully extended they form ladder-shaped fronds. Hard little buds can be found along the stems, already sprouting little leaves in late spring. If laid in a box of moist soil and kept shaded they will root down and make new plants. 46cm–1m/18–39in.

P. s. (Divisilobum Group) 'Dahlem'. I collected this fern and *P. s.* 'Herrenhausen' from a German nursery. *P. s.* 'Dahlem' produces tall, upright elegant fronds, making a perfect companion for hostas in cool, damp, shady places. May exceed 1m/39in.

P. s. (Divisilobum Group) 'Herrenhausen' differs from *P. s.* 'Dahlem' in having much more finely divided fronds which lie more horizontally, thus creating a large rosette of lacy design, perfect by the edge of a shady walk.

P. s. 'Divisilobum Densum'. This form is less elegant, but no less attractive. The light green pinnae are longer at the base, forming broadly pyramidal-shaped fronds. They are also more closely packed, creating a heavily ruffled effect. This fern needs a cool, moist spot to show its best. 46cm/18in.

P. s. 'Pulcherrimum Bevis' is one of the most distinctive ferns, Its pinnae are not congested but set at wide intervals to form an upright frond, incurved towards the tip, looking as if someone had pulled it through a half-closed hand. It was discovered by a farm-worker in a Somerset ditch about 120 years ago.

II | Classified Plant Lists to Help with Garden Planning

W HEN I COME TO PLANT A NEW BED in my garden, I find it confusing to consider all the possible plants which might be available, so it helps me to simplify my choice by classifying the enormous range of plants into groups from similar environments. In the following lists the plants are grouped under headings that indicate roughly the same kind of conditions or situations. I hope you may find some selections which suit your climate and soil.

It is sometimes possible to mix plants from overlapping associations, such as meadow plants and edge of woodland groups, but not from extreme conditions, such as full sun and deep shade. These lists are not grouped along strictly ecological lines. In my garden design I choose plants from different countries around the temperate world and plant them together. Thus I will combine plants from Japan, North America and Europe, provided they all are adapted to similar conditions.

Basically it is common sense to put plants where they will survive. Aesthetically I have found it very helpful to have a little knowledge of the native environment of my plants, to know something of the landscape, the trees, bushes, grasses and other plants with which they grow in the wild.

Now, for the lists. I include variegated plants, selected forms, and some cultivars which are familiar to us in gardens. It would be impossible to include every plant that may be known or grown. I tend to include those most familiar, and which I have grown myself.

The genus *Miscanthus* includes many improved forms, giving us some of the most beautiful ornamental grasses. They make strong, non-invasive clumps, provided the soil does not dry out. When fresh the shining, silken, purple-tinted flower heads look like shuttlecocks, eventually drying and curling to look like feather dusters.

THE POND EDGE AND SHALLOWS

These are swamp plants, that is, those, which need to be in very wet soil throughout the growing season. Some, indicated by a 'W', will also grow in shallow water. To be saturated in winter and then dried out in summer will not do. Some can be planted a little further from the water's edge – or even in a garden where there is no visible water, but where plenty of moisture can be maintained all the year. I am not including water-lilies, or the many submerged and floating aquatics which are dealt with fully in books on water gardening. Those marked 'R' are very rampant, or too huge for a small garden. So some of them will turn up again in the lists that follow, where I group the plants according to size and situation. I should mention that Gunnera needs to have its crown well above the water level even though it looks superb by a pond or lake.

W *Acorus gramineus* 'Variegatus'
W *Butomus umbellatus*
W *Calla palustris*
Caltha leptosepala
Caltha palustris
Caltha palustris var. *alba*
W *Caltha palustris* var. *palustris*
Caltha palustris var. *palustris* 'Plena'
Caltha palustris var. *radicans*
Caltha palustris var. *radicans* 'Flore Pleno'
Cardamine pratensis 'Flore Pleno'
Cardamine raphanifolia
W *Carex elata* 'Aurea'
W *Carex riparia* 'Variegata'
RW *Cyperus longus*
Darmera peltata
R *Eriophorum latifolium*
Geum rivale
RW *Glyceria maxima* var. *variegata*
R *Gunnera manicata*
R *Gunnera tinctoria*
R *Houttuynia cordata*
R *Houttuynia cordata* 'Chameleon'

R *Houttuynia cordata* 'Flore Pleno'
W *Iris laevigata*
W *Iris laevigata* 'Variegata'
W *Iris pseudacorus* var. *bastardii*
W *Iris pseudacorus* 'Variegata'
W *Iris* × *robusta* 'Gerald Darby'
Iris setosa
Iris sibirica
W *Iris versicolor*
W *Iris versicolor* 'Kermesina'
Leucojum aestivum 'Gravetye Giant'
Leucojum vernum var. *vagneri*
Ligularia 'The Rocket'
Lysichiton americanus
Lysichiton camtschatcensis
Lythrum salicaria
Lythrum virgatum
W *Menyanthes trifoliata*
Mimulus cupreus 'Whitecroft Scarlet'
Mimulus guttatus
Mimulus hose-in-hose form
Mimulus lewisii
Mimulus ringens
Myosotis scorpioides
R *Onoclea sensibilis*
W *Orontium aquaticum*

Osmunda regalis
Persicaria bistorta 'Superba'
RW *Phalaris arundinacea* var. *picta* 'Picta'
W *Phalaris arundinacea* var. *picta* 'Feesey'
Phormium tenax
Pontederia cordata
Pontederia cordata var. *lancifolia*
Primula bulleyana
Primula florindae
Primula japonica
Primula prolifera
Primula pulverulenta
Primula pulverulenta Bartley hybrids
Primula sikkimensis
RW *Ranunculus lingua*
RW *Sagittaria sagittifolia*
Senecio smithii
Trollius chinensis
Trollius europaeus
Trollius pumilus
Trollius stenopetalus
RW *Typha angustifolia*
RW *Typha latifolia*
Typha minima
W *Zantedeschia aethiopica*
W *Zantedeschia aethiopica* 'Green Goddess'

LARGE PLANTS FOR DAMP SOIL IN SUN

These are plants for soil that is not saturated, but remains damp all summer. Some shelter from drying winds is vital for the larger leaved plants. Sometimes north-facing sites can be a blessing, where there is adequate light overhead, but not direct scorching. These plants are superb where there is plenty of room, where invasive plants, in particular the persicarias, helianthus and eupatoriums, will not be forever regretted, and where the scale of planting requires handsome architectural features.

However, they are not only for owners of parks and lake-sides. Many can be used, in smaller numbers and in smaller groupings, provided that the invasive members are avoided. It is astonishing how one really magnificent plant can add style and dignity to a small and simple setting.

Plants marked 'R' are rampageous or heavy seeders, and must be used with care.

Aconitum carmichaelii 'Arendsii'
R *Angelica archangelica*
Artemisia lactiflora
Aster novae-angliae, cultivars
Aster novi-belgii, tall cultivars
Astilbe rivularis
Boltonia asteroides
    var. *latisquama*
Campanula lactiflora
Centaurea macrocephala
Cephalaria alpina
Cephalaria gigantea
R *Chaerophyllum hirsutum*
    'Roseum'
Delphinium elatum, varieties
Eupatorium purpureum
R *Fallopia sachalinensis*

R *Filipendula rubra* 'Venusta'
Gunnera manicata
Gunnera tinctoria
Hedychium densiflorum
R *Impatiens glandulifera*
    'Candida'
Inula magnifica
Leucanthemella serotina
Ligularia dentata
Ligularia 'Gregynog Gold'
Ligularia 'The Rocket'
Ligularia przewalskii
Lilium pardalinum
Lythrum salicaria
Persicaria amplexicaulis
Persicaria weyrichii
Phormium tenax

Phytolacca americana
Phytolacca polyandra
Rheum palmatum
Rheum palmatum
    'Atrosanguineum'
Rheum palmatum
    var. *tanguticum*
Salvia guaranitica
Salvia uliginosa
Sanguisorba canadensis
Thalictrum aquilegiifolium
Thalictrum delavayi
Thalictrum flavum subsp.
    glaucum
Vernonia crinita
Veronicastrum virginicum
Zantedeschia aethiopica
    'Green Goddess'

LARGE PLANTS FOR DAMP SOIL NEEDING SHELTER FROM WIND AND SUN–SCORCH

Aruncus dioicus
Astilboides tabularis
Cardiocrinum giganteum
Datisca cannabina
R *Matteuccia struthiopteris*
R *Petasites japonicus*
Phlox paniculata
Rodgersia aesculifolia

Rodgersia pinnata
Rodgersia podophylla
Rudbeckia laciniata
Rudbeckia laciniata
    'Goldquelle'
Rudbeckia laciniata
    'Herbstonne'
Telekia speciosa

Thalictrum delavayi
Thalictrum delavayi
    'Hewitt's Double'

LARGE GRASSES FOR DAMP SOIL

Fargesia nitida,
    and other bamboos
Arundo donax
Cortaderia selloana
Cortaderia selloana 'Pumila'
Cortaderia selloana
    'Sunningdale Silver'

Miscanthus sacchariflorus
Miscanthus sinensis
    'Silberfeder'
Miscanthus sinensis
    'Gracillimus'
Miscanthus sinensis
    'Variegatus'

Miscanthus sinensis
    'Zebrinus' etc.
Phalaris arundinacea var. *picta*
R *Spartina pectinata*
    'Aureomarginata'

MEDIUM–SIZED PLANTS FOR RETENTIVE SOIL IN SUN

Achillea ageratum
    'W. B. Childs'
Aconitum 'Ivorine'
Alopecurus pratensis 'Aureus'
Amsonia tabernaemontana
Anaphalis margaritacea var.
    yedoensis
Anemone hupehensis
Anemone × *hybrida*
Anemone tomentosa
Aster × *frikartii* 'Mönch'
Aster lateriflorus 'Horizontalis'
Aster, other species and
    cultivars

Astilbe chinensis var. *taquetii*
Astilbe hybrids
Astrantia major
Astrantia maxima
Bergenia, species and cultivars
Camassia cusickii
Camassia leichtlinii,
    and variants
Campanula 'Burghaltii'
Campanula latifolia
Cautleya spicata 'Robusta'
Chelone obliqua
Deschampsia cespitosa
Echinacea purpurea

Eupatorium rugosum
Euphorbia griffithii 'Fireglow'
Euphorbia palustris
Euphorbia sikkimensis
Filipendula purpurea 'Elegans'
Filipendula ulmaria 'Variegata'
Gentiana asclepiadea
Gentiana lutea
Geranium endressii
Geranium himalayense
Geranium pratense,
    and cultivars
Geranium clarkei
    'Kashmir White'

Low planting at the water's edge opens up a view across two ponds separated by a narrow, grassy walk where you can stand to watch the fish or dragonflies.

Geranium sylvaticum
Geranium wallichianum
Helenium autumnale, cultivars
Hemerocallis, species
    and cultivars
Hosta sieboldiana and others
Inula hookeri
Iris chrysographes
Iris delavayi
Iris ensata
Iris sibirica
Knautia macedonica
Leucanthemum maximum,
    all cultivars
Leucojum aestivum
Lilium species
Lobelia cardinalis, and cultivars
Lobelia siphilitica
Lobelia × speciosa
    'Vedrariensis'
Luzula nivea
Lychnis chalcedonica

Lysimachia ciliata
Lysimachia clethroides
Lysimachia ephemerum
Lysimachia punctata
Lythrum virgatum
Mimulus cardinalis
Molinia caerulea cultivars
Monarda didyma, and cultivars
Morina longifolia
Panicum virgatum 'Rubrum'
Persicaria bistorta subsp. *carnea*
Persicaria bistorta 'Superba'
Persicaria campanulata
Persicaria macrophylla
Phlox pilosa
Phormium cookianum
Physostegia virginiana
Polemonium caeruleum
Polemonium foliosissimum
Potentilla atrosanguinea
Potentilla atrosanguinea
    var. *argyrophylla*

Potentilla 'Gibson's Scarlet'
Potentilla nepalensis
    'Miss Willmott'
Ranunculus acris 'Flore Pleno'
Ranunculus constantinopolitanus
    'Plenus'
Rheum alexandrae
Rudbeckia fulgida var. *fulgida*
Rudbeckia maxima
Sanguisorba obtusa
Scabiosa caucasica
Schizostylis coccinea
Stachys macrantha
Stokesia laevis
Tradescantia Andersoniana
    Group
Trollius species and cultivars
Verbena corymbosa

SMALL AND LOW–GROWING PLANTS FOR DAMP SOIL IN SUN

Adonis amurensis
Adonis vernalis
Ajuga reptans, cultivars
Aquilegia flabellata
Aster tongolensis
Astilbe chinensis var. *pumila*
Astilbe, dwarf hybrids
    including 'Sprite'
Bergenia stracheyi
Cardamine pratensis
    'Flore Pleno'
Cardamine quinquefolia
Colchicum autumnale
Colchicum speciosum
Colchicum, other species
    and cultivars
Crepis aurea
Dodecatheon meadia,
    and other species

Erigeron 'Dimity'
Erigeron roseus
Erythronium californicum
    'White Beauty'
Erythronium dens-canis
Erythronium 'Pagoda'
Erythronium 'Sundisc'
Filipendula vulgaris
Fritillaria camschatcensis
Fritillaria meleagris
Fritillaria pallidiflora
Gentiana, species
Geum 'Borisii'
Geum rivale, cultivars
Heuchera, species and
    cultivars
Iris cristata
Lysimachia nummularia
Lysimachia nummularia
    'Aurea'

Mentha pulegium
Narcissus pseudonarcissus
Narcissus, species and smaller
    hybrids
Nierembergia repens
Ourisia coccinea
Ourisia macrophylla
Persicaria affinis
Persicaria milletii
Persicaria vacciniifolia
Primula denticulata
Primula rosea
Solidago, dwarf varieties
Trifolium repens
    'Purpurascens'
Veronica gentianoides
Viola cornuta
Zigadenus elegans

PLANTS FOR SHADE AND PART SHADE IN DAMP SOIL

The site may be shaded by trees and tall shrubs, or it may be a generous border along a north wall. Every effort must be made to conserve moisture by enriching the soil and mulching, especially where tree and shrub roots are present below. If there are many of these roots near the surface, such as close under hedges, or immediately under some large, densely shady trees, the soil will be too dry, and most of the following plants will not survive (except where rainfall is plentiful).

LARGE AND MEDIUM-SIZED PLANTS

There are few large plants which can grow in deep shade, but many flourish best in, or even need, the moister atmosphere and shelter from wind provided by surrounding shrubs and trees. Most of them enjoy direct sunlight for part of the day (preferably not mid-day), especially if it is partly flecked and broken by tree foliage high above. In the garden they grow well in gaps between tall bushes, at the edge of plantings of trees and in sunny woodland glades, or in north, north-east and north-west-facing borders with open sky overhead but little direct sun (not bone-dry under eaves).

Aconitum × *commarum* 'Bicolor'
Aconitum carmichaelii
Aconitum lycoctonum subsp. *vulparia*
Aconitum, other species and hybrids
Anemone × *hybrida*
Anemone tomentosa
Aquilegia formosa var. *truncata*
Aquilegia, long-spurred hybrids
Aquilegia vulgaris
Arisaema species
Arum italicum subsp. *italicum* 'Marmoratum'
Aruncus dioicus
Aruncus dioicus 'Kneiffii'
Brunnera macrophylla cultivars
Cardiocrinum giganteum
Carex pendula
Dicentra spectabilis
Digitalis grandiflora
Digitalis purpurea
Euphorbia amygdaloides 'Purpurea'
Euphorbia amygdaloides var. *robbiae*

Gentiana asclepiadea
Geranium maculatum
Geranium phaeum
Geranium sylvaticum
Geranium wallichianum
Geranium, other species
Gillenia trifoliata
Helleborus species and cultivars
Heuchera americana
Heuchera cylindrica 'Greenfinch'
Hosta, including variegated forms
Kirengeshoma palmata
Lamium orvala
Lilium, species
Meconopsis betonicifolia
Meconopsis cambrica
Mertensia ciliata
Mertensia sibirica
Pachyphragma macrophyllum
Paeonia emodi
Paeonia 'Late Windflower'
Paeonia lactiflora
Paeonia mlokosewitschii
Paeonia obovata var. *alba*

Paeonia veitchii
Persicaria virginiana
Phalaris arundinacea var. *picta* 'Feesey'
Phlox paniculata, and cultivars
Phytolacca, species
Polygonatum, species and hybrids
Polygonatum verticillatum
Ranunculus aconitifolius
Roscoea cautleyoides
Roscoea purpurea
Salvia glutinosa
Selinum tenuifolium
Selinum wallichianum
Thalictrum aquilegiifolium
Thalictrum delavayi
Thalictrum delavayi 'Hewitt's Double'
Thalictrum diffusiflorum
Tricyrtis species and cultivars
Valeriana phu 'Aurea'
Veratrum album
Veratrum nigrum
Veratrum viride

LOW-GROWING PLANTS FOR PART SHADE IN DAMP SOIL

Adiantum species
Ajuga reptans, cultivars
Arisarum proboscideum
Buglossoides purpurocaerulea
Chiastophyllum oppositifolium
Convallaria majalis
Corydalis cheilanthifolia
Corydalis lutea
Corydalis ochroleuca
Cystopteris fragilis
Dicentra formosa
Eranthis hyemalis
Erythronium californicum
Erythronium dens-canis
Erythronium oregonum
Erythronium, garden hybrids
Fragaria × ananassa 'Variegata'
Galanthus, species

Hacquetia epipactis
Hosta, dwarf species
   and varieties
Lamium maculatum
Lathyrus vernus, and varieties
Leucojum vernum
Lysimachia nummularia
   'Aurea'
Omphalodes cappadocica
Omphalodes verna
Phlox divaricata subsp. *laphamii*
   'Chattahoochee'
Phlox pilosa
Potentilla alba
Primula denticulata
Primula elatior
Primula, hybrids
Primula vialii

Primula vulgaris
Pulmonaria species and
   cultivars
Ranunculus ficaria
Speirantha convallarioides
Tellima grandiflora
Tiarella cordifolia
Tiarella wherryi
Tiarella, varieties
Viola cucullata
Viola odorata
Viola riviniana
   Purpurea Group
Viola, other species
Waldsteinia ternata

PLANTS FOR SHADE IN DAMP SOIL

These are plants that do not need direct sunlight, which can be harmful to many of them by wilting and scorching their leaves. But they do need subdued light, perhaps speckled through the overhead foliage of trees. Some, with hard leaves, will stand more sun, but flourish best in shade.

LARGE AND MEDIUM-SIZED PLANTS

Actaea, species
Anemonopsis macrophylla
Brunnera macrophylla and
   cultivars
Cardamine heptaphylla
Deinanthe bifida
Diphylleia cymosa
Geranium phaeum
Helleborus species and
   varieties
Hosta sieboldiana

Hosta, other large species
   and cultivars
Iris foetidissima
Kirengeshoma palmata
Mertensia virginica
Pachyphragma macrophyllum
Petasites japonicus
Podophyllum hexandrum
Polygonatum odoratum var.
   pluriflorum 'Variegatum'
Smilacina racemosa

Symphytum species
Trachystemon orientalis
Tricyrtis hirta
Tricyrtis macropoda
Tricyrtis, other species
Uvularia species

LOW-GROWING PLANTS FOR SHADE IN DAMP SOIL

Anemone nemorosa,
     and cultivars
Anemone ranunculoides
Anemone, other low species
Asarum, species
Cardamine trifolia
Cardamine quinquefolia
Cardamine pentaphylla
Clintonia andrewsiana
Coptis trifolia
Cornus canadensis
Corydalis cava
Corydalis, other species
Dicentra formosa, and varieties
Epimedium grandiflorum
Epimedium, species

Galax urceolata
Galium odoratum
Glaucidium palmatum
Helleborus niger
Hepatica nobilis and cultivars
Heucherella cultivars
Hylomecon japonica
Jeffersonia dubia
Linnaea borealis
Maianthemum bifolium
Melittis melissophyllum
Mitella breweri
Mitella caulescens
Oxalis acetosella
Oxalis oregana
Pachysandra terminalis

Phlox divaricata subsp. laphamii
     'Chattahoochee'
Phlox stolonifera
Primula vulgaris, and varieties
Sanguinaria canadensis
Saxifraga cuneifolia
Saxifraga fortunei
Saxifraga umbrosa
Trillium chloropetalum
Trillium grandiflorum
Trillium rivale
Trillium, other species
Vancouveria hexandra
Viola sororia
Viola, other species

FERNS FOR SHADE OR PART SHADE IN DAMP SOIL

Adiantum pedatum
Adiantum venustum
Asplenium scolopendrium
Asplenium trichomanes
Athyrium filix-femina
Athyrium niponicum var.
     pictum
Blechnum penna-marina
Blechnum spicant
Blechnum tabulare
Cystopteris bulbifera

Cystopteris fragilis
Dennstaedtia punctilobula
Dryopteris erythrosora
Dryopteris filix-mas
Dryopteris goldieana
R Hypolepis millefolium
R Matteuccia struthiopteris
Onoclea sensibilis
Osmunda regalis
Osmunda, other species
Polypodium vulgare

Polystichum aculeatum
Polystichum lonchitis
Polystichum munitum
Polystichum setiferum
Polystichum setiforum
     Acutilobum Group
Polystichum setiforum
     Divisilobum Group
Polystichum setiforum
     Plumosodivisilobum
     Group

A FEW GRASSES AND SEDGES FOR DAMP SHADE

Carex morrowii 'Variegata'
Carex pendula
Cyperus eragrostis
Hakonechloa macra 'Aureola'
Luzula nivea
Luzula sylvatica 'Marginata'
Milium effusum 'Aureum'

Further Reading

Bowles, E. A. *My Garden in Spring*, David & Charles 1972, Timber Press 2003

Bowles, E. A. *My Garden in Summer*, David & Charles 1972, Timber Press 2003

Bowles, E. A. *My Garden in Autumn and Winter*, David & Charles 1972, Timber Press 2003

Chatto, Beth *Beth Chatto's Garden Notebook*, Dent 1988

Beth Chatto's Gravel Garden, Frances Lincoln and Viking (USA) 2000

Beth Chatto's Woodland Garden, Cassell Illustrated and Stirling (USA) 2002

The Dry Garden, Dent 1978

Farrer, Reginald *The English Rock Garden*, T. C. & E. C. Jack Ltd

Hillier's Manual of Trees and Shrubs (5th ed., 1981), David and Charles

The RHS Plant Finder 2004–2005, Dorling Kindersley

Lloyd, Christopher *Christopher Lloyd's Garden Flowers*, Cassell 2000

The Well-Tempered Garden, Cassell (revised edition) 2001

Foliage Plants, Viking (revised edition) 1985

Lucy, Gerald *Essex Rock: A look beneath the Essex landscape*, Essex Rock and Mineral Society 1999

Perry, Frances *Water Gardening*, Country Life 1938

Phillips, Roger, and Martyn Rix *Perennials*, Pan 1991

Shrubs, Pan 1989

Bulbs, Pan 1981

Rice, Graham and Elizabeth Strangman *The Gardener's Guide to Growing Hellebores*, David and Charles and Timber Press 2001

Robinson, William *The English Flower Garden*, John Murray 1993

Sackville-West, Vita *In Your Garden*, Michael Joseph 1953; Frances Lincoln 2004

Speichert, C. Greg and Sue *Encyclopedia of Water Garden Plants*, Timber Press 2004

Swindells, Philip *Waterlilies*, Croom Helm and Timber Press 1983

Thomas, Graham Stuart *Ornamental Shrubs, Climbers and Bamboos*, John Murray 1992

Perennial Garden Plants, Dent 1993

Plants for Ground-Cover, Dent 1977

Index

Page numbers in *italic* refer to the illustrations

Laurel, Cherry *see Prunus laurocerasus*
Lenten Rose *see Helleborus* x *hybridus*
Leopard Lily *see Lilium pardalinum*
Leptinella, 84
    L. potentillina, 81
    L. squalida, 27, 244
Leucanthemella serotina, 181, 227, 259, 273
Leucanthemopsis alpina, 149
Leucanthemum, 227
    L.maximum, 179, 227, 275
Leucojum aestivum, 154, 179, 227, 275
    L.a. 'Gravetye Giant', *182*, 227, *227*, 272
    L. vernum, 168, 227, 277
    L.v. var. *vagneri*, 227, 272
Levesley, Philip, 227
Ligularia, 50, 126, 142, 144, 227–8
    L. dentata, 84, 126, 161, 163, 177, 196, 227–8, 273
        L.d. 'Desdemona', 84, 227
        L.d. 'Othello', 227
    L. 'Gregynog Gold', *19*, 126, 179, 228, 273
    L. hodgsonii, 163, 228
    L. macrophylla, 228
    L. przewalskii, 54, 228, 273
    L. 'The Rocket', 54, 84, 126, 177, 179, 228, 272, 273
    L. wilsoniana, 228
Lilac, Chinese *see Syringa swedinzowii*
Lilium, 228–9, 275, 276
    L. auratum, 164
    L. bulbiferum var. *croceum*, 179
    L. concolor, 228
        L.c. var. *pulchellum*, 163
    L. x *hollandicum*, 228
    L. lancifolium, 27, 164, 228
    L. martagon, *104–5*, 158, 228
        L.m. var. *album*, 228
    L. monadelphum, 159, 179, 228, *228*
    L. nanum, 160
    L. oxypetalum, 160
    L. pardalinum, 111, 164, 228–9, 273
        L.p. var. *giganteum*, 111
    L. regale, 161
    L. speciosum, 181, 184, 185, 229, 238
        L.s. var. *album*, 228
    L. superbum, 229
Lily *see Lilium*
Lily-of-the-Valley, 26, 107, 168
    see also Convallaria majalis
limestone soils, 157–8
Linaria, 149
Linnaea, 173, 229
    L. borealis, 173, 229, 278
        L.b. subsp. *americana*, 229
Linnaeus, Carl, 229
Liquidambar, 64, 73
    L. styraciflua, 25, 38, 185
Liriodendron tulipifera, 25, 64–5
Liriope, 99
    L. muscari, 181, 184
Little Grassy Wood, 65
Lloyd, Christopher, 211, 249
Lobelia, 229–30
    L. 'Bees' Flame', 229
    L. cardinalis, 156, 180, 229, 275
        L.c. 'Queen Victoria', 181, 229, *229*
    L. fulgens, 229
    L. siphilitica, 229, 230, 275
        L.s. 'Alba', 230
    L. x *speciosa* 'Vedrariensis', 181, 229–30, 275

Loosestrife: Purple *see Lythrum*
    Yellow *see Lysimachia*
Lunaria rediviva, 168
Lungwort *see Pulmonaria officinalis*
Lupinus polyphyllus, 164
Luzula nivea, 263–4, 275, 278
    L. sylvatica, 177, 264
        L.s. 'Aurea', 264
        L.s. 'Marginata', 82, 264, 278
Lychnis chalcedonica, 230, 275
Lysichiton, 84, 201
    L. americanus, *18*, 40, 81, 156, 230, *230*, 272
    L. camtschatcensis, *16*, 81, 154–6, 177, 230, *230*, 272
        L.c. x *americanus*, 92
Lysimachia, 230, 256
    L. ciliata, 87, 177, 181, 230, 275
        L.c. 'Firecracker', 177, *230*
    L. clethroides, 230, 275
    L. ephemerum, 181, 230, 275
    L. nummularia, 153, 230–1, 275
        L.n. 'Aurea', 177, 231, 275, 277
    L. punctata, 82, 231, 275
        L.p. 'Alexander', 231
    L. vulgaris, 153, 209, 231
Lythrum, 231, *231*, 256
    L. salicaria, 153, 177, 231, 272, 273
        L.s. 'Blush', 231
        L.s. 'Feuerkerze', 181
    L. virgatum, 177, 231, 272, 275
        L.v. 'Rose Queen', 231

M

Macleaya, 231–2, 252
    M. cordata, 232
    M. microcarpa, 232
        M.m. 'Kelway's Coral Plume', 232, *232*
Mahonia japonica, 53, 185
    M. repens, 97
Maianthemum bifolium, 173, 232, 278
Maidenhair Fern *see Adiantum*
maintenance, 137–47
    fertilizers, 145–6
    large areas, 132–5
    see also mulching; soil; weeding
Male Fern *see Dryopteris filix-mas*
Maltese Cross *see Lychnis chalcedonica*
Malus tschonoskii, 52, 53
manure, farmyard, 145
Maple *see Acer*
Marsh Blue Violet *see Viola cucullata*
Marsh Fern *see Thelypteris palustris*
Marsh Helleborine *see Epipactis*
Marsh Marigold, 154, 162, 163
    see also Caltha palustris
Marsh Spurge *see Euphorbia palustris*
Marsh Violet *see Viola palustris*
marshes, 152–7
Masterwort *see Astrantia*
Matteuccia, 266
    M. struthiopteris, 88–9, 91, 169, 268, *268*, 273, 278
May Apple *see Podophyllum peltatum*
May Lily *see Maianthemum bifolium*
Mazus radicans, 244
Meadow Cranesbill *see Geranium pratense*
Meadow Rue *see Thalictrum*
Meadow Saffron *see Colchicum autumnale*
meadows: damp meadows, 157–64

flood-meadows, 152–7
Meadowsweet *see Filipendula*
Meconopsis, 33, 208, 231, 232–3
    M. aculeata, 160
    M. betonicifolia, 91, 109, 162, 185, 221, 232, 276
    M. cambrica, 26, 232, 276
    M. grandis, 232
    M. napaulensis, 232
    M. quintuplinervia, 232
    M. regia, 232
    M. x *sheldonii*, 232
    M. villosa, 232–3
Melittis melissophyllum, 233, 278
Mentha, 233
    M. aquatica, 153
    M. x *gracilis* 'Variegata', 233
    M. longifolia, 233
    M. pulegium, 233, 275
    M. suaveolens, 233
    M. x *villosa*, 233
Menyanthes trifoliata, 154, 177, 233, *233*, 272
Mertensia, 233–4
    M. ciliata, 164, 233, 234, 276
    M. sibirica, 164, 276
    M. virginica, 184, 234, 277
Metasequoia, 38, 73
    M. glyptostroboides, 37, 144
mice, 132
Michaelmas Daisy, 172
    see also Aster
Milium effusum, 71, 167, 264
    M.e. 'Aureum', 26, 185, 262, 264, 278
Milkweed *see Euphorbia*
Mimulus, 234
    M. x *burnettii*, 234
    M. cardinalis, 234, 275
    M. cupreus, 234
        M.c. 'Whitecroft Scarlet', 234, 272
    M. guttatus, 82, 164, 177, 234, 272
    M. hose-in-hose form, 82, 272
    M. lewisii, 164, 234, 272
    M. luteus, 234
    M. ringens, 234, 272
    M. variegatus, 234
    M. 'Wisley Red', 181, 234
Mint *see Mentha*
Miscanthus, 28, *54*, 90, 143, 239, 253, 264, *270*
    M. sacchariflorus, 32, 40, 66, 128, 144, 264, 274
    M. sinensis, 264
        M.s. 'Gracillimus', 32, 40, 264, 274
        M.s. 'Malepartus', 264, *264*
        M.s. 'Morning Light', 264
        M.s. 'Silberfeder', 66, 128, 177, 181, 264–5, 274
        M.s. 'Variegatus', 177, 265, 274
        M.s. 'Yaku-jima', 265
        M.s. 'Zebrinus', 32, 128, 144, 177, 179, 264, 265, 274
Mitella, 234
    M. breweri, 184, 234, 278
    M. caulescens, 234, 278
Moccasin Flower *see Cypripedium*
Molinia caerulea, 275
    M.c. subsp. *arundinacea*, 180, 181, 265
        M.c. subsp. *arundinacea* 'Transparent', 265
    M.c. subsp. *caerulea* 'Variegata', 40, *60*, 90, 181, *231*, *264*, 265
Monarda 'Beauty of Cobham', 234

M. 'Cambridge Scarlet', 234
M. 'Croftway Pink', 234
M. didyma, 170, 234, 275
    M.d. 'Beauty of Cobham', 179
M. 'Schneewittchen', 234
Monkey Musk *see Mimulus*
Monkshood *see Aconitum*
Montbretia *see Crocosmia*
Moor Grass *see Molinia caerulea* subsp. *arundinacea*
Morina longifolia, 160, 179, 234–5, 275
Morris, Sir Cedric, 175, 213, 260
moss, in lawns, 138
Mother of Thousands *see Saxifraga stolonifera*
Mountain Bluebell *see Mertensia ciliata*
Mountain Fern *see Blechnum spicant*
Mouse-tailed Arum *see Arisarum*
mulching, 61–3, 142, 147
    bark, 61–3, 133–5, 147
    farmyard manure, 145
    hop waste, 28, 147
    maintaining large areas, 132, 133–5
    mushroom compost, 147
    peat, 61
    straw, 61, 66, 132, 133, 147
Myosotis scorpioides, 38, 82, 154, 177, 234, 235, 272
    M.s. 'Mermaid', 235

N

Naked Ladies *see Colchicum autumnale*
Narcissus, 235, 275
    N. cyclamineus, 235, *235*
    N. poeticus, 158, 235
        N.p. var. *recurvus*, 65
    N. pseudonarcissus, 235, 275
    N. 'Thalia', 27–8, 71
    N. 'Tresamble', 27–8, 71
    N. triandrus, 235
Nasturtium officinale, 154
Neillia, 25
Nepeta govaniana, 235
    N. sibirica, 163, 179
Nicotiana alata, 57
    N. sylvestris, 57
Nierembergia repens, 181, 235, 275
Nothofagus, 41
Nuphar, 154
Nymphaea, 154
    N. 'James Brydon', *120–1*
    N. 'Rose Arey', *120–1*
Nymphoides peltata, 188

O

Oak *see Quercus*
oak woods, plants of, 166–7, 170
Obedient Plant *see Physostegia virginiana*
Oehme, Wolfgang, 239
Omphalodes, 235
    O. cappadocica, 169, 235, *235*, 277
        O.c. 'Cherry Ingram', 235
        O.c. 'Starry Eyes', 235
    O. verna, 235, 277
        O.v. 'Alba', 235
Onoclea, 266
    O. sensibilis, 8, 26, 83, 85, 171, *174*, 177, 268, *268*, 272, 278
Ophiopogon planiscapus 'Nigrescens', 99, 106, 181
Orchids, 158

Acknowldegements

I am grateful to many people who have helped and encouraged me to write this book, both directly and indirectly. Most of all, to my late husband. Throughout our life together I absorbed, like a sponge, talk of plants and their habitats. From Andrew's patient, lifelong study I learnt much that I know about plants and their needs. It is a never-ending study from books, and from practical experience in our own particular environment. As part of his lifetime research into the ecological associations of many plants we grow in our gardens; he translated German, Russian and French botanists into English. This work is now in the hands of James Hitchmough, Head of the Department of Landscape at Sheffield University.

I am much indebted to the late Graham S. Thomas for his sound and constructive criticism of my original manuscript. With much patience, and far greater experience, he spared me from many pitfalls which strew the path of would-be horticultural writers. But I begin to think that a gardening book, like gardens, does not exist that has no flaws!

I should like to acknowledge several writers whose works are currently out of print, but which I consulted when writing the original edition of *The Damp Garden*. I had beside me Alan Bloom's excellent book *Moisture Gardening*. His garden at Bressingham, Norfolk, was established, and his name as a great plantsman was known in Europe and the United States before I had begun to be a gardener. To my delight, we exchanged visits – and plants – and enjoyed wandering round each other's gardens, Mr Bloom generously sharing his great stores of knowledge and experience.

The most comprehensive book I know on the specialized subject of pond construction and water plants is *Water Gardening* by Frances Perry, published by Country Life in 1938. If you can get hold of a copy second hand, I recommend it. There are practical ideas in it for everyone, from the most modest garden to the most expansive. The Wisley Handbook No. 29 *Water Gardens* by Ken Aslet is a delightful little book, if you can find it, giving the names and habits of the best-known and best-loved water plants. As well as providing very good instructions, with illustrations, for the construction of pools that most of us could envisage in our gardens, there is also plenty of sane advice. I like the list of equipment that comes in handy, like floating plastic bowls and waders. It has been superseded by more recent RHS publications.

I am glad to have this opportunity to give credit to my staff, whose enthusiastic and conscientious teamwork brings my plans and ideas to life. In winter as well as summer their wholehearted involvement and hard work have made my gardens grow. Fine ideas would be of little use without such support.

I would also like to say thank you sincerely to our visitors and postal friends from far away. Without them the gardens would not have developed, nor could continue. Their appreciation of our efforts gives us fresh energy and inspiration to do better. Chrissy McDonald drew and painted the garden plan on pages 14 to 15. I wish to thank my Company Secretary, Tricia Brett, who has patiently trawled through *The RHS Plant Finder* to revise the many name changes that have occurred in recent years.

In their original editions, my two books, *The Dry Garden* and *The Damp Garden*, gained something very special with the exquisitely sensitive drawings of the late Margaret Davies. She involved herself so completely with my ideas and feelings about plants and design that sometimes I felt we were two parts of one whole. Her plans and diagrams form the basis of those in this book but in place of her plant portraits are Steven Wooster's photographs. He brings the eye of an artist to the camera lens. Because more pictures were to be introduced into this revised edition it became necessary to précis some of my original writing, which remains in the paperback edition. I am indebted to my editor, Erica Hunningher, for so conscientiously undertaking this task without losing important information.

DONE
PG